Sound and Fury

Also by Eric Alterman

Who Speaks for America? Why Democracy Matters in Foreign Policy (1998)
It Ain't No Sin to Be Glad You're Alive: The Promise of Bruce Springsteen (1999)

Sound and Fury

The Making of the Punditocracy

Eric Alterman

CORNELL UNIVERSITY PRESS ITHACA AND LONDON

First published 1992 by HarperCollins Publishers
First HarperPerennial edition published 1993
First printing, Cornell Paperbacks, 1999

Printed in the United States of America

Cornell University Press strives to use environmentally responsible suppliers and materials to the fullest extent possible in the publishing of its books. Such materials include vegetable-based, low-VOC inks, and acid-free papers that are recycled, totally chlorine-free, or partly composed of nonwood fibers. Books that bear the logo of the FSC (Forest Stewardship Council) use paper taken from forests that have been inspected and certified as meeting the highest standards for environmental and social responsibility. For further information, visit our website at www.cornellpress.cornell.edu.

Library of Congress Cataloging-in-Publication Data

Alterman, Eric.
   Sound and fury : the making of the punditocracy
/ Eric Alterman.
      p.   cm.
   Includes bibliographical references and index.
   ISBN 0-8014-8639-4 (pbk.)
   1. Journalism--Political aspects--United States. 2. United States--Politics and government--20th century. 3. Mass media--Political aspects--United States 4. Television and politics--United States. 5. Press and politics--United States. 6. Talk shows--United States. I. Title.
PN4888.P6A48   1999
071'.3--dc21   99-42030
DNLM/DLC   CIP
for Library of Congress

Paperback printing
10 9 8 7 6 5 4 3 2 1

FSC FSC Trademark © 1996 Forest Stewardship Council A.C.
        SW-COC-098

TO MY PARENTS AND TO THE MEMORY OF THEIR PARENTS

לְדֹר וָדֹר

Contents

I live in New York and I have not the vaguest idea what Brooklyn is interested in.

—Walter Lippmann, *Liberty and the News* (1920)

I can speak to almost anything with a lot of authority.

—Fred Barnes on *The McLaughlin Group* (1992)

Introduction

On what forecasters like to call "an unseasonably warm" February morning in 1990, my friend Loring and I rode the subway to the Capitol, where Vaclav Havel, the new president of Czechoslovakia, was to address a joint session of Congress. Our friend George had secured two guest passes for the occasion but misinformed me when I asked him whether I needed to wear a tie. I was therefore barred at the door until I managed to convince the head of security that a sports jacket and a beat-up old wool scarf worn as an ascot represented "formal deeplomatic vear in mine country." Tragedy narrowly averted, we entered the chamber and took our seats with the senators and representatives.

Havel entered the hall to a thunderous standing ovation. It was quite a moment, and even the tough guys in the press gallery were fighting back tears. This modest, diminutive playwright, fresh from facing down the guns of the Soviet empire and leading his country in a democratic revolution, had been invited to share his wisdom in the hall that sits at the rhetorical center of what was now, undisputedly, the most powerful nation in the history of the world. Never in my adult life had I witnessed so unambiguous a victory for the forces of sweetness and light.

But for all the emotional power and moral uplift of the occasion, I still left the hall depressed. Havel was not exactly at his best, but he was still Vaclav Havel. He explored many of the great themes of personal and political responsibility with uncommon wit and originality and was certainly the only person in the chamber's history to offer even a brief plug for a Hegelian interpretation of the dialect of historical consciousness. But the sense that I was being addressed by a political leader who felt no compulsion to speak down to his audience, to insult its intellect with empty-headed rhetoric and pander to its egocentricity with kitschy encomiums, was almost wholly new to me. Seated above Havel's lectern, with that eerie, lost-in-space smile of his, was Vice-President Dan Quayle. The hall exploded when Havel declared that Marxism had been wrong, although the representatives did not bother to listen to his explanation of just what the Marxists were wrong about. ("Consciousness precedes being, and not the other way around," Havel stated.) How is it, I wondered, walking back toward Union Station to catch a train home, that the Czechs and Slovaks managed to elect this exquisitely eloquent, intellectually challenging moral champion as its president on their very first try, while more than two hundred years after our revolution, we remain mired in arguments about flag factories and Willie Horton?

If ideas have consequences for society, then so, too, does their absence. Jay Leno and David Letterman get plenty of mileage out of current politicians' day-to-day squabbles, but our lack of coherent political discourse really is a serious problem. Our politicians' rhetoric is so riddled with misinformation, mindless cliché, and meaningless spectacle that it has ceased to have any relevance to the problems it alleges to address. Even the candidates hardly pretend to believe themselves any longer. The forms of American political communication—nine-second television sound bites, negative advertisements, and ceaseless fundraising—have buried even the possibility of fruitful debate. And the political system has coasted so long on the fuel of its own irrelevance that the people who operate it have lost both the imagination and the inclination to rethink its premises. Meanwhile, back in the real world, America's problems proliferate. Our economy declines, our cities collapse, our environment deteriorates, and Washington fiddles.

It is dangerous, Thucydides reminds us, to uncouple words from things. We begin by fooling others and end up fooling ourselves. Because American politicians' words are so thoroughly uncoupled from the things about which they speak, the role of setting the parameters of our national debate, of determining what problems require urgent attention and what issues may prove to be important to the national interest, must fall elsewhere. In our case, that means the media. Nothing else remains. As our political parties have transformed themselves into little more than glorified fundraising operations, and voluntary civic, ethnic, and labor-related organizations have retreated into local politics or been shunted to the sidelines by megabuck special interests, the only place where national political communication and exchange can take place is within the elite television and print media outlets.

The problem here is that for a variety of reasons—some commercial, others cultural—the media is not up to its task. First, the most the obvious criticism: the media is owned by international corporate conglomerates whose interests frequently conflict with those of the larger public. Equally troubling are a series of more subtle barriers to honest communication, such as the role of journalistic "objectivity." Almost everyone seems to agree that objective reporting is something to which a journalist should aspire. Yet the rules of objective reporting often prevent the media from providing exactly the kinds of contextual information that allow readers, viewers, and listeners to understand what is truly going on. This not only impedes our ability to judge a story's significance, but also gives politicians enormous latitude with the truth. Much of even the most conscientious objective journalism consists of the "misstatements" that politicians would like their constituents to believe.[*]

Because objectivity is the principle by which virtually all important elite journalism defines itself, the only participants in the media's discourse licensed to provide context sufficient to allow people to form even a remotely well-informed political viewpoint are the pundits. Only the pundits are accorded both the authority and the audience necessary to explain, in language a concerned citizen is likely to understand, why such-and-such proposal is either healthy or catastrophic for the future of the republic. Only the pundits are invested with a responsibility to point out when a group of politicians are conspiring against the many on behalf of the few. Only the pundits are allowed to make the necessary connections between a scandalous rip-off of the public trust and a massive buyout of a political party. In that segment of the media in which our political discourse takes place, the pundits alone have the power and the obligation to point to a naked emperor and observe that he has no

---

[*]A minor example in this case makes a major point. On March 24, 1990, the *New York Times* reported that President Bush had announced himself to be opposed to statehood for the District of Columbia because, the president said, "its funds come almost exclusively from the Federal government." Instead of seeking to discover whether the president's insistence was true or false, the report merely quoted an opposing politician, in this case Jesse Jackson, calling Mr. Bush "unfair" for his attempts to "disenfranchise six hundred thousand American citizens." The story wholly conformed to the *Times'* demanding standards of objectivity but was nevertheless based on a falsehood. As the *Washington Post* did happen to mention in its story the same day, only 14 percent of the district's budget is provided by the Federal government. Objectivity, in the unfortunately typical case of the *Times* report, had absolutely no relevance to truth. See Philip Shenon, "Statehood for Capital Opposed by President," *New York Times*, 24 March 1990, and Ann Devroy and R. H. Melton, "President Opposes Statehood," *Washington Post*, 24 March 1990, p. A1.

clothes on—without first attributing it to "sources close to the alleged parade route."

It is the argument of this book that our economy, our security and, most particularly, our democracy, are imperiled by the decrepit state of our national political discourse. We lack the ability, as a nation, to conduct a simple, sensible, and civil conversation about the choices we face. Unless we diagnose the disease and begin to treat it, the sick state of the American body politic will certainly worsen. The net result will be not only the amplification of what George Will calls the "tawdry ferocity" of American debate, but the increasing paralysis of our political system in the face of the most daunting set of challenges America has faced since we slept though the birth of Fascism more than half a century ago.

I do not argue that the dominance of our national political dialogue by political pundits is the only serious roadblock to the achievement of a vibrant political culture in the United States. The power of money in American politics is an ongoing scandal. So is our inability, liberal and conservative, to deal honestly with the unspoken fissures in our society deriving from racial prejudice, religious conflict, and class-based stratification. Our shameful education system turns out so many illiterate citizens that intelligent political participation is all but impossible except for a decreasing minority. And political corruption, individual alienation, and a general civic laziness have led large numbers of Americans—perhaps even a majority—to remove themselves from political life. Finally, the omnipresent influence of television, coupled with the increasingly short attention span of the viewing audience, has reduced much of the discourse to a kind of semiotic shorthand, designed to trigger the emotions without disturbing the mind. Many of these carefully constructed sound bites are nothing more than advertising slogans lifted directly from Hollywood or Madison Avenue.* Few last long enough to form a coherent thought, much less outline a sensible political program.

Owing to the dominance of form over content—in this case, media forms drowning out political content—the elevation of one issue or viewpoint over that chosen by the competition is a function less of any real-world concern than of the twin dictates of television production values and the mores of Washington's Insider political culture. Working together over the past couple of decades, these two forces have spawned something I call the *punditocracy*. The punditocracy is a tiny group of highly visible political pontificators who make their living offering "inside political opinions and forecasts" in the elite national media. And it is

---

*"Where's the beef," "make my day," "read my lips," etc.

their debate, rather than any semblance of a democratic one, that determines the parameters of political discourse in the nation today.*

Defining who is and who is not a pundit at any given time can be a tricky matter. *Webster's* informs us that a pundit is "a person of great learning"; William Safire's *Political Dictionary* expands the definition to "a political analyst, usually associated with a sizable broadcasting outlet." Broadly speaking, pundits are the people anointed by the media to give their opinions on things. Political pundits give their opinions on things political. Whether these people bring any special expertise to their subject is wholly at the discretion of those doing the anointing. The ability to call oneself an expert on a particular topic is a useful, but hardly necessary, qualification.

The punditocracy, like what used to be the Soviet politburo, has full-fledged members, candidate members, and membership hopefuls. Not all pundits are invited into the punditocracy, and not all members of the punditocracy are professional pundits. As with the ex-Communists, relationships are in a state of constant flux and rarely conform to an easily discernible hierarchy.

A few extraordinarily visible perches within the insider media automatically confer to their holders a seat at the punditocracy banquet table. These include the chairs on NBC's *The McLaughlin Group* and *Meet the Press*, CBS's *Inside Washington*, ABC's *This Week*, and CNN's *The Capital Gang* and *Crossfire*, as well as regular slots on all-news cable stations such as CNN, MSNBC, and the Fox News Channel. The punditocracy's print portfolio consists of the op-ed columns of the *New York Times*, the *Washington Post*, and the *Wall Street Journal*; the top editorships of the *New Republic* and the *Weekly Standard*; and the Washington-based columns in the newsweeklies. The most celebrated commentators—super-pundits like George F. Will, William Safire, and William Kristol—earn mountains of money and play a role in insider culture analogous to that of Leonardo DeCaprio or Brad Pitt in Hollywood. Their colossal incomes derive, however,

---

*Evidence of the American people's alienation from their political system is not exactly difficult to come by. The Times Mirror Company publishes a monthly poll of just how much attention Americans pay to the news. An extensive survey of this data indicates that to say that it takes a major war (or a tax cut) to get more than half the country to sit up and pay attention to politics is no exaggeration. At one point in 1990, more Americans were aware that George Bush hated broccoli than that he had ordered the invasion of Panama. See Times Mirror Company, "The American Media: Who Reads, Who Watches, Who Listens, Who Cares," 15 July 1990. This phenomenon has important implications for any consideration of the revival of American democracy, most of which are beyond the scope of this book. For an excellent discussion of many of them, however, see the Kettering Foundation's pamphlet "Citizens and Politics: A View from Main Street America" (1991), discussed in the conclusion of this book, and E. J. Dionne's thoughtful work, *Why Americans Hate Politics* (New York: Simon and Schuster, 1991).

not from their newspaper columns or their television commentaries, but from the inevitable celebrity appearances that these positions automatically generate.

For those without access to the television personality/syndicated columnist route, admission to the punditocracy becomes largely a matter of conflating a career as former secretary of something or other with a healthy dose of self-promotional talent. Henry Kissinger and William Rogers, for instance, both were secretaries of state for Richard Nixon. Kissinger became a super-pundit; Rogers was never heard from again. In addition to his regular column syndicated by the *Los Angeles Times* and carried in the *Washington Post*, Kissinger is a regular "expert" on *Nightline*, *The NewsHour with Jim Lehrer*, and many other network and public television outlets. He is also frequently given massive amounts of space to vent his feelings in *Time* and *Newsweek*. Kissinger is the lodestar against which all former officials' pundit careers are measured. His closest competition comes from Zbigniew Brzezinski, Jimmy Carter's national security adviser, who has shadowed Kissinger for his entire professional life. Brzezinski has no syndicated column, but he is a talk-show/newsweekly/op-ed page fixture whenever a crisis materializes. It may be no coincidence that both men speak heavily accented English and therefore sound "intellectual" to American audiences. It is certainly no coincidence that Ted Koppel—a figure invested with nearly divine powers within the punditocracy realm—considers these two men to be perhaps the most intelligent political analysts in the United States.*

Beneath the Kissinger/Brzezinski stratosphere hovers a seemingly limitless—usually male—supply of former officials of past administrations ready and willing to share their expertise on today's issues with the larger public. Those who have successfully trained themselves to speak in short sentences and communicate in snappy slogans are rewarded with limited associate memberships in the punditocracy. When a crisis occurs in their "area," they are suddenly besieged with calls from bookers at *Nightline*, *Crossfire*, and *The NewsHour*; editors from the major op-ed pages and newsweeklies; and reporters seeking a sound bite to confirm what they already intend to say. The terms and duration of their memberships depend on a number of factors, including the length of the crisis and the pundit's ability to impress the gatekeepers who make the appointments. The Persian Gulf War was worth a lifetime of *New Republic* articles and strategically placed op-eds for military experts appointed by the networks

*Another exceptionally talented performer during the 1980s was Jeane Kirkpatrick, who managed, despite the perceived disadvantages of being a Democrat, an academic, and a woman, to catapult into the first rank of ex-officialdom.

to walk the audience through the minefields of Kuwait. An invitation from *The NewsHour* to discuss, for example, a trade dispute between the United States and the European Community, however, will result in little more than the fifteen minutes predicted by Andy Warhol and prescribed by the show's producers.

The outer limits of the punditocracy are composed of a short list of televisually sophisticated academics. While these "experts" are not necessarily respected in their respective fields, they are, without exception, adept at responding to questions with a minimum of professional jargon and a maximum of clarity and brevity. The ability to begin sentences with a folksy, "Well, Ted," or "That's an interesting point, Jim," is useful too. On extremely rare occasions, it is possible for a single book or magazine article to propel a writer straight into the center of punditocracy debate. Just what confluence of events is necessary to accomplish this is not wholly clear, but academics Allan Bloom and Paul Kennedy and one-time political apparatchiks Frances Fukiyama and Kevin Phillips have all traveled this path in recent years. Of course, it did no harm whatsoever that each of the works in question was championed within the punditocracy before the political explosion that opened the riches of temporary membership to their authors.

In the 1990s, the advent of three all-news cable stations (CNN, the Fox News Channel, and MSNBC), coupled with the growth of the Internet, vastly inflated the outer reaches of the punditocracy by opening up dozens, if not hundreds, of new slots in news programming. This inflation had the effect of producing many new stars, most of whom were lawyers, and of creating a second and third string of pundit wannabes who could be viewed—or downloaded from the Internet—virtually every moment of every day. Curiously, the explosion of the punditocracy did nothing to devalue the insider positions. The Sunday shows and op-ed pages remained in charge, but they commanded a much larger universe. The enormous gulf discovered by pollsters separating the members of the twenty-four hour punditocracy and the general public on the issue of President Clinton's fitness for office during the period of the Lewinsky scandal, however, demonstrated the potential for an anti-punditocracy backlash in the public at large.

In most cases, however, the public's views are not relevant. The public does not possess the means nor, apparently, the inclination, to interfere in Washington's policy apparatus in any but the most exceptional cases. This is particularly true in matters relating to foreign policy. It is not the populace's views that are defined by the pundits, but those of the Washington insiders—that informal aristocracy of the powerful, the influential, and the well-connected in whose hands either fate or a presidential appointment has placed the levers of national power. The people who inhabit the insular world of Insider Washington are largely divorced from the travails that can make everyday life in the United States such a struggle. They live in neighborhoods like Georgetown, Cleveland Park, and Chevy Chase, with green lawns, safe playgrounds, good schools, and an extra room for the maid. Their biggest problem in life, according to one Washingtonian magazine survey, is traffic.

Within insider culture, social status rests not so much on wealth as on proximity to power. How much money you earn is less important than whether you have been to Katharine Graham's (or, even better, "Kay's") for dinner. Wisdom is judged not on the depth of knowledge but the speed with which it is acquired. If you have to wait for the polls to close to hear who won an election somewhere, forget it. The only returns worth mentioning are those gleaned from exit polls. The only scandals worth raising an eyebrow over are those about to break. To know who is about to be appointed assistant secretary of state for Near Eastern and South Asian affairs is a great deal more impressive than knowing where the hell either place is. Insiders intimidate outsiders in cocktail party conversation by implying that they know more about a particular policy than they can, in good conscience, say. (This has always been Henry Kissinger's secret.) Even worse, insiders possess the unspoken potential to end a conversation by responding, "Oh, really? The Under Secretary and I just flew back on the Concorde together, and he says you don't know what you're talking about." And it is in this tiny but powerful universe that the intellectual sovereignty of pundit power reigns supreme.

The power of the punditocracy takes many forms. One can identify examples of political pundits entering the history books directly. Pat Buchanan has used his status as a pundit to run for president three times now. Buchanan is, of course, a special case, and he is unlikely ever to win his party's nomination, but a pundit presidential candidate has been inevitable for more than a decade, ever since the punditocracy achieved its prominence as the primary locus of our national political discourse. On announcing his first candidacy in December 1991, Pat Buchanan could credibly brag that "No other American has spent as many hundreds of hours debating the great questions of our day on national television." With seven weekly television appearances, two regular columns, and a popular newsletter, Buchanan was able to enlist the support of his conservative minions through infinitely greater access to the American people than any mere representative or senator. As a result of his unmediated televisual relationship with his constituency, Buchanan was able to overcome accusations that he was both an anti-Semite and a "pacifist isolationist" regarding the Gulf War—accusations that would likely have sunk the aspirations of any professional right-wing politician limited to the usual sound-bite responses.

On a less grandiose but equally significant scale, we have seen a number of direct pundit interventions into national and international politics. Ironically, we may have the punditocracy to thank for the man who sat just "a heartbeat" from the presidency for four years. When Dan Quayle launched his aggressive insider campaign for the vice-presidency, he first conspired with his close friend, *Washington Times* pundit and former Reagan administration official Kenneth Adelman. "We should have a little boomlet over this," advised Adelman, sitting by the pool with the then-unknown senator. A few days later, on August 10, 1988, a column appeared in the *Washington Times* under Adelman's name entitled, "Why Not Dan Quayle?" George Bush apparently read and heavily underlined it. Days later, Quayle was asked to appear on ABC's *This Week with David Brinkley.* James Baker, the most powerful and influential figure in the Bush campaign save Bush himself, told Quayle not to do it. But George Will intervened and apparently, in Quayle's view, outranked Baker. Quayle did the show and got the job.

Pundit interventions in international politics are rarely so heavy handed, but politically no less significant. *New York Times* columnist William Safire, for instance, went on a rampage in 1989 against Germany's sale of poison gas to Libya, calling it "Auschwitz in the Sand," and comparing it to a "final solution" for the Jews. Chancellor Helmut Kohl complained to his American visitors that "this Safire fellow has done more damage to German-American relations than any other individual." But Safire's story turned out to be true, and the Kohl government was forced to instigate a criminal investigation and change its export laws. When George Will challenged Ferdinand Marcos' democratic credentials on *This Week with David Brinkley,* Marcos responded by calling a snap election on the air, setting in motion a process that yielded the "People Power" revolution of 1985. Lyndon Johnson once said that the *Washington Post* op-ed page under editor Russell Wiggins was "worth two divisions" in Vietnam, while the *Jerusalem Post* likened *New Republic* owner Martin Peretz to a similar percentage of the fighting force of the Israeli military. Punditocracy efforts, as is discussed later in the book, were absolutely essential to President Bush's efforts to convince Congress to approve his decision to go to war in January of 1991. When, in the war's bloody aftermath, White House Chief of Staff John Sununu quipped that the only pressure on the United States to intervene on behalf of the Kurds was "coming from columnists," these same columnists reminded him that, six months earlier, they were "the only ones supporting the use of force to liberate Kuwait." Within two weeks of the invasion, the president had reversed himself and accepted an open-ended commitment to defending the lives of the Kurds.

But these are rare cases. Usually, the punditocracy's influence is invisible and therefore unprovable. No politician can credit a television talk show or newspaper op-ed column with influencing his policies, lest he compromise his reputation for independence. Not a single political pundit earned a mention in Ronald Reagan's memoirs: not even Pat Buchanan, who served as White House director of communications, or George Will, who coached the president's debating tactics, touched up his speeches, and frequently hosted dinner parties Reagan attended.

Nevertheless, it is difficult to imagine a president who could have paid more attention to political pundits than Ronald Reagan. In addition to hiring Buchanan and befriending Will, Reagan was a dedicated fan of *The McLaughlin Group* and was known to bang on the tables at Camp David when one of its members took issue with one of his policies. He appeared at the *Group*'s birthday party; visited its host, John McLaughlin, at his home for dinner; and appointed McLaughlin's wife to be secretary of labor. Reagan was also known to call members of *Agronsky and Company* after the show. The president took the editorial pages of Sun Myung Moon's *Washington Times* so seriously that when Buchanan entered the White House, he proceeded to allow his entire communications staff to languish in bureaucratic limbo while he devoted himself to the only work he thought truly mattered: planting articles and ideas in the *Washington Times*' far-right Commentary section.

Even more important than the ability to influence the president's mind is the ability to fashion his intellectual environment. Walter Lippmann observed nearly fifty years ago that "he who captures the symbols by which the public feeling is for the moment contained, controls by that much the approaches of public policy." These approaches are exactly where the influence of the punditocracy is so powerfully pervasive. As right-wing media critic Jude Wanniski observes, "If politicians are able to decide what the electorate wants, they have to have the parameters of the debate communicated to them by the scriveners." By determining these parameters, the punditocracy can create for a president either a hostile or sympathetic context in which to pursue his agenda. James Fallows, a speechwriter in the Carter White House, recalls that "what was on the op-ed pages provided the boundaries of what we were allowed to say in the speeches. Underlings in the government, like me, could move the ball up and down the playing field, but the columnists defined the field." Part of Fallows' job, therefore, was to contact op-ed writers to convince them to address issues which the president was preparing to approach. In one particularly illustrative case, Fallows actually ghostwrote a *New Republic* editorial himself to legitimate a discussion of its subject by his employer, the president of the United States.

The Carter presidency predated the explosion of pundit television, and the "punditocracy effect" had not yet reached its present proportions. The fruition of its influence can be seen in the 1985 invention of the "Reagan Doctrine" by *New Republic* editor, *Washington Post* and *Time* columnist, and *Inside Washington* regular panelist Charles Krauthammer. On the basis of a few throwaway sentences in the president's State of the Union address, Krauthammer created a concept that brought coherence to what had previously been just an amalgam of rag-tag drug runners, terrorists, Islamic fundamentalists, Maoist revolutionaries, and a few hapless democrats pacing the Capitol hallways for taxpayer handouts. As "freedom fighters" for the Reagan Doctrine, these sorry fellows were transformed into romantic agents of the "restoration" of "democratic militance," fighting to turn back Soviet gains at "the limits of empire." In addition to considerably flattering Reagan's intelligence, Krauthammer's rhetorical umbrella vastly increased the limits of the ideological and financial tribute that high-powered Washington influence peddlers were able to wrangle out of Congress for the Afghans.

Similarly, when in March 1983 Ronald Reagan unveiled his "dream" of a nuclear astrodome–protected United States that would render Moscow's nuclear missiles "impotent and obsolete," a healthy portion of the punditocracy underwent what one writer called "a mass conversion reminiscent of that decreed by King Ethelbert of Kent in the sixth century." Led by Kissinger and Brzezinski, the punditocracy created an ideologically inspired smokescreen on behalf of the strategic defense initiative (SDI) that enabled the Reagan administration and its allies in Congress to soak up tens of billions of tax dollars on what was clear to all disinterested parties to be a perfectly pinheaded scheme.* The fact that 98 percent of the members of the National Academy of Scientists in relevant scientific fields believed that SDI would never "provide an effective defense of the entire U.S. civilian population" and only 4 percent expected such a system to be "survivable and cost-effective at the margin" did not carry much weight in Washington. The history of supply-side economics, moreover, discussed at length in Chapter 8, can be

---

*Kissinger described SDI as "a major contribution to Western strategy . . . perhaps [Reagan's] greatest contribution to strategic theory" ("How to Deal with Gorbachev," *Newsweek*, 2 March 1988, pp. 42, 47). Zbigniew Brzezinski, Robert Jastrow, and Max Kempleman chose the almost comically appropriate biblical incantation that "faith can move mountains" in support of their own version of the system (see "Defense in Space Is Not Star Wars," *The New York Times Magazine*, 27 January 1985, p. 47).

charted along similar lines as the earlier discussion. Within the confines of Washington's punditocracy-driven insider debate, when reality and ideology come into conflict, it is the former, almost uniformly, that gives way.

For the first half-century of its existence, political punditry was simply a branch of journalism. A newspaper column was considered the reward for a particularly distinguished career as a reporter or, in rare cases, a mark of incipient political genius. The first Washington pundits arose in the decade between 1910 and 1920 as a complement to increasingly objective news reporting. During most of the previous century, journalists had few pretenses about their prejudices, and owners frequently used their newspapers as political weapons. Neither had much incentive to divorce their opinions from the news and, hence, equally little interest in explicitly labeled commentary. Washington was, for most of this period, a backwater swamp compared to New York or Chicago, and journalists with literary pretensions wisely steered clear of it.

The first truly influential Washington pundit, Walter Lippmann, was in many ways the least typical. Lippmann had earned himself a national reputation as a New York editorial writer and columnist, as well as a best-selling author, when complications in his personal life led him to relocate down South in 1936.* Lippmann's newspaper analyses were so vastly superior to those that preceded his arrival that he single-handedly raised both the social status and the professional standards of his chosen profession. His columns provided other journalists with an intellectual standard to which they might aspire and his readers with an education in the principles of foreign policy as the young republic grew to superpowerdom. Equally important, he offered high officials the opportunity to challenge, refine, and ultimately communicate their own ideas before attempting to chisel them in the stone of government edict.

But Lippmann was less a journalist than a public philosopher. The pundits who followed him did not have the option of simply applying their genius to the daily rush of events and knocking off something brilliant before lunch. They compensated by combining journalistic investigation with a bit of context, a few explicitly stated opinions, and the kinds of inside dirt that could not comfortably be included in a straight news story. Some, like James Reston of the *New York Times*, rested their reputations on their journalistic prowess. Others, like Joseph Alsop, earned reader loyalty through a combination of Lipp-

---

*Lippmann fell in love with the wife of his best friend, Hamilton Fish Armstrong, and the two left their respective spouses in New York to begin a new life together.

mannian hauteur, Restonian legwork, and virulent anti-Communism. As their influence grew steadily during the postwar era, a few pundits developed their own political constituencies and achieved the ability to throw their weight around Washington the way any senator or representative might. In Lippmann's case, his endorsement of a presidential initiative was said to be roughly equal to the combined clout of either four U.S. senators or the Speaker of the House. But the numbers of the select few whose views mattered in the success of a given government policy were truly minuscule. Beyond Lippmann, Reston, and Alsop, it is difficult to name more than a dozen pundits whose influence lasted longer than a single decade between 1930 and 1980.

The nature of the job and the power of its practitioners began to change during the 1970s, when television discovered punditry and vice versa. Once again Lippmann was the pioneer, and once again his example spawned an offspring that bore him only passing resemblance. In the early 1960s, *CBS News* took the extraordinary step of devoting a series of television interviews to a man whose only celebrity derived from his fame as a political columnist.[*] In the final year of that decade, Post/Newsweek stations took the equally remarkable step of devoting a weekly television show to the opinions of a group of journalists, none of whom was named Walter Lippmann. *Agronsky and Company* eventually spawned a series of imitators, opening the doors of stardom and riches to its beneficiaries and vastly increasing both their visibility and ambitions.

Because of its tangled roots in personal journalism, political commentary, and television production values, the punditocracy never developed a recognizable code of ethics. This situation was further complicated by the entry into the profession in the early 1980s of large numbers of political operatives who could not even pretend to consider themselves journalists. No longer a means of rewarding the profession's most distinguished members, the jobs opened up to political deal makers, speechwriters, press flacks, and professional ideologues. During this period, the political column came to be seen as the stepping stone to riches, fame, and kingmaker status all in one. Even better, there were almost no rules about how such success might be achieved. John McLaughlin, himself credibly accused of (and sued for) extremely offensive sexual harassment, feels free to attack the character and credibility of Anita Hill without so much as mentioning his own sordid history.[†] George Will coaches the president on his debating

---

[*]The first "Conversation with Walter Lippmann" aired on August 11, 1960.
[†]McLaughlin settled the case out of court for an undisclosed payment. See Chapter 5 for details.

techniques and then judges his performance a few days later. Morton Kondracke and Fred Barnes of Fox News Channel's *The Beltway Boys* sell their dinner conversation to wealthy American Express Platinum Card holders, "by invitation only." Kondracke, together with Robert Novak, happily accepts thousands of dollars in payments from the Republican party, ostensibly in return for sharing his political wisdom at a gathering of its governors. Novak and his partner, Rowland Evans, have created something approaching a mini pundit conglomerate, hosting two television shows, publishing three newsletters, sponsoring pricey off-the-record briefings by cabinet officials for corporate fat cats, and—like Barnes and Kondracke—auctioning off their dinner conversation to starstruck fans. If anyone objects to the coziness of these arrangements, their beneficiaries are shocked that anyone would question their integrity.

Just why this class of commentators came to cohere as the most influential determinants of the shape of American political discourse in the early 1980s may be clearer to future historians than it is today. The most convincing explanation lies in the coupling of the collapse of the punditocracy's competition with the inexorable expansion of the empire of media dominance in all aspects of American cultural life. In many ways, the pundits won the fight because they were the only guys left standing in the ring. The bull market in pundit influence coincided with the collapse of the bipartisan establishment that had guided American foreign policy for the previous five decades. This process began in Vietnam, which sapped the self-confidence of the "Wise Men" and destroyed the trust the American political system had invested in them. It continued through Watergate, the oil crises of the 1970s, and the debilitating stagflation of the same period. The rise of the New Right provided the final shove over the ledge. Political parties by and large disappeared during this period as well, in part because of internal divisions on both sides and in part because the onset of the electronic campaign made their infrastructure obsolete. The community of academic experts on whom our national political discussion had previously relied took the same opportunity to withdraw to the academy—partially as a result of Vietnam-related divisions and partially as a result of an increasing obsession with social-scientific arcania. Independent intellectuals of the *Partisan Review* model also slipped off the public's screen during this period, falling victim to the balkanization of public culture and the collapse of the socioeconomic foundation that supported their professional lives.

An equally important factor was the pundits' ability to hitch themselves successfully to Ronald Reagan's rising star. Whether right-wing pundits became influential during "the Reagan revolution" or influential pundits became right-wing is a chicken-and-egg problem. Either way, the punditocracy proved that it could read election returns as well as any legislature. Most newspaper publishers and the lion's share of public affairs television funding originated on the Right, as well; their prejudices were suddenly unleashed by the newfound respectability Reagan accorded them. Suddenly, views that had been considered Cro-Magnon just months earlier became sophisticated. While a tiny cadre of stalwarts managed to hold fast to their liberal instincts during this period, most professed to see new wisdom in cutting taxes for the rich, threatening war with the Soviets, and cracking down on vodka-guzzling welfare queens. The punditocracy hardly required a weatherman to determine which way political winds were blowing.*

A final addition to the dominance of misinformation and misinterpretation in American political discourse was the punditocracy's ever-expanding pretension to expertise in areas its members could not really be fairly expected to master. This is less a reflection on the talents of the men and women who people the punditocracy than on the increasingly impossible demands of their jobs. In Lippmann's day, both the world and the American role within it appeared a great deal simpler. When David Halberstam returned from two years in the Congo in the mid-1960s, his boss, James Reston, sent him over to see Lippmann. When he arrived, the pundit asked him, "When I understood Europe they told me I needed to understand Asia. Now that I've been trying to get Asia, they tell me I need Africa. What can you tell me about Africa?" When Halberstam gave up daily reporting and was approached by a syndicate about beginning a regular column, he remembered this story and decided the entire idea was futile. Even in Lippmann's later days, punditry was becoming increasingly difficult to defend as an intellectual enterprise.

Today, a good column has become harder than ever to write, not only because issues have proliferated and increased in complexity, but also because this has become increasingly obvious inside Washington, owing to an explosion in the specialized fields of policy research and political consultancy. The most defensible columns are those that spe-

---

*Several rightist organizations have spent a great deal of their funders' money convincing Americans that the media is biased on behalf of liberals. I would not argue that the media is not biased, or that this bias does not manifest itself on certain issues—particularly abortion—in a politically liberal direction. But the bias is more cultural than political. It is urban, secularist, pseudo-sophisticated, wholly ahistorical, and tremendously cowardly in the face of concerted government or corporate pressure. Overall, conservatives benefit more from these biases than do liberals, but the point is arguable.

cialize in a particular beat or speak with an intensely personal voice while addressing larger issues from something approaching a human scale. The problem with beat columns, however, is that they force pundits down the same hole into which reporters historically fall: they become prisoners of their sources. The latter, more personal style can have great value when done well. But the temptations toward laziness, self-satisfaction, and plain old burnout are more than most pundits can resist. Only a negligible number of pundits manage to pull off the simultaneous feats of intellect, reporting, and integrity required to write an honest analytical column about the panoply of issues facing America. The number who manage to present a coherent, contextual viewpoint on television is zero.

As with virtually every aspect of life it touches, television has degraded the quality of political punditry, coarsening its language and destroying what remained of its Lippmann-era sophistication. The level of political analysis on even the best of these shows is usually a notch below that heard on *Friends*. Moreover, because virtually everyone in Washington journalism entertains at least a daydream of the riches and fame that only television can bring, even good journalists are tempted to imitate increasingly rich and famous performers, and so television's simpleton virus flows throughout the entire political discourse. Even in the unlikely event that a pundit has no wish to become rich and famous through television, he must nevertheless address himself to the particular pseudoreality television has created.

During the 1990s, the size of the punditocracy exploded, and its frivolousness increased exponentially. The O. J. Simpson case, the death of the Princess of Wales, the trial of the au pair Louise Woodward in the so-called nanny murder, and the JonBenet Ramsey investigation, combined with the media's obsession with President Clinton's relationship with Monica Lewinsky, drove nearly all serious discussion of larger problems from the public domain. The endless talk of sex and murder in the American public sphere made it nearly impossible for interested citizens to feel themselves to be participants in a larger conversation about the nation's future. The public frequently condemned the media's relentless focus on sex and tawdry tabloid topics, but the producers of these shows insisted that they had no other way to attract large numbers of viewers. The result was an endless cycle of cynicism on both sides and an ever-widening gap between the rulers and the ruled. "Ignorance is correctable," notes the social critic Neil Postman, "but what shall we do if we take ignorance to be knowledge?" By allowing the punditocracy to determine the content of its political dialogue, the American political system has committed itself to a path that all but guarantees the acceleration of the destructive pathologies threatening our common future. What follows is an examination of how this catastrophic situation came to pass.

THE BIRTH OF A NOTION

"I wish we had never come to Washington. New York is so much nicer and the people there are much more amusing; they dance ever so much better and send one flowers all the time, and then they never talk about first principles."

—Sibyl Lee, in Henry Adams' *Democracy* (1880)

CHAPTER ONE

The Road to Lippmanndom

The word *pundit* is a bastardization of the Hindi honorific *pandit*, which confers on its holder the implication of great learning. *Pandit* derives from the Sanskrit *pandita*, meaning "scholar." Its metamorphosis into the American vernacular owes a great deal to the wives of a group of Rochester, New York, professional men who joined together in 1854 to found a club "devoted to the serious and conscientious investigation of the truth." Not much in the creativity department, apparently, the men decided to call their club "The Club." Their wives, however, thinking all this high-mindedness to be a bit much, took to referring to the group as "The Pundit Club" in a facetious reference to the Eastern title. The members were well acquainted with the word's connotations; one of its members, the Reverend Doctor McIlvaine, had given a report to the group entitled "Observations on the Sanskrit Language," and soon, in good spirits, they adopted the appellation as their own.

The term meandered into the American public dialogue via an article in the *Saturday Review,* dated 1862, in which the author noted a point on which "the doctors of etiquette and the pundits of refinement" were likely to differ. The final stage of its etymological development seems to have come from the pen of Henry Luce, who founded *Time* magazine in 1923. Luce adopted the term *pundit,* which he derived, most likely, from another well-known club—this a group of Yale undergraduates—and applied to the *New York World* editorial writer Walter Lippmann.

It is particularly fitting that Lippmann should have the honor of being the first journalist so zinged with the moniker, since the art form did not begin to approach its current level of pretension until he chose journalism as a profession on graduating from Harvard in 1910. Pre-Lippmann, journalists had been considered incompletely evolved life-forms on the American social scale. Reporting was seen a job for winos, perverts, and those without sufficient imagination to become successful gangsters. The notion of a young man choosing to be a journalist rather than a professor of political philosophy at Harvard, as Lippmann had done, was akin to that of a guest at a society cocktail party refusing a glass of Dom Perignon and inquiring, instead, if the hostess could come up with a cold Schlitz.

The emergence of Walter Lippmann as America's semi-official public philosopher in the 1920s and 1930s represented the fulfillment of a kind of circular journey for American journalism. In the days of the American revolutionary press, politicians, journalists, pundits, and pamphleteers were by and large the same people. Politicians owned and published newspapers and pamphlets, and probably no one even thought to separate fact from opinion. The press played an absolutely essential role in the creation of a revolutionary consciousness among the colonists, stoking a vibrant public discourse in the late 1760s and early 1770s from resistance to rebellion. To achieve this transformation, they created an ideology that was both angry and inspirational. Firebrands Samuel Adams and Thomas Paine used the printing press to turn what were seen as little more than obnoxious restrictions sent over by the king into an irreconcilable conflict between freedom and slavery. The most important pundits of the time were, therefore, by definition the most important journalists and politicians as well.

With victory over the British assured, the pundit-politicians turned their attention to the shaping of the new nation. Between 1787 and 1788, Alexander Hamilton, together with James Madison and John Jay, published the eighty-five essays that made up the Federalist papers in the semiweekly *New York Independent Journal* in support of the proposed constitution under the nom de plume "Publius." Their opponents, less well remembered although equally well regarded at the time, used the names "Brutus," "the Federal Farmer," and "Cato" in response. Both sides provided a standard of scholarship and eloquence against which all subsequent political punditry would pale.

The American opinion magazine, in which so much of the modern punditocracy is today housed, owes its pedigree in large measure to the wit and energy of Benjamin Franklin. A copy of the *British Spectator*, founded in 1711, landed in Franklin's hands when he was a young man, and he "bought it, read it over and over, and was much delighted with it." The sixteen-year-old

Franklin then began his punditry career by stealth—slipping columns underneath the door at his brother's newspaper and signing them "Silence Dogood." Between April and October 1722, the *New England Courant* published fourteen such letters, in which the fictional Mrs. Dogood complained of political and religious hypocrisy, championed feminist rights, and laughed at Harvard. James Franklin was so angry and embarrassed when the author's identity was revealed that he ran his precocious brother out of town. Young Benjamin was forced to move to Philadelphia, where he worked at various printing trades, finally founding his *General Magazine* in 1741.*

During the early life of the republic, newspapermen did the bidding of politicians and were rewarded in kind, with no questions about where allegiances lay. Building on the success of his Federalist experience, Hamilton founded the *New York Evening Post* in 1801, where he frequently dictated the editorials verbatim. Ten years earlier, during George Washington's presidency in Philadelphia, Thomas Jefferson promised the revolutionary poet Philip Freneau a $250-a-year clerkship at the State Department and complete access to all of his correspondence in return for establishing the pro-Jefferson *National Gazette*.

The cozy printing-contract-for-friendly-partisan arrangement continued through 1860, when the founding of the Government Printing Office put an end to the president's store of newspaper venture capital. Before that, Andrew Jackson set something of a record, carrying fifty-seven journalists on the public payroll. They were, according to John Quincy Adams, without exception "the vilest purveyors of slander during the last electioneering campaign," which by the way, Adams lost.†

The carrying of a newspaperman on the public payroll was no doubt helpful to the scribe's standard of living, but it was hardly necessary. James Gordon Bennet, the profession's first Washington correspondent,

---

*"Without Freedom of Thought," wrote Mrs. Dogood, "there can be no such Thing as Wisdom and no such Thing as Publick Liberty. . . . Whoever would overthrow the Liberty of a Nation, must begin by subduing the Freeness of Speech." See Karl E. Meyer, *Pundits, Poets and Wits* (New York: Oxford University Press, 1990), p. xvii. The letters themselves can be found in Benjamin Franklin's *Letters to the Press*, ed. Verner W. Crane (Chapel Hill, NC: University of North Carolina Press, 1950). The full name of Franklin's magazine was *The General Magazine and Historical Chronicle for All the British Plantations in America*. Unfortunately for Franklin's place in the record books, however, he went to press three days after his employee, Andrew Bradford, brought out his short-lived *American Magazine*.

†See John Tebbel and Sarah Miles Watts, *The Press and the Presidency* (New York: Oxford University Press, 1985), p. 78. Adams' quote may deserve greater credibility than his political interests might imply. These appointments were drawn from a pool described by fellow editor John Fenno as "the most ignorant, mercenary, and vulgar automatons that ever were moved by the constantly rusting wires of sordid mercantile avarice." Quoted in Allen Nevins, *American Political Opinions, 1895–1922* (Port Washington, NY: Kinnikat Press, 1928), p. 7.

ably demonstrated the prevailing standards of fairness and objectivity in his first *New York Herald* dispatch, published on January 2, 1828, when he disclosed that "it will be found that the Jacksonian party are the truest friends of the country, and that they will encourage every interest but favor none." Although wealthy publishers and their hired editors did enjoy the prerogative of purely editorial columns, these were often nothing more than a harmless vanity: the true editorializing was done in the news columns.

For the first twelve or so decades of the republic, the only generally recognized names in the journalism profession were those of the wealthy owner-publishers, crusading editors, and the syndicated feature writers, the vast majority of whom were humorists and satirists. Many belonging to the first category did enjoy a significant degree of influence over the opinions of their literate publics. The late *New York Times* pundit Arthur Krock saw the forerunners of his profession at work at the Cincinnati Liberal/Democratic convention of 1872, at which publisher-journalist Horace Greeley was nominated for president. Scheming quite openly to deny their print colleague his ambition were four powerful editors who called themselves the "Quadrilateral": Henry Watterson, the legendary publisher of the *Louisville Courrier-Journal*; Murat Halstead of the *Cincinnati Commercial*; Sam Bowles of the *Springfield (Mass.) Republican*, and Horace White of the *Chicago Tribune*. The editors were so impressed with one another's wisdom that each printed the editorials of the other three in his paper.[*] The plot failed, due to the fact that Greeley's assistant, Whitelaw Reid, was inexplicably admitted to the inner councils of the cabal.

The incident may mark the beginnings of the all-important institution of the syndication of individual pundits. The technological phenomenon of newspaper syndication itself, the foundation on which pre-electronic punditry rested, came on the heels of the invention of the telegraph, when, in May 1846, the *New York Tribune* and the *New York Herald* began running identical wire dispatches from Washington.[†] The most widely syndicated writers were, however, rarely political. The *New York Sun* syndicated the work of Henry James. McClure's syndicate handled the work of Robert Louis Stevenson, Mark Twain, Henry Cabot Lodge, Rudyard Kipling, Jack London, and Arthur Conan Doyle. William Randolph

---

[*]Greeley was nominated on the Liberal Republican and Democratic tickets. He lost to Republican U. S. Grant, which is just as well, since Greeley died before the electoral college cast its ballots. See Arthur Krock, "The Early Personal Journalists," in *Walter Lippmann and His Times*, Marquis Childs and James Reston, eds. (New York: Harcourt, Brace, Jovanovich, 1959), pp. 83–110.
[†]This development led to the formation of the Associated Press three years later.

Hearst's syndicate—the great-grandfather of today's King Features—featured the sardonic skepticism of Ambrose Bierce before he disappeared into the Mexican Civil War and the prophetic satire of Chicago wit Finley Peter Dunne, whose barkeep, Mr. Martin J. Dooley, rivals Huckleberry Finn and Jay Gatsby as modern punditry's favorite fictional oracle.

Before punditry could play a significant role in political debate, however, "straight" American journalism needed to rid itself of the opinionated arguments that were its foundation. The initial seeds of objective reporting appeared in New York in 1851, in part as a reaction to the perceived excesses of the crusaders. First and foremost among the guilty, no doubt, was Horace Greeley. Though not quite as vociferous as the *Liberator*'s William Lloyd Garrison, Greeley barely stopped to take a breath as he and his newspaper, the *New York Tribune*, thundered against war, social inequality, and the South's peculiar institution. In addition to sponsoring the foreign-correspondent career of an unknown European journalist by the name of Marx, Greeley's *Tribune* can take credit for founding the institution of the modern editorial page.* The great American historian and former *New York World* editorial writer Allen Nevins described Greeley's creation as follows:

> a page treating a wide variety of topics in a variety of manners, though pursuing a consistent policy: achieving a level of genuine literary merit; produced by a body of editors, not by a single man and representing their united elevated judgment and information; and earnestly directed to the elevation and rectification of public opinion.

What Greeley did not do, or make any pretense of doing, was remove the same opinions from his news pages. His former managing editor,

---

*Greeley's hiring of Karl Marx is a wonderfully ironic episode in the history of both the political philospher and American journalism. Marx himself hated writing his columns, and complained to a friend that "this continual journalistic hack-work is getting on my nerves. It takes up a lot of time, destroys any continuity in my efforts and in the final analysis amounts to nothing at all" (quoted in Neil A. Grauer, *Wits and Sages* [Baltimore: Johns Hopkins University Press, 1984], p. 7). Looking at his published letters, however, it is hard to work up much sympathy. Unbeknownst to Greeley and his managing editor Charles Dana, Marx had subcontracted out at least nineteen of these London-based dispatches—those dealing with revolution and counter-revolution in Germany and published between October 1851 and October 1852—to his uncredited German partner, Friedrich Engels. The articles stopped arriving, however, because the paper cut the fee for them by 50 percent, from ten dollars to five. With his family sick and hungry, the author "did not have the penny to go read newspapers." Why he needed to read newspapers, however, when Engels was doing all the work, Marx does not explain. The entire correspondence between Marx and Engels on the subject is reprinted in Karl Marx and Friedrich Engels, *Selected Letters: The Personal Correspondence, 1844–1877*, ed. Fritz J. Raddatz (Boston: Little, Brown, 1980), pp. 34–51. The "did not have a penny" quote appears on page 51.

Henry J. Raymond, did not appreciate what he considered to be the over-wrought prose of his ex-employer, and on September 18, 1851, he responded with the launching of the *New-York Times*. In a thinly veiled jibe at Greeley, he promised his readers on page one of the inaugural issue that "We do not mean to write as if we were in a passion unless that should really be the case; and we shall make a point to get into a passion as rarely as possible."

If one wished to chart the earliest antecedent in the search for the journalistic Holy Grail of "objectivity," one might do well to begin with Raymond's first issue. His paper was intended to emulate the *Times* of London in its aspiration toward a journalism of authority and complete-ness. Raymond's *Times* did introduce a new note of decency and restraint into political journalism, but a man who served as chairman of the Republican National Committee and managed Abraham Lincoln's sec-ond presidential campaign is not really an appropriate model for aspiring objectivists. Moreover, Raymond's impact was slight and, after his death in 1869, the profession came to be dominated by E. L. Godkin, the com-bative British aristocrat who campaigned against American imperialism, government corruption, and unsound money.

The editor of the *New York Evening Post* and *Nation* magazine for nearly three decades, Godkin was said by William James to be the most influen-tial writer of his generation. A combative generation it must have been. Godkin called President Cleveland an "international anarchist" and com-pared the modes of operation inside the nation's yellow journals to those of Hell, gambling houses, brothels, and brigands' caves, noting that, judged purely on the basis of intellectual integrity, the newsrooms finished a poor fifth.* With the influence of Godkin and the continuing preemi-nence of old-time publisher-editors like Watterson of Louisville, Kentucky, Samuel Bowles I and II of Springfield, Massachusetts, and William Allen White of Emporia, Kansas, another serious stab at the virtues of newspaper objectivity would have to wait until nearly the end of the century.

In 1896, a Chattanooga publisher named Adolph Ochs purchased the ailing *New-York Times*. Ochs was a man with big plans. On August 19, 1896, the paper's readers awoke to a "business announcement" explaining that it would henceforth be the policy of the paper "to give the news, all the news, in concise and attractive form, in language that is parliamentary in good society" and "to give it impartially, without fear or favor, regardless of any party, sect, or interest involved." Adolph Ochs' *Times* would be an

---

*The *Nation*, America's oldest continuously publishing political magazine, was founded by the architect Fredrick Law Olmstead in 1865. Godkin, its founding editor, sold it to his *New York Evening Post* in 1881, where it was issued as a weekly supplement for the next thirty-three years.

"independent newspaper" that would "tolerate no tampering with the news, no coloring, no deception." It would stand for "the fullness, trustworthiness and impartiality of its news service." Ochs' pronouncement was soon reprinted in papers across the country.

In addition to his grand public gesture, Ochs instituted a number of new features in the newspaper, all of which were directed toward attracting a new kind of readership. He began with a weekly financial review and followed up with a list of "Buyers in Town," listed court cases and records, and included a column called "The Merchants' Point of View." Most reporters expected these changes to make the *Times* duller than ever but, to their astonishment, the paper attracted thousands of new readers and the flow of advertising increased fantastically. Soon enough, the paper that had been losing $1,000 a day when Ochs purchased it became the "Business Bible" of New York and a veritable money-printing machine for Mr. Ochs. Circulation skyrocketed from 9,000 in 1896 to more than 120,000 nine years later and to 343,000 by 1920.

The economic foundation of Ochs' success can be gleaned from the incredible urban growth statistics of the period.[*] New York was exploding with new wealth and a newly well-educated population. By providing commercially oriented information to consumers and removing both the crusading tone adopted by Greeley and Godkin and the sensationalist ravings of the yellow journals of the time, Ochs managed to invent a new and tremendously profitable form of American journalism and a status symbol for an emerging commercial class.

As Christopher Lasch observes, this new press attracted exactly the kinds of readers advertisers were eager to attain:

> well-heeled readers, most of whom probably thought of themselves as independent voters. . . . Responsibility came to be equated with the avoidance of controversy. . . . Some advertisers were also willing to pay for sensationalism,

---

[*]The percentage of the American labor force engaged in non-agricultural work jumped from 41 percent in 1860 to 62 percent in 1900. Bank deposits tripled between 1865 and 1885, then quadrupled in the twenty years following that. The population of New York City jumped from 1 million to 1.5 million between 1880 and 1890. Meanwhile, illiteracy declined from 20 percent of the population to 10.7. See Arthur M. Schlesinger, *Rise of the City, 1878–1898* (New York: Macmillan, 1932). For more recent data and interpretative material, see Sam Bass Warner, Jr., *The Urban Wilderness: A History of the American City* (New York: Harper and Row, 1972), and Charles N. Glaab and A. Theodore Brown, *A History of Urban America* (New York: Macmillan, 1976). The literacy figures in particular had enormous implications for politicians. When "Boss" William Macy Tweed instructed his henchmen to destroy copies of New York's anti-Tammany newspapers in the 1860s, he worried not about the editorials, but only about their cartoons. "My constituents can't read," Tweed explained, "but damn it, they can see pictures." Tweed died in prison in 1878. See Stephen Hess, "The Ungentlemanly Art," *The Gannet Center Journal* (spring 1989): p. 122.

though on the whole, they preferred a respectable readership to sheer numbers. What they clearly did not prefer was "opinion." It did not guarantee the right audience. No doubt they also hoped that an aura of objectivity, the hallmark of responsible journalism, would also rub off on the advertisements that surrounded the increasingly slender columns of print.

Historians generally consider Ochs' *Times* to be the first example of a newspaper dedicated to objective journalism. But what Ochs and company sought to achieve in the *Times* was less the goal of objective journalism than the appearance of it. As Godkin's successor, Oswald Garrison Villard, demonstrated in his 1933 book *Some Newspapers and Newspaper-Men*, the *Times* was still what Garrison called "a class paper, pure and simple." Its dedication to impartiality fell by the wayside when it proved ideologically inconvenient. Vociferously opposed to the Russian Revolution, the *Times* reported that Petrograd had fallen six times, been on the verge of capture three more times, been burned to the ground twice, and been in absolute panic twice and in revolt against the Bolsheviks on six different occasions, and insisted that the regime was on the verge of collapse over ninety times. None of these impending catastrophes, Charles Merz and Walter Lippmann pointed out in the *New Republic*, had much foundation in fact. But for the purposes of delineating the history of punditry, the *Times'* failure to be "objective" in its news columns is less important than the impression it created: that "objectivity" was possible and desirable, and that any responsible newspaper had better strive for it if its owners wanted to be rich, powerful, and admired like those of the *New-York Times*. As a result, during the next two decades, smaller-scale imitations sprouted up across America.

Although the professional developments it inspired were gradual, Ochs' philosophical departure was, in fact, a radical change. Without at least the pretense of objective news reports as a counterpoint, it is impossible to imagine punditry's occupying anything like the political role into which it has grown in the twentieth century. Absent a professionally sacred faith in objective news gathering, there would be no call for political pundits to comment on it and interpret it. This relatively banal observation goes a long way toward explaining why the United States is the only Western country to enjoy (if that be the word) the presence of a pundit class: it is the only nation in which the aspiration toward objectivity dominates the profession of quality journalism. Where journalism drops the pretense of reporting only fact, the need for opinion writers, dedicated, ideally, to placing the news in a larger and more useful context for readers, diminishes accordingly.

Around the same time that newspaper publishers were beginning to emulate Ochs, the young Walter Lippmann attempted, in three remarkable studies of the American media, *Liberty and the News* (1920), *Public Opinion* (1922), and *The Phantom Public* (1924), to grapple with some of the more complex interrelationships between imperfect journalism and the fragilities of modern democratic practice. Given the limits of even the best American journalism and the inability of average citizens to grasp even the most basic facts about their leaders and institutions, how, Lippmann asked, could a functional republic be forged?

Reality, to Lippmann (and to Ochs, no doubt), was something picturable, like a baseball box score or a stock market quotation. He titled the most impressive chapter in *Public Opinion*, the most demanding of his studies, "The World Outside and the Picture in Our Heads." The problem with journalism, according to Lippmann's critique, was its inability to focus the lens correctly on the more intricate manifestations of reality. "News comes from a distance," Lippmann complained, "it comes helter-skelter." Journalism works fine, Lippmann explains, "when it can report the score of a game, or a transatlantic flight, or the death of a monarch." But where the picture is more complex, "as for example, in the matter of a success of a policy, or the social conditions among a foreign people—where the real answer is neither yes or no, but subtle and a matter of balanced evidence," then journalism "causes no end of derangement, misunderstanding and even misrepresentation."

The inherent limitations on journalists, moreover, are compounded by the inability of the general public to understand and assimilate the imperfect information it receives. The thirty-three-year-old public philosopher is rather harsh on his fellow citizens, but contemporary information surveys would seem to bear him out:

> The mass of absolutely illiterate, of feeble-minded, grossly neurotic, under-nourished and frustrated individuals, is very considerable, much more considerable there is reason to think than we generally suppose. Thus a wide appeal is circulated among persons who are mentally children or barbarians, people whose vitality is exhausted, shut-in people and people whose experience has comprehended no factor in the problem under discussion. The stream of public opinion is stopped by them in little eddies of misunderstanding, where it is discolored with prejudice and far-fetched analogy.

The net result of imperfect journalism consumed by ignorant people is, in Lippmann's view, the creation of a "pseudo-environment," in which a perverse kind of democratic politics takes place.

Hardly the "omnicompetent" agrarian yeoman of Jeffersonian theory, the private citizen, or "outsider" as Lippmann called him, had a vision of political realities hardly better than that of a deaf spectator in the back row of a sporting event. "He does not know what is happening, why it is happening, what ought to happen; he lives in a world which he cannot see, does not understand and is unable to direct." "We must assume," therefore, "that a public is inexpert in its curiosity, intermittent, that it discerns only gross distinctions, is slow to be aroused and quickly diverted; that, since it acts by aligning itself, it personalizes whatever it considers, and is interested only when events have been melodramatized as a conflict." The danger arises when the members of the populace become the "inevitable victims of agitation and propaganda." The victors in such a system are "the quack, the charlatan, the jingo, and the terrorist." The result, both for democracy and for intelligent governance, is disaster.

At first, in the 1919 articles that became *Liberty and the News*, Lippmann suggested addressing the problem simply by improving the quality of the journalism Americans received. He complained that reporting was not a "dignified profession for which men will invest the time and cost of an education, but an underpaid, insecure, anonymous form of drudgery, constructed on catch as catch can principles." Merely to value the reporter in terms of his "real importance to civilization" would go some distance in alleviating the problem.

By the time he published *Public Opinion* three years later, however, Lippmann had grown increasingly pessimistic. Journalism did not offer much hope. Even if undertaken relatively objectively, it could not create the "mystical force called Public Opinion" merely by "acting upon everybody for thirty minutes in twenty-four hours," when all other public institutions had failed to do so. Instead, in one of the strangest intellectual excursions of his career, Lippmann proposed the creation of "intelligence bureaus" made up of what he called "special men"—social scientists whose job it would be to model reality like a DNA molecule and explain it to the confused citizenry. His prototype was the government's Bureau of Standards. In Lippmann's plan, the group would act as a kind of social scientific House of Lords, which, freed from the pseudo-realities of democratic politics, would be able to inform and persuade in a such a manner that citizens would be protected from their own ignorance and gullibility.

For all the brilliance and prophetic qualities of Lippmann's diagnosis, he never did come up with a sensible solution. He wisely abandoned his intelligence bureaus in *The Phantom Public*, but failed to replace them with a workable alternative. Fortunately for the history of punditry, however, Lippmann did offer a kind of stopgap answer to the problem: the services of one Walter Lippmann. Through his newspaper column, his books, and later his television appearances, Lippmann interposed himself between the inadequacies of incomplete, biased, and stereotyped "objective" journalism and the mass of confused, ignorant, and just plain lazy American citizens who were otherwise defenseless against the emotional pull of their pseudo-environments. In doing so, he filled what was and remains an absolutely crucial vacuum in the functioning of American democracy.

While the governing elite—the "insiders," as Lippmann called them— sought to manipulate the news media to "manufacture the consent" of the governed, Lippmann worked diligently to inform himself on the great issues of the day and then educate his readers to a point at which they might intelligently judge the actions of their leaders. "In this," Lippmann contended at the end of his career, he and other pundits performed an "essential service . . . to find out what is going on under the surface and beyond the horizon; to infer, to deduce, to imagine and to guess what is going on inside, what this meant yesterday and what it could mean tomorrow." In this selfless pursuit, political punditry would do "what every sovereign citizen is supposed to do but has not the time or the interest to do for himself."

The theory's fault line lies in its vulnerability to human idiosyncrasies. To work effectively, the theory required that two enormous assumptions be true: first, that the pundit could accumulate, through disinterested inquiry, the requisite insider information from those who control it— rather than through some implicit quid pro quo of sympathy and support; and second, that the pundit would continue to identify with the interests of the outsider class over those of the insider elite (despite the fact that virtually their entire professional and social lives were likely to be dominated by interaction with that same ruling class). Should either of these two assumptions be undermined, the pundit becomes not an agent of democracy but an accomplice to its subversion.

It is right and proper that one of the richest American political biographies of the past generation had as its subject Walter Lippmann. Lippmann was born with the American Century, exactly one hundred years after the Constitution, and spent his entire professional life seeking to educate his countrymen about the risks and responsibilities that their tremendous power entailed. From the period in which Teddy Roosevelt called the twenty-six-year-old writer "the most brilliant man of his age in the United States" through the days in which Lyndon Johnson drove him out of Washington, so angered by Lippmann's refusal to endorse his war in Vietnam that Johnson took to making bawdy jokes at Lippmann's expense in the presence of foreign dignitaries, no other private individual played so central a role in the shaping of the nation's political debate.

Lippmann's own rise to preeminence coincided with America's rise from a massive, untamed industrial giant to the most influential power the world has ever seen. Given the relative ignorance that even the most sophisticated Americans exhibited about the foundations of international diplomacy and the vast ambitions of the emerging foreign policy elite, it seems fair to conclude that if Walter Lippmann had never existed, America would have had to invent him.

Lippmann was not the first full-fledged Washington pundit. David Lawrence, the founder of *US News and World Report*, began adding a tag line identifying his pro-business, anti-labor opinions to his *New York Post* dispatches in 1915. When the *Post* began syndicating him a year later, he fulfilled the basic criteria for Washington punditry, nearly twenty-five years before Lippmann joined him: he wrote his column from Washington, he was nationally syndicated, and he had been given full authority by his superiors to vent his opinions.

Lawrence and his journalist colleagues, however, formed an intensely parochial and self-contained fellowship. When Arthur Krock first arrived in 1919, he found what he called "a small group of pompous frauds" dominating the Washington press corps, "identifiable not only by their disinclination to do legwork, which was great, but in most cases by their attire. They habitually wore frock coats and silk hats, dropped big names in profusion, carried canes and largely made contacts with their single news source in the noble saloons of the period." Before Lippmann came to the city in 1939, Washington punditry was important only to Washingtonians—and to them not terribly so.

Lippmann began his career as a regular political commentator in November 1914, having already published two considerable works of political inquiry, when he appeared on the masthead of the first issue of the *New Republic*. Herbert Croly, the magazine's editor-in-chief, and Willard and Dorothy Straight, its financiers, were deeply committed to Roosevelt's Bull Moose Progressivism. Lippmann, by his own account, was positively in love with the Moose himself. But the romance soured almost immediately when the magazine, opposing Woodrow Wilson's foray into Mexico in December 1914, gently chided Roosevelt for trying to goad the president into a full-scale invasion. Roosevelt went on a rampage, damning the *New Republic*'s editors as "three circumcised Jews and three anemic Christians."

With Teddy raging, Woodrow Wilson saw his opening and launched a personal lobbying campaign for the magazine's support, inviting Lippmann to his summer home in Shadow Lawn, New Jersey. There the president expertly massaged the young writer's ego, showing him secret cables and soliciting his advice. Probably no pundit has ever survived a personal session with a president and classified war cables without soon convincing himself of the merit of the man's viewpoint. When it was over, Lippmann returned to New York and convinced Croly as well. Shortly thereafter, he received his first invitation to dine at the White House.

From dinner at the Wilson White House to the days of his banishment from Lyndon Johnson's Oval Office more than half a century later, Lippmann dealt with the tension inherent in his business in a decidedly ambivalent fashion. He professed the need for "airspace" between the worlds of power and punditry but freely ignored his own advice. Time and again, Lippmann proved all too easily misled by powerful insiders who encouraged him to mislead his powerless outsiders, with disastrous results. In the matter of the still unsolved 1948 murder of the journalist George Polk in war-torn Greece, Lippmann lent his name to a white-washed investigation that dishonestly served the interests of U.S. Cold War diplomacy. Whether calling a 1933 speech by Hitler "genuinely statesmanlike" and "evidence of good faith" or accepting the Pentagon's 1965 assertion that the bombs it was dropping on North Vietnam did not "kill anybody" because "they're political bombings," Lippmann found himself being made to look ridiculous by history. On these occasions, as on many others, Lippmann simply accepted the word of power as sufficient evidence of its good faith.

Throughout his early life, Lippmann had benefited from the patronage of great and powerful men, to whom he attached himself with an enthusiasm that Michael Kinsley has named "the American sycophancy." From the time that he abandoned his radical Greenwich Village pretensions and metaphorically moved uptown to the luxurious and well-funded liberalism of the *New Republic*, Lippmann wedded himself to the views and interests of the American elite. Party meant nothing to Lippmann. His only loyalties were to the influence of his ideas and the idea of his influence.

As his friend James Reston observes, "One of the interesting things about Lippmann was that he did more to argue for the principle of detachment and was [himself] more attached" to politicians than any other columnist. Reston attributes Lippmann's weakness on the issue to his need for social status and his "fascination for the social whirl." Lippmann loved, according to Reston, "going to embassies and philosophizing after dinner and he liked to be asked to the White House. It's true that people talk about money as corruptive, but the social life is much more so than money."

After the war and a short, unhappy return to the *New Republic*, Lippmann was recruited for what may have been the best job in the history of journalism: editorial writer for *New York World*. Since the *World* turned out its final heartbreaking issue on February 27, 1931, America has yet to see a paper so literate, so exciting, and so faithful to the *Front Page* legends with which modern underappreciated journalists still console themselves. The *World* was a monument to the possibilities of drinking, lying, gambling, and relatively honest daily journalism.

Under editor Frank Cobb, the *World* invented the home and hearth of modern punditry, the op-ed page, and amassed a staff of writers that would make any modern editor cry. Heywood Broun, who began as a sportswriter, moved his pro-labor column to the op-ed page where he fiercely defended its leadership from the attacks of the Hearst chain and the Republican president. The rest of the constellation included Maxwell Anderson, the future playwright; James M. Cain, the future novelist; and Allen Nevins, the future historian.

Cobb was diagnosed with inoperable cancer in 1923 and left Lippmann as editorial editor-in-chief. Although his editorials were unsigned, Lippmann, by now the author of four celebrated books and countless magazine articles, had grown into a New York society celebrity. He found his counsel sought after in many quarters, including Calvin Coolidge's White House. Needless to say, he emerged from his meeting with Coolidge with renewed sympathy for the president's predicament.

In the history of political commentary, 1923 is a seminal year for another important reason: the debut of *Time* magazine. Henry Luce's prospectus for his new magazine estimated that the number of American college graduates had reached 1 million by this time. Despite rising education levels in the country, the vast majority of people outside New York, Boston, and Washington, D.C., had almost no access to quality information about the state of affairs in the world—with the exception of those who read Walter Lippmann. Television did not enter into most American lives until the 1950s, and commercial radio, which began in the 1920s, was a medium devoted primarily to the insights of commentators like Jack Benny and George Burns. Few if any syndicated columnists paid much attention to foreign events, and most local newspapers did not run the Washington columnists who did.

In the coming decades, Luce and *Time* would share with Lippmann the battleground for the college-educated mind in America. But in the 1920s, *Time* still held only the promise of power and influence. Its tiny New York staff clipped and pasted from other sources, throwing in generous helpings of American "corn" as demanded by Luce. The early 1920s *Time* was not terribly political, and it was not until the 1930s that the voice of Luce, with its emphasis on small-town Presbyterian virtues, virulent anti-Communism, and the U.S. imperial mission in Asia, came to dominate its news coverage.

When the *World* finally expired in 1931, Lippmann moved to the Republican *Herald-Tribune* and began writing his regular column, "Today and

Tomorrow." Having turned down offers of a chair at Harvard, the presidency of the University of North Carolina, and journalism jobs at the *New York Times*, the *World Telegram*, and the Hearst chain, it was hardly an overstatement when *Time* announced that, at age forty-one, its cover boy, Walter Lippmann, had become the "Moses," the "Prophet of Liberalism." The fact that a writer identified with daily journalism could be considered for so wide a range of honors, much less turn them down, bespoke a cultural revolution in society's perception of the profession for which Lippmann was almost singularly responsible. Before a distinguished crowd assembled by the Academy of Political Science at a dinner given in his honor, Lippmann defined what he considered to be the tenets of progressive politics, under fire from Left and Right during the dark days of the depression:

> Who but a political hack can believe that . . . the fate of the nation hangs upon the victory of either political party. . . . Who can believe that an orderly, secure and just economic order can be attained by the simple process of arousing the people against the corporations. . . . Is it vain to suppose that our problems can be dealt with by rallying the people to some crusade that can be expressed in a symbol, a phrase, a set of principles or a program? If that is what the progressives are looking for today, they are looking in vain.

Lippmann's liberalism had, by 1931, lost all vestiges of its former radicalism. He had long ago given up, as Reston notes, "bleeding for the poor." The problems faced by modern government, he recognized, were post-ideological and managerial in nature. Thirty years before Daniel Bell sounded his clarion call to the New Class/managerial elite, Lippmann enlisted liberalism in the search for a "more civilized and rational" organization of the corporate economy. While some of his former colleagues at the *New Republic* were calling for a vote for the Communists, Lippmann's liberalism was now completely self-identified with the exercise of power.

Thus did Walter Lippmann fulfill the role he had envisioned for his philosopher kings in *Public Opinion*. By convincing both the rulers and the ruled that his work was integral to their well-being, he created a central role for political pundits in the political power structure of the emerging superpower. The American people needed him to understand their world. The government depended on him to explain its role, both to the citizenry and to itself. Both political punditry and elite journalism grew in status as a result. As Lippmann negotiated these trends in the 1920s and early 1930s, the role of other pundits also expanded in the public's consciousness. Evidence of the increasing importance of pundits of all political stripes can be seen in the text of a resolution proposed but not passed at the 1938 convention of the American Society of Newspaper Editors:

> This society sees in the increasing of the press of syndicated columns of opinions and interpretation—for which individual papers assume no responsibility—a threat to the independent thought of the newspaper public. It fears that predigested opinion, sweetened with rhetoric and garnished with Olympian pronouncements, may come to be accepted by too many readers as an easy substitute for fact and individual thought.

Among the beneficiaries of this growing influence were Dorothy Thompson, the fiery anti-fascist, and Drew Pearson, the schmaltzy and sentimental liberal populist. On the Right, know-nothing yahoos like Westbrook Pegler and pro-business Chamber of Commerce voices like David Lawrence also grew in prominence.

Lippmann's most significant role during this period was the one he played in educating the young republic for its coming role as world superpower. Although it had grown to be the only nation powerful enough to frustrate the Nazi conquest of Europe, the United States was nevertheless still in its infancy in terms of the sophistication of its foreign policy. Franklin Roosevelt's 1933 inaugural address had contained exactly one paragraph about foreign affairs. When the war struck eight years later, the country was still obsessed with the domestic sources of economic depression, and even its ruling elite were relatively ignorant of the international roots of both the depression and the war. During the interventionist/isolationist debate that preceded Pearl Harbor, Americans began to get a taste of the kinds of questions that had riveted Europe since the Peace of Westphalia. Could alliance with warring countries prevent American entry into the war? Could a swift and early intervention prevent a long and bloody late one? Could America prosper with hostile nations and ideologies controlling Europe and the seas around us?

Public debate, however, remained mired in a Norman Rockwell painting. Senator Harry Truman spoke for many when he explained, "if we see that Germany is winning, we ought to help Russia and if Russia is winning, we ought to help Germany and that way let them kill as many as possible." Wall Street, by and large, concurred. As the editors of the *Wall Street Journal* put it, "The American people know that the principal difference between Mr. Hitler and Mr. Stalin is the size of their respective mustaches."

But Walter Lippmann, with the self-selected members of the infant foreign policy establishment, was laying the foundation for a far grander and in many ways more ominous path. Lippmann saw, in the wake of Europe's exhaustion, a vision of a powerful and expansive American empire. As if intoxicated by this vision, Lippmann proclaimed, as war raged overseas, "What Rome was to the ancient world . . . America is to be in the world of tomorrow." The country, he worried, "cling[s] to the mentality of a little nation on the frontiers of the civilized world, though we have the opportunity, the power, and the responsibilities of a very great nation at the center of the civilized world." In a prophetic critique of this vision, the progressive historian Charles Beard took Lippmann to task for the "ornate, glistening, masculine" language he used in this passage without sufficiently considering the consequences that empire would bring.* But by the time the United States entered the war in December 1941, the die had been cast. Lippmann's side emerged victorious in the war for the elite mind and now needed only to draw the blind, ignorant spectators onto the new playing field as well.

For a brief, thirty-year century, the United States would indeed become the new Rome, fighting wars and reordering the lives of people in countries whose names its citizens could not pronounce. An ambivalent general in this effort, Lippmann nevertheless enlisted countless majors and admirals, ensigns and privates, into the struggle to build a new empire. In the end, it proved a bitter and, in many respects, self-defeating effort. Most intoxicated journeys are. But through his remarkable talent for synthesis and persuasion, Walter Lippmann helped forge a new role in the American political dialogue for a tiny class of journalists and commentators who chose to emulate his example. If it was not exactly the road to an "omnicompetent" citizenry, it was at least a means of educating a new class of American leaders for the burdens that providence—together with Nazi Germany—had placed on our doorstep.

---

*Rome conquered, ruled and robbed other peoples from the frontier in Scotland to the sands of Arabia," wrote Beard,

> from the Rhine to the Sahara, and then crumbled to ruins. Does anybody in his right mind really believe that the United States can or ought to play that role in the future, or anything akin to it? America is to be "what Great Britain has been to the modern world." Well, what has Great Britain been to the modern world? Many fine and good things, no doubt. But in terms of foreign policy, Britain swept the Spanish, the Dutch, the French and the Germans from the surface of the seven seas. During the past three hundred years Britain has waged numerous wars on the Continent to maintain, among other things, the balance of power. Britain has wrested colonies from the Spanish, the Dutch, the French, and the Germans, has conquered, ruled and dictated to a large part of the globe. Does anyone really believe that the United States can or ought to do all these things, or anything akin to them?"

See Charles A. Beard, "Giddy Minds and Foreign Quarrels: An Estimate of American Foreign Policy," *Harper's Magazine*, September 1939, pp. 349–50.

CHAPTER TWO

Lippmanndom

In the spring of 1944, Henry Luce's *Life* magazine rejected an excerpt from Walter Lippmann's book *U.S. War Aims* because he found it "too anti-Russian." The problem was that Lippmann was simultaneously ahead of and behind his time. Had Lippmann offered the piece four years earlier, when Luce's *Time* was calling Joseph Stalin "the world's most hated man," he might have made a sale. Had he waited three more years, by which time Luce was calling Lippmann "naive" and *Life* was proclaiming that the Soviets were "intent upon bringing chaos, the collapse of civilization and the Communization of the European continent," then the piece might have gone over better too. But Lippmann submitted an essay noting that the Soviet Union was a totalitarian country when Luce's publications were calling Stalin "a great wartime leader" and the Russians "one hell of a people," who "look like Americans, dress like Americans and think like Americans." In the dawn's early light of the Cold War, the ideological constructs of American politics were in constant flux. As Lippmann learned to his dismay, timing was all.

The Cold War braced Washington like a gust of frigid wind. Two months into his presidency in June 1945, Harry Truman, president of short memory, observed that Americans had no reason to be "afraid of Russia." "They've always been our friends," he insisted, "and I can't see any reason why they shouldn't always be." Truman certainly found his reasons. Like Luce and the rest of postwar Washington, he became increasingly frustrated with Stalin's truculence and the Soviet unwillingness to abide by

U.S. interpretations of wartime accords relating to Eastern Europe and the Middle East. U.S. politicians, led by Truman, did their best to create a sense of permanent crisis, fanning the flames of Cold War hysteria to what Truman's trusted adviser Clark Clifford accurately predicted would be "considerable political advantage." The city's temperature heated up so quickly that by March 1948, Joseph and Stewart Alsop reported, "The atmosphere in Washington today is no longer postwar, it is prewar."

The pundits played a key role in the creation and communication of America's new Cold War ethos. Even if they could not by themselves convince the majority of the American people of the righteousness of the enterprise, they could at least give the impression they were trying.* This was more than enough incentive for their recruitment. The new establishment's Wise Men, flush with victory over Germany and Japan, saw as their next task nothing less than the remaking of the world. For this they needed allies, and the printing press had proven itself every bit as mighty as the sword. The worldwide Pax Americana that men like Dean Acheson, George Marshall, Robert Lovett, and John J. McCloy planned to build was one that had precious little in common with prewar, isolationist America. If their vision was to have any hope of realization, the energetic cooperation of those who had earned the ear and the trust of the newspaper-consuming public would be required. The pundits, pleased to learn of their new significance, were not exactly reticent about shouldering the Wise Men's burden. As their ranks and their appetites expanded, they stepped into their Cold War boots and marched lock-step into the brave new world of American empire.

Between Franklin Roosevelt's 1933 inauguration and the big victory party twelve years later, sleepy white Washington mushroomed into a full-blown American city, brimming with Ivy-educated bureaucrats and Wall Street lawyers. The new city manufactured only one thing—words on paper—and those with the ability to master this craft came to enjoy some of the same advantages of position and prestige enjoyed by Duke Snider in Brooklyn or Joe DiMaggio in the Bronx.

It may be useful to think of Washington as a palace court where the pundits played multiple roles: they were courtiers, but they served as both advisers to and communicators for the crown. Because the courtiers shared the basic assumptions of the court itself, but were ostensibly free to write whatever they pleased, the pundits were seen to be uniquely credible and hence well situated to parlay their positions into small fiefdoms of influence.†

*There is really no scientifically respectable measure of this.
†I am indebted to Marcus Raskin for this metaphor.

No longer treated by the truly powerful as mere newsmen, the most important pundits acquired some of the status of Washington's great families and most powerful political institutions. They had access to the highest reaches of the government and in turn were expected to exercise good judgment about just how much truth was healthy for Americans to hear. By endorsing fundamental assumptions of the Cold War agenda and relaying its implications to their audiences, the pundits were able to perform two important functions on behalf of burgeoning empire: they carried on the political and cultural conversation of the capital with regard to this new endeavor, and they behaved as a politically articulate surrogate for the masses of uninformed and politically disinclined citizens for whom they alleged to speak.[*]

Excluding Lippmann much but not all of the time, the insider pundits depended heavily on their sources to provide information that would distinguish their columns from those of their competitors. Although a certain degree of literacy was required, a fluid writing style was not really important. The necessary talents were, rather, the ability to get one's telephone calls answered and an aptitude for typing these answers up simply and quickly. A first-rate column depended on a steady stream of titillating tidbits that the writer could spin into an eight-hundred-word morality play.

The extent of each insider pundit's dependence on those in power varied from writer to writer. At one end of the spectrum was Lippmann; at the other stood those writers who consciously tailored their thinking to reflect the political fashions of the moment. They did so, ironically, in the hopes of being treated more like Lippmann: praised for their wisdom, invited to the best dinner parties, and called on by the president for their advice.

Few pundits were actually able to achieve Lippmann's status of both adviser to and interpreter for the crown. Most were dangled just close enough to keep them in the court but outside the circles in which the truly powerful discussed business. Most went along for the ride quite willingly, happy just to be present somewhere near the creation. When necessary, top government officials had any number of pundit-manipulation tools available to them. There was personal flattery; there were confidential briefings; and there were personal friendships, school ties, and institutional connections. Occasionally, and most effectively, there was a whiff of raw power. In one especially chilling instance, one of the most influential pundits of the era found himself arrested in a Moscow bathroom for having made a homosexual pass. The Soviets agreed to hush up the incident once they discovered the writer's identity, but the CIA obtained its own confession. Allen Dulles, the agency's director, placed it inside his

[*]In Washington, then as now, politics is culture.

private safe and informed President Eisenhower of its existence. The document was shown to people in the military, Congress, and the national security bureaucracy. Eisenhower apparently went to the trouble to make certain that a copy be made for president-elect Kennedy as well. The threat that lay behind this type of blackmail need never be explicitly carried out to achieve its desired effect.[*]

Frequently, officials in power would take responsibility for satisfying the insider-tidbit needs of individual pundits on a regular basis. Lippmann's voice was by far the most closely watched. But he was also the most difficult to control, so supremely confident was he in his own analytical powers. Still, he met regularly with the likes of government officials George Kennan and Dean Acheson and found much in their plans he could endorse. Arthur Krock of the *New York Times* was perhaps the easiest fish to feed, and his tank was regularly sprinkled with classified data provided by his Princeton clubmate, James Forrestal. Joseph Alsop, who alternated with Lippmann in the *Herald-Tribune* and would soon come to rival him as the most influential voice inside the political establishment, regularly received thick folders from State Department Soviet specialist, Charles Bohlen, a fellow alumnus of Harvard's Porcellian Club. Lippmann's protégé, the ace *Times* reporter and later columnist James Reston, it was widely noticed, would often publish important stories regarding "big planning at State" after he lunched with Dean Acheson at the Metropolitan Club. Bruce Cumings, the leading American historian of the Korean War, goes so far as to see "James Reston's lips moving, but Acheson speaking" in the series of columns Reston wrote explaining the changing bases of U.S. policy that led to the Truman administration's embrace of South Korea in early 1950.[†]

Sometimes the pundit/power relationship became so confused that it was impossible to tell who was manipulating whom. Perhaps the most

---

[*]I have in my possession copies of six separate documents that refer to the confession, all signed by Lewis L. Straus, then head of the Atomic Energy Commission, that contain lengthy discussions of this document, including the names of all parties involved and mention of its possible use as an instrument of blackmail.

[†]Acheson's opponents, notes Cumings, especially Senator McCarthy, denounced his famous January 12 "Press Club" speech, in which he explicitly excluded Korea from the U.S. defense umbrella, thereby allegedly giving the North Korean Communists "the green light" to attack. Many historians and political scientists, he notes, point to the speech as a classic example of the failure of deterrence. Though Acheson explicitly omitted it, Reston interpreted the speech to mean that Korea, like Japan, was now included in those areas where "the US had direct responsibilities." Cumings finds the weird accuracy of Reston's judgment fascinating and wonders whether "Reston knew that Acheson privately backed containment in Korea" or whether he simply "got the speech wrong." "Since the North Koreans were still poring over Acheson's words," he notes, "they must have again scratched their heads about whatever it was Acheson had said in January." See Bruce Cumings, *The Origins of the Korean War*, vol. 2: *The Roaring of the Cataract, 1947–1950* (Princeton, NJ: Princeton University Press, 1991), pp. 416–19, 436–39.

illustrative example of this phenomenon can be found in the conversion to internationalism undergone by Senator Arthur Vandenberg, although the actual turn of events remains a matter of some controversy. Vandenberg, a frightfully vain and self-important man, planned to run for president in 1948. Ronald Steel, basing his account on an interview with Walter Lippmann, argues that Lippmann, with Reston's assistance, convinced the senator in the summer of 1945 that no self-respecting presidential candidate could hope to lead this country without first jettisoning the immature vestiges of Republican isolationism. Together they wrote the senator's seminal speech, which praised the United Nations, abandoned isolationism, and decapitated the philosophy that had characterized the Republican party for decades.

Reston, however, remembers it differently. He cannot recall any involvement on Lippmann's part. His own role, he says, was limited to reading a speech Vandenberg was planning to give on the floor of the Senate denouncing the Soviets for their interference in Poland and suggesting that Vandenberg consider adding a section endorsing the continuation of the wartime alliance as a means of addressing Soviet paranoia about the security of its borders. "What changed his mind," argues Reston, "was not the speech, but the reaction to it. He became a hero to all the people who had thought he was just a big blowhard." Among those who lauded Vandenberg's heroism were Lippmann and Reston. The *Times* reporter noted a "brave and statesmanlike" address given by the senator. Whatever the exact inducement, Vandenberg's conversion all but crippled the once-proud tradition of main-street Republican isolationism.*

As Cold War tensions came increasingly to dominate public debate, Lippmann, as the perceived voice of history and reason, grew in stature. His first twenty-five years in the public arena had earned him enough political and intellectual capital that he came to be viewed as almost a separate branch of government. During the war, the British embassy had appointed one official whose responsibility it was to keep Her Majesty's Government appraised of the great man's thoughts and vice versa. Lippmann had become better able to explain government policy to the Amer-

---

*Vandenberg proved even more malleable in the future. When Reston outlined a $20 billion, four-year European recovery plan (eventually to become the Marshall Plan) in the summer of 1947, Vandenberg telephoned to tell him he was out of his senses, that "no administration would dare come to the Senate with a proposal like that," and that he himself would never support "any such goddamned foolishness." Nine months later, on March 1, 1948, Vandenberg himself rose in the Senate to begin debate on it. These quotations from Vandenberg appeared in a sanitized version in James Reston's column of June 20, 1960, and later in Reston's memoir, *Deadline* (New York: Random House, 1991), p. 168. See also Patrick Lloyd Hatcher, *The Suicide of an Elite: American Internationalists and Vietnam* (Stanford, CA: Stanford University Press, 1990), p. 206.

ican people and place it in a sensible political and historical context than was the government itself. When White House or State Department officials thought of seeking support in Congress for a new proposal for postwar reconstruction, they frequently floated it by Lippmann, even before approaching the relevant committee chairman.

With the collapse of Henry Wallace's Progressive Party in the 1948 election, the increasingly conservative Lippmann came to represent the liberal pole in the Cold War debate. His traditionalist balance-of-power orientation was as far as any insider pundit would go toward advocating the kind of foreign policy compromises that might catch the attention of some McCarthyite vigilante. On Lippmann's left, Drew Pearson continued to reach large numbers of people with his populist preaching and melodramatic scandal mongering. But Pearson's influence in insider circles derived exclusively from the fact that every once in a while he put somebody in jail.* I. F. Stone, on the other hand, toiled alone with his wife, Esther, in northwest Washington on an extraordinarily learned and intellectually acute newsletter, combining the moral outrage of Jeremiah with the investigative skills of Philip Marlowe. But until the New Left

---

*Pearson was not much on journalistic ethics. His motto was "We will give immunity to a very good source as long as the information he offers is better than what we have on him." But if a man can be judged by the enemies he makes, Pearson might well have been a saint. The *Congressional Record* is filled with politicians protected by immunity who reach never-to-be-equaled heights of eloquence in their zeal to sully his name. Senator Kenneth McKellar of Tennessee once took the floor of the world's greatest deliberative body to call Pearson "an infamous liar, a revolting liar, a pusillanimous liar, a lying ass, a natural-born liar, a liar for living, a liar for daytime, a liar for nighttime, a dishonest ignorant corrupt and groveling crook. . . ." McKellar later fainted in the cloakroom. Not to be outdone, Senator Walter George of Georgia branded Pearson "an ordinary, congenital, deliberate and malicious liar." Representative Philip Bennett of Missouri labeled him "a dishonest, unreliable, vicious character assassin." Senator William Jenner of Indiana found him to be "a filthy brain-child conceived in ruthlessness and dedicated to the proposition that Judas Iscariot was a piker." And the infamous Theodore Bilbo of Mississippi said Pearson would "go down in history as 'Pearson-the-sponge' because he gathers slime, mud and slander from all parts of the earth and lets them ooze out through his radio broadcasts and through his daily contributions to a few newspapers that have not yet found him out." See Oliver Pilat, *Drew Pearson* (New York: Pocket Books, 1973).

Pearson's exploits on behalf of decency were of such force that Joseph McCarthy once felt compelled to sneak up on him in the men's room at the Sulgrave Club and either kick him in the groin or "belt the bloody and half-conscious Pearson in the mouth." According to the groin version, published in Pilat, the two men were separated by Richard Nixon before the fight could really get going. According to James Reston, however, an inebriated McCarthy beat up Pearson before he and Nixon stumbled around Washington for a half-hour trying to find McCarthy's car. See Reston, *Deadline*, p. 226. McCarthy had previously referred to the pundit as "the diabolically clever voice of international Communism . . . a Moscow-directed character assassin . . . a journalistic fake and a prostitute . . . a degenerate liar" and "a twisted, perverted mentality." The Pilat version has McCarthy wondering aloud whether "to kill Pearson or just to maim him" as well. See also the wholly unreliable *Drew Pearson's Diaries 1949–1959*, ed. Tyler Abel (New York: Holt, Rinehart, Winston, 1974).

adopted him as one of its patron saints during the antiwar movement in the late 1960s, Stone, a self proclaimed "Jeffersonian Marxist," remained a virtually anonymous figure to the establishment and largely irrelevant to the shaping of the insider mind.

Because the owners of newspapers and newspaper chains were more likely to be sympathetic to the appeals of racism, Christian fundamentalism, and laissez-faire capitalism than they were to unions, health care, and democratic socialism, populists of the far Right were far more common in the ranks of American punditry than the occasional Pearson or Stone. Westbrook Pegler was probably the most widely read of these. Pegler's ironically titled column, "Fair Enough," occasionally descended into what H. L. Mencken would term "Ku Kluxery," and his attacks on the Hearst family finally cost him his job in 1962. But by that time, he had lost his thunder to an upstart Yalie named William F. Buckley, Jr.

If the Left was largely irrelevant, however, the far Right was important only insofar as it could make mischief. Joe McCarthy proved that this potential was considerable indeed and could be ignored only at the peril of one's career. But Pegler, Buckley, and their cohorts had no direct impact upon the shaping of the insider mind nor the forging of its consensus. Although some of them may have lived or worked in Washington, they did not live and work at what Stewart Alsop called "the Center."

The Center, according to Alsop, was "the Washington which a political journalist sees with his tunnel vision." More than a place, it was a state of mind. The Center was where the action was. It was where men of goodwill met to hammer things out. "Extremists" and "ideologues" of all stripes abhorred the Center, but the truly Central knew that this was where political rhetoric on behalf of unarguable principles was turned into policies and sometimes wars. Defining these principles for the powerful people who made them and the powerless people who fought and sometimes died for them was the essential business of the Cold War Washington pundit.

Postwar debate over the course of United States–Soviet relations peaked early. In July 1947, George Kennan published "The Sources of Soviet Conduct" in *Foreign Affairs* magazine under the pseudonym "X." Soon after, Lippmann responded with a series of fourteen successive columns that, collected together in a small book, helped give the Cold War its name.

In his article and the earlier "Long Telegram," where he first delineated the theoretical basis of his argument in a classified cable from Moscow, the not-so-anonymous Kennan argued on behalf of a U.S. "policy of firm containment, designed to confront the Russians with unalterable counter-force at every point where they show signs of encroaching" via "the adroit and vigilant application of counter-force at a series of constantly shifting geographical and political points." Arthur Krock, who had been shown an earlier version of the essay by Forrestal, cleverly promoted it in the *Times*, implying that the document was somehow far more significant than he could in good conscience say. Other pundits soon picked it up, and by the time the article snowballed into *Life* and *Reader's Digest*, it had been elevated, as Kennan notes, "to the status of a 'doctrine' which was then identified with the foreign policy of the administration."

Lippmann's brilliant critique of Kennan's argument stands today as a remarkable prophesy of the problems that containment presaged for U.S. foreign policy. Lippmann predicted that even if successful, the policy cost would outweigh its benefits. To implement it would entail "recruiting, subsidizing, and supporting a heterogeneous array of satellites, clients, dependents and puppets." This would require a massive military apparatus with interventionary capabilities dwarfing anything the world had previously seen. In addition to the expense, the United States would be left vulnerable to these very puppets, who could fly the flag of appeasement in our faces to manipulate us into defending a murderous status quo on the basis of no stronger common interest than a shared antipathy for Communist revolution. "My strongest impression," Lippmann wrote, "is that the Russians have lost the Cold War and they know it." The task at hand was to "push toward a settlement which permits the recovery of Europe and the world, and to relax the tension, to subdue the anxiety, and to end the panic."

The "X" debate probably constitutes the apex of postwar punditry. Despite Kennan's ostensible anonymity, the argument itself was conducted publicly and served to focus attention on the American role in the world with considerable seriousness, integrity, and respect for the intelligence of the public mind. Although Kennan has since come to agree with Lippmann's critique more than his own argument (just as Lippmann, toward the end of his career, would echo Charles A. Beard's critique of the 1939 Walter Lippmann), the two men conducted what amounted to a public seminar for an entire generation of American leaders previously unschooled in the discipline of international diplomacy and power politics. Writers and thinkers of all political stripes weighed in with minds more open to the various possibilities than would be possible for the next forty years. The discussion was both educative, to return to the aspirations Lippmann voiced in *Public Opinion*, and conducive to public inquiry and community conversation, as Dewey had hoped. The catch, however, was how tiny this community had become. It would be tendentious to blame pundits for this, but just the same, it is impossible to ignore the fact that, aside from Lippmann's column or Kennan's X article, the greater American public enjoyed precious few opportunities to consider intelligently the arguments that would determine the course of the nation's foreign and domestic policies for the next half-century. Containment developed its own momentum, independent of the ostensible object of its affections, and none of the appointed agents of community conversation ever saw fit to question its fundamentals again. Still, one should not lose sight of the moment without tipping one's hat to Lippmann's prescience. Posterity has borne out his arguments, rather than those of Kennan, the lifelong scholar and Sovietologist—an astonishing accomplishment for a man in a business so fleeting as that of a newspaper pundit.

Helpful in this debate, as well as many others, was an enviable talent for criticism that singed but did not burn. In addition, Lippmann had an exceptional ability to cast aside his sweeping principles on behalf of particulars when they had already become accomplished facts. Regardless of what he may have believed about the relative powers of nationalism and Communist subversion in the service of revolution, Lippmann nevertheless managed to find reasons to support military aid to the Greek colonel's regime, U.S. military intervention in Korea (although limited to air and sea power), and even, briefly, French and U.S. military involvement in Vietnam. He went to great psychological lengths to convince himself that the makers of U.S. foreign policy shared his basic views and adhered to them with a similar dedication to honor and candor. As he wrote in 1952, "The real problem of our foreign policy is not in its objectives, on them there is fairly general agreement." The real problems, quite simply, lay with the "control and administration of the policy." The same year, when Communists accused the United States of engaging in germ warfare in Korea, Lippmann insisted that the accusations must certainly be false because "the two highest responsible men in the U.S. government—who would have to give the orders to conduct germ warfare—have said on their word of honor that there is no truth of any kind in the charges. Both of these men happen to be old personal friends and I believe them." This faith was absolutely essential to the job description of an aspiring Washington pundit and to all those who labored inside the Center. It was this faith, more than anything, that collapsed in the wake of Lyndon Johnson's war and ended Lippmann's career as Washington's ambassador from the world of history, philosophy, and context.

Lippmann once observed, during the height of the Vietnam War, that if Lyndon Johnson ever did become inclined to negotiate with Hanoi, "the most powerful voice against it would be that of Joseph Wright Alsop." A distant cousin of Theodore and Franklin Roosevelt, Alsop was the only pundit in the Cold War debate whose political and intellectual influence could begin to approach Lippmann's.* He cut his political teeth on the New Deal and maintained his column and his impressive influence for the next forty years.

Alsop arrived in Washington in 1935. An obese, twenty-seven-year-old aesthete from Harvard and Groton, he landed a job at the *Herald-Tribune*, owing to his mother's friendship with its owners. But Alsop had talent and an unquenchable relish for the game of insider politics. A self-taught polymath and scholar with aristocratic tastes and a Spenglerian demeanor, Alsop cut a distinctly odd figure on the Washington political circuit. His accent has been described alternately as "a clerk in a not-very-good London hotel trying to make people think he went to Harrow" and "Charles Laughton playing Oscar Wilde." His Georgetown dinner parties were legendary, and Washington socialites still talk about them wistfully. Often on hand as a kind of living family heirloom was Alice Roosevelt Longworth, Uncle Teddy's daughter and a wonderfully tart-tongued old woman. Mrs. Longworth, who once congratulated Dorothy Thompson on having her "menopause in public and making it pay," admitted that she knew that "whenever I go over to Joe's house I am working for him. I don't mind a bit. I know Joe uses me. Good heavens, he uses everyone." In between the exquisite food and wine, Alsop would ask his guests for a bit of "general conversation," before launching forth on his Subject, the American position in the world. Later in the week, the speech would appear, in slightly amended form, in Alsop's column.

With Robert E. Kinter from 1937 until the war, with his brother Stewart from 1946 to 1958, and alone thereafter until 1974, Alsop wrote a highly literate column that leaned in equal parts on his erudition, his ideological fixation, his dinner party guest lists, and his considerable legwork. On the night of June 24, 1950, Assistant Secretary of State Dean Rusk, Secretary of the Army Frank Pace, Under Secretary of the Air Force John McCone, State Department Director of Policy Planning George Kennan, and Justice Felix Frankfurter were all located by their underlings at Alsop's dinner table and were informed that the North

---

*During the Cold War's early days, Alsop and his brother had launched a campaign to remove Truman's defense secretary, Lewis B. Johnson, from his job. Johnson had offended Alsop by observing that there was too much "fat" in the U.S. military budget. The campaign was successful; the Alsops almost single-handedly sent Johnson to the unemployment lines. But it disgusted Lippmann, who, in a rare personal rebuke, called the writers "little boys playing with matches." Alsop never forgot that and, according to one of his close friends, constantly made disparaging remarks about Lippmann and his wife thereafter. (The source for these remarks insists on remaining anonymous.)

Korean Army had crossed the Yalu into the Southern zone. They had been discussing the Romanian threat to Yugoslavia, when the guests realized something was up. But "no one," according to brother Stewart, "was tactless enough to ask what the something was—that is contrary to the Washington ground rules."

Merle Miller once likened Alsop's views on Communism to those of Pope Innocent III regarding the Children's Crusade: "While we sleep, they go forth and conquer the land." He was obsessed with what he saw as the nation's need to prove its collective manhood and was forever wondering whether this or that president was "man enough" to stop the Reds at some critical juncture. But, unlike many fervent anti-Communists at the time, Alsop's obsession stopped at the river's edge. His history during the depths of the 1950s Red Scare was a distinctly honorable one, particularly when compared to the relative silence of Lippmann and his peers. He and his brother, Stewart, launched a crusade on behalf of Robert Oppenheimer when Atomic Energy Commissioner Lewis L. Strauss and the hawkish physicist Edward Teller were smearing the atomic scientist in an attempt to remove his security clearance. Alsop wrote a book in defense of Oppenheimer that Strauss, whose influence probably exceeded that of J. Edgar Hoover at the time, determined would receive no mention in any important print forum.[*] Alsop also defended State Department official Owen Lattimore, whom he considered to be a "perfect fool," because, Alsop insisted, "There is a difference between foolishness and treason." In 1954, when Henry Wallace was called in to testify before McCarthy's Senate Subcommittee on Internal Security, Alsop spent all day on the phone trying to find a lawyer willing to defend the former vice-president. On domestic matters, Alsop showed a patrician's concern for middle-class problems and sensibilities that might generously be considered generous, given the limited contact he had with the common folk. "Joe was the kind of liberal," says his friend Tom Braden, "who thought it was a good idea for men of property—who wanted to remain men of property—to keep an eye on the social problems of the masses."

Alsop's clout (and that of insider punditry) was symbolized by the fact that on a cold and snowy January night in 1961, the president of the United States, just hours into the job, saw fit to interrupt his inauguration-night festivities to shoot the breeze with his friend, the conservative Republican columnist. It was Alsop who, more than anyone else, helped convince the candidate Kennedy of the existence of a phantom "missile

---

[*]Joseph W. Alsop and Stewart Alsop, *We Accuse: The Story of the Miscarriage of American Justice in the Case of J. Robert Oppenheimer* (New York: Simon and Schuster, 1954).

gap" with the Soviets, a notion he conjured up on the basis of wholly man-ufactured, or perhaps imaginary, evidence. During the Johnson adminis-tration, the president was heard to accompany his decision to increase troop levels in Vietnam by fifty thousand American boys with the quip, "There, that should keep Joe Alsop quiet for a while."

Alsop's influence during the 1950s and 1960s derived in part from his dinner parties, but more important, though, was the civilized manner in which he incorporated the foreign policy worldview of the far Right into polite society. Like Lippmann, Alsop did much to elevate the level of community conversation. Also like Lippmann, his effectiveness fell victim to body counts in Vietnam. But whereas Lippmann was too aware of the limitations of anti-Communist warfare for political comfort, Alsop was undermined by his inability to recognize these limits once the Zeitgeist reversed itself after the January 1968 Tet Offensive.

Having played a key role in propping up Chiang Kai-shek's collapsing regime in China during the war, Alsop became obsessed with the Com-munist takeover there and professed to see the hand of Maoist manipula-tion behind every turn of events on the Asian mainland. This was particularly true of Vietnam. Alsop began predicting the enemy's immi-nent collapse as early as June 1964 and never let go. After Tet, when much of the establishment was looking to extricate the nation from the Vietnam debacle, Alsop could only conclude that those who failed to sup-port the war "had gone collectively insane." Should the United States withdraw, he promised, McCarthyism would run rampant and "the Amer-ican future would hardly bear contemplation." The morning after his long-time friend Bobby Kennedy made a speech wondering whether the United States could ever win the war in Vietnam, Alsop left three mes-sages with his receptionist to please tell his close friend, the senator from New York, that he was a traitor to his country.[*] He also flew to Vietnam to lecture correspondents like David Halberstam and Neil Sheehan: "you'll be like those fools who lost their jobs in China. I tried to help them. I tried to warn them, but they never listened. I testified at their hearings, never fear, I shall testify for you as well."

Alsop continued writing his column through 1974, but he forfeited the fear and respect he had engendered more than seven years earlier by his fanatical devotion to the failed war effort and the men who lied about it.

*   *   *

[*]Alsop's capacity for self-delusion on Vietnam was apparently limitless. He told Joan Braden that "the minute Robert Kennedy got to the White House, he would tear into Vietnam like a tiger. Robert Kennedy would not have permitted his country to lose a war." Quoted in Joan Braden, *Just Enough Rope* (New York: Villard Books, 1989), p. 151.

Of all the giants who walked the earth in punditry's golden age, by far the kindest, gentlest, and most inspirational was the chief Washington correspondent of the *New York Times*, James Barrett "Scotty" Reston. Arthur Krock held the bureau's weighty title for two decades but relinquished it to Reston in 1953 when he realized that it was the only way to keep the forty-three-year-old Reston from accepting an offer to be editor of the *Washington Post*. In all his years in punditry, stepping aside for Reston was probably the most graceful act Krock ever performed. It was certainly his greatest contribution to the quality of the profession.

The two men could not have been more different in demeanor. Tom Wicker remembers his first sighting of Krock in the Washington newsroom. "He would stalk though the office, carrying a statesman's girth with more aggressive dignity than anyone in Washington, his head cocked back to allow his gaze to play scornfully on the gods, a Churchillian cigar cocked toward his hat brim like a banner of war." Because Wicker was writing the introduction to a collection of Krock's columns, one can safely conclude that these were the most generous words he could bring himself to utter. Now here is Russell Baker on his first glimpse of Reston:

> There was an old-fashioned, boyish look about him. With black hair, slightly curly, and a wide mouth that smiled readily, and a brow so serene that it seemed never to have scowled, at first glance he looked as if he might have stepped down from an old photograph over the velveteen settee in a 1912 parlor. The eyes told a rather different story. He had the shrewdest, wisest, most disconcerting gaze I had ever seen on an honest man. Old fashioned or not, he was the most self-confident person I had ever met. . . . It was love at first sight.

Krock insisted that everyone who worked at the bureau call him "Mister Krock." When a senior reporter asked him how long he was expected to keep up this ridiculous formality, Krock replied, "as long as you care to stay here." Later, even the delivery boys would call his successor "Scotty." Krock was a respectable journalist, although one wonders just how effective he would have been with a less august calling card. In his memoirs, he bragged of knowing eleven presidents, "one way or another." But Krock's reputation derived far more from his talents as a crony to great men than as a reporter or commentator on them. He tended to seek favors of the wealthy, as when he borrowed Joseph Kennedy's (now infamous) Palm Beach winter home for vacations, and proved more than willing to repay them in kind.* He wrote complicated, convoluted sentences that often obscured whatever meaning he might have intended. This impressed people, but it did not guide their thinking much. Although his sponsorship could be important, as in the case of Kennan's containment brief, the slightest trace of his influence on the period is difficult to discern today. It was almost as if his entire Washington career had been a prelude to the era of Scotty Reston.

Reston, almost as much as Lippmann, helped to define his profession by his example. When he took over the *Times* bureau and began his column in 1953, he was already recognized as the best reporter in Washington. He seemed to travel behind a kind of force-field of good fortune, somehow marrying the high ideals of hard-charging reporter and Protestant clergyman. Reston was no philosopher. Neither was he much of an intellectual. But he was a brilliant reporter with a genius for homespun

---

*Krock had a particularly tortured relationship with Lippmann. Krock "envied and detested" Lippmann, according to Reston, and Lippmann's feelings toward Krock can probably be characterized as "detestation laced with contempt." (Tom Braden, interview by author, and James Reston, interview by author. The quotations are Braden's.) In *Walter Lippmann and His Times*, the collection of essays in honor of Lippmann edited by Reston and Marquis Childs, Krock manages to contribute an eighteen-page essay without ever mentioning the honoree's name. On another occasion, speaking of the close relationship developed by Lippmann with President Kennedy (whom Krock had once helped win the Pulitzer Prize for literature), Krock told a colleague, "I may be getting old and I may be getting senile but at least I don't fall in love with young boys like Walter Lippmann." See Halberstam, *Powers That Be*, p. 546.

While the rivalry may have been in part professional, it was almost certainly cultural as well. Lippmann was born a wealthy, upper-crust German Jew. He attended the Sachs School and Harvard, where he later supported Jewish quotas as a means of limiting the population of Jews there. Krock, also Jewish, hailed from south central Kentucky and had to drop out of Princeton for lack of money, eventually earning only a junior college degree from the Lewis Institute in Chicago. When Krock asked in 1937 to be made editorial page editor of the *Times*, he was told by C. L. Sulzberger that the sensitive German-Jewish owners of the *Times* were not about "to put a Jew in the showcase." Krock protested that his mother, whom he liked, was not Jewish (actually, she was half-Jewish), while his father, whom he did not like, was. According to Jewish law, he insisted, he was a gentile. Sulzberger was not impressed. "Arthur," he replied, "how do you know all that if you aren't Jewish?" See Talese, *Kingdom and the Power*, p. 232.

In adition to cultural and intellectual differences, the enmity between the two was sparked by an incident at the *World* back in the 1920s, where Krock, who had been hired by Joseph Pulitzer to "ride herd" as a sort of ombudsman, was overheard by Lippmann talking on the phone to the investment firm of Dillon, Read and Co., where he moonlighted as a consultant. Lippmann, who was said to have a penchant for listening at doorways, became convinced that Krock was passing along inside dope on a future editorial likely to affect stock prices. He banished Krock from ever appearing on the *World* op-ed page again. Krock maintained that he was merely discussing a past editorial, but he understood that as he was now known to be an adversary of Lippmann's, his professional growth at the *World* was likely to be stunted. So he left for the *Times*. (Differing versions of this story can be found in Steel, *Lippmann and the American Century*, pp. 200–201, and Arthur Krock, *Memoirs: My Sixty Years on the Firing Line* [New York: Funk and Wagnalls, 1968], pp. 61–63.) For Reston's characterization, see *Deadline*, p. 146.

American wisdom. Reston, as Murray Kempton once observed, was not a man of the Left or Right but of the *Times*. He was the perfect pundit for an America that saw itself living in a post-ideological age.

Born in Clydebank, Scotland, of poor, devout Presbyterian parents, in a home where all four Restons had to sleep in a single bed, young James grew to manhood in Dayton, Ohio, with an immigrant schoolboy's belief in the virtue of his adopted nation. He was a man who, as late as 1975, could say without irony, "This is a country in which good prevails over evil."

Reston was hired by the *Times*' London bureau on September 1, 1939, the day Hitler invaded Poland. He took a brief leave of absence to work for the London-based Office of War Information, where he authored his first book, *Prelude to Victory*. In the darkest days of the conflict, Reston seemed able to breathe new life into shopworn American clichés. The author preached, "We cannot win this War until it ceases to be a struggle for personal aims and material things and becomes a national crusade for America and the American Dream. . . . We must strengthen the things that unite us and remove the things that divide us. We must look forward to the future with the faith in each other and in the rightness of the American Dream." A reviewer called it the work of a "valuable propagandist."

As a Washington reporter, Reston was in a class by himself. His success in persuading Chinese diplomats to leak the details of four-power negotiations under way at Dumbarton Oaks in 1944 earned him both a Pulitzer Prize and an FBI investigation.[*] Reston's energetic use of multiple sources, coupled with his subtle and unthreatening ability to exploit the power and influence of his employer, set a standard against which the Washington press corps still measures itself. Moreover, Reston benefited from the special cachet that derived from Lippmann's patronage. Lippmann was often willing to help young journalists up their respective ladders, but his mentoring relationship with Reston was understood by all to be one of unique respect and affection. Reston would work the town, finding everything out, and then Lippmann would sit Reston and the rest of Washington down to explain what it all meant. "He used my legs, and I used his brain," remembers Reston, "It was a wonderful relationship."

As a columnist, Reston was exceptional for his unexceptionalness. Earnest, moderate, and ostentatiously unpretentious, he was a kind of pundit's Ward Cleaver. Reston had, as David Halberstam notes, "a nice feel for the country" and he wrote in "wonderful quick, illuminating sentences." As a six-year-old boy, Reston explains in his memoirs, he used to respond to

---

[*]Reston's conduit to the Chinese, he later revealed, was the former student intern at the *Times*, Joseph Ku. After he returned to China from the *Times*, Ku reappeared as a member of China's delegation to the Dumbarton Oaks conference. Author's interview with James Reston.

inquiries about his life's ambition by telling whoever asked him that he would "preach the gospel to the heathen." Like many others, Joseph Alsop, who competed with Reston as a reporter in the same way that he competed with Lippmann the philosopher, found Reston a bit much to take on the inspiration front. He would frequently pick up the paper and complain, "There is one of Scotty's Sunday Presbyterian sermons again."

Inside the palace court, Reston sought to soothe tempers and encourage everyone to simmer down and work everything out. Outside the Beltway, Reston's task was to reassure a worried populace that things were not as bad as they seemed. In his valedictory column, published in August 1987, Reston wrote, "despite the recent silliness in Washington . . . things here are seldom as good or bad as most people think they are." An unkind Alexander Cockburn supposed that "There has not been a day in the past two thousand years that Reston would not have been capable of writing those words."

What distinguished Reston's column, aside from its author's infectious decency, was just how closely it mirrored "responsible" opinion within the councils of government. As he was the first to admit, Reston did not have Lippmann's intellectual self-confidence or Alsop's thirst for political combat. The combination of Reston's unquestioning belief in the ultimate good intentions of the American government and his ability to communicate his own uncynical patriotism led him to identify almost completely with the interests of the government as defined by the government. There was little that Americans could not accomplish, Reston seemed to reason, if we would just quit bickering and set our collective nose to the grindstone. Yes, "Life, tyranny and the pursuit of capitalists is the Russian way of life." Yes, the "underdeveloped world, still in the agony of transition, remains vulnerable to the sorcery, the subversion, and the techniques of Communist organization and conspiracy." But "one wonders whether Berlin would be divided if we further West had a little more faith in ourselves." All that was needed, Reston reasoned, was "a patient, well-informed people, both attentive and unafraid, who know what this great country stands for and are willing to die for it if necessary."

This good-versus-evil paradigm dominated Reston's ruminations from the early days of Hitler's rise throughout much of the Vietnam War. If Reston happened to hear of reports of anti-American riots in Latin America, his immediate reaction would be to peg a story on Communist infiltration south of the border. His first move was to call the director of the CIA. Reston's deep, unyielding faith in America and its government made him all the more convincing as an advocate to the public at large, even when what he was advocating was transparent nonsense.

Reston's role in the pantheon of pundit history is partially distorted by the fact that his influence derived far less from his columns than from his stewardship of the *Times* bureau. The seminal moments in his career—convincing the *Times* to tone down its front-page story revealing the upcoming Bay of Pigs invasion in 1961 and standing foursquare behind the decision to publish the Pentagon Papers a decade later—were the actions not of a pundit but of an executive. Young Washington reporters looked to Reston's example not because they were inspired by his column, but because they wanted to be *Times*men themselves. But the Presbyterian sermons, the columns about Washington's mood and its weather, and the occasions on which he would literally turn over his column to Dean Acheson or Henry Kissinger became inseparable from the accomplishments of Reston the journalistic hero.[*] Reston once admitted to a reporter, "If you spend your life as a hatchet man—and there's something to be said for that—then eventually you find that everybody's out to lunch when you call. You're left with only your own opinion. I wouldn't like that, because my own opinions aren't that good." Instead Reston relied on what he called "compulsory plagiarism" of "well-informed officials" in "high level quarters."

Reston's modesty about his own considerable gifts makes it difficult not to like and admire the man, but his contribution to the development of Washington punditry remains problematic. By providing a model for virtually all aspiring Washington pundits—one that was far more accessible than the unapproachable genius of Walter Lippmann—Reston defined an essentially passive profession for his imitators. The pundit's job is less to point out the foibles of a particular policy than to smooth over conflict and encourage bipartisanship. Altogether too eager to accept the government's word as truth, Reston acted, unwittingly, as a kind of advance man for U.S. government policy and a public relations executive for its favored supporters. No one, not even Acheson, exploited this vulnerability better than Kissinger. During Nixon and Kissinger's infamous 1972 Christmas bombing of Hanoi, Reston wrote that Kissinger "has said nothing in public about the bombing in North Vietnam, which he undoubtedly opposes. If the bombing goes on . . . Mr. Kissinger will be free to resign." The only problem with the story, however, was that the bombings were Kissinger's idea.[†] He feigned anguish to Reston, on "deep

---

[*]Reston once titled a column, "By Henry Kissinger with James Reston."
[†]Reston's column so infuriated Nixon that he had his staffers secure Kissinger's phone logs. These proved that Kissinger had spoken with Reston on the day he denied giving him "an interview." When Haldeman discovered this, he confronted Kissinger, insisting, "You told us you didn't give Reston an interview but in fact, you did talk to him." Kissinger responded, "Yes, but that was only on the telephone." See Seymour Hersh, *The Price of Power: Kissinger in the Nixon White House* (New York: Summit Books, 1983), pp. 630–31.

background" no doubt, to deceive Congress and the country at large. In this deception, Reston was his invaluable accomplice, all the more helpful because he liked, admired, and needed to believe Kissinger himself.

The generation of Washington pundits that emerged in Lippmann's wake owed as much to Reston's example as to that of his mentor. Lippmann had single-handedly elevated the profession, socially and politically, to a point at which it grew from undisguised flackery to a complicated amalgam of critical examination, community conversation, and somewhat better-disguised flackery. Lippmann's example attracted a better-educated, more ambitious, and socially better-born element into journalism, and the most ambitious of these people often lusted for invitations into punditry's relatively exalted ranks. But his example was unapproachable, and in Scotty Reston eager young reporters saw a model of power and prestige to which they might reasonably aspire. The fact that Reston's reputation sprang less from his original thoughts than from his dogged reporting further minimized the psychological space between his revered status and the unsung hacks who envisioned themselves in his place.

Lippmann's immediate successors, pundits like Marquis Childs (the 1960s version of Rowland Evans and Robert Novak) and David Broder—men of the Center all—earned their daily bread in Reston-like fashion: not through the acuity of their analysis, but with the timeliness of their access. They were certainly better educated than their forebears, and their dinner parties were considered more desirable invitations. But Joseph Kraft, the main contender for Lippmann's abandoned crown, manifested his wisdom not by writing difficult philosophical tomes as Lippmann had, but by passing along the ministrations of kings, shahs, and prime ministers.*

Like Vladimir and Estragon, the Washington of the 1960s waited impatiently for the next Lippmann to appear on the scene. But the issues had become too diffuse and the pundit class too expansive for anyone to dominate the public dialogue quite as thoroughly as he had. No one inherited Lippmann's ability to define the political limits of the Center's debate. Instead, the post-Lippmann generation merely reinforced the borders set by others, attempting all the while to inject some drama and

---

*In his article, "The Most Famous Journalist in the World," *Washington Monthly*, March 1975, p. 13, James Fallows quotes this story from an undated *Village Voice* column: "Writing in the *New Yorker* about OPEC [Organization of the Petroleum Exporting Countries], Kraft is awfully above himself in this article. He meets the secretary general of OPEC, Dr. Khene. 'When I greeted him in French,' reports Kraft, 'he was visibly pleased.' I should say so. If a fellow said to you, 'Bonjour, Monsieur, je suis Joseph Kraft, meilleur écrivain, homme le plus intelligent parmi tous les columnists du monde,' you might be pleased too."

status into what otherwise would have been considered the most insignificant minutiae of insider politics. This was clearly a corruption of both the Lippmannian and Deweyite ideals, but it was not one worth getting terribly excited about; for, outside of the notable exceptions discussed earlier, until the mid- to late 1970s few pundits were influential at center stage. While the politicians attended to domestic policy, the bipartisan political establishment embodied by the likes of Acheson and McCloy managed, with Lippmann's assistance, to keep the portfolio of American foreign policy under control.

Beginning in the late 1960s, however, the calculus of power and influence inside Washington began to change. The civil rights movement challenged the primacy of the politicians in the making of domestic policy, while the Vietnam quagmire proved the second generation of foreign policy Wise Men to be less masterful than their forebears in asserting control. In addition, the growth of television redefined the terms of the American political debate, and the rise of competing forces in the wake of the establishment's failures destroyed the Center's confidence as the leading political class. The net result was the slow formation of a restructured insider political constellation in which the role of the emerging pundit class would be enormously enhanced, just as its voice became simultaneously more vulgar and increasingly belligerent. Nothing symbolized this development better than the replacement on punditry's center stage of Lippmann, Alsop, and Reston by the deeply ideological and ceaselessly televised voices of George F. Will, Patrick J. Buchanan, and Rowland Evans and Robert Novak.

CHAPTER THREE

Post-Lippmanndom: The Rest and the Rightest

On the evening of August 11, 1960, CBS newsman Howard K. Smith turned to Walter Lippmann and asked the father of all softball questions: "Could you tell me why you felt that way then and why you feel the way you do now?" The nationwide, prime-time broadcast signaled the beginning of a new era in American politics: the marriage of television and political punditry. By creating an annual special broadcast devoted exclusively to Lippmann's opinions about the world, CBS had broken an old barrier. Never before had network television spent an entire one-hour program inquiring the view of someone who was neither an elected politician nor a Hollywood entertainer. Punditry, in its most exalted form, could now be called on to stand in for both of them.

Before appearing on television, Lippmann had done little to disguise his contempt for the medium. "Television," he insisted, was the "prostitute of merchandising," whose primary influence had been to "poison the innocent" and "debase the public taste." But the camera was kind to Lippmann, and the first show met with virtually unanimous public acclaim. Lippmann soon upped his television fee to a remarkable $15,000 for one hour-long interview a year and $10,000 for each additional discussion.

Looking back on Lippmann's annual televised appearances from the vantage point of more than thirty years, one can see in them the defining characteristics of the modern-day punditocracy. Lippmann brought prestige to television and television brought Lippmann riches. But the riches were not without a long-term cost. In Lippmann's last interview, conducted in February 1965, the pundit committed some of the most egregious errors of his career. (On Johnson's B-52 raids: "They're political bombings and . . . I don't think they kill anybody.") In the ensuing decades, the power of television, coupled with the right wing's post-Vietnam counter-revolution, would shape the American political dialogue in ways that could not but have depressed and disturbed the man who helped inaugurate them.

During the course of the August 11 interview, Lippmann outlined what he considered to be the most important qualities of presidential leadership. A great president, he explained, must have "the ability to see what matters in the excitement of daily events. He must be able to see through the latest headline to what is permanent and enduring." Just as important was the president's ability to "articulate":

> He must be able to talk in language which not the lowest common denominator understand, but the best—what you must lead in a country are the best of the country and they will carry it on down. There's no use of the president trying to talk down to a fellow who can just about read and write. Let somebody else do that. He must talk to the people who teach the man to read and write.

Both of Lippmann's criteria are consistent with the generally suspicious attitude he had demonstrated toward democratic governance four decades earlier. But they are also borne out by the quality of the American political dialogue as it developed over the course of those forty years. Daily American journalism, and its most prestigious tributary, Washington punditry, did not succeed in creating a vanguard of highly educated, sophisticated political consumers of the type Lippmann pined for in *Liberty and the News*. Instead, they helped create a dichotomy between Washington insiders, who had access to relatively unfiltered sources of information about the United States and the world, and the rest of us. Historically, Lippmann had concerned himself primarily with the former, despite the fact that the bulk of his readership could be found in the latter.

To television executives, who judged success or failure exclusively on how many millions of people sat still for commercials, the insider audience was meaningless. Television could not cordon off an op-ed page for its highbrow customers. The medium addressed itself exclusively to the masses. If elite audiences found something they enjoyed in the wasteland, well, that was unobjectionable; but it was also irrelevant. The numbers, and therefore the money, were in stupidity. Network executives liked to congratulate one another about their commitment to the "public interest," but they had a curious definition of the word. In one of the great moments in the history of inadvertent truth-telling, then–CBS president Frank Stanton once explained, "A program in which a large part of the audience is interested is by that very fact . . . in the public interest."

When Lippmann delineated the foundation of presidential leadership to Howard K. Smith in the summer of 1960, he hit on precisely the two qualities a political figure might have in which television had the least interest: invisible, subterranean long-term forces and the need for a sophisticated, relatively well-educated elite to elevate national political discussion.* To ask a television audience to think about something it cannot see is folly; the medium is entirely visual. Similarly, although television executives might have been willing to relinquish most of their audience in order to bask in Lippmann's reflected glow once a year, the heart and soul of the industry clearly belonged to poison and prostitution. Because no other pundits commanded the degree of deference enjoyed by the great man, if they wanted a piece of the television's phenomenally remunerative action as well, stupid or not, they had better learn to play by television's rules.

Lippmann's 1960 appearance may have marked the beginnings of political punditry's passage into the phosphorescent universe, but the true origins of highbrow television punditry lie not with Lippmann, but with Edward R. Murrow. Murrow vaulted into the American consciousness during the wartime raids on London. He was a radio reporter then, leaving the job of commentary to the likes of Raymond Gram Swing, a moderate liberal with a spooky voice, and Elmer Davis, whose voice so engaged the president that Roosevelt called on him to run the Office of War Information.† These radio pundits were popular, but could not hope to match the drama of Murrow's dispatches. When CBS radio anchor H. V. Kaltenborn came on the radio "calling Ed Murrow, calling Ed Murrow," an

---

*One is today depressed, though hardly surprised, to note that the strongest criticism Lippmann voiced for the Eisenhower administration was for its refusal to demand sufficient taxes to pay for an adequate education system for America's children. ("And once you've failed to educate a child, you've failed, and you can't make that up later" [*Conversations with Lippmann*, pp. 8–11].)

†"You know the one I mean," said the president, "the one with the funny voice." See Richard J. Barnet, *The Rocket's Red Glare* (New York: Simon and Schuster, 1990), p. 224.

entire nation sat transfixed as Murrow's dramatic baritone brought them the story of the century, with full special effects courtesy of the Luftwaffe. Through his radio broadcasts, Murrow became a national hero, single-handedly demonstrating the journalistic possibilities of the medium. Amid the drama of the gunfire, however, Murrow and his staff did not concern themselves with the niceties of objective journalism. Nobody would have stood for it. This was the good war, with all of the good guys on the same side, and the rules of objectivity did not apply. As in the early stages of print journalism, the punditry and the reporting were one and the same.

After the war, television gradually replaced radio as the primary news and entertainment medium in the United States, and Ed Murrow made the transition with little difficulty. Murrow's CBS television career is most notable for his famous piercing of the armor of Senator Joseph McCarthy. The fact that Murrow is remembered as the white knight of the McCarthy era is less a tribute to his foresight or bravery, however, than to the increasing primacy of television in the American cultural universe. The February 1954 broadcast that helped end the McCarthyite scare came four years after McCarthy began his noxious campaign and long after Alsop, Reston, and Martin Agronsky had begun to attack him. But because McCarthy was a heartland rather than a Beltway phenomenon, the influence of these condemnations was minimal. And if Truman or Eisenhower did not have the courage to denounce his antics, then, by 1954, only one political institution had the power to do so.

Murrow's dramatic program provided the stake that pierced the vampire's heart, but it also signaled the beginning of the end of Murrow's own effectiveness within the profession he helped build. Destroying McCarthy somehow stained Murrow in the eyes of his employer. Shortly afterward, CBS began to move the show around the schedule and restrict the extent of Murrow's broadcast time. In 1955, he was further weakened when the Alcoa Corporation discontinued its support of the program after Murrow featured a lengthy interview with J. Robert Oppenheimer and an unflattering report on Texas real estate in the same program. Oppenheimer was still damaged goods, despite McCarthy's self-immolation, and Alcoa had been planning to increase its investments in Texas. CBS began to limit Murrow to an occasional documentary series, referred to contemptuously on Madison Avenue as "See It Now and Then." Within four years of Murrow's 1954 McCarthy triumph, his show was history. Two years after that, so was Murrow, having been systematically emasculated by the network that to this day never ceases to invoke his name.

In retrospect, Murrow's sins were two. He was overly intellectual, and he was not sufficiently anti-Communist. This remained the case despite the fact that Murrow had gone to great lengths to inoculate himself against exactly these charges. His celebrity interview program, *Person to Person*, was a deliberate attempt to convince Americans (and CBS corporate executives) that Murrow was a member in good standing of the apolitical celebrity aristocracy that ruled the American entertainment industry.

On the anti-Communist front, Murrow had also done his utmost to protect himself. In March of 1947, Murrow failed to come to the aid of his friend and colleague, William Shirer, whom he had hired in Berlin in 1938. Shirer's radio program was unceremoniously canceled by CBS founder and czar William Paley when its commercial sponsor, a shaving soap manufacturer, found Shirer's name on a blacklist of accused Communist sympathizers. The sponsor soon reversed itself in the face of a massive public outcry, but Paley refused to budge. Murrow, according to Shirer, declined to expend any of his professional capital on the matter and immediately distanced himself from his old friend. Shirer was not a Communist, but this was hardly the point. He was an unapologetic liberal, and in March of 1947, that was just as bad. As Irving Kristol would explain six years later, "there is one thing the American people know about Senator McCarthy; he, like them, is unequivocally anti-Communist. About the spokesmen for American liberalism, they feel they know no such thing."

Although Murrow had helped destroy McCarthy, television executives were not nearly ready to bask in the glow of their newfound political power. But by allowing McCarthy to self-destruct on his program, Murrow appeared to have crossed the invisible barrier that journalism had set up between fact and opinion. Objective journalism had given free reign to McCarthy's antics, and so the unmasking of them was, by definition, not objective. Murrow's opinions were not an issue during the war, because they generated no controversy. But no matter how much McCarthy had done to discredit witch hunting, handing him the pistol with which to shoot himself appeared to be an act of political bias. So nervous were CBS executives about challenging any aspect of political power, even in this backhanded fashion, that William Paley suggested offering McCarthy thirty minutes of unrestricted air time for a rebuttal.

After Murrow, television commentary was returned to its respectful norm, offering politicians a platform from which to pontificate without much interference from the men behind the cameras. Until the Lippmann broadcast on CBS, explicit political opinions on television remained the exclusive property of politicians, starlets, and the ubiquitous man on the street.

Non-Lippmann punditry did not make a significant impression on television again until 1968, when ABC news, trailing in the ratings and constantly strapped for funds, introduced the notion of regular commentaries on its nightly broadcast. (ABC expanded its newscasts from fifteen minutes to thirty in late 1967; CBS and NBC had done so in September 1963.) The stable of commentators included Bill Moyers, James J. Kilpatrick, and Gore Vidal. The network's intention was to provide an inexpensive way to flesh out the program and give it a unique identity. Private polling indicated that viewers liked the commentaries but thought they lacked star quality; the constant rotation prevented the audience from making an emotional investment in any one of the commentators. The obvious answer was for the network to concentrate on just one or two personalities. Howard K. Smith, the conservative, and Frank Reynolds, the liberal, thus became television's first daily pundits, paid to tell you not only the news, but also what to think about it. Soon Eric Sevareid was added to Walter Cronkite's broadcast to offer political commentary.

But executives at both CBS and ABC grew uncomfortable with the phenomenon of commentary on the evening news. The commentators themselves proved uncontrollable and unpredictable. More serious, however, was the fact that Washington pundits had so successfully defined the parameters of thoughtful analysis that TV news executives had come to associate "responsible" commentary with "access to information on a 'background' or off the record basis." Because their New York–based anchors were excluded from "the main business of gathering information—across a lunch table or on the cocktail circuit in Washington," television commentary struck them as "bland and predictable." That a person could be expected simply to comment intelligently on national affairs without having achieved the status of a Washington insider was considered by these executives to be beyond the pale. Quickly banished, in large measure, from the network news programs, political commentary soon became the sole purview of the Sunday morning talk-show ghetto.

The fickle romance between television and punditry was finally consummated when the Washington Post Company discovered a format that answered the needs of both sides: the pundit sitcom. The idea was that instead of merely relaying information, each pundit would portray himself as a stock character, thereby giving viewers a chance to identify, either positively or negatively, with an entertainment personality rather than just a boring journalist. The show that discovered this formula, *Agronsky and Company*, was launched in December 1969. Here, for the first time, were print pundits not named Walter Lippmann being asked to give their opinions on the news without bothering to invite the politicians along. Host Martin Agronsky borrowed the format from public television's *Washington Week in Review*, founded in February 1967. But the PBS show simply asked straight reporters who covered a beat to explain their stories in a bit more detail, with the other members of the roundtable occasionally chiming in with a question. Had anyone offered an opinion without first attributing it to a major political figure, he would likely have been hooted off the air. The Agronsky show improved the entertainment quotient of this formula by inviting pundits and encouraging them to argue. The facts, so well respected on PBS, were disputed on *Agronsky and Company*, and its members were encouraged to develop distinct characters.

The show's secret weapon for many years was the late Peter Lisagor, the gregarious Washington correspondent for the *Chicago Daily News* and a living relic of the Ring Lardner/*Front Page* days, when men were men and reporters were broke. Lisagor used to delight in "sticking little needles into [Southern conservative] James J. Kilpatrick," as Jack Germond recalls, "and watching all the hot air come out of him."

It was on *Agronsky*, after the death of Lisagor, that George Will honed his act before taking it on the road. Will's withering witticisms dominated the dialogue on any given program, but not quite to the point at which the other regulars were prevented from defining their own personalities. Martin Agronsky was a grandfatherly presence of the liberal, anti-Communist Center. Hugh Sidey, *Time*'s White House correspondent and perhaps the most determinedly sycophantic newsman ever to grace the profession, was Mr. Samgrass, journalistic valet to presidents great and small.[*] Carl Rowan, among the only prominent blacks in America to give public voice to J. Edgar Hoover's concern about subversives in Dr. King's entourage during

---

[*]Sidey's musings provided countless presidents with a direct conduit to *Time*'s four million readers with minimal journalistic interference. Reminiscing on the first part of his career, Sidey observed that, yes, as he looked back, "We were too easy on Eisenhower. . . . We were too easy on Kennedy. . . . I might also say we were too easy on Nixon. . . ." Even Ronald Reagan would look to Sidey with the knowledge that, as late as December 1986, the pundit would literally turn his weekly column over to the Communicator in Chief, offering the beleaguered president the opportunity to sound off against his enemies in the Iran-Contra affair unimpeded by commentary or context. President Bush's reputation for extreme caution was not endangered in the slightest when *Newsweek* reported that he expected Sidey to "treat him favorably" during his presidency. Sidey was the only pundit invited by the Bushes to attend the official state dinner in honor of Mikhail Gorbachev at the spring 1990 summit. His hard-hitting report: "In the White House, candlelight and the aura of history soften the edges, bringing everyone closer together. That magic was at work Thursday night." See Jonathan Alter, "Bush's Media Tastes," *Newsweek*, 9 April 1990, p. 6, and Hugh Sidey, "Capitalists over Corn Bread," *Time*, 11 June 1990. Sidey's self-criticism appeared in "The Presidency and the Press," in *The LBJ School of Public Affairs, University of Texas at Austin, Conference Report* (Austin, TX: University of Texas, 1977), p. 80.

the 1960s, held fast to his Great Society heritage.* James J. Kilpatrick, the former segregationist firebrand, jettisoned his separate but equal shtick, but he kept his courtly Southern gentlemen, proud-to-be-a-Confederate routine in order to harrumph at Rowan. The *New Yorker*'s Elizabeth Drew evoked a censorious New England schoolteacher, one who told us that the homework she was giving us was for our own good, and one day we would thank her for it. To anyone not caught up in the rhythms of Capitol life, either personally or vicariously, the show was about as much fun as a proctology exam. But over time, *Agronsky and Company* developed a strong following in the Center. Power Washington would straighten its tuxedo and fasten its garters before going to cocktail parties and honorary dinners and recapping the arguments of its favorite players.

From the standpoint of pundit history, the primary function of the Agronsky show was the creation of a new kind of stardom for its participants. Certainly no certified players in the insider game could admit to allowing so mass-directed a vehicle to influence their thinking on the important issues of the day. Rather, the show allowed a few chosen pundits to develop television personalities identifiable to a mass viewership. This led to enormously lucrative speaking engagements, along with the kind of recognition inside Washington that usually attends only the starting five of a small-town varsity basketball team. Neither would go ignored within the journalism profession.

The successful marriage of television and punditry was just one aspect of the black box's increasingly dictatorial power over American politics. Television's transformation of American cultural life is beyond the scope of this book (it may be beyond the scope of human analysis). In many ways, television has simply replaced our lives with itself. In Mark Crispin Miller's memorable phrase, "Big Brother is you, watching." The average American family keeps its television humming more than seven hours each day. Since 1961, the majority of Americans surveyed have deemed it their most believable news source since 1961, with a more than two-to-one margin over newspapers since 1968. As Richard Schickel observes, "Television has

---

*When, in March 1967, Martin Luther King called the Vietnam War "a blasphemy against all that America stands for," Rowan wrote that "King was listening most to one man [among his advisers] who is clearly more interested in embarrassing the US than in the plight of the Negro or the war-weary people of Vietnam." The following Sunday, he insisted that the civil rights leader had an "exaggerated appraisal of how much he and his crisis techniques were responsible for the race-relations progress that has been made." Rowan also raised the specter of "Communists influencing the actions and words of the young minister," although he insisted that he, personally, did not "endorse what King and many others consider a 'guilty by association smear.'" See Neil A. Grauer, *Wits and Sages* (Baltimore: Johns Hopkins University Press, 1984), pp. 204–06.

come to provide the only meaningful context for that speculative enterprise: the idea of America; the only external reality that matters."

Print may have looked down its nose at television, but once Lippmann joined in, even its most revered insiders had no choice but follow suit. The suggestive power of television is such that a raised eyebrow or a feigned expression of surprise could be subliminally more convincing to the unschooled viewer than a year's worth of well-reasoned columns. Politicians and pundits alike were therefore forced to remain exceedingly respectful of the medium's distorting and trivializing potentialities. Nowhere was this more evident than in the twisted history of the domestic politics of the Vietnam War.

Vietnam, David Halberstam has observed, was the first war in American history whose end was declared by an anchorman. When, on February 27, 1968, Walter Cronkite decided to shed his Olympian objectivity and explain in plain language on a special CBS news broadcast that the war simply did not work, Lyndon Johnson turned to his press secretary, George Christian, and admitted that it was all over: If he had lost Walter Cronkite, he had lost Mr. Average Citizen.

There were ten thousand television sets in America when the Japanese bombed Pearl Harbor and 10 million by the time the North Korean troops crossed the Yalu River. The night that Cronkite came before the cameras to denounce the Vietnam War effort in 1968, that number had reached 100 million. The U.S. Air Force could bomb every outhouse in Indochina to ashes, but if it could not convince the most trusted man in America that it was winning, then it might as well not bother. When Cronkite closed his broadcast with the tag line "And that's the way it is," that was the way it was, for all practical purposes, in the minds of tens of millions of Americans. Whether Cronkite was correct in his assessment made little difference; he was Walter Cronkite—that's the way it was.[*]

Cronkite was an anchorman, not a pundit. But on that historic broadcast, Cronkite combined television's persuasive powers into the most powerful pundit portfolio in the history of the business. Cronkite's status as an impeccably objective anchor certified his opinion with a kind of irresistible force. That "objectivity" could be enlisted on behalf of a political opinion was well known to the governing establishment. Its manipulation had become an essential ingredient in creating what theologian Reinhold Niebuhr called the "necessary illusion" providing "emotionally potent

---

[*]During the Nixon administration, the president's political advisers briefly considered attacking Cronkite for his alleged bias. But staffer Dwight Chapin told his colleague Lyn Nofziger, in a memo dated February 15, 1971, that "taking on Walter Cronkite cannot do us any good whatsoever. It is like taking on the Lord himself." See Bruce Oudes, ed., *From the President: Richard Nixon's Secret Files* (New York: Harper and Row, 1989), p. 218.

simplifications" required to win the support of the average American voter. Lippmann had a similar concern in mind when, in *Liberty and the News*, he spoke of the "manufacture of consent." But the fact that these manipulations could be used to overturn the policies of the government, and that television now felt sufficiently confident to try it; this was something new, something revolutionary, something dangerous.

A second important result of the Cronkite broadcast was its confirmation that on matters of both war and peace, the government itself was no longer to be trusted. The Vietnam War had been a lie from start to finish, and it contaminated the credibility of almost everyone who touched it. Americans were slow to digest the fact that their leaders had misled them, but soon all of the institutions that had invested themselves in Vietnam began to suffer similarly, both from loss of internal self-confidence and from a decline in public trust. Congress did not have the courage to put an end to the war by cutting off its funding or to go the distance with the president in seeking to prosecute it to an ever more grisly end. Meanwhile, the civil rights and anti-war movements were creating what appeared to be a crisis atmosphere in the country, in the face of which Washington's pontification seemed impotent and pathetic.

Equally significant was the deterioration of the Center, whose best and brightest had nurtured the political illusions that sustained the war for so long. With their children denouncing them as war criminals and their former academic colleagues signing petitions to bar them from setting foot on their campuses, the men who so proudly had guided the nation's struggle against the dark forces of Communism lost the will to continue. As America confronted collapse in Vietnam, the entire establishment seemed to enter into a period of extended nervous breakdown. While some of the war's architects continued to put on a brave front, most faded back into the oak-paneled woodwork from whence they came. Meanwhile, academia became so thoroughly divided and disgusted by the war effort that it, too, began a process of withdrawal from the political dialogue. At the vortex of foreign policy and national politics, the only political institution to emerge strengthened by the debacle was the one that had been instrumental in unmasking its deceptions: the news media. By the end of the 1960s, however bruised and battered by the war and their role in promoting it, the media alone, it seemed, was left standing in the mud-splattered ring of the American public dialogue. And it was left to the pundits, the media's most prestigious component, to forge a new American consensus.

Owing their multifaceted political, ideological, and social connections to the men who conducted the war, the insider pundits were not among the first to comprehend the bankruptcy of America's Indochina policies.

One pundit who did not shrink from the war and its implications, however, was James Reston. This was true in part because Reston's immunity to Johnson's bellicose rhetoric had been strengthened by his close relationship with Lippmann.

Lippmann had insisted all along that the United States was essentially an air and sea power. Vietnam offended Lippmann's sense of proportion, as well as his conception of the country's natural advantages. Johnson's conceit, he argued, "was based on a totally vain notion that if we do not set the world in order, no matter what the price, we cannot live in the world safely. If we examine the idea thoroughly, we shall see that it is nothing more but the old isolationism of our innocence in a new form." Until Lyndon Johnson escalated his pursuit of the Vietnam War beyond, as Lippmann saw it, all reason, Lippmann had never burned his bridges to an administration or questioned anything more fundamental than the "control and administration" of its policies. With Johnson, however, Lippmann's treasured lines of comity were broken by a man whose pride and stubbornness were unmatched.

Lippmann had initially gone out of his way to be friendly to Johnson, and he muted his criticism of Vietnam during the early part of the American commitment. But as the president allowed himself to be drawn deeper into the Indochinese mud, the two men grew obsessed with what each saw to be the other's duplicity. Johnson used to tell Vietnam dissenters in Congress to "go ask Walter Lippmann" next time they wanted a dam built in their districts and delighted in making off-color remarks about Lippmann at diplomatic gatherings. Lippmann, meanwhile, gradually withdrew from the very insider contacts with which he had defined the profession. Shortly before he went into unhappy exile in Manhattan in May 1967, Lippmann was using language he had not had occasion to use since he stopped hanging around with John Reed at *The Masses.* Johnson's America, he wrote, "was no longer the historic America," but a "bastard empire which relies on superior force to achieve its purposes."

When the course of the war seemed to bear out Lippmann's prognosis, Reston proved readier than most to entertain the implications. He supported his Vietnam correspondents down the line and indulged in not a whit of the grumbling about their having "gone native" that characterized the conversations of so many Washington insiders. Moreover, in part because he had children of counterculture age, Reston did not axiomatically reject its political analysis, though he was at great pains to understand its vehemence.

Thus, Reston came to view Vietnam with what was an extraordinarily open mind for a Washington insider. In January 1968, the U.S. district attorney approved indictments against five individuals, including the baby doctor Benjamin Spock and Yale chaplain William Sloane Coffin, Jr., for counseling young men to resist the draft. Exactly one day after the indictments were handed down, Reston invited one of the defendants, Marcus Raskin of the Institute for Policy Studies, to lunch at the Metropolitan Club. The symbolism of the engagement spoke volumes both about Reston and about the new legitimacy the antiwar movement was acquiring in the mind of the establishment. "Maybe it is a good thing," Reston wrote of the resisters' decision to seek arrest:

> The country has been arguing for months now about a great many other things: Is bombing effective or not? Should we negotiate with the Vietcong and the National Liberation Front or not? But this case of Coffin and Spock has raised even more fundamental questions: Is the policy of the United States in Vietnam morally right or wrong? Who is 'committing offenses against the United States'—the people who oppose the war or the people who want to continue it and expand it?

It was not only Vietnam, however, that led Reston to reassess the panoply of beliefs that had sustained the Washington consensus during the postwar years. The war had lifted a scab on the nation's conscience and left in its place a visible, festering wound. Reston did not shrink back from this wound. Rather, he examined it, carefully, tentatively, in the hopes of determining just how infected the body had become. The deeper Reston looked, the more troubled he became. Of Martin Luther King, Jr.'s assassination, he wrote, "The nation is appalled by the murder of Martin Luther King, but it is not appalled by the conditions of his people. It grieves for the man, but not for his cause. This is the curse and tragedy of America. This is the real crime of which the assassination of Dr. King is but a hideous symbol."

Nineteen sixty-eight would prove to be a traumatic year for the United States, a year of political assassination, orgiastic violence, and immense psychopolitical tension. But it was not merely the counterculture that had stressed the system near its breaking point. A significant proportion of the voters who shocked Lyndon Johnson into early retirement by supporting McCarthy's peace crusade in New Hampshire voted for George Wallace in the general election. The discovery of the "Silent Majority"— the 56 percent of those polled who thought that Mayor Daley's cops had used an appropriate level of force in senselessly beating both student protesters and visiting news media before national television cameras— threw what remained of the Center into a state of confusion. About the only thing that Washington pundits could agree on, as Joseph Kraft admitted, was that "most of us . . . are not rooted in the great mass of ordinary Americans."

With Richard Nixon's election in 1968, the competition between ideological currents within the insider dialogue came to a head. In the first place, Nixon faced something with which no Cold War president had ever had to deal: an unapologetic intellectual opposition. In Anthony Lewis, who began appearing on its op-ed page in June 1969, the *New York Times* had found a writer who alone among influential commentators was willing and able to articulate the moral outrage against the American government that characterized the antiwar movement.* "The war," he thundered, constituted "a crime against humanity," causing "the most terrible destruction in the history of man." Today, Lewis tends to see the war as less a "conscious evil" than just a "combination of miscalculation and ignorance." Yet his language, published day after day on the *Times'* op-ed page, was probably the most powerful that had ever been used to criticize an American president in so prestigious a forum.

Significantly, Lewis did not write his column from Washington. He had intended to, and found a house in the capital, but when he went to his new office, he decided almost immediately to move out of town. "I realized," Lewis recalls, "that I could not live [there] because I could not write about public figures the way I wanted to. . . . When I see people regularly I find it very hard to be unabashedly critical." But even in Washington itself, voices were cropping up that appeared to embrace a rejection not only of the war, but of the entire Cold War ideology that had produced it. Ignored for more than three decades, I. F. Stone suddenly became a celebrity, as more than seventy thousand subscribers read his radical newsletter, *I. F. Stone's Weekly*. Tom Wicker, the former *Times* bureau chief, joined Lewis on the op-ed page of the *Times* and adopted a similarly antiwar perspective. The *Washington Post* hired former community organizer Nicholas Von Hoffman and gave him a column (albeit in the Style section) in which to vent some old-fashioned left-wing moral outrage. And the *Washington Star* found a deceptively polite, well-mannered New England lady named Mary McGrory who, once she got interested in Vietnam, found she could write about nothing else. As what McGrory termed the "infectious choler that is rising from the city" under Lyndon Johnson gave way to the "continuing spiral of obliviousness from the White House" under Richard Nixon, her rage grew in scope and intensity, but it never overpowered the wonderfully

---

*Ironically, Lewis was offered the role because publisher Punch Sulzberger had asked him to fly back from London to discuss a new job, which was filled by the time he arrived. Sulzberger felt guilty, and Lewis got his column. (Author's interview.)

measured tone of her carefully constructed prose. "Senators used to tell me," explains McGrory, "you're not funny anymore. Why aren't you ever funny anymore? What they meant was, 'Please shut up about Vietnam.' "

Even Reston, although still a hopeless sucker for Kissinger, was sufficiently shocked by the lies and mendacity of the Nixon administration to adopt an entirely new vocabulary with regard to the symbols of American power and prestige. In response to Nixon's initial defense of his lawlessness—that his subterfuge was undertaken in the name of "national security"—Reston wrote, "And the tragedy is that more crimes and brutalities have been done in the name of 'national security' in this country than in the name of anything else." This was indeed an amazing moment. Here was the most important political commentator of the day, the man who helped censor his own newspaper on behalf of the Bay of Pigs invasion, debunking the most sacred words of his generation as not merely a sham but a mask for "crimes and brutalities."*

But in politics, unlike science, not every action causes an equal and opposite reaction. Some actions cause reactions that far exceed the power and scope of their initial inspiration. The insinuation of "movement" values into the thinking and writing patterns of insider pundits, however tentatively, created a reaction that, over time, would sweep away not only the emerging Left but also the cinders of the old establishment, leaving in its wake a new political and intellectual formation that would cripple liberal and moderate political culture for decades to come.

The rise of the New Right began almost immediately with the collapse of the Center. Richard Nixon was a man with an almost bottomless capacity for resentment, and he resented nothing and no one so much as the men and women who wrote about him each day in the great newspapers of the country.[†] As he explained to Patrick Buchanan:

> If you consider the real ideological bent of the *New York Times*, the *Washington Post, Time, Newsweek,* and the three television networks, you will find overwhelmingly that their editorial bias comes down on the side of amnesty, pot, abortion, confiscation of wealth (unless it is theirs), massive increases in welfare, unilateral disarmament, reduction of their defenses and surrender in Vietnam.

*Reston later qualified this by adding, "The statement that 'More crimes have been committed with the excuse of national security' is absolutely right. But it doesn't follow from that that anytime they proclaim that national security is at stake that you reject it. It may be true. It was true during the missile crisis" (James Reston, interview by author).

[†]Safire now says that his biggest misjudgment of Nixon's character resulted from his underestimation of the president's hatred and contempt for the press, which he had previously interpreted to be Nixon's respect for personal privacy (William Safire, interview by author).

Nixon was certain that he, not the these self-selected Ivy League smarties, understood what the American people wanted from their president, and whatever criticism he received from them he filed under the category of hostile conspiracy. Spiro Agnew spoke for his boss in a series of November 1969 speeches when he attacked the national news media for "giving the American people a highly selective and often biased presentation of the news" and blamed it for the continuing salience of the antiwar movement, singling out for special contempt "the effete corps of impudent snobs who characterized themselves as intellectuals."

Insider punditry continued to grow in influence as Nixon's stature fell, but it was a nervous growth, unsettled by the fact that Nixon was playing a new kind of extra-Constitutional hardball. Reporters' phone lines were tapped, the FBI was unleashed against them, and the White House even hired a private investigator to search the home of *Post* pundit Joseph Kraft. The Agnew attacks, moreover, proved a brilliant tactic in creating a political atmosphere more palatable to Nixonian conservatism. Newspaper publishers worried that their high-minded commentators were out of touch with American values, and Nixon's visible hostility gave them great incentive to address this. Finding pundits whose views were "rooted in the great mass of ordinary Americans" may have been beyond the capacities of the media barons, but responding to direct political pressure—that was something they understood.

The distinguished careers of William Safire and George F. Will owe a great deal to this historical moment. Safire, a Nixon speechwriter, was brought on the staff of the *Times* amid great controversy in 1973. David Halberstam spoke for many when he wrote to the publisher that Safire "was not a Conservative . . . but a paid manipulator. He is not a man of ideas or politics but a man of tricks." Safire did not do much to assuage the fears of his colleagues when, in his earliest columns, he suggested that Nixon "reestablish the confidentiality of the presidency" by setting off "a public bonfire of the tapes on the White House lawn."

The *Washington Post*'s op-ed page was also in the market for an insider pundit to take up the conservative banner. Alsop was no longer effective, having discredited himself over Vietnam,* and editor Philip Geyelin could not afford to match the *Times*'s offer to Safire, though he "struggled like

---

*Alsop served in Manila with MacArthur and caught the last plane out of the city before it fell. He was interned by the Japanese as a civilian (despite his military status) and turned over to the Americans in a July 1942 prisoner exchange at Madagascar. He returned with General Claire Chennault to China and threw himself into the arms of Chiang Kai-shek, where he displayed, in Barbara Tuchman's words, "a relentless animus to destroy the credibility of Chiang's detractors." It was Alsop who drafted the generalissimo's infamous and ultimately successful telegram to Roosevelt, demanding that General Stillwell be replaced there. See Barbara Tuchman, *Stillwell and the American Experience in China, 1911–1945* (New York: Macmillan, 1970), p. 358.

hell" to try. As a consolation prize, Geyelin settled on a young ex-professor and Republican speechwriter whom his deputy, Meg Greenfield, had recommended. George Will was brought onto the page, where he quickly developed a flair for enlisting the likes of Edmund Burke and G. K. Chesterton on behalf of his hawkish sentiments, on a trial basis. But, as Geyelin recalls, Will had not as yet developed even an "elementary sense of journalistic propriety." When Geyelin told Will that his trial period had ended and the Washington Post Writers Group was ready to syndicate him nationally, Will asked, "Does this mean I have to stop writing speeches for Jesse Helms?"

The fact that neither Safire nor Will was a journalist in his pre-pundit life explained much about the post-Lippmann direction the profession had taken. Most of the journalists who could have been expected to be nominated to be columnists and commentators came to be classified as "liberal" during this period. Like Reston, their work had led them to the conclusion that the United States required a period of retrenchment to deal with its own seething internal tensions. A few hard-liners remained committed to Cold War contests and Vietnam-like wars, but by and large, the nonpolitical response to Vietnam and, later, Watergate, was to try to think more modestly about the nation's ambitions in the future. To find pundits who could convincingly argue the opposite—that what the United States and the world required was an even greater dose of military adventure—publishers had to turn outside the profession to professional ideologues like Will and Safire.

Like Nixon, the far Right had always suspected a liberal (and usually Jewish) conspiracy of dominating the media, but because the movement had traditionally been in thrall to its lunatic fringe, it had trouble distinguishing its crazier notions from those with which a significant portion of Americans could be expected to identify. In William F. Buckley, Jr., however, the Right found itself an amazingly fortuitous spokesperson. Although his influence on the political mainstream was initially negligible, Buckley's achievements were nevertheless significant. First, his magazine, *National Review*, founded in November 1955, managed to unify conservatism's politically palatable elements into the beginnings of a cooperative movement. Before the days of Buckley's journal, organicist, religious conservatives who traced their lineage to Burke and the American philosopher Russell Kirk did not feel they had much to say to economic conservatives, who looked to Adam Smith and the Austrian economist Freidrich von Hayak as their lodestars. The former viewed capitalism with considerable suspicion, entailing, as it did, the Shumpeterian "creative destruction" of the class-based order on which the organicists placed so much emphasis. The *National Review* pioneered what it called a "fusionist movement," which, according to Buckley, offered necessary "godfatherly moral attention" to the "concrete and observable services" rendered by capitalism.

Buckley's second crucial contribution consisted of his successful expunging of some of the movement's loonier elements. According to Marvin Liebman, one of Buckley's most stalwart foot soldiers, in the "dark ages" before the *National Review* was formed, the conservative movement was an "ooze . . . dominantly made up of bigots, anti-Semites, anti-Catholics, the KKK [Ku Klux Klan], rednecks, Know-Nothings, a sorry lot of public hucksters and religious medicine men."*

Third, and no doubt by far the most pleasurable for him, Buckley was able to present himself to literary taste-making society as a perfectly dashing sort of fellow, a conservative without fangs, without a tail, and congenitally incapable of sipping his vichyssoise with the wrong spoon. As children, the Buckleys had been tutored in apologetics, art, ballroom dancing, banjo, birdwatching, building boats in bottles, calligraphy, canoeing, carpentry, cooking, driving, trotting horses, French, folk-dancing, golf, guitar (Hawaiian and Spanish), harmony, herb-gardening, horsemanship, history of architecture, ice skating, mandolin, marimba, music appreciation, organ, painting, piano, playing popular music, rumba, sailing, skiing, Spanish, speech, stenography, swimming, tap-dancing, tennis, typing, and woodcarving. As an adult, Buckley's famous charm and ever-growing celebrity status offered uncounted avenues for him to insinuate his political philosophy into mainstream forums, particularly in the omnipresent universe of television celebrities. In the days when Ronald Reagan was still a B-movie actor, Buckley proved the movement's most effective ambassador.

Buckley began a syndicated column in 1962 and in 1966 introduced *Firing Line*, a television show that proved a boon both to the movement and to Buckley's personal stock within mainstream culture. His half-serious 1965 campaign for mayor of New York City also earned him considerable capital as a social commentator, so much so that by 1968, Richard Nixon felt he needed to court Buckley's support to shore up his Right flank. With Nixon in the White House, Buckley and his lieutenants set about building a movement that would be capable, some day, of electing its own presidents, rather than merely attaching itself to the lesser of two evils.

Like Moses (and Mikhail Gorbachev), Buckley would eventually be able to lead his people out of the land of Canaan, but not quite so far as the promised land. In the 1970s Buckley's celebrity as a television host, a spy novelist, and a jet-set bon vivant displaced his image as a far-right ideologue. With his patrician instincts and countless liberal admirers, he ultimately lost touch with the middle-American grassroots conservatism

*See Phil McCombs, "Revelation from a Right-Winger," *Washington Post*, 9 July 1990, Style section, p. 1. Buckley says his friend exaggerated a bit (William F. Buckley, Jr., interview by author).

of Nixon's silent majority and the New Right leaders building on it.[*] Before the *National Review,* Buckley recalls, "conservatism was considered philistinia," and he found "obsequy to populism" to be "unnecessary and demeaning." But the New Right's minions were nothing if not proud Philistines. Like William F. Buckley, Jr., they hated Communists; but they hated liberals even more. The movement that Buckley and his magazine had helped create and effectively fronted for was, by the late 1970s, ready to be taken to places where he himself could not comfortably go.

The New Right was a movement built on middle-class grievance. The reaction to the events of 1968 had demonstrated an American middle class that was made distinctly uncomfortable by what it considered to be the increasing influence and lurch leftward of much of the national media that accompanied Vietnam and Watergate. These anxieties, along with the fires of class and racial resentment, were consistently stoked by the Nixon administration and its supporters in the New Right. The stagflationary macroeconomic impact of the Vietnam War, followed by the oil shocks of the 1970s, was shrinking disposable incomes. This put greater stress on the value of progressive tax rates and welfare for the poor. Conservative social movements sprouted in response to unpopular Supreme Court decisions relating to abortion, school prayer, and racial integration. And Americans felt helpless observing the military adventurism embarked upon by the Soviet Union and the explosion of anti-American nationalism throughout the Third World. With the humiliation and denial that comes with losing a war, and the collapse of the Cold War foreign policy elite, these forces gave aid and comfort to ideas that only a decade earlier had been the exclusive province of Westbrook Pegler's end of the spectrum. They also swept away the tentative (and often misguided) efforts liberals were making to scale down America's global ambitions and redistribute some of its wealth and power.

In the conservative ideological attack of the early 1970s, all the uncomfortable changes the country was undergoing were welded together into a single critique of "liberal elite culture." Like the vulgar Marxists a number of them had once been, the right-wingers saw an unspoken conspiracy ruling American political and cultural life in which everyone and everything was connected to everyone and everything else. It was a kind of bargain-basement Hegelianism: the entirety of American culture moved as if guided by a single dialectical spirit. Harvard and Yale, feminism and taxes, school prayer and Soviet power, abortion and pornography, Communist revolution

---

[*]Not all liberals found Buckley's charms irresistible. *New York Daily News* columnist Lars-Erik Nelson says, "Buckley exists to wrap up peoples' base, greedy, bigoted, low-life, mean and nasty views into high-faluting language so that they don't have to go around thinking that they are just mean, stupid and nasty, but instead have a philosophy like Buckley's" (Lars-Erik Nelson, interview by author).

and gay rights; all of these social ills and more stemmed from the same source of political/cultural malaise, namely, the post-Vietnam victory of the "New Class" and the "permissive" culture it foisted on the nation.*

The New Class, according to neoconservative godfather Irving Kristol, was made up of "scientists, teachers, and educational administrators, journalists and others." The New Class had somehow manipulated Americans to believe that they were an evil people who rained death and destruction on Vietnam to feed their own sick compulsions. As for Watergate, although the liberal press had carried out a successful coup d'état (in Norman Podhoretz's judgment) to please its own vanity, it succeeded only in increasing its own appetite. In the aftermath of Vietnam and the establishment's failure of will, the New Class radicals had swallowed the entire establishment—the Council on Foreign Relations, the Trilateral Commission, Harvard, and the lot—and annexed the Supreme Court. Among the most dangerous aspects of the tactics of these people, moreover, was the stealth with which they went about their ideological mission. Although they spoke of social justice, what the New Class was really after was the triumph of socialism.

The ranks of the neoconservatives were largely composed of former sectarian Marxists of mostly Jewish academic origin who transferred their intellectual allegiance to capitalism and American military power but retained their obsession with theological disputation and political purity. The impresario at the center of this attack was Irving Kristol, a one-time Trotskyist who had since become a passionate defender of capitalism. The job of the neoconservative intellectual, Kristol once remarked, was "to explain to the American people why they are right and to the intellectuals why they are wrong." Beginning with the early days of the Nixon administration, this is just what they began to do. Spreading the word was a costly proposition in America, however. There were think-tanks to be started, journals to be founded, scholarships to be offered, and university chairs to be endowed. Like Willie Sutton, Kristol had to go where the money was— in this case, downtown about thirty blocks to the once-forbidden Philistine city of Wall Street.

The money tree did not bear immediate fruit. Historically, as Kristol observed, business wanted "intellectuals to go out and justify profits and explain to people why corporations make a lot of money." Kristol had a far more ambitious agenda in mind, but first he needed to convince the businessmen that they needed him. In this effort he could not conceiv-

---

*My favorite example of this dialectical pattern came in George Will's 1991 equation of the dangers faced by the United States in the Persian Gulf War with those embodied by the threat of multiculturalism. Runner-up would be Norman Podhoretz' 1986 equation of New York City's anti–sex discrimination law with support for the Sandinistas. See George F. Will, *Newsweek*, 22 April 1991, and Norman Podhoretz, 20 March 1986.

ably have cultivated a more valuable ally than Robert Bartley, the editor of the *Wall Street Journal*'s editorial page. Both men were already fierce Cold Warriors, but Bartley, tutored by Kristol, soon enlisted in the New Class war as well. The ideology of the New Class, according to Bartley, was fomenting "something that looks suspiciously like a concerted attack on business." To thrive and prosper in the upcoming battle for control of the American economy, businessmen and their allies needed to publish or perish. The *Journal*'s editorial pages soon became a hotbed of neoconservative counter-revolution, and Kristol, a regular contributor.

Once business began to pony up the cash necessary to fight a media class war, the terms of the Washington's insider debate began to change. With tens of millions of dollars solicited from conservative corporations, foundations, and zillionaire ideologues like Nelson and Bunker Hunt, Richard Mellon Scaife, Joseph Coors, and the Reverend Sun Myung Moon, the new conservative counter-establishment (so-named by then journalist Sidney Blumenthal) did a masterly job at aping the institutions of the establishment's Washington and replacing them with its own. Unable to transform (or blow up) the liberal think-tank the Brookings Institution, the conservatives created the American Enterprise Institute (AEI), the Center for Strategic and International Studies (CSIS), the Heritage Foundation, and a host of smaller ideological shops to drown out the liberals and moderates with their own analyses.* In need of a newspaper to run its second-string pundits and give jobs to its wives and children, they embraced the Moonie-financed *Washington Times*, which came to serve as a daily crib sheet through which right-wing insiders could keep tabs on their ideological stock exchange.†
Having made insufficient progress colonizing the Council on Foreign Relations, the conservatives founded the Committee on the Present Danger (CPD), a Cold War–obsessed cadre of disaffected, hawkish Wise Men and newly respectable neoconservative intellectuals. The group, which would eventually furnish fifty-nine members of the Reagan national security team, including the president himself, dedicated itself to the notion that "the principal threat to our nation, to world peace, and to the cause of human free-

---

*These foundations did more than just promote the spread of conservative ideas. According to Sidney Blumenthal, the Heritage Foundation, at the suggestion of Robert McFarlane and Oliver North, transferred $100,000 to a front group controlled by partners of Iran-Contra moneyman Spitz Channell. Heritage President Edward Feulner wrote, "My colleagues and I have discussed your proposal in some detail and we are pleased to respond in a positive way." When this was discovered by the Congressional investigative committees, then-Congressman Richard Cheney quashed the investigation by threatening to call up the records of every non-conservative think-tank in Washington. See Sidney Blumenthal, *Pledging Allegiance: The Last Campaign of the Cold War* (New York: Harper and Row, 1990), pp. 29–30.

†Among the neoconservative brethren whose sons, daughters, and wives enjoyed regular Moonie-financed paychecks were Norman Podhoretz, Ben Wattenberg, Richard Grenier, and honorary neoconservative and Contra frontperson, Arturo Cruz.

dom is the Soviet drive for dominance" and its "long-held goal of a world dominated from a single center—Moscow."*

The newly sophisticated right-wingers recognized that they required a combination of political and cultural strategies to transform the American political debate. Had they relied on a strictly insider-based battle plan, the old Center could have ignored them at relatively little cost. And if the Right had kept to an exclusively grassroots organizing model, they would likely have seen their champions co-opted. But together, the two strategies worked synergistically and created a momentum that seemed, by the election of 1980, to sweep away virtually all traces of the old-guard elite.

It is impossible to determine whether the pundits provided the cannon shots that softened up the underbelly of respectable Centrism or the cavalry that broke through the final line to victory. Certainly no soldier in the conflict was given a more prominent position from which to declare victory. And none seemed to relish the fight more than the Mutt-and-Jeff combination of Rowland Evans and Robert Novak.

The dynamic duo began writing their column in 1963, strictly as a news-gathering enterprise. Evans, a Main-Line Philadelphian who wears custom-made suits and throws Alsop-like dinner parties, took care of the diplomatic beat. Novak, a beer-bellied tough guy who buys his suits off the rack, wore out the shoe leather in the Capitol. The column was ideologically balanced, treating insider politics the way *Popular Mechanics* treats cars and *Stereo Review* treats tape decks. Novak may have slugged a *New York Times* reporter at the 1964 Republican convention, but he also slugged a Goldwater Republican for balance.

As with the neoconservatives, the duo's flight to the hard Right was a reaction to the incipient leftward forces that they termed "McGovernism." In the three months just before the 1972 election, thirty-seven of their ninety-three pre-election columns assaulted either McGovern or his political views, accusing him of, among other things, consorting with "zealots with long hair, bizarre costumes and peace signs." This strategy coincided perfectly with the political direction mapped out personally by Nixon to destroy the McGovern campaign by associating him with "Abby [*sic*] Hoffman, Jerry Rubin, Angela Davis, among others," whose support of McGovern "should be widely publicized and used at every point."

Because of their excellent sourcing inside the political establishments of both parties, the columnists' anti-McGovern rampages had a considerable effect on the coverage of the 1972 election. In one of the most influential

---

*Note the inverted historical parallel between the CPD and William Allen White's committee to influence Americans to intervene in World War II. See "Common Sense and the Common Danger," in *Policy Statement of the Committee on the Present Danger: Alerting America* (Washington, DC: Pergamon/Brassey, 1984), p. 3.

columns ever to be written during a presidential election, Evans and Novak helped coin the famous phrase "acid, amnesty and abortion" to describe McGovern's political positions. The quote was attributed to "a liberal senator whose voting record differs little from McGovern's." The speaker warned that "Once middle America—Catholic middle America in particular—finds this out, he's dead." The "Triple A" slogan, as it came to be called, was picked up by Reston and given much wider circulation as a slogan for McGovern opponents.* With the McGovern campaign, Evans and Novak leaped over the line that allegedly distinguished straight reporting from avowed partisanship. In the admiring words of the rigidly Marxist Alexander Cockburn, the journalists took Mao's advice and "put politics in command."

The same tendencies that helped create the "Triple A" political firestorm were also at work in a column that would have an equally important effect on the Carter-Ford presidential election of 1976. In this case, the authors wrote a blistering attack on a Kissinger aide named Helmut Sonnenfeldt. According to an Evans and Novak report of March 22, "Intense debate was set off when Secretary of State Henry Kissinger's right-hand man declared in a secret briefing that permanent 'organic' union between the Soviet Union and Western Europe is necessary to avoid World War III." The column, based on a leak of Sonnenfeldt's speech to a group of U.S. diplomats in London, set off a political crisis for Kissinger both in Congress and inside the ethnic communities that Ford needed to sway to win the 1976 election. "Of all my columns," Novak insists thirteen years later, "that is the one I am most proud of. It really showed the hypocrisy of the Kissinger State Department and it really nailed them." As Sonnenfeldt would later explain to a Congressional panel called to discuss the matter, however, his concept of an "organic relationship" was diametrically opposed to the notion that the columnists sought to portray with the phrase, "permanent 'organic' union"—a phrase he never used. The speech implied a greater Soviet tolerance for diversity in Eastern Europe, rather than reliance upon the use of force.

As a result of the column, Sonnenfeldt and his patrons Gerald Ford and Henry Kissinger were ceaselessly attacked in the Eastern European ethnic media, and the KGB even picked it up to try to show the Romanians and the Poles that the United States supported their subjugation. Candidate Ronald Reagan attacked Ford relentlessly for his support of Eastern Europe's "permanent enslavement." Finally Ford was asked, at his second debate with Jimmy Carter, if he accepted the permanent domination of Eastern Europe by the Soviet Union. "There is no Soviet domination of Eastern Europe," replied the soon-to-be ex-President.

---

*According to McGovern, the column was a "dishonest one, which distorted my position in a way I could never catch up to" (George McGovern, interview by author).

Aside from its arguable electoral impact, the defection of Evans and Novak to the far-right end of the spectrum was crucial in the shaping of insider political dialogue for a number of reasons. The fact that the two were so powerfully wired into the main currents of the Republican party and the national security bureaucracy made their column impossible to ignore, lest inside dope be missed. Its appearance three times a week on the *Washington Post* op-ed page gave its far-right ideological interpretations the establishment's seal of approval. Moreover, their breathless, Pearson-like prose, coupled with Novak's well-rehearsed Joe Six-pack television persona, gave Washington insiders the impression that Evans and Novak spoke for (and with) that elusive silent majority for whom everyone in Washington always seemed to be looking. This fusion had the effect of softening up the right-wing borders of polite insider society and creating an opening for Evans and Novak's intellectual betters to exploit and expand.

Ready and willing were Will and Safire, who together set the standard for political punditry in the late 1970s as Lippmann and Reston had done two decades earlier. When these men began writing their columns, each had something to prove. Safire needed to show that he was more than just a Nixon flack, and Will, that he was more than a nerd with a copy of *Bartlett's*. Will's opportunity came when he joined Buckley's brother and conservative New York senator James Buckley in calling for Nixon's impeachment back in 1973, rather early in the impeachment-calling-for game. Safire never fully emerged from Nixon's shadow during the Watergate period but demonstrated a bit of previously undetected moxie when he found out that his friend Henry Kissinger had been bugging his calls and lying to him about it.[*] Safire had made his journalistic reputation during the Carter years, when he tirelessly pounded away at the unorthodox financing techniques of Carter's budget chief, Bert Lance. His congenial personality had already won over many of his enemies at the *Times*' Washington bureau, and his energetic, though biased, reporting struck many liberals and conservatives as model punditry for an ideological era, however marred by his incessant hammering at such memorable scandals as "Koreagate," "Oilgate," "Peanutgate," "Angolagate," "Lancegate," "Billygate," and Safire's own personal favorite, "Double Billingsgate."[†]

[*]When Safire originally wrote about the incident in *Harper's*, Kissinger called it a "fairy tale" riddled with errors resulting from "a desire to claim inside information he in fact never possessed." Safire, in turn, assailed this "blustering deceit on Kissinger's part." The two have since made up; Safire says that "the statute of limitations on Henry has run its course" (William Safire, interview by author). The quotes appear in Charles Michener, Philip S. Cook, and Thomas M. DeFrank, "Puppet and Puppet Master," *Newsweek*, 3 May 1975, p. 71.
[†]Safire today admits that, psychologically, he may have been seeking to minimize the relative importance of the crimes committed by his former boss with this silliness (William Safire, interview by author).

Both Will and Safire shared almost all of the basic tenets of the counter-establishment thesis, including its critique of the New Class and its permissive culture, but they were most effective in using the Vietnam War stick to beat liberals into submission and to destroy the ideological underpinnings of the Carter presidency. "The real lesson of Vietnam," wrote Safire in January 1979, "is that the perception of America's weakness of will invites aggression; that Moscow is willing to use its clients/states to bring about a Pax Sovietica; and that there is no turning away from our allies anywhere without a cost in lives and human freedom everywhere." Similarly, Will was angered to learn that, as late as 1978, Carter still considered the civil war in Vietnam to be an internal affair. The reason Carter deserved to be dumped onto the ash heap of history, argued Will, was his inability to see that the "Western democracies are, whether they know it or not, in the fifth decade of a war with totalitarians." Fortunately, "today the Soviet regime is so grotesquely ignorant and arrogant, so boorish and bullying, that its cruelty and recklessness may awaken Americans from their dogmatic slumber."

The difference between the Lippmann/Reston regime and that of Will/Safire is instructive. Lippmann and Reston had allied themselves with the establishment. By the time of the Will/Safire regime, the old establishment was disintegrating, and the new power pundits threw their lot in with the nascent counter-establishment. Their constant stream of ideological invective toward the Carter presidency helped to destroy the insider political foundation on which it had tenuously rested. It is impossible to separate these efforts from those undertaken in the heartland by the moral majority, California's tax revolters, and the New Right's direct-mail maestros. But within Washington, where the tone and parameters of the national political dialogue were determined, punditry was clearly king.

The remarkable rise in the fortunes of Washington pundits that accompanied their destruction of the Carter administration could be seen through the prism of the city's social life. In December 1977, Barbara Walters held a dinner party in honor of the newly cordial Egyptian and Israeli ambassadors. The real news of the evening, however, had nothing to do with the headliners. Aside from Carter aide Hamilton Jordan's oafish comments to the wife of one of the dignitaries, the most significant aspect of the dinner was the social pecking order it revealed. It was Walters, not Henry Kissinger or Zbigniew Brzezinski, who elicited from Anwar Sadat the prime-time pledge to visit Jerusalem. In his opening toast, Art Buchwald feted the hostess for "bringing together two men who have been ideologically miles apart, who fought each other over the years—Hamilton Jordan and Bill Safire." Reports of this historic moment appeared later in Safire's column.

The Washington represented in this room was, for most practical purposes, the only Washington that mattered. There was television, in the regal form of Ms. Walters, staging the entire event. There was the editor of the *Washington Post*, Ben Bradlee, and the *New York Times*' Most Important Pundit William Safire, listening to off-the-record speeches by pundit Buchwald and proto-pundit Kissinger on the subjects of Safire and Kissinger. Jordan, who had been given honorary status as Safire's equal by virtue of his relationship with the president, cracked under the pressure and reverted to his Georgia frat-boy self.* At the end of the evening, when Safire went home to write his column, it was clear to everyone where lasting power in Washington genuinely lay.†

In the Carter years, dinner parties like Walters' expressed a world in which the pundit, Safire, slightly outranked the president's most trusted adviser, Jordan. Immediately after the 1980 election, however, punditry ascended still further. Even before Ronald Reagan had a chance to warm his presidential seat, George Will threw a series of dinner parties at which the host outranked everyone but the guest of honor. The pundit who hosted the Reagans and the rest of power Washington at these dinners was a different animal than the one Lippmann had envisioned when he invented the business more than four decades earlier. In the first place, Will had become no less a television star than a revered newspaper pundit. In contrast to Lippmann's reluctant annual appearances, Will expounded from the black box twice a week. Lippmann was a failure at maintaining his distance from high public officials, but he did profess to try. Will, on the other hand, flaunted his political friendships and made no apologies for them. While Lippmann did his best to moderate the military appetites of his countrymen, Will encouraged them, siding in almost all disputes with those who argued for war. Lippmann did not have much journalistic training: a few months as a cub reporter and a stint as an assistant to Lincoln Steffens. But Will had none at all. A former professor and Republican aide, Will saw himself as practicing not a higher form of journalism, but a new kind of political partisanship, one in which the weapons of choice were television stardom, presidential access, and a regular newspaper column, in declining order of significance.

---

*While gazing down the Egyptian Ambassador's wife's cleavage, Jordan pulled on the woman's elasticized bodice and loudly declared that he "always wanted to see the pyramids." A little later, he stood up and announced, "This administration has to piss." For the gory details, see Sally Quinn, "Where Did All the Good Times Go? Where Have All the Good Times Gone: The Trials and Separations of the Carter Crowd and the Washingtonians," *Washington Post*, 18 December 1977, Style section, p. 1.

†When Jordan's sidekick Jody Powell left the White House to try his hand at columnizing, Safire penned him a note reading, "No more the trappings of power, just the real thing." See Eleanor Randolph, "William Safire, Right to the Core: The Columnist and His Novel Look at Abraham Lincoln," *Washington Post*, 24 August 1987, Style section, p. 1.

Perhaps the most important difference between Lippmann and Will was the fact that in Lippmann's day, there had been only Lippmann. By the time that bow-ties and steel-rimmed glasses became fashionable among young conservative operatives, Will was at the head of an ever-expanding pundit class. The numbers were still tiny, but the job had become a reasonable ambition for well-educated, socially ambitious young men who, fifty years earlier, would not have allowed a journalist into their living rooms. No longer was it astonishing to find a newspaper commentator who had studied political philosophy at Oxford and Princeton. No longer was it amazing to find one who earned more than the president. And it seemed hardly worth noting that, however many papers may have carried Will's column, he was better known for what he looked like than for what he wrote.

When Lippmann, Reston, and Alsop ruled the day, the political spectrum they embodied was not much narrower than that defined by the Reagan-era pundit class. But it was less self-consciously militant and had a far healthier respect for the complexity of world affairs and the difficulty most Americans experience in incorporating the details of politics and policy into their busy lives. In the age of Reagan, politics had suddenly become simple. All that was required for peace and prosperity was for America to start acting more American: to be tougher, to be stronger, and to feel better about itself. The pundits had, in Lippmann's day, been merely one voice in a complex public debate over what direction the country should take in world affairs. But because of the influence of television, the legacy of the Vietnam War, and the ever-increasing inanity of the American electoral process, the new pundit class—the punditoc-racy—was virtually alone in setting the tenor of public debate and determining the scope and parameters of political discussion.

The net effect of these changes lay the groundwork for untold political damage to the American people and the political system during the decade of the 1980s. Lippmann, however loftily, had envisioned a group of pundits like himself, who would shield the republic from the force of its emotion and arm it with the means to defend itself intellectually against the charlatan, the terrorist, and the jingo. The punditocracy that he indirectly spawned, however, worked hand in glove with these same forces. For its access to information and social status, it attached itself to the very rulers against whom it was supposed to be guarding. And for its income it relied on a medium dedicated to "poisoning the innocent" and "debasing the public taste." Lippmann may not have intended to plant these seeds, but it was clear that by the dawn of the Reagan era, his inheritors would gladly reap their harvest.

THE REAGAN PUNDITOCRACY

Now judge, judge I got debts no honest man could pay.
The bank was holdin' my mortgage and they was takin' my
* house away.*
Now I ain't sayin' that makes me an innocent man.
But it was more 'n all this, judge, that put that gun in my
* hand.*

—Bruce Springsteen, "Johnny 99" (1982)

CHAPTER FOUR

The Triumph of George Will

I t is a strange observation to make about a man who has—
and has done—virtually everything, but William F. Buckley,
Jr. never has lived up to his potential. Buckley is a pioneer
of the conservative political organization and of public affairs television.
But by the time the two came to rule American public life in tandem, the
Israelite himself had become something of a museum piece. When his
friend, charter *National Review* subscriber Ronald Reagan, was elected
president in 1980, George Will, William Safire, Patrick Buchanan, and
Robert Novak had long surpassed Buckley's influence within both insider
and conservative movement audiences. On *Firing Line*, in particular,
Buckley was badly dated by his good manners. Although occasionally
high on genuine intellectual fireworks, the show was notoriously lacking
in sitcom fundamentals. Yes, there was Buckley, playing the old Mr. Chips
role, but beyond that, it was all so . . . civilized.

But Buckley's television career did leave one extremely important legacy to the punditocracy. It derived not from *Firing Line*, but from his short-
lived career as Gore Vidal's partner as an ABC commentator during the
1968 Republican and Democratic conventions. It was during that engagement that the two pundits set a standard for intelligent political dialogue
against which future political commentators would one day be measured.

A generation ago, ABC was something of a semiprofessional news organization. Its executives' desperation to attract viewers overrode their
desire to be taken seriously as a credible and responsible voice in the polit-

ical dialogue. While planning their 1968 election coverage, these executives were searching for something that would truly distinguish their coverage from that of Walter Cronkite and company on CBS or Huntley and Brinkley on NBC. The idea for pairing Buckley and the unpredictable Vidal came from Buckley himself, albeit in a back-handed manner. The network asked him to name a liberal with whom he could profitably spar during the convention coverage, and Buckley replied that he would appear with any non-Communist, but he would prefer it not be that "philosophical degenerate" Gore Vidal. "Bingo," said the men at ABC.

The network's reporting of the 1968 Republican gathering, like the convention itself, came off without incident. The Miami gathering was marred only, in Buckley's view, by Vidal's insistence during their debates that he had based the "entire style" of the transsexual hero of his novel *Myra Breckenridge* on Buckley. Buckley replied that Vidal was "immoral" and held American culture in "disdain," but there the colloquy ended. Buckley tried to convince the producers to allow the two commentators to make their presentations separately for the ensuing Democratic convention, but it was no go: a star had been born.

Amidst the violent chaos that was the 1968 Chicago Democratic convention, Buckley and Vidal began to argue over the provocational potential of the student protesters' raising of a Vietcong flag the night before. Buckley compared it to the raising of a hypothetical Nazi flag during World War II. Vidal then insisted that "as far as I'm concerned, the only sort of pro- or crypto-Nazi is yourself." "Now listen, you queer," retorted the conservative elder statesman, "stop calling me a crypto-Nazi or I'll sock you in the goddam face and you'll stay plastered." The evening degenerated from there.

The incident drew itself out in a long and fruitless exchange in *Esquire*, wherein Vidal implied that Buckley was not only a homosexual but also an anti-Semite.[*] Buckley considered a lawsuit, eventually concluding a complex legal agreement with *Esquire* instead. Of greater significance than the legal machinations, however, were the prescient observations of Buckley's friend, the conservative literary critic Hugh Kenner. Kenner admonished his friend for sacrificing the seriousness of his intended purpose on the altar of celebrity. "What you have in fact done is accept a role as a Celebrity. You will be playing William F. Buckley, Old Antagonist of Gore Vidal." Buckley may have regretted his exchange with Vidal, but, once again, he was merely embodying the Zeitgeist before its time. Call-

---

[*]For a nice illustration of things going around and coming around, see Buckley's discussion of Vidal's alleged anti-Semitism in William F. Buckley, "In Search of Anti-Semitism," *National Review*, 30 December 1991.

ing one's opponent a queer and threatening, if only metaphorically, to plaster him so that he stayed plastered, would be considered the height of good manners in the punditocracy within a decade.

The pundit who best embodied the remarkable increase in the power, prestige, and prosperity that the profession enjoyed in the Reagan era was not Buckley but a man he had hired briefly to be the *National Review*'s Washington correspondent and book editor. Riding the crest of a harmonic convergence between the rise of the television-based punditocracy and the victorious revolt of the New Right, George Will achieved, in the Washington of the early 1980s, a cultural presence among insiders akin to that of the patron saint of a small Sicilian village. Completely unknown when Nixon won his second term in 1972, Will saw his shadow loom larger over Ronald Reagan's Washington than the monument at Seventeenth Street. That barely one in ten "real" Americans recognized his face was irrelevant. In the media's most influential outlets, Will's bow-tied, bespectacled visage was everywhere: in the *Washington Post,* in *Newsweek,* on *Agronsky and Company,* on *This Week with David Brinkley,* on *The ABC Evening News,* on *Nightline,* and in the ad copy for *Newsweek, Agronsky and Company, This Week with David Brinkley, The ABC Evening News,* and others. To earn so much free and favorable media attention in most provincial capitals, one generally has to overthrow a regime and name oneself emperor for life.

Will's star rose so quickly that there is almost no charting it. When discovered by then–deputy *Post* editorial page editor Meg Greenfield in 1973, Will was just, according to Greenfield, "a snotty-nosed little kid" in a room full of politicos at a conference at Kenyon College. (Actually, he had, at age twenty-five, already been hired at *National Review*.) One writer described him as looking like an usher at a Whiffenpoof's concert. Born in suburban Illinois of mildly socialist parents, Will served as senior-class president and captain of the track team before earning degrees from Trinity College, Oxford, and Princeton. He taught political philosophy at Michigan State and the University of Toronto before joining the staff of Republican Senator Gordon Allott in 1970. Allott's defeat two years later left Will unemployed, until Buckley discovered in him a kindred soul and user of large words. "He came along at a time when there was a seismic change in American politics," observed NBC vice-president Tim Russert. "Someone had to explain why Ronald Reagan's conservatism was sweeping the country, and he filled the vacuum."

Will filled the vacuum so powerfully that, by the mid-1980s, a front-page *Wall Street Journal* story would call him "perhaps the most powerful journalist in America—rivaling—and some say surpassing—such famed pundits of previous decades as the late Walter Lippmann." But Philip Geyelin, a Lippmann protégé who, as *Post* editorial page editor at the time, had made the final decision in January 1974 to go ahead with Will's column, considers Will's work "demeaning to the profession." However the quality of Will's criticism was judged, there was no mistaking the power and influence his unofficial status as First Pundit seemed to carry. In case anyone had missed the point about his unparalleled access to the new president, Will opened his first column of the Reagan era approximately six inches from the era's new desk, "the one under which John-John played hide and seek."* When Will irritated Reagan by calling the president "incontinently eager" to placate the Soviets, the president immediately called him in for a thirty-minute conference. He was received, according to one journalist, "like some head of state." And when Will was forced to defend his coaching of Reagan in the presidential debates one Saturday evening on *Agronsky and Company*, the president phoned him at home immediately after the show aired, just in time for Will to mention it to 6 million people on *This Week with David Brinkley* the next morning.

Before he began filing reports from the Oval Office, Will had spent the second half of the 1970s on the front lines of the New Right panzer divisions, relentlessly attacking what he calls "the infantilism; impatience; hedonism; inability to defer gratification that produced the cultural dissolution of the sixties." His July 1973 call for Nixon's impeachment gave his right-wing politics the oomph required to distinguish him from the typical Kilpatrick/Buckley fare then available, and his 1977 Pulitzer Prize for commentary sanctified his growing reputation as the counter-establishment's boy wonder. But it was his television performances, coupled with his remarkably nondeferential friendship with the newly elected Ronald Reagan, that marked Will as the avatar of the emerging punditocracy.

Just as Lippmann had defined the pundit profession in the 1930s and 1940s, so Will redefined it at the dawn of the Reagan era, thanks to his unique ability to master every level of the pundit business simultaneously. A useful way to think about the then-just-emerging punditocracy is to envision four concentric rings conforming (coincidentally) to the inner circles of Dante's *Inferno*. Each circle feeds into the smaller circle inside it, and each represents a different degree of a single political-philosophical continuum. At the center of it all lies George Will: television commentator, syndicated columnist, occasional political philosopher, and close personal friend of Ron and Nancy.

---

*Will also felt compelled to note that his buddy the president was "wearing a suit of blue-plaid that is . . . bold enough by Washington standards to set off an alarm" (George F. Will, *Newsweek*, 2 February 1981).

With Will in the center ring are his fellow cast members on the various pundit network sitcoms, each conforming to a personality type with which viewers can be expected to identify.* The epicenter of the punditocracy includes only those shows on which journalists and commentators are invited to be pundits—to pontificate regardless of expertise. "Old-fashioned politician meets the old-fashioned press" programs do not qualify. If the politician is invited to the party, as happens on CNN's *The Capital Gang*, it is with the express condition that he or she be prepared to behave like a pundit.

To argue that few people outside the Washington Beltway watch these shows is to misunderstand the nature of punditocracy's power and influence. Washington watches them, and that's what matters. Those pundits who make the final cut are its most admired stars. The people who select the regulars and the topics are among its most powerful moguls. But there's a catch: despite their ostensible freedom to discuss almost anything, virtually all the pundits' discussions are devoted to the same issues and formed with White House guidance.†

The second smallest ring, surrounding television, is newspaper and newsweekly syndication. The reach of a syndicated column is not nearly as wide as that of a regular television spot, but for most pundits it is a necessary foundation on which to build an empire. The column attracts the attention of television producers and talk-show hosts. Columns are also taken quite seriously inside the government's massive public relations apparatus, which works in a kind of parallel universe with that of the punditocracy, trying to shape opinion by virtue of its ability to control the national agenda and its ability to reward those pundits who support it

---

*For example, one reason for the successful reinvention of David Brinkley's career in the early 1980s appears to be his talent for filling the gaping hole in the "national grandpa" role left by Walter Cronkite's retirement. The show's producers reinforced this image by casting the Eddie Haskell–like Sam Donaldson opposite Brinkley, no doubt to highlight Brinkley's reassuring calm and sardonic wit.

†Drawn from the *Washington Post*'s television listings, these were the topics covered on the weekend of December 2, 1989:

Evans and Novak; live from Malta
Newsmaker Saturday; live from Malta
Inside Washington; topics include the summit . . .
The Capital Gang; topics include the summit . . .
The McLaughlin Group; issues are the summit . . .
Journalists Roundtable; topics are the Soviet-U.S. summit
Sunday Today; live reports on the Malta summit
CBS News Sunday Morning; live coverage of the summit
This Week with David Brinkley; the Malta summit
Newsmaker Sunday; live from Malta, the Summit at Sea
Face the Nation; The U.S. Soviet Summit
(Thanks to Jack Shafer.)

with increased access to the president's inner sanctum. The only columnists who qualify for this ring, however, are those who either work or are read in Washington, preferably both. Garry Wills and William Pfaff may be great columnists, but they might as well be writing in Albania from the standpoint of insider influence. With syndication in nearly five hundred subscribing papers and semipermanent ownership of one of only two bimonthly columns in *Newsweek*, Will has few rivals as king of the highbrow syndicated pundits.

The punditocracy's third ring is made up of the smaller, limited-circulation periodicals in which mainstream political ideas are discussed and—defining the term quite loosely—debated, along with those television shows and op-ed pages in which "experts" are given the opportunity to sell their views to a larger audience. The membership of this ring fluctuates seasonally with the insider Zeitgeist. One week, terrorism experts are all the rage on *Nightline*; the next, one would have to blow up a failing savings and loan to be called. There are two explicit categories of the punditocracy here, although each performs roughly the same function of injecting ideas into the two smaller, more influential rings. The print section of the third ring is made up of regular contributors to the *New Republic* and the *Post*'s Outlook section, with regular input from the *National Review, Commentary*, the *National Interest*, the *Public Interest, Foreign Affairs, Foreign Policy* and, every once in a while, special contributors to op-ed pages of the *New York Times*, the *Washington Post*, and the *Wall Street Journal*. Historically, insiders have taken note of articles appearing on the op-ed page of the *Christian Science Monitor* or the *Los Angeles Times*, but hard and fast examples of this phenomenon are difficult to come by. Perhaps three times in a decade, an article in a source with no direct ties to Washington insiderdom will also have an impact. This happens occasionally with the *New Yorker*, the *New York Review of Books*, the *Atlantic*, and, more recently, *Daedalus*. The best recent example of this phenomenon may be the *New Yorker*'s 1982 serialization of Jonathan Schell's *The Fate of the Earth*, which almost single-handedly challenged the primacy of the Reaganite nuclear agenda. Will got his start in this subsection of the ring when he was appointed Washington correspondent of the *National Review*. Since then, however, his presence has been a ghostly one, hovering over the "ideas" discussion without actually entering it.

The television subsection of the third ring is made up of those academic experts and former government officials who are sufficiently expert in the medium to be able to speak in short, uncomplicated sentences. The divisions here can be a bit confusing. When Sovietologist Marshall Goldman appeared on *The MacNeil/Lehrer NewsHour* to predict the imminent overthrow of Mikhail Gorbachev—as he appeared to do every few months from the moment Gorbachev came to power—he was working the third ring of the punditocracy. But when David Gergen and Mark Shields appeared on the same show on the same evening to argue about whether Gorbachev liked broccoli, they were back in the center ring. The televised segment of the third ring had been the exclusive province of Harvard liberals John Kenneth Galbraith and Arthur Schlesinger, Jr. until Milton Friedman and his conservative legions came along in the mid-1970s. Today, its much larger, though constantly fluctuating membership is largely determined by the young, overworked bookers on *Nightline* and *The NewsHour with Jim Lehrer*, with considerable input from that morning's op-ed pages.* Ironically, although his dominance of the first ring would seem to disqualify him, Will is a player even in this ring. He has been designated an all-around Wise Man by the producers at ABC News—the only full-time commentator the network employed during the Reagan years. Thus, Will is frequently invited on *Nightline* as an expert on matters from homelessness to violence in the cinema, about which he does not even pretend to have any specialized knowledge. This last category—the designated public philosopher—is perhaps the most exclusive insider club of all.

The fourth and final ring of the punditocracy arose in the late 1990s with the advent of all-news cable television. Larry King is the king of this realm, but it is populated with countless mini-, would-be, and wanna-be Kings. MSNBC, CNBC, Fox News Channel, and CNN rotate any number of available slots for experts in various arcane subjects depending on the scandal of the week. Geraldo Rivera managed to remake his reputation with a King-like program focusing on the O. J. Simpson trial and expanded it, in the era of Monica Lewinsky, into a mini-empire. Chris Matthews followed with his program, *Hardball*, as did Keith Olbermann, with *White House in Crisis*, and John Gibson on MSNBC. Fox News, however, had more trouble establishing itself and was forced to turn to the ghoulish cyber-gossip Matt Drudge to try to create a genuinely cable-friendly personality. The "experts" on these shows have moments of fame that are often one-fifth of the fifteen minutes that Andy Warhol predicted for all of us. George Will would never be caught, alive or dead, on any of these cable programs.

Once again, the contrast with Lippmann is instructive. Lippmann made his initial reputation as a thinker by writing lengthy philosophical treatises—the most significant of these being *Public Opinion*. The columns were a product of the intellectual capital acquired in writing them. But

---

*National Public Radio, which invites a wider spectrum of commentators than do television's public affairs programs and succeeds occasionally in offering offbeat perspectives, is nevertheless guided by similar principles.

George Will did not even attempt to write a serious book until 1983's *Statecraft as Soulcraft*, and the work proved to be an embarrassment. ("Reads in long stretches like Monty Python's shooting script of *Bartlett's*," wrote one reviewer in the *Washington Monthly*.) For Will, whose pretensions to being taken seriously as a political philosopher were no less earnest than Lippmann's, the television screen and the 750-word column proved the entire basis of his claim. His reputation, as his published oeuvre made clearer and clearer, rested not on thoughtfulness but on cleverness. But for the purposes of achieving Lippmann-like brightness in the pundit constellation of the 1980s, cleverness was more than sufficient.[*]

Of course, it might be argued in Will's defense that by the time he achieved Lippmann-like prominence, the reading and writing of books had become largely irrelevant to the American political dialogue. This is only partially true. Books cast an evanescent shadow on the insider dialogue. Power Washington does not generally read books. But its inhabitants like to sound well read anyway and are therefore required to refer to them occasionally. Sometimes a book is mentioned so frequently within the punditocracy that people feel compelled to buy and thumb through it—just to see what all the fuss is about. (This is particularly true in the ever-burgeoning genre of confessionals by former White House aides.) Usually, however, insiders keep up exclusively by reading reviews. For most functional purposes, the review becomes the book. A good review can be

*A second characteristic shared by Lippmann and his inheritor is the embarrassingly gossiped-about love affair. Rumors of a relationship between the self-declared "thoroughly married" George Will and Lally Weymouth, globetrotting reporter, daughter of *Post* owner Katharine Graham, and former main squeeze of Left executioner Alexander Cockburn, were initially dismissed by Washington wags as too good to be true. When the rumors panned out and Will left his wife and children to buy a $990,000 house a few blocks away from his family in Chevy Chase only to see, according to the *Washingtonian*, his office furniture left on his front lawn with a note reading "Take it somewhere else, Buster," the cocktail party circuit exploded. Will and Weymouth both denied that the relationship had been romantic and threatened to sue the *Washingtonian*. The magazine offered to write a correction if it would be allowed to investigate the matter and interview Will's friends. The matter was dropped there.

Will's ex-wife Madeleine, whose father owned the diner that Will patronized as a liberal Trinity College undergraduate, had formerly been employed as the treasurer-secretary of GFW Inc. at a salary of $30,000 annually. As part of their May 4, 1989, divorce settlement, she was awarded $460,021 from the "defined benefit plan" that GFW maintains at Alex Brown & Sons, a brokerage firm. She also received the Will house, worth more than $1 million, and an undisclosed amount of child support. Following her stint at the Will corporation, she worked as Ronald Reagan's director of the Office of Special Education and Rehabilitative Services in the Department of Education from 1983 to 1989. According to a November 28, 1989, General Accounting Office audit, 79 percent of her employees thought she had "negatively influenced the management of their organizational units."

Since breaking off with Weymouth, Will apparently found love again with former Reagan White House communications worker Mari Maseng, thirteen years his junior. The couple was married at Will's home on October 12, 1991. Maseng was a top strategist in Bob Dole's 1996 campaign.

its author's ticket to *Nightline* or *The NewsHour,* or at least to an appearance on MSNBC, and the reviewer usually benefits by making new friends.

Although they are, for the most part, only collections of his columns, Will's books sell well and are almost always respectfully reviewed. Writing for the *New Republic* in early 1982, soon to be a famous pundit and also soon to be a close friend of Will's, Charles Krauthammer called Will "the undisputed leader of [Conservatism's] House of Lords." Will repaid the favor by devoting an entire column to Krauthammer's first collection of essays, published four years later, comparing the writer to the distinctly un-Krauthammerian strikeout king Dwight Gooden and observing that it had become "widely recognized" that his new friend was now "the best new, young writer on public affairs."

In examining the relationship of the punditocracy's four rings to one another and to the shape and scope of the insider dialogue, it would be tempting to argue that television has come to dominate our political dialogue so forcefully that it is really the only forum that matters today. It would be tempting but, as Richard Nixon once said, it would be wrong. Television is a vacuum that sucks in everything in its path, but like the bag on the vacuum cleaner handle, it changes its shape with the content of whatever is filling it. This is not to say that the form of the medium is not the overriding determinant of its content. It is. But the process is a dialectical one. The derivative ideas bandied about on the average pundit talk show derive from somewhere. Television is the dominant medium in the punditocracy and, for most Americans, it is the only visible part. But, like the passengers on the *Titanic,* we ignore the rest of the iceberg at our own peril.

Because television is the only medium that can make a pundit fabulously wealthy, impress his or her parents and high school rivals, and still leave the rest of the day free for putzing around, it is the focal point of most pundits' ambitions. The *New York Times* forbids its employees from appearing regularly on any pundit shows. It can do so because it is perhaps the only print institution whose power and prestige can offset the loss of money and fame that television offers. Still, its employees gripe about the policy a great deal, and a handful have moved to less fastidious outlets in pursuit of television's riches.*

Most papers, unlike the *Times,* are pleased to see their reporters on television, preferring not to think about journalistic difficulties this cre-

---

*The *New York Times* management considers it demeaning for its reporters to accept regular stints as television commentators and forbids their doing so more than once a month. The *Los Angeles Times* is also said to have a policy that discourages its reporters from appearing regularly on any program. But, given the fact that the *Los Angeles Times'* Washington bureau chief Jack Nelson's weekly appearances on *Washington Week in Review* do not violate the policy, it is difficult to imagine just what the restrictions might be.

ates. The attraction of television for the journalist is not merely fame, but also money—a great deal of it—and it is the easiest money imaginable. With the right kind of television exposure and political biases, and an energetic speaking agent, a pundit can earn an extra $10,000 or $20,000 a week at lunch and still keep most of the day free for golf.

Again, the pioneer here is not so much Lippmann or Buckley, both of whom indulged their fondness for money quite unabashedly, but Will. Back in 1975, when the Agronsky show was still the only ticket to sitcom stardom, Will explained the secret of his success to the late British journalist Henry Fairlie: "He said that his column was important to him because it got him on TV. And the Agronsky show was important because it got him on the lecture circuit. He told me I should be doing the same thing, because, if you choose your audiences right, you could give the same speech every time." In the Reagan era, despite fees that hovered in the vicinity of $20,000 a pop, Will had more invitations than he could possibly accept. Nancy Reagan recalls in her memoirs that, after her operation for breast cancer, Will came to see her one morning in the hospital, "just back from one speaking engagement and then on to another at noon."

The appearance of greater influence that accompanies television stardom is part of an endless cycle that leads to even greater television stardom. Of the *Washingtonian*'s fifty "most influential journalists" in the capital in 1989, only nine were print reporters who did not appear on television.[*] When one combines regular speaking fees with six-figure television consultancies, not to mention the psychic gratification that comes with pontificating before millions of people, the price—being recognized in airports and fancy Washington restaurants—does not sound terribly onerous.[†] The complications that arise from trying to think in television's terms—the denigration of linear intellectual progressions; the dominance of superficial form over content; the inability to communicate nuance, paradox, and cultural relativism—these are difficult drawbacks to get overly exercised about in the face of the benefits.

Much of insider Washington did make a show of getting quite exercised when then–*New Republic* editor-in-chief Michael Kinsley, widely recognized as the sharpest liberal mind of his generation, opted to step down from his influential perch at the magazine to accept a lucrative job fighting with Pat Buchanan on CNN's *Crossfire* every night. Yes, Kinsley

---

[*]Jack Germond and Jules Whitcover coauthor a column for the *Baltimore Sun.* Germond appears on television each week; Whitcover does not. Germond appeared on the *Washingtonian*'s list; Whitcover did not.
[†]Morton Kondracke once explained to the wife of another *New Republic* editor that his life's ambition was to walk into a room and see people whisper to one another, "there goes Mort Kondracke." Philip Terzian, interview by author.

allowed, he feared the job might, over time, make him "dumber." It is often an extraordinarily dumb show.* But Kinsley's "main feeling is that life ought to be an adventure, and what the heck." Few beneficiaries of television's largesse are even this self-critical. Former McLaughlin group member Jack Germond justifies his television appearances with the quip, "It is a half-hour of being a dancing bear to make a better living." Will, on the other hand, becomes indignant at the suggestion that too much television may be bad for his brain. "Anyone who goes to reread the stuff, as I have, will agree with me. I think this rubbish about my doing too much is mostly jealousy, and the rest is not understanding my lifestyle."

Will's "lifestyle" was one of the important new wrinkles he brought to the job of power pundit. Will's publicly affectionate relationship with the First Couple flew in the face of all known journalistic ground rules and certainly conflicted with the idealized notions of which Lippmann had spoken half a century earlier. By coaching, socializing with, and generally cavorting with the people who ran the country and making no apologies for it, Will trampled on the Constitutional provision embodied in the First Amendment that entrusts the press to guard against the illegal and unwise exercise of power. Whether he actually did favors for his powerful friends was almost less important than the fact that he saw no reason to justify the appearance of having done so. For if fame, riches, and plenty of time to go to baseball games were the primary penalties for throwing most of journalism's principles out the window, then its less exalted practitioners might, quite understandably, become a good deal more cynical about trying to live up to them in the first place. That Will took refuge in his status as a columnist, arguing that, unlike a typical reporter, his political prejudices were secret to no one, did not really clarify matters. Rightly or wrongly, punditry is still considered the most prestigious sinecure in the journalism business. None of the pundit shows that ruled the discourse bothered to distinguish between bona fide pundits, journalists hoping to be pundits, and guests who behaved like pundits even though they were forced to masquerade during the week as old-fashioned journalists. Because the rules of punditry had never been codified or even much discussed in the profession, Will's behavior infected nearly all aspects of the journalism profession. In the past, punditry merely offered greater freedom to journalists to escape the stultifying rules of objectivity. But in Will's case, it seemed to cloud the basic issue of which side punditry—and by extension, high-powered Washington journalism—was

*No less so when I appeared on it.

really on: were the pundits with the politicians, or were they with the rest of us?

Will defended himself in part by minimizing the intimacy of his friendship with the president. Although the Reagans were frequent guests at Will's Chevy Chase dinner table, Will explained, "When Ronald Reagan comes to my house, I say, 'Hi. Here are my guests,' and then my wife takes him, sits down at the table with him. I mean it's not a close personal relationship." But the First Lady and First Pundit could often be spied lunching at the Jockey Club together, and Nancy listed Will, along with Meg Greenfield and Katherine Graham, among the "pals" who called her with support and encouragement during the "dark and hurtful time" of the Iran-Contra affair. When Will received an invitation to a White House Christmas party, he refused, on the grounds that other journalists were to be invited as well.

Of even greater notoriety than Will's personal relationship with the First Couple were his professional ties to its "more colorful" half. Privately, Will seemed to concur with Clark Clifford's characterization of Ronald Reagan as something of an "amiable dunce." Before Reagan won the Republican nomination, Will called him "the unsurpassed master of Jeremiads." Reagan biographer Lou Cannon reports that Will "wondered how anyone so uninformed could reach the top of the American political system." Will was "particularly annoyed," Cannon noted, by Reagan's "substitution of anecdotes for analysis." He considered the president's thinking to be "terribly banal . . . Durango, Colorado, Rotary thought." But these reservations did not appear to interfere with either Will's social relationship with the Reagans or his political championing of the president once he landed the job. Will helped write a 1982 speech that Reagan gave before the British House of Commons. He accepted a nonpaying appointment to the Board of Visitors of the U.S. Naval Academy and openly politicked to get superhawk John Lehman appointed secretary of the Navy. These machinations also coincided with his (now-ex) wife's high-level appointment in the Department of Education.

Phil Geyelin, Will's editor at the *Post* op-ed page during the 1970s, recalls telling Will that he should not have been sitting in the Reagan family box at the 1976 Republican convention and that he should have resisted the temptation to write Reagan's speeches for him as well. Will apparently disregarded Geyelin's advice and, in the summer of 1983, Will's conduct itself became a political issue. During the 1980 election season, Will spied a copy of a purloined Carter briefing book in Reagan adviser David Stockman's kitchen and failed to inform his readers, editors, or producers. Even more egregiously, Will helped coach Reagan in his debate with President Carter and then, presenting himself on *Nightline* as an impartial observer, credited his student with a "thoroughbred performance."

All of the issues that had troubled other journalists about Will were brought to the forefront by "Debategate." Previously, he had been able to ascribe such criticism to the fact that "journalists are spurning choices not really open to them." Finally, as the denunciations grew in vehemence and the *New York Daily News* publicly expunged him from its editorial pages, Will was forced to respond. He argued that the Carter papers looked unimportant to him, and as for coaching Reagan, all he had done was to ask Reagan "a recondite question bristling with references to Resolution 242 and 'the green line,' " regarding the Arab-Israeli peace process. Reagan, he felt compelled to add, "did not distinguish himself." Will insisted that as a columnist, rather than as a journalist, he was correct to accept the invitation to help prepare the president for his debate, and he argued that Lippmann, Krock, Alsop, "and others have had various relationships with presidents from Woodrow Wilson on."[*]

Debategate divided the ranks of the punditocracy. Lining up against Will was most of the journalistic establishment. Arguing that it was fine for Will to coach Reagan one minute and set himself up as an allegedly impartial judge of his performance the next were Hugh Sidey and his occasional ventriloquist, Ronald Reagan. Ben Bradlee later complained that if it had been up to him, "I would have canned him [Will] on the spot."

But far from resulting in Will's losing his job, the controversy only added to the Willian lore, further blurring the lines between the watchdogs and the watched. The *Daily News* reinstated him, and soon the kingdom of Will was bigger than ever. It is ironic that Will was professionally beyond the reach of Bradlee, the editor of his flagship newspaper and then the nation's most respected newspaperman. By the end of the controversy, Will's political status was so great that he was beyond virtually all accepted journalistic rules and practices. When it was all over, a *Wall Street Journal* reporter asked Will just where he drew the line between personal and professional relationships. "I don't," he replied.

The talents that made Will a ubiquitous presence in the Washington media for the past three decades and the most powerful and influential television pundit of his era bore precious little relevance to those embodied by any journalist before him, Lippmann and Reston included.

---

[*]Moreover, Will could not resist mentioning, he was frequently invited to dinner with Reagan and other celebrities, and they all had a marvelous time together. There was, for instance, that "small dinner" the previous winter "with Reagan, who enjoyed himself enormously—which is easy to do when Lee Iacocca is present and feeling feisty" (George F. Will, 10 July 1983).

When former *Washington Post* Moscow correspondent Robert Kaiser returned home from Soviet assignment, he called George Will on the recommendation of a mutual friend. The two men had dinner, and Kaiser said to Will, "you know, George, you really ought to go to the Soviet Union. It's different than you imagine it." Will's face looked, Kaiser recalls, as if the suggestion had been made by someone who recently returned from a stay in an insane asylum. That Kaiser seemed to believe that a pundit's ability to pontificate about a place could in some way benefit from his having observed it firsthand was an indication of just how long he had been away from Washington.

Charles Krauthammer, Pulitzer Prize–winning pundit and close friend of Will's, has rightly praised his comrade for single-handedly injecting a Burkean sensibility into the American political consciousness. Indeed, as Krauthammer points out, Will is in many ways at philosophical odds with the phenomenon known as Reaganism. Almost alone among prominent American conservative pundits, Will confronts head on the philosophical contradiction between simultaneous loyalty to Adam Smith and Edmund Burke. "Capitalism," Will worries, "undermines traditional social structures and values: it is a relentless engine of change, a revolutionary inflamer of appetites, enlarger of expectations, diminisher of patience." Will is contemptuous of "the most familiar and fashionable" conservatives, who, "complacently . . . define the public good as whatever results from the unfettered pursuit of private ends." It is foolish, he insists, "to treat laissez-faire economic theory as a substitute for political philosophy." It is for statements like these that some vociferous conservatives consider Will an unserious parvenu. Ex–*National Review* writer Joseph Sobran calls Will's conservatism, "a toothless, coffee-table Toryism, nicely calculated for liberal consumption."

At the core of Will's philosophical project is his distinction between "statecraft" and "soulcraft." Like most Marxists, Will insists that the state has a positive role to play in the shaping of its citizens' cultural consciousness. What distinguishes Will from the Marxists are the values he seeks to inculcate. "The United States acutely needs," Will argues, "a real conservatism, characterized by a concern to cultivate the best persons and the best in persons. It should express renewed appreciation for the ennobling functions of government." Singularly among his peers on the Right, Will supports increased taxation and additional government spending on such projects as child nutrition, prenatal care, and aid to dependent children. These communitarian functions are not only morally sound, he argues, but they contribute to the civility of the American polity, a value Will prizes almost above all.

That Will has managed to navigate a coherent philosophical position within the swamps of American political discourse is no mean achievement. But the achievement, however impressive, is undermined by the manner in which it has been achieved. Will does not earn his millions on the basis of his refined Tory philosophy. Rather, Will achieved his unique perch in American political culture—a perch the writer William Henry III has called "a national version of the smartest boy in the class"—on the strength of his television persona and the bellicosity of his foreign policy views. Although Will does have a smooth pen and an enviable ability to speak precisely and concisely on television, the seriousness of his purpose is marred by a terminal addiction to intellectual name-dropping, a writing style that veritably drips cuteness, and a shameless fealty to his social set in the pages of his columns.

Bathed in the phosphorescent glow of the cathode rays, George Will was glibness itself. Bon mot after mot seemed to spin off Will's tongue as if placed there by the ghosts of Burke and Chesterton. Aside from his eccentric Tory demeanor and shameless Anglophilia, Will was most revered for his pioneering work in the art of the sneer, both literal and figurative. The Will sneer took many forms. He would quiz Jesse Jackson on international monetary policy in a manner intended to make the presidential candidate look foolish. He would deliberately oversimplify the writings of Jean-Paul Sartre to the point, literally, of absurdity. ("Existentialism seems to be the belief that because life is absurd, so philosophy should be too.") And, quite frequently, Will would deploy obscure historical references to illustrate the fact that he was smarter and better read than the person about whom he was writing, particularly if that person was the leader of a rival superpower. In this last strategy, one begins to sense considerable insecurity. Will once bragged in an interview, offering no evidence, that when he goes "to hear old Gorbachev, I've read more Marx than he has." In a 1979 column on Soviet expansionism, he observed that "It is not that Brezhnev reads Marx before bedtime (any more than Richard Coeur de Lion went around constantly reciting the Athanasian Creed)." Will liked this argument so well that eight years later he observed of Gorbachev, "The problem is not that Gorbachev reads Lenin nightly, any more than Richard Coeur de Lion went around reciting the Athanasian Creed."

Will's ability to fashion a compact alliterative put-down on almost any occasion further added to his fame. When in January 1982 Will observed on *This Week* that President Reagan "loved commerce more than he loathed Communism," the city reacted as if Will had written a sequel to *Remembrance of Things Past*. Will himself was forced to admit that he had come up with "the most quoted . . . sentence yet written about the Reagan administration," drawing on his sound bites the way Lippmann drew on *A Preface to Morals.*

Having been chastened in the most painful and public manner conceivable—the revelation from a Mr. Timothy Dickinson that he was supplying Will with his simulated erudition, followed by a full week of Doonesbury variations on this theme—Will began, in the late 1980s, to lay off a bit on the quotes. But the early Will years contained some pretty hard going for those seeking to discern a consistent intellectual theme amidst the maddening crowd. In a 1973 column on Hubert Humphrey, Will found occasion to call into service the thoughts and reputations of Robert Kennedy, Eugene McCarthy, Roger Branigin, Lyndon Johnson, Barry Goldwater, Alexander Bickel, Ambrose Bierce, Samuel Johnson, James Boswell, and Charles Maurice de Talleyrand. In a 1976 discussion of what ails the English ("Englishness does"), Will enlisted George Santayana, Muriel Spark, Peter Drucker, the *London Economist,* Randolph Churchill, Napoleon, Henry James (twice), and Arthur Koestler. In his 1978 encomium to the reactionary Russian mysticism of Aleksandr Solzhenitsyn, Will augmented his argument by recruiting Augustine, Aquinas, Richard Hooker, Pascal, Thomas More (twice), Edmund Burke, G. W. F. Hegel, Alexis de Tocqueville, Henry Adams, Irving Babbitt, Paul Elmer, Peter Viereck, and "others" (twice) whom Will believed to constitute a "submerged but continuous tradition that shares Solzhenitsyn's anxiety about American premises and the culture they produce."*

To atone for his intellectual pretensions, Will likes to show his readers and viewers that he, too, can be a regular guy. In print, he most often does this by inserting dialogue from "Dennis the Menace" into his argu-

---

*George F. Will, 18 June 1978. By the end of the 1990s, Will had grown strangely lackadaisical about his quote mongering. In a 1989 column about the rejuvenated German question, Will wrote, "Someone—Clemenceau perhaps—said he loved Germany so much he wanted there always to be more than one." The quip in truth belonged to François Mauriac, who noted, "I love Germany so much that I am happy there are two of them." When I wrote to Will, wondering about his source, I received the following reply, dated August 11, 1989, signed by a Mr. James Martignon, "Assistant to Mr. Will":

Dear Mr. Alterman,

Thank you for your enquirery [*sic*] and information concerning columns that Mr. Will has written. The François Mauriac quote will make a fine addition to our files. It is quite possible that this is the quote that Mr. Will was referring to in his May 7th column. It is difficult to tell, for Mr. Will reads a great deal of information. His memory is excellent, but it would be impossible to find the exact source of every quote and meet deadlines. That is the reason for "Someone—Clemenceau perhaps—said . . . ," and not a direct quotation credited to Clemenceau. It is possible that either both (and possibly others) have made this statement concerning Germany. Whatever the case, Mr. Will appreciates that you were concerned enough to provide additional sources of information to our office. They will indeed make a fine addition to our files.

ments. Here is Will on the 1980 election: "Gadzooks! If a Republican majority emerges, it may do so wearing galoshes." Here is Will, at the foot of Reagan's desk once more, worrying about presidential panic: "Gadzooks! Is there a panic detector, akin to a smoke detector, that sniffs anxiety in the air?" Here is Will defending himself against charges that he should not have coached Reagan in his debate: "Nobody says 'Gadzooks! George Will favored Ronald Reagan.'"

Another favorite trick of Will's is the insertion of a contemporary American city or political issue within a well-known classical quotation. Here is Will on Topeka: "Et tu, Topeka?" On Iowa: "Et tu, Iowa?" On Indiana, "Et tu, Indiana?" On Nicaragua: "Et tu . . . ?"

Another foundation on which Will's stylistic edifice rests is the clever, almost offhand plug of the author's friends in politics and the media. John Danforth, Will observes, is "one of the most judicious and least flamboyant members" of the Senate and "the only person ever to receive degrees from the Yale Law School and the Yale Divinity School on the same day." An equally accurate description might read, "Senator Jack Danforth, the godfather of my daughter Victoria. . . ." Will devoted ten full columns to Robert Bork's brilliance during his 1987 Supreme Court battle and threw in a full-page plug in *Newsweek* for Bork's "masterpiece of American reflection," *The Tempting of America*, published on the heels of Bork's Senate rejection. Nowhere in this avalanche of verbiage did Will find the space to mention that he had been an usher at his subject's wedding.[*] Sometimes Will had trouble juggling all these plugs. Will's friends and political allies Richard Scammon and Ben Wattenberg were touted as "the Butch Cassidy and Sundance Kid of electoral analysis," while just three months later, David Stockman and Martin Anderson were said to be the "Butch Cassidy and Sundance Kid" of budgetary politics.

The chief beneficiary of Will's encomiums was his friend the president, a man whose foremost achievement, according to Will, "has been in convincing the country not that he knows the future, but that he knows his own mind." Will truly seemed to lose patience with his advisee only when he thought Reagan was letting his wishy-washy advisers tone down his hawkish instincts. The communitarian values Will paraded on domestic policy bore no relevance to Will's opinions on foreign policy. When it came to foreign nationals, Will—who sat out Vietnam with a married student deferment—was spoiling for a fight.

From the beginning of the Reagan era, Will was on the lookout for a conflict somewhere, in which the United States might win a proxy war

---

[*]It did, however, contain the following prediction: "The bad news for Biden is that . . . the confirmation process [for Bork] will be easy" (George F. Will, 2 July 1987).

against the Soviets. It would be necessary "during our watch," he wrote, to "take one of their pieces off the board." The notion that, above all, Americans needed to win a war—any war—led Will to celebrate the use of force at virtually every opportunity. His harshest attacks on the administration came when its leaders opted for a policy of relative restraint. When American marines were killed in Beirut, Will called for an attack on Syria. This act of war was necessary because "terrorism serves Syrian interests" and "such attacks could probably not have occurred without the knowledge of Syria, which controls the road by which the truck had to approach to attack sites; Syrian occupation is a necessary precondition for such attacks." During the Beirut crisis, Will found hysterically funny the notion put forth by then–Senate majority leader Howard Baker that the United States should use retaliatory military force if and only if the attackers could be identified "with precision and exactness." "What is this," he guffawed, "the Warren Court conducting foreign policy? Who will read the suspects their Miranda rights?"[*]

In an almost perfect repudiation of Lippmann's credo, Will argues that in moments of diplomatic tension, politicians should do their utmost to inflame popular passions in support of the escalation of violence. "Intelligent behavior," Will explained to Peter Jennings during the 1985 TWA 847 hostage crisis, "flows not from keeping one's passional and rational capacities separated, but from reasonably relating a proper passion—in this case, cold fury—to action." When the Soviets shot down the KAL 007 jetliner over the Sea of Japan in 1983, Will likened the public mind to wax, noting that "it is easiest to shape when hot." Here Will steps down from his customary elitist disdain for the popular will for the purpose of manufacturing the consent necessary to carry out a policy of force and violence. Will's hatred for the Soviets and those nations he deems to be "terrorist" overrides virtually all of the elegant moral distinctions on which he prides himself when writing of the American (or West Euro-

[*]George F. Will, 10 November 1983. Will takes an interesting leap of logic here. Among the bloodiest terrorist attacks of the 1980s was that unleashed by Sikh militants in 1985 on an Air India 747 bound from Montreal to London, which killed 329 people. The perpetrators learned their craft at a private paramilitary camp in Dolomite, Alabama, where U.S.-supplied mercenaries were trained for military action in Central America and elsewhere by an American citizen named Frank Camper. The U.S. government must certainly have known of the existence of the camp, yet did nothing to shut it down. By Will's rules of great-power machismo, both Canada and India would have been justified in bombing Alabama. "Great nations," after all, Will teaches, do not concern themselves with the measurement of justice to "persons who are instruments of other nations' interests." If Americans complained, Canada could always read us our Miranda rights. For details about the camp and Camper's role in training the terrorists, see Leslie Cockburn, *Out of Control* (New York: Atlantic Monthly Books, 1987), p. 26. For the "Great nations" quote, see George F. Will, 10 February 1983.

pean) polity. But, in some cases, this proclivity spills over into his domestic analysis, leading the armchair psychologist to conclude that Will appears to have a problem with the "other," whether at home or abroad.

Will's difficulty in empathizing with society's victims can lead to comical results. The most notorious of these was the evening in September 1984 on which Will and his family were given tickets to a Bruce Springsteen concert by Max Weinberg, the E Street Band's drummer. Dressed in full bow-tie regalia, with cotton pads stuffed in his ears, Will somehow heard in Springsteen's "Born in the USA" a "grand, cheerful affirmation" of American life.[*] The song in question tells the story of a working-class youth in trouble with the law and forced by the courts to go to Vietnam "to kill the yellow man." In Vietnam, he loses his brother at the battle of Khe Sahn, only to return to a hometown in which his factory job has been eliminated. It is a "grand, cheerful affirmation" of American life in much the same way that Aleksandr Solzhenitsyn's *The Gulag Archipelago* is a grand, cheerful affirmation of the Stalinist penal code.

Will's America is a country that was "born on the farm and moved to town, leaving behind the Jeffersonian vision." This is a country, needless to say, of upstanding white Christian folk. Consider George Will on the homeless. The most conspicuous aspect of the problem to Will is the "simple matter of public order and hygiene . . . getting these people off the streets." "The community," he argues, "has some rights here. If it is illegal—and it is and ought to be illegal—to litter the streets, frankly, it ought to be illegal for people who must survive on panhandling, among other things, to sleep on the streets." The homeless are explicitly excluded from the Will "community" in this analysis, and their stubborn demand to sleep on the streets in full view of Will and his friends should be punished. "Should society arrest them?" Will was asked. "Not arrest them," came the response, "but move them off to some place where they are simply out of sight and no longer a visible . . . public nuisance."

Will's reputation as a thoughtful, communitarian conservative, his support for child welfare programs, and his concern for the effect of state "soulcraft" had the effect, during the Reagan years, of increasing the credibility—and therefore influence—of his less generous impulses. It was so much more impressive for Will to call for random retaliation upon

[*]George F. Will, 13 September 1984. The Will column led to a wonderful comedy of errors when the politicos in the Reagan campaign read it and tried to secure Springsteen's endorsement. Springsteen told all the president's men to get lost. Reagan had to make do with quoting Springsteen in his New Jersey campaign appearances and went on to enlist the celluloid psychotic killer, Rambo, the summer of 1984's other cultural icon, for his campaign. Walter Mondale's campaign also tried, unsuccessfully, to claim Springsteen's endorsement, based on the fact that he had refused it to Reagan. In fact, the last presidential candidate the great man had voted for was George McGovern.

the Lebanese or Syrian population, as well as the internal exile of the homeless (regardless of Constitutional liberties), because he had earned his moral capital, so to speak, by virtue of his support for higher taxes. Because of the civilizing veneer of his elegant philosophical distinctions, Will could not be dismissed, with much of the Reagan coalition, as morally retarded or ideologically obsessed. Yet the snideness of his tone seemed to brook no principled opposition. This proved an enormously effective combination throughout the 1980s, as Will maintained his status as Lippmann's rightful heir without doing any of the difficult philosophical explication that marked Lippmann's career and precious little of the interpretive work that had characterized Lippmann's idealized notions of the educative function of punditry.

Instead of setting himself above the battle with Lippmann, or astride it, with Reston, Will threw himself into combat on behalf of the winning side, while at the same time posing as the battle's most distinguished arbitrator. In this regard, his position in the public dialogue had less in common with that of Lippmann than with one of Lippmann's early patrons, President Woodrow Wilson, during the early stages of the Great War. Wilson, too, had pretended to mediate a conflict from above while simultaneously scheming to support those he expected would be its victors. The result was American entry into the war and the disastrously misguided peace settlement that Wilson later engineered. Without stretching the metaphor overmuch, one could say that Will's hypocrisy in this regard accomplished for honest political punditry approximately as much as Wilson's chicanery did for the notion of disinterested peaceful mediation.

Toward the end of the Reagan era, Will decided, for reasons still unknown, to forswear his executive privileges. Offended by George Bush's supplications to the party's far Right in early 1986, he launched a premeditated attack on Bush, whose self-effacing efforts to secure his right flank Will found distasteful. The columnist insisted that "the unpleasant sound Bush is emitting as he traipses from one conservative gathering to another is the thin, tinny 'arf,' the sound of a lapdog." The day before that column appeared, Will told a Florida audience "if he [Bush] survives it, the power of the written word is gone."

Washington was scandalized. Here it was, only 1986, and George Bush had already lost the Will primary. Bush called a meeting of his staff and urged them not to get too depressed over the Will thing. Will insisted that he meant the column as a kind of "shot across Bush's bow." Why, for goodness' sake, asked Will-watchers, would the First Pundit wish to shoot across the bow of the one man who could keep him within spitting distance of John-John's favorite desk? Could it be that Will felt his journalistic manhood threatened by his close association with the increasingly befuddled First Lame Ducks? Would that have anything to do with Will's decision to write a baseball book as well?

Shortly after publishing the "lapdog" column, Will sent Bush a handwritten note suggesting that the two Firsts get together mano-a-mano and discuss their differences. "Thanks, but I'm booked up," replied the grudge-holding Skull and Bones Man. "Criticism is one thing, personal attack another."

Will was never taken into the inner circle of the Clinton administration and, hence, was among the president's most fervent critics throughout the entire Clinton era, particularly during the Lewinsky scandal and impeachment process. Will's wife, Mari Maseng Will, played a key role in Robert Dole's unhappy 1996 presidential run. One could occasionally discern Will cadences in Dole speeches and Dole talking points in Will columns. When Dole was trounced, this diminished Will's influence, but not his celebrity. He continued to appear every seven days on ABC's *This Week*, to write his column in the *Post* and *Newsweek*, and to publish the occasional collection of essays. His vituperative attacks on President Clinton made his occasional darts at George Bush seem gentle indeed. Ironically, it is as a sportswriter that Will's gifts have been most evident. His collections of essays on baseball are so meticulously reported and sparely written that many observers have been given to wonder just what this brilliant sportswriter could do if he ever turned his attention to politics.

CHAPTER FIVE

Attack of the McLaughlinites

First aired in April 1982, *The McLaughlin Group* proved to be a breakthrough in the history of pundit television. Only two shows before it had eliminated the politician and allowed journalists to question one another, and both were boring. *The McLaughlin Group* may have been simultaneously annoying, irritating, aggravating, grating, and galling—but boring it wasn't.

In achieving its landmark status, the show broke a number of once-sacred pundit barriers. In the first place, some panelists were only nominally journalists. John McLaughlin was himself a journalist in the sense that somebody who takes his car into the shop to get it fixed a great deal is a mechanic. He had always kept the company of journalists—leaked to them, perhaps, and gone to their dinner parties. But he had hardly been spending his time wearing out shoe leather. During the period from 1983 to 1988 during which McLaughlin held the title of Washington editor of the *National Review*, his column was regularly ghostwritten by his assistants. "Sometimes he would change it," recalls one former ghost, "sometimes it would sail right through." Among the other panelists, Patrick Buchanan had spent a grand total of two months as a reporter before becoming an editorial writer and beginning his distinguished career as a conservative polemicist, part-time government official, and presidential aspirant. Robert Novak had, during the 1960s, been among the most respected and hard-working journalists in Washington, but in the decade preceding the launching of *The McLaughlin Group*, Novak's intense conservative bias had overtaken his reputation as a straight-shooting journalist.

The regular cast had no blacks or women. The atmosphere was soaked in the same country club locker-room machismo that drifted out of the White House in the Reagan years. *Rolling Stone* national affairs editor William Greider, an occasional substitute, recalls a pre-show run-through in the show's early days in which McLaughlin, Novak, and panelist Morton Kondracke spent the whole time telling "incredibly crude and sexist jokes" about prostitutes in Bangkok. When the group discussed a Texas gubernatorial candidate's insistence that Mexican brothels were the only places a young man could "get serviced" in West Texas, Jack Germond noted that this comment was offensive to the West Texan sheep population.

The show's success derived from McLaughlin's ability to conduct it in a fashion owing more to roller derby than to public-affairs television. The discussions were fast-paced and extremely short on both attributed information and contextual nuance. Few topics lasted more than seven or eight minutes, and some were abruptly cut off in less than thirty seconds, depending on McLaughlin's moods. Panelists were quick to personalize their criticisms of one another and insult each other's manhood whenever the opportunity arose.

As in any good sitcom, each of the regular panelists played a stock character. McLaughlin was the ringleader—a combination Catholic school headmaster and circus announcer. Patrick Buchanan played the tough Irish cop with twinkly eyes and a heart of granite. Robert Novak portrayed a beer-guzzling, middle-class construction worker whose idea of a good time was to sic his German shepherd on welfare queens and pinko student demonstrators. Morton Kondracke, with his much-abused yuppie steel-rimmed glasses and his altar-boy haircut, was the guy who always sat at the front of the class waving his arms at the teacher only to forget the answer once he was finally called on. His waffling responses almost always gave Novak the opportunity to call him a weenie and to threaten to take away his lunch. The balding, proudly overweight Jack Germond—by far the most attractive character of the lot—was the sort of pundit Fred Mertz would have been had Ethel ever let him out of the house: willing, just barely, to undergo the torture long enough to pick up his check each week.

The McLaughlin Group advertised itself not as a group of Lippmann-like sages or Seymour Hersh–type investigators, but as a collection of "federal authorities," giving "inside opinions and forecasts." Excluding Germond, the words "I don't know" or even "I think" or "I believe" were not to be found in any of the panelists' vocabularies. Whether it was the guerrilla strategy of Afghan mujahedeen or the next open-market operation by the Federal Reserve Board, the members of the group always seemed to have just gotten off the phone with the guy in charge.

Judged strictly on its entertainment value, the show worked just fine. Germond harrumphed, Buchanan huffed and puffed, and Kondracke hemmed and hawed until Novak pounced. McLaughlin would then close out the discussion by saying something like "Okay, let's get out. On a scale of one to ten, one being Adolph Hitler's *Mein Kampf,* ten being the Ten Commandments, George Shultz's Middle East peace plan rates what on the scale of divine inspiration, Mor-TAHN?"

Washington loved to hate it. *The McLaughlin Group* quickly surpassed *Agronsky and Company* as the pundit show to watch. Journalists and pundits alike vied with one another for the ever-important rotating seat. (*New Republic* editor Michael Kinsley lost his spot in the rotation, however, when his magazine carried testimony of McLaughlin's reliance on ghostwriters.) Occasionally, a mere politician would be granted the honor of sitting in. But it had to be a politician with special qualities; somebody with the modesty and charm of, say, Ed Koch.

The Reagan White House understood just how important television punditry had become in political tastemaking and displayed a nice touch for symbolism when it arranged for special pundit briefings to be conducted in the Reagan family theater for members of the group and the rest of the network's weekend pundit line-up. At these Friday morning briefings, White House officials would come by and give "not for attribution" information to the lucky few. The boys would then hustle straight to their tapings, where the tidbits and leaks were repeated verbatim, either in the form of predictions or inside scoops.

These predictions, ironically, were among the best researched and most firmly grounded of all those offered by the show's guests. A series of tracking polls by *Regardie's* magazine showed the average group member's accuracy to hover between 12 and 25 percent. Often, when McLaughlin would find himself approaching a taping without any inside kitty, he would turn to one of his young assistants for help. These assistants, sensing the opportunity to begin a politically useful rumor, would literally fabricate one. In one instance, recalls former issues consultant Tom Miller, he told McLaughlin that Assistant Secretary of State Chester Crocker was in trouble for his insufficient dedication to Reagan Doctrine causes in Southern Africa. McLaughlin went on the air to predict that Crocker might soon be removed. Crocker, according to Miller, was forced to deny the story and was undoubtedly a bit wary of raising his profile on issues dear to the heart of the Reaganites for a while thereafter.

Inside the Beltway, group members were Washington's rock stars. Reagan would watch the show at Camp David and bang his fists on the table when a panel member failed to take his side. At one McLaughlin party, Reagan dropped by and read a speech about the group written for him by his new Director of Communications, former and future panelist Patrick Buchanan.* The historically right-wing General Electric Corporation (GE), which took over the show's sponsorship from the Edison Electric Institute, soon began to spend many millions of dollars to advertise the show and to give it free to any PBS station. "Don't miss it. The people who run this country never do," warned the Orwellian advertising copy. "Listen to the voices of authority."

McLaughlin reveled in his increasingly powerful role as media kingpin. He soon adopted GE Chief Executive Officer Jack Welch on the Washington social circuit, inviting him over for dinner with his (now-ex) wife's new boss, Ronald Reagan. Ann Dore McLaughlin, who engineered her husband's resounding Senate defeat and had been public relations director for a small Catholic college before that, managed to get herself named secretary of labor. In between she had worked for Donald Regan in the White House, for Union Carbide, and for Nixon's infamous Committee to Re-elect the President (CREEP). Whether her position in the cabinet was likely to influence McLaughlin's treatment of the president on the show was a question so déclassé that no one even thought to raise it publicly.

While not as thoughtful as Will or as feared and respected as Safire, John McLaughlin nevertheless appeared in the early 1980s to be the living Zeitgeist of American politics—the Frankenstein of the Buckley-Vidal experiment run amuck. A pure creation of the nexus of media power, corporate money, and the conservative insider boys' club, McLaughlin had no discernible political beliefs. A man of tremendous appetite for power, riches, and control over the lives of those around him, McLaughlin was a modern-day Citizen Kane, building a television empire of media hot air on the basis of a quick wit and a talent for ideological body-surfing. Having lived his adult life on the fringes of political power and ideological obsession, McLaughlin found himself, at the height of the Reagan era, with three television shows and eight full hours of air time each week. In terms of frequency of television appearances, his only real competition was Lucy and Ricky Ricardo. An ex-Jesuit, ex-anti-Nixon, dovish Senate candidate, as well as an ex-pro-Nixon, hawkish "Watergate priest," the story of

* "*The McLaughlin Group* serves as a most tasteful television program alternative to professional wrestling, live from Madison Square Garden," read the President. "Thank you for making that half hour every weekend something very special to look forward to. I wouldn't miss it; I can't afford to."

McLaughlin's rise, fall, and rise again rivals that of the man from Whittier for self-reinvention in the service of political opportunism.

McLaughlin's achievement was tainted, however, not only by the damage inflicted on American politics by the deification of his brand of lightning-fast, quarter-inch-deep political analysis, but also by personal flaws that his celebrators and sponsors were willing to ignore in the face of his success. To the youthful underlings who worked in his office, McLaughlin was a petty tyrant and, according to the testimony of at least three women, an insatiable sexual harasser. McLaughlin settled one lawsuit over his sexual harassment tactics and faced the possibility of at least two others.[*] That

---

*On Petty Tyranny: Former marine officer and McLaughlin employee Tom Liddy regards McLaughlin as a "brilliant" and "inspiring" boss. Once, when Liddy came back to his old haunt for a visit during a three-week vacation from the marines, McLaughlin took him into the office, shut the door, and said, "I understand you're free for three weeks. I want you to work here." When Liddy protested that it was his only vacation and that he would like to be able to spend some time with his family, McLaughlin replied, "Look, I really need you." Three weeks later, Liddy left the office, picked up his mortar platoon, and flew to Okinawa. The young man's characterization of McLaughlin as "demanding, but not overly demanding" would appear to be ludicrously generous, until Liddy himself raises an excellent point: "Don't forget, I was raised by Gordon Liddy."

On Alleged Sexual Harassment: These stories do not have such endearing punchlines. According to several former employees, some still friendly with McLaughlin, he would personally insult a number of his female underlings, telling them that they were "fat" or "stupid" and that they "would be out on the street were it not for him." It was the responsibility of one staffer to cut the pieces of McLaughlin's chicken sandwich into the right sizes and shapes. Kara Swisher, now at the *Washington Post*, was once buzzed into McLaughlin's office and told to make her boss toast. When she refused, McLaughlin called it "a very serious toast situation" and threatened—seriously, according to Swisher—"If I ask you to make toast and you don't do it, I can fire you."

One McLaughlin staffer had the task of arranging the pens and pads in McLaughlin's suitcase in exactly in the order he preferred. "If one of the pens was out of place," the staffer noted, "it was a national security emergency." All were expected to run, literally, into McLaughlin's office whenever he buzzed them. (McLaughlin loved his buzzer.) There they were told where to stand, like chess pieces, until dismissed.

The staff's basic attitude, says Anne Rumsey, a former employee, was that "Yes, he was a lunatic but he has this, this, and this going for him so I'll try to stick it out." Rumsey quit after only six weeks at the job, after McLaughlin asked her to walk him to the elevator, only to thunder, "I've been told that you spend a lot of time on the phone with your friends. Do you value your job?" While McLaughlin was reading Rumsey's resignation letter, she was out collecting his laundry.

When Linda Dean, a former office manager, began her lawsuit alleging sexual harassment by McLaughlin, she swore that McLaughlin told her that "he needed a lot of sex" and that if she would stick by him, "he would take care of every material desire she had." McLaughlin, according to Dean, insisted that he "owned" her and on several occasions touched her "intimately and against her will." She was eventually fired but since has settled her lawsuit and refuses to discuss the matter with reporters.

The complaint also discussed the case of another female receptionist who, according to Dean's sworn testimony, complained in a letter to her employment agency that McLaughlin he could rise to where he has in American political culture with only quiet whispers of resentment is an indication of just how successful success had become in Ronald Reagan's Washington. That McLaughlin would still feel free to pass judgment on the propriety of Chuck Robb's, Paul Reuben's, and other people's sex lives on his show—to say nothing of his tasteless and unseemly attack on Anita Hill's testimony regarding her alleged harassment at the hands of Clarence Thomas—says something even uglier.

As a young Jesuit seminarian, John McLaughlin was expected to weave small whips with thongs on the end and, occasionally, engage in self-

---

had "behaved improperly toward her by committing acts which the receptionist perceived to be sexual harassment." The receptionist, when reached by telephone, refused to discuss the incident.

A third female McLaughlin employee, Sharon T. Wulbern, also appears in the court record. Having read of Dean's suit in the *Washington Post*, Wulbern (her name is spelled three different ways in the documents) told Dean's lawyer that Dean's accusations mirrored "quite a bit of my experience," containing "all the things I had been experiencing." Wulbern was terminated by McLaughlin in January 1989. These accusations appear in her own deposition, parts of which were printed in the court records.

A fourth female former employee confirms that McLaughlin made unwanted sexual advances toward her on more than one occasion, including once on a business trip to Mexico. Both Kara Swisher and Tom Miller, a former issues consultant to McLaughlin, recall instances of McLaughlin "leering" at the fourth woman and making suggestive sexual comments to her. McLaughlin, according to the recollections of Swisher and Miller, occasionally put his arm around the woman in a way that struck both of them as surprising and undesired.

McLaughlin also liked to make personal comments about his young female employees. Anne Rumsey recalls him telling her one day that her sweater was too tight. "He was very touchy," recalls Swisher. "I think that sexual harassment is like pornography. You know it when you see it. People can tell you look nice and there will be no menace to it. With John McLaughlin, there was menace." Miller recalls McLaughlin asking an employee whether she liked her sex rough. McLaughlin's own court filings contain references to a conversation with Dean about having sex in an airplane. When a Supreme Court decision on sexual harassment was handed down during Miller's tenure on the job, he showed it to Beverly Larson, a high-level staffer, to give to McLaughlin as a warning. Swisher, too, says she met with *The McLaughlin Group*'s executive director, Margaret Suzor, to complain of McLaughlin's alleged sexual harassment, with no results.

McLaughlin's interviews are littered with strange ruminations about the relationship between power and sex. He told one reporter, "Power as an experience is as intense as sex. Power is more pervasive and unremitting. Sex has periods of remission." But he has refused to discuss any and all accusations about sexual harassment, except to deny those laid out in Dean's lawsuit, including the fact that anyone in his office ever complained to him about alleged sexual harassment. A spokesman for GE, who continues to fund McLaughlin, calls it "a private matter." Because the suit has been settled, it is unlikely that the accusations will ever be given a public airing. (The above is based on *Dean v McLaughlin* [DC Cir 1 88-CV-02185 1989], and on the author's interviews with Tom Miller, Tom Liddy, Kara Swisher, Anne Rumsey, and Anon. [a female former McLaughlin staffer who wishes to remain anonymous for fear of retaliation].)

flagellation. He was also expected to wear a chain made of barbed wire around the upper thigh, the better to battle feelings of sexual arousal. The pain was prescribed to remind the young men that the "flesh has an inclination toward evil." After the seminary, McLaughlin went on to earn three graduate degrees before becoming an editor at *America* magazine, the Jesuit weekly. There McLaughlin began to develop his unique public persona, traveling the country giving lectures on such subjects as "Intimacy outside Marriage" and "Intimacy before Marriage and the Swedish Experience (Parts I, II, III, and IV)."

In 1970, the Jesuit sex expert shocked virtually everyone who knew him when he announced that he would switch parties to challenge Rhode Island Democrat John Pastore for the U.S. Senate. McLaughlin campaigned as a high-profile Republican dove, calling for an even quicker withdrawal of U.S. troops from Vietnam than George McGovern was pushing for at the time and supporting a rapprochement with both Cuba and China. He lost big, but his candidacy somehow won him an appointment in the Nixon White House.[*]

McLaughlin began his tenure as a relatively low-level speech writer and special assistant to Nixon on refugees and other matters that Nixon didn't care too much about. But, as the Nixon ship began to sink from the weight of its Watergate baggage, McLaughlin made his break for the captain's bridge. Larry Speakes, who was working in the Nixon press office during the Watergate crisis, was having trouble getting any White House staffers to show their faces to the television cameras on the lawn. McLaughlin volunteered one afternoon, gave a boffo performance, and one day later four network crews showed up in his office. A staffer turned to Speakes and warned, "My god, he's a monster and I've created him."

McLaughlin called Nixon, "the greatest moral leader of the last third of this century." He defended the president's 1972 Christmas bombing of Hanoi, the mining of Haiphong Harbor, and Nixon's frequent taking of the Lord's name in vain. He called the latter, "a form of emotional drainage . . . a form of release, almost therapy." As late as May 9, 1974, barely ninety days before Nixon finally ended our Long National Nightmare, McLaughlin was still insisting that Nixon was a "moral man thirsting for truth." The accusations leveled against him were "erroneous, unjust, and contain elements of hypocrisy," he asserted, predicting that Watergate would be a mere "footnote to a glorious administration."

[*]In a typically accurate Evans and Novak column entitled "The Vetoed-Writer Priest," the dynamic duo reported that "combined pressure from the Republican right, Capitol Hill Democrats, and even the White House itself has just about killed a unique scheme to install a left-of-center Roman Catholic priest as presidential speech-writer." Rowland Evans and Robert Novak, 13 June 1971.

The press had a good time with McLaughlin's rather atypical Jesuit lifestyle. McLaughlin lived in the Watergate and earned $33,000 a year while publicly defending a man whose presidency seemed to have decidedly little in common with the teachings of Jesus Christ. McLaughlin made no pretense of donating his salary to the Jesuit community, as is customary, and his attempts to justify his lifestyle on theological grounds had a decided lack of conviction. He told friends that yes, he did live in the luxurious Watergate, but his apartment faced a gas station and he only rode the trash elevator. His friend and former campaign manager Ann Dore, not yet Ann Dore McLaughlin, was a frequent hostess at McLaughlin's parties, leading many in the Jesuit order to wonder just how faithfully McLaughlin was adhering to his vows of celibacy. Having extricated himself from a high-profile censure by the Jesuit authorities with an agreement to leave the White House, McLaughlin did everything but chain himself to his White House desk when Nixon finally fled for San Clemente. As late as September 30, Evans and Novak were still able to report that "the notorious Father John McLaughlin" was still on the job. Seventy-two hours later, McLaughlin was eligible for unemployment.

After leaving the order and marrying the previously wed Dore in a 1975 civil (not Catholic) ceremony, McLaughlin gradually worked his way back into the media limelight. He was hired in 1980 by a local Washington radio station to co-host a talk show but was fired a year later for talking too much. Soon, however, McLaughlin was frying even bigger fish. He had convinced his wealthy friend Richard Moore to pony up the funds to create a new kind of public affairs program. The pilot for *The McLaughlin Group*, featuring Jack Germond, Robert Novak, the distinguished black journalist Chuck Stone of the *Philadelphia Daily News*, and Judith Miller of the *New York Times*, was hardly promising. Miller lectured, Elizabeth Drew–style, and Stone was stone silent. But it did attract the corporate sponsorship of an electric utility trade association, the Edison Electric Institute. When McLaughlin replaced his black and woman panelists with Patrick Buchanan and Morton Kondracke, the juggernaut was launched.

The show's chief strength was its weird personal chemistry. McLaughlin's chief adversary in the group was Robert Novak. The two men started out the program in 1982 as close friends and political allies. But McLaughlin grew upset with Novak's monopolizing of the show's air time and tried to force him to shut up. He did so by refusing to tell Novak which days he would be invited and by literally thumbing his nose at Novak when the time came to cue him. Novak endured, but the animosity welling up in each man, coupled with their naturally theatrical tendencies, made for surprisingly interesting theater. When they finally did blow up, it was

McLaughlin who exploded; but in the interim, each man would needle the other, and the viewer was left to wonder what was real and what was not.* Both men were frequently approached in airports and asked how they could stand the other. The other group members were asked how they could stand either one.

Unlike McLaughlin, Novak was well liked by his peers, and it was generally understood that, politics aside, he was a pretty harmless fellow. On the tube, however, the only clear difference between "Robert Novak" and "Archie Bunker" was that the former got more air time. Despite—or perhaps because of—its bellicosity, the Novak character seemed to go over well in the heartland, earning Novak in the area of $7,500 a lecture. The reason insiders continued to read his column, however, was not the television shtick but his continued devotion to the kind of inside dope that political junkies mainline.

The Evans and Novak column played a crucial role in helping to form and execute what it called the "Reagan revolution." As "pragmatist" battled "ideologue" for the limited attention span of the president, the column worked as a kind of tribal drum for the warrior faction. From David Stockman to Ollie North, important administration principals could read the column in the *Post* three mornings a week and determine their own standing in the grand struggle. Stockman told stories of posting notices on what he called the "Bob Novak bulletin board" to manufacture the appearance of a "David Stockman for OMB [Office of Management and Budget] director" movement. "At the time Mr. Novak wrote the item in his column, it was a movement of 3 or 4 people, if you include the minority of my staff that favored the idea," wrote Stockman. By the time it was over, Stockman had the job and went on to become the most influential member of the Reagan cabinet.

Congressional bomb-throwers like Phil Gramm, Malcolm Wallop, Jack Kemp, and Newt Gingrich received free public relations from the column worth millions of dollars. Hardly a week went by without some "brave," "tough," "canny," or "strong" action by one of these men, usu-

---

*Finally, in the summer of 1988, McLaughlin spontaneously combusted. Needling McLaughlin about his chameleon-like political views, Novak accused McLaughlin on the air of tailoring his views to fit the contours of what might be a Democratic administration, given Michael Dukakis' then-strong standing in the polls. At the commercial break, McLaughlin exploded, turning "beet-red in the face" and screaming at the top of his lungs "VILE! VILE! VILE!" Novak said he expected McLaughlin to have a heart attack any minute. Germond, who is a long-time friend of Novak's, said to his buddy, "If you want to tell this guy to go fuck himself and walk, I'm with you." McLaughlin managed to compose himself by the time the commercial break ended. Novak gratefully declined Germond's offer but left the group to form his McLaughlin-like show on CNN—hosted by the ubiquitous Buchanan. (Author's interviews with Robert Novak, Jack Germond, Patrick Buchanan, and Morton Kondracke.)

ally accompanied by some previously unrevealed tidbit designed to portray them in as favorable a light as was humanly conceivable. Among the most historically significant of these morality plays was a column published in May 1986 in which a hitherto unknown "star player in the long, hard fight to keep alive the Nicaraguan contras" found himself endangered by "the gray and faceless officials" of the Reagan National Security Council (NSC) staff. Oliver North, about to be reassigned to the Marine Corps by his gray, faceless, and certainly luckless boss, John Poindexter, managed to retain his job in large measure as a result of the Evans and Novak column (along with another by Suzanne Garment of the *Wall Street Journal*). At the NSC, North could continue his sideline business of selling arms to the Ayatollah and funneling the profits to the Nicaraguan contras undisturbed.

In most cases, Novak and his partner went to the trouble of getting their facts down right, only to explode them in a wildly imaginative interpretation. But they could be mighty careless at times. An unsuspecting reader who accepted everything Evans and Novak have reported in recent years would find himself believing, as Michael Massing once demonstrated, in the reality of a "direct Soviet intervention in Poland" during the 1981 Solidarity crisis; an "imminent move by the Soviets from Afghanistan into Pakistan" in September 1984; and the sad fact that as of January 1985, "Mikhail Gorbachev is no longer considered the heir apparent" in the Kremlin. Somehow, Novak's popularity and influence only seemed to increase with the outlandishness of his views and reporting.

Seated across from Novak in McLaughlin's studio was the cherubic Catholic crusader and recent presidential candidate Patrick J. Buchanan. Buchanan's decision to announce for the presidency in December 1991 came as no surprise to anyone who had closely observed his career in the punditocracy. He carefully considered the idea four years earlier, but demurred in favor of the more conventional politician, Representative Jack Kemp. By the time Buchanan reversed himself, however, the displacement of "real" politicians at the center of the political dialogue was considerably further advanced. All of a sudden, in 1991, there was nothing ridiculous about the idea of moving from the small screen to the White House without having to earn any interim qualifications.

Buchanan was a popular and much admired character in Reagan's Washington. (George Bush is the only Republican president since Eisenhower who has managed to survive a presidency without Buchanan by his side.*) Throughout the 1980s, Buchanan was no less ubiqui-

---

*And look what that got him.

tous on television than Novak. He was a widely syndicated columnist, the co-host of *Crossfire* each night, a regular on *The McLaughlin Group*, and the host of Novak's own pundit CNN roundtable, *The Capital Gang*. (Novak thought he could not be nasty enough if he had to act as a fair-minded host as well.) Because of his extensive government experience, moreover, Buchanan is also treated as an honored former official. During one Middle East hostage crisis, Ted Koppel found it necessary to book him on *Nightline* twice in three days.

Buchanan may have had his own column, but unlike Novak, or even Will, he made no pretense of being a reporter. Rather, he was a professional right-winger. As Reagan's White House director of communications, Buchanan was the only member of the president's inner circle to speak favorably, at least in the abstract, of treason. During the Iran-Contra scandal, when the first "Buchanan for President" boomlet began, its standard-bearer gave inflammatory speeches, insisting, "If Colonel North ripped off the Ayatollah and took $30 million and gave it to the contras, then God bless Colonel North." During a particularly tense Congressional debate on contra aid, Buchanan drew the lines as follows: "With this vote on contra aid, the Democratic Party will reveal whether it stands with Ronald Reagan and the Resistance or with Daniel Ortega and the Communists." When the AIDS virus first hit the national news, Buchanan pooh-poohed the national trauma. "The poor homosexuals," he wrote, "they have declared war upon nature and now nature is exacting an awful retribution." Buchanan regularly refers to gay men as "perpetrators" and argues that "by buggering one another" and "committing promiscuous sodomy," they "threaten doctors, dentists, health workers, hemophiliacs and the rest of society by their refusal to curb their lascivious appetites." It is a measure of Buchanan's own inimitable style that both his almost–presidential campaign and his 1988 memoirs began with the same cri de coeur, "Let the bloodbath begin."

Despite what appears, even to most conservatives, to be a deeply extremist worldview, Buchanan sits comfortably at the hub of punditocracy life. An October 1991 charity roast of Buchanan featured tributes from two Republican ex-presidents, one Democratic presidential candidate, two almost–Democratic presidential candidates, the House minority whip, and leaders from every wing of both parties.* The evening testified to Buchanan's role in polite Washington society as a kind of

---

*"Compassion. Warmheartedness. Generosity of Spirit," said Richard Nixon, "the last words that come into my head when I think of Pat Buchanan." See Lloyd Grove, "Fresh Roasted Conservative," *Washington Post*, 17 October 1991, Style section, p. 7.

white man's Louis Farrakhan.* Just as intelligent blacks might ignore the weird, nonsensical, and often hateful pronouncements the black Muslim leader makes on the grounds that he peppers them with statements that appear sensible and well conceived, so, too, Patrick Buchanan was embraced into the bosom of insider Washington, despite views that fall somewhere in the twilight zone between Goldwater and McCarthy—that is, between conservatism and hate-mongering. ("McCarthy was cheered because for four years he was daily kicking the living hell out of people most Americans concluded ought to have the living hell kicked out of them," wrote Buchanan of his hero.)

But despite his engaging manners and charming persona, Buchanan is a man at war with his surroundings. The secret to his success—aside from his considerable talent as a writer and debater—is his ability to conduct this holy war in a huggable fashion. Buchanan comes from a deeply religious Irish Catholic family that prized loyalty and discipline above all. To impress on Buchanan what the loss of the soul through mortal sin meant, Buchanan's father would light a match, grab his son's hands, and hold them briefly over the flame, saying: "See how that feels: now imagine that for all eternity." It was in this atmosphere that Buchanan imbibed the religious dogma that he has so effectively preached in American political life. It was in his lower-middle-class, Scotch-Irish Catholic household that Buchanan came to his most important political understanding: "Before we believe, we know."

The Buchanans' disillusionment with contemporary life dates from the day Pope John XXIII issued Vatican II, liberalizing canon law and sanctioning all kinds of behavior that the family had been taught to consider deviant and dissolute. "Our political and social quarrels now partake in the savagery of religious wars because they are, at bottom, religious wars," Buchanan writes. The cultural civil war, with which Reagan dealt "in a very gentle fashion," according to Buchanan, "is a conflict between what might be called the Right, which proceeds from Christian beliefs and values, and the counterculture, which proceeds out of secularist beliefs and values. Its manifestations can be seen in the move to equate homosexuality with normal heterosexual activity, tolerance of pornography, [the belief that] anything goes so long as it doesn't hurt another individual." Buchanan proudly observes that he comes "from the tradition that my great grandfathers tried to overthrow the

*I asked Buchanan what he thought of Farrakhan, and he was surprisingly generous. He said that Farrakhan was "part healthy and part unhealthy. He has turned the worst people in prisons away from crime, drugs, and alcohol, but what is bad about it is the hatred of Whites. Conversion is important, however, and both Farrakhan and [Charles] Colson believe in it." (Patrick J. Buchanan, interview by author.)

government of the United States. . . . The idea of standing up to an establishment is a great tradition."

To Buchanan, the "establishment" is the same radical-thinking and socialist-inspired monolith that destroyed Nixon and McCarthy. Its institutions, like the pro-contra, pro-MX missile *Washington Post*, appear to him as "the untethered attack dog of the American left." Congress, to Buchanan, is guilty of "complicity in permitting the enemies of the U.S. to consolidate a military beachhead on the mainland of North America." Buchanan delights in upsetting the sensibilities of respectable Washington by championing the cause of accused Nazi war criminals and paying no heed to the sensitivities of the American Jewish establishment. Some of the Nazis, he claims, may be innocent. Others may not be. But, Buchanan insists, "There is political cowardice so thick you can cut it with a knife. If these guys were accused of being communist spies on behalf of the Soviet Union in World War II, you wouldn't have to ask me, there would be ten thousand reporters working on their behalf demanding a hearing."*

Add to this strange mixture of intolerance and good-heartedness, of religious certitude and political savvy, of blind idolatry of anti-Communism and Catholic conservatism a street fighter expelled from Georgetown University for punching out two D.C. policemen, and you have an enormously effective spokesman for a radical, reactionary minority. Buchanan imagines that he speaks for approximately one-third of the country, "people to the Right of Ronald Reagan."

The triumph of Buchanan over Buckley as the unadulterated voice of the conservative movement is a significant one. While the political philosophies expressed by the two men were quite similar, their cultural differences spoke volumes about the transformation of American politics between the late 1950s and the early 1980s, and about the changes in the role of the punditocracy. Buckley, the grandson of a Texas sheriff, was a self-styled aristocrat. Although he hoped to reconfigure and repopulate the important elite institutions in America, his bottom line was protecting the privileges of the privileged. The movement Buckley headed was as

---

*The "attack dog" quote, given to a rally of the faithful in Lafayette Park across the street from the White House, is reprinted in *Newsweek*, 19 January 1987, p. 18. The "Congress" quote comes from Patrick J. Buchanan, "Whom Will History Indict?" *Newsweek*, 7 July 1987, p. 21. The "Nazi" quote is from the author's interview. I am deliberately avoiding the question of whether Buchanan's thirst for combat with the Jewish establishment crosses over into anti-Semitism because the issue is too complex and too sensitive to do justice to in this context and has, in any case, been the subject of oceans of verbiage already. For the record, I have discussed the issue at some length in the 5 November 1990 issue of the *Nation* and generally find persuasive William Buckley's far longer dissection of it in his essay on anti-Semitism in the 30 December 1991 *National Review*, later published as *In Search of Anti-Semitism* (1992).

much about skiing in Gstaad or yachting in the Caribbean as killing Commies. Buchanan's politics, however, were steeped in the cultural resentment of the New Right. The working-class Catholic boys of Washington's Gonzaga High School were not recruited by Yale and could not have afforded the tuition anyway. Buchanan's conservative movement was not about teaching the liberals at Yale to repent; it was about dynamiting the place to kingdom come. It was an angrier, less sophisticated movement than Buckley's, but one that had learned the lessons of mass political organizing and political intimidation from its enemies in the antiwar, feminist, and civil rights movements. It was a movement, moreover, whose spokesman in the punditocracy participated in politics not at its periphery, as Buckley had, but at its center, literally displacing the politicians whom Buckley had sought only to influence.

Sociologically speaking, the most interesting member of the McLaughlin roundtable was *New Republic* senior editor Morton Kondracke. Like Novak, Kondracke grew up in Joliet, Illinois. He earned his spot on *The McLaughlin Group* after a career as a straight reporter of moderately liberal leanings at the *Chicago Sun-Times* before being hired by *The New Republic* in the mid-1970s. On *The McLaughlin Group,* however, under pressure from his fellow Jolietite, Kondracke soon began to change his stripes. On issue after issue, he developed greater sympathy for the line of reasoning coming out of the Reagan White House. Instead of fighting back when Novak would impugn his manhood on the issue of this or that proposed nuclear attack somewhere, Kondracke would insist that he could be every bit as mean and nasty as his tormentor. Just point out the enemy, and Kondracke, too, would support the funds for others to fight and die for the cause.

The easiest explanation for Kondracke's shift across the spectrum was simple gullibility. Despite his veneer of insider sophistication, the man was a journalistic yokel. His hero in life had been James Reston, whose photograph he carried around in his wallet for a brief time. Like Reston, Kondracke generally believed what his sources inside the government were telling him. But while Reston may have been a bit easy to mislead, he was at least dealing with a group of men whom he knew extremely well and about whose characters he could form independent judgments. Kondracke seemed incapable of distinguishing the lies and the liars. During the Carter years, it was the liberals who were doing the lying, and so he was a liberal. During the Reagan years, he became a conservative.

In the new era, Kondracke saw in Reagan a man who had "cast a kind of golden glow over the past four and a half years," his programs representing a return to bedrock American values and optimism, shielding the country from bitter realities such as burdensome debt, social inequity, and international challenge. "Reagan," Kondracke wrote, "is a kind of magic totem against the cold future." When Kondracke's "magic totem" was later revealed to have sold weapons to the Ayatollah and lied about it while funneling the profits to illegally arm the contras in Nicaragua, Kondracke was reluctant to give the story much weight. "As scandals go," he wrote, "the Iran mess wasn't much . . . the Administration did wrong but in defensible causes."* Kondracke did admit that Reagan's decline restored what he called "the reality principle." "He has been a good leader and a political genius," said the critic who Buchanan called his "left-wing comrade," and "he was on the right track for his time. . . . But he is, after all, an ordinary mortal in need of criticism. It's good to know that, but the truth still hurts."†

Unlike the rest of the group, who would revel in argument like pigs in a manure pile, Kondracke seemed adrift when asked to think on his feet. Sometimes this led him to positions that were entirely nonsensical, even by the considerable standards of *The McLaughlin Group.* When McLaughlin made the prediction that Mikhail Gorbachev's politics would turn out to be similar to those of Olaf Palme, the late Social Democratic leader of Sweden, Kondracke replied, "Yeah, what happened to Palme? He got shot." Did Kondracke mean to imply that Palme was shot for his political views? Was he saying that Gorbachev faced similar dangers to those faced by the president of one of the world's wealthiest, most stable democracies on his way home from the movies? When I asked him, he had no idea.

Like many apostate liberals, Kondracke dates his loss of faith from the Vietnam War. Kondracke explains that the "arrogance of the journalistic profession reached its height" with the Tet Offensive. "The same people who are now heroes, Halberstam, Sheehan, they should have written the goddam story and just shut up about whatever the solution was. They stopped being reporters and started being pundits . . . and they killed Diem."‡ The quote is instructive. Ngo Dinh Diem was killed by his own troops with no objections from the American embassy in 1963. Halber-

---

*Kondracke later retracted this. (Morton Kondracke, interview by author.)
†The first half of the quotation appears in Fallows, "Washington's New Celebrities." The Iran-Contra quotes come from Morton Kondracke, "Reagan Stumbles and Can't Recover—A Sad Spectacle," *Los Angeles Times,* 15 January 1987, pt. 2, p. 5. Note: When the scandal initially broke and McLaughlin surveyed his panelists about whether they believed Ronald Reagan knew about the transfer, Kondracke replied, "I hope he didn't know." Pressed after his evasion, Kondracke replied, "If he did know, he's a liar. . . . I'll say he didn't know." This segment was rebroadcast on McLaughlin's five-hundredth-show anniversary, 13 October 1991.
‡Halberstam calls Kondracke's quote "ridiculous. We were reporters for print organizations and we were going against the conventional wisdom of the time. It was real reporting. Mort is dumb and lazy and this kind of reporting is alien to him. Perhaps one day Kondracke will write a book as brilliant as Neil Sheehan's *A Bright Shining Lie* but I doubt it." Regarding Kondracke's assertion that the reporters "killed Diem," Halberstam notes, "I doubt Morton would be willing to say that to my face." David Halberstam, interview by author.

stam and Sheehan undertook some of the most distinguished reporting in the history of the profession, forcing John Kennedy to exclaim at one point, "Why can I get this stuff from Halberstam when I can't get it from my own people?" One need not be a Freudian psychiatrist to wonder what motivates a comfortable, well-remunerated Washington pundit to blame heroic war reporting for "killing" the president of South Vietnam.*

In addition to his duties at the *New Republic* and *The McLaughlin Group*, during the 1980s Kondracke was also a frequent guest commentator on *This Week with David Brinkley* and the sole host and interviewer on PBS's weekly foreign policy show, *American Interests*. (The latter is funded by counter-establishment cash deriving from the far-right Olin and Smith-Richardson foundations, along with the Maytag Corporation.) He was a triweekly columnist for the *Wall Street Journal* and, later, the Washington bureau chief of *Newsweek*. (The latter job did not work out as Kondracke assumed; one of the prerogatives of his job was to assign reporters to research his children's homework assignments.) Early in the 1990s, he was kicked off the *New Republic*'s masthead and forced to decamp to *Roll Call*, a Capitol Hill weekly. Later in the decade, he moved with Barnes to Fox News Channel, where the two were given their own show, called *The Beltway Boys*.

One searches in vain for an explanation as to exactly what professional quality propelled Kondracke to his exalted status within the punditocracy. He is not an engaging sitcom character like Buchanan, a likable buffoon like McLaughlin, or an easily hatable Novakian villain. Unlike Will, who has made a career of being a know-it-all, Kondracke plays the part of a man without a clue. Neal Freeman, the producer of *American Interests*, says he chose Kondracke to be the host because, "Mort is conducting his education in public," and on television, "that earnestness comes through."

What Freeman is saying but would never admit is that the Kondracke persona is effective explicitly because of its owner's mediocrity as both a thinker and a reporter. Why did Richard Nixon choose Kondracke as the sole interviewer for his May 1990 comeback interview? Was Nixon worried about the tough going-over he might receive from Kondracke, or was he confident that he would receive questions like "How do you feel toward [George Bush]? Do you feel toward him as though he's your kid brother . . . ?" Might the man Kondracke called a "rehabilitated senior statesman" have been in the market for a journalist willing to ask him if he had yet made peace with "the enemies who brought down his presi-

*The irony thickens when one recalls that both Halberstam and Sheehan were forced to hide out in the home of the U.S. embassy press attaché because of death threats from Diem's security forces. See William Prochnau, "Halberstam's War," *Gannett Center Journal* (Fall 1989): pp. 25, 28.

dency: the liberals, the media, and the bureaucrats" while leaving out Nixon's most important enemy, the United States Constitution? How about an interviewer who is willing to assert, offering no proof whatsoever, that "it has been fairly established that anything your administration did during Watergate had been done by the Johnson administration and by the Kennedy administration," and then follow it up with "Why do you think the system conspired to get you?"

With Hugh Sidey getting on in years, the system needs a reporter who is wholly incapable of embarrassment when prostrating himself before whatever powers might happen to be. The value of this kind of "reporting" and "analysis" is obvious from the perspective of Nixon and the others who sit under the glaring light of Kondracke's grueling technique. But why do editors and producers seek him out? What lies at the bottom of what John Gregory Dunne would call the "Krondrackoid" phenomenon? Herein lies the true mystery.

One of the few—if not the only—lasting contributions Ayn Rand made to the history of literature was her creation of the character Lancelot Clokey in her novel *The Fountainhead*. Clokey was the author of *The Gallant Gallstone* and, according to the town's most powerful critic, Elsworth Toohey, "a worse piece of trash was never put down on paper." But Toohey and his equally cynical and manipulative critic friends praised *The Gallant Gallstone* to the sky in their newspaper columns because they believed that "the little people" needed role models like themselves to continue to justify their small-minded, bourgeois lifestyles. Soon, two hundred thousand copies had been sold and *Gallstone* was on the lips of all the town's glitterati. Clokey, "a total nonentity who'd done nothing more outstanding than eating, sleeping, and chatting with neighbors," soon lost all perspective and began, quite understandably, to believe that he actually was a brilliant social critic and public philosopher. Like the Clokey-reading public, he was deluded, but he was happy. But Rand completed *The Fountainhead* in 1943, and so Clokey never made it on *The McLaughlin Group*.

After Robert Novak left to form *The Capital Gang* on CNN in 1988, McLaughlin added *Newsweek* reporter Eleanor Clift, Chicago columnist Clarence Page, and *New Republic* White House reporter Fred Barnes to the lineup. Clift and Page, both engaging and attractive personalities with mildly liberal politics, helped McLaughlin answer the frequent criticism that the show ignored women and blacks. Barnes, a preppy, pro-Bush Republican, melded perfectly with the group's collective persona. When asked by McLaughlin whether he could discuss silicon breast implants "with authority," he replied—perfectly straight-faced—"I can speak to almost anything with a lot of authority." He now does so each week to the Fox News Channel's tiny audience with Kondracke.

Baltimore Sun veteran Jack Germond rounded out the group, rolling his eyes upward and gently subverting the gravitas with which the others called for an immediate declaration of war over this outrage against the common decency or that insult to all Americans. Germond played along with the rest of the boys when the subject was politics. He remains the kind of reporter Novak once was, devoting himself to the minutiae of the political system. Germond's distaste for ideological politics, coupled with Kondracke's conversion, has allowed the others to cast him as "the liberal" in the discussion, when in fact he is no such thing. Germond is a pure pragmatist. He may have some sympathy for old-style liberal programs, but he is much more likely to look at things as they are and say "Why?" than to look at them as they never were and say "Why not?" He also left the show in the late 1990s, apparently no longer able to bear its host.

The value of casting an apolitical fixer as the show's liberal during the Reagan era was considerable, as it severed the legs of any truly liberal alternative without further discussion. Few developments were more helpful to Ronald Reagan's effort to de-legitimize liberal solutions to America's problems than the growth of conservative-dominated television punditocracy. With Novak, Buchanan, and later Barnes attacking from the Right, and Kondracke agreeing from the so-called Left, Ronald Reagan's brand of genial reaction came to appear downright reasonable. Centrist solutions became liberal by virtue of the show's skewed political geography, and truly liberal ideas were marginalized entirely.

Unapologetic liberals were occasionally trotted out as guests, but they often sounded as if they were filing from another planet. What reasoned reply can be offered to a panel member who insisted that black teenagers were unemployed because "these kids don't want to work," or that the only way to deal with Muammar Khadaffi was to "slit his throat with no fingerprints," or that the reason the National Organization for Women differed so strongly with the administration was because the group was "twenty-five percent lesbian"? To even engage these issues on such far-out ideological territory is to admit defeat. Christopher Hitchens, columnist for the *Nation* and Socialist bon vivant, managed one McLaughlin invitation. Seconds before the show ended, Novak referred to Cuban drug runners as Hitchens' "friends." (Hitchens later retorted by calling Novak a "polecat" and a "McCarthyite bum" on *Crossfire*.) When historians one day seek to understand how George Bush and Lee Atwater succeeded in making "liberalism" a dirty political word in 1988, they will need to look no further than the tapes of five upper-middle-class white guys sitting around a television studio talking about how black families "are just going to have to stop relying on government and politics to solve [their] problems."

In addition to its decimating effects on liberal participation in the insider dialogue, one of the most damaging legacies of *The McLaughlin Group* was its implied notion that any idea, no matter how complex or enormous, could be boiled down to a yes-or-no question or a letter grade on a sliding scale. On one show, McLaughlin asked his fellow panelists to give "a grade on the planet Earth." McLaughlin gave it a "B," and I quote his justification in its entirety: "overcoming nationalism and a general spirit of internationalism."

As was frequently the case, his response was rather thick with irony. Of all the offenses that can be laid at the feet of McLaughlin and the politics that he and the group represent, the most galling is their smug ethnocentrism and paternalistic hubris. On the very same show in which McLaughlin gave his generous grading to the planet and the century for its "internationalism," group members had gone on record voicing some of the most distasteful xenophobic statements ever heard in punditocracy debates. We learned from Fred Barnes that "The United States is the center of the world. . . . All the smart people and entrepreneurs are winding up in the U.S." Morton Kondracke observed that "the more we know about the Japanese ways of living and Chinese and Korean, the less we like them. I mean, they're rigid, they're nasty, you know, they're still Confucian and all that." These statements recalled a CNBC "McLaughlin" show in which the host flew into an uncontrollable fury over the refusal of the president of Mexico to speak English on his program. While discussing the subject of bilingualism with Hispanic politician Linda Chavez, McLaughlin became suddenly enraged by the fact that two presidents of Mexico had been graciously invited to be interviewed by McLaughlin and both proceeded to speak in their native language. Their insistence, he raged, necessitated an "elaborate simultaneous translation which is a yawn as far as the audience is concerned." "When are they going to get into the twentieth century down there?" he demanded of his befuddled guest. "When is someone going to show some leadership and say to the Mexicans, 'Look, it's good for us that I speak English.' . . . Somebody should tell the president of Mexico that when he appears on American television, he should speak English."

Perhaps the most intriguing fact about John McLaughlin was his own self-awareness. During one hectic afternoon when all of Washington seemed to be calling, McLaughlin explained himself. His assistant Kara Swisher asked him, "Why do so many people kowtow to you?" McLaughlin "got down really low on his desk, almost like he was a lizard," recalls

Swisher, looked up at her, and replied, "They're all whores. Every one of them, they're all whores. And so am I. But I've got the TV show."

The main change during the 1990s in the world of what Calvin Trillin calls "the Sabbath gasbags" was the enormous increase in the degree of cutthroat competition among them. Because of the healthy demographics of the respective audiences of these Sunday shows, advertisers were willing to pay premium prices for their relatively meager audiences. It was therefore crucial to all the networks to try to keep these shows as lively as possible. Yet because of the size of the egos involved, as well as the natural caution exhibited by network executives when dealing with age-old institutions, change came slowly and painfully.

At ABC, the avuncular but increasingly baffled David Brinkley was not-so-gently forced from the perch he occupied for so many years as host of *This Week with David Brinkley*. The transition was anything but smooth. Brinkley chafed at being put out to pasture before he made his own decision to retire. He soon signed a contract with Archer-Daniels-Midland—the much-indicted agribusiness giant that underwrote the show—to act as its pitchman on special commercials made explicitly for his former show. These commercials had the effect of unleashing a veritable firestorm of criticism on Brinkley, who was roundly accused of prostituting his decades of hard-earned journalistic credibility and attempting to confuse his former audience to boot.

Moreover, while the show certainly had plenty of time to prepare itself for the end of Brinkley's career as host, evidence of advance preparation was hard to find in the aftermath. At first the show's producer could not decide on a new name. The two new hosts, Sam Donaldson and Cokie Roberts, were badly mismatched. Roberts, smooth as silk, was nonplussed by everything. Donaldson, however, wearing a bad wig, losing more than a step intellectually as he passed seventy, and obnoxious in the first place, seemed at times willing to sabotage his colleagues' conversation if they did not pay sufficiently respectful attention to whatever he thought he was saying. Donaldson's antics had the effect of undermining the considerable strengths of his co-panelists. After his departure from the Clinton administration, George Stephanopoulos had given a gentle tap on the politician/pundit revolving door and joined William Kristol, who had gone through the same door a few years earlier after his tenure as Vice-President Dan Quayle's chief of staff. George Will, who had been occupying the seat for nearly two decades, had traveled though the same portal, although from a much less exalted level on the governmental ship. These three commentators were as intelligent as anyone appearing regularly on television, and Stephanopoulos effectively stretched the network's reigning definition of acceptable liberal ever so slightly toward where it had once been. Again, however, during the punditocracy portion of the show, these three had a hard time making themselves understood under the constant hectoring of Donaldson and the occasional tut-tutting of Cokie Roberts. Although the Sunday shows retained their agenda-setting function for the rest of the week, ABC's *This Week* achieved this primarily by attempting to draw their guests into making newsworthy statements, rather than through the quality of their pundits' analysis.

The chaos at the post-Brinkley *This Week* left Sunday open to a new dominating force, and the vacuum was soon filled by a re-energized *Meet the Press* under the guidance of the grisly, hard-working NBC News Washington bureau chief Tim Russert. Russert entered the punditocracy just as Stephanopoulos, Will, and Kristol had—through the political revolving door. Before becoming king of Sunday morning, Russert had been an adviser to senior New York Democrats Governor Mario Cuomo and Senator Daniel Patrick Moynihan. Russert's career as a pundit was based on a combination of his abilities as reporter, interviewer, and commentator. A powerful personality, he dominated his show to a degree that no other host could, save, perhaps, Ted Koppel, who filled only one of these roles. While *Meet the Press* became by far the most important of the Sunday gabfests in the 1990s, it also fell victim to Russert's desire to chase celebrity newsmakers regardless of the quality of their alleged expertise. On separate occasions, therefore, he debased the quality of insider discourse by inviting into it the right-wing blowhard Rush Limbaugh as a commentator, rather than an object of curiosity; the nefarious cyber-gossip, Matt Drudge, for the same reasons; and the hate-mongering, anti-Semite Louis Farrakhan as a newsmaking guest, although in the absence of any Farrakhan-related news.

The quality of debate can be seen most clearly on *The McLaughlin Group,* where, during the final minutes of one show in June 1998, the host decided to focus the group's attention on what he had determined to be the problem of contemporary American culture: men being regarded as "inseminating instruments, superfluous after that." Another show, this one in April 1998, focused on the release of the sexual dysfunction drug Viagra. Fred Barnes called the new pill, "the greatest thing for trophy wives since joint banking accounts . . . [but] bad for gigolos." McLaughlin opined that the hope of better sex would inspire Americans to work out more, and surprised his copanelists with the argument that frequent ejaculation leads to a healthy prostate.

Over at *The Capital Gang*, former McLaughlinite Robert Novak made a strange and costly foray into black politics late in the decade. During President Clinton's trip to Africa, Novak insisted that many black Americans should be grateful for the fact of slavery because "African-Americans in government, in business, in athletics, in show business" would not be Americans without the slave trade. The following week, however, Novak was forced to apologize and pronounce slavery an "unmitigated evil." He went so far as to insist that his original quotation was merely intended to explain that "our society was enriched by African-Americans." During this period Novak also embraced to his bosom the racist, anti-Semitic demagogue Louis Farrakhan. Like the black Muslim preacher himself, Novak blamed Farrakhan's unpopularity on the Jews. "He is viewed with such loathing by the Jewish community that any effort to talk to him to pursue racial harmony is prohibited. A lot of what Farrakhan is saying echoes the Republican philosophy. He was knocking on the door, and no one would answer," complained Novak, soon to convert from Judaism to Catholicism.

The rest of the old-line Sunday lineup featured the also-ran *Face the Nation* on CBS and the upstart *Fox News Sunday* on Rupert Murdoch's network. Neither made much of an impact on punditocracy debate save for those moments in which one of either show's guests made a newsworthy comment. This proved rare, however, because both shows were forced to bottomfeed from the list of guests who were not desired by either *Meet the Press* or *This Week*. Of these two, Fox's show, hosted by former Bush speechwriter Tony Snow, skewed rightward, as did all of Murdoch's media properties. CBS remained in its responsible, inside-the-Beltway, hard-news mode on *Face the Nation*.

The rest of the Sunday schedule was dominated by a gaggle of shows, including a Sunday version of CNN's *The Capital Gang*; *Reliable Sources*, also on CNN; and Kondracke and Barnes' show, *The Beltway Boys*, which they formed after leaving McLaughlin for more Murdoch money. These shows were reinforced throughout the week by any number of programs that appeared every night on the various cable networks: *Crossfire, Politics Today, Larry King Live, Geraldo, Hardball with Chris Matthews, Imus in the Morning, The Big Show with Keith Olbermann* (later replaced by yet another McLaughlin-hosted show and a version of *Equal Time* featuring Oliver North), *Watch It with Laura Ingram, Hanitty and Colmes, The Drudge Report,* and *Special Report with Brit Hume,* augmented by the daily broadcasts of *Nightline* on ABC, *The NewsHour with Jim Lehrer,* and *The Charlie Rose Show.* Given all these options, a crazed pundit fan could watch all pundits virtually all the time.

As with professional sports, the rapid expansion of the number of teams playing did not do much to improve the quality of play. As *Time* magazine essayist and regular *Capital Gang* panelist Margaret Carlson noted, "the less you know about something, the better off you are. What's good TV and what's thoughtful analysis are different. That's been conceded by most producers and bookers. They're looking for the person who can sound learned without confusing the matter with too much knowledge. I'm one of the people without too much knowledge. I'm perfect."

CHAPTER SIX

All the Views Fit to Print

Heartless and dumb"; "vicious and unbelievable"; "scathing and cruel." These are the adjectives Nancy Reagan chose to describe, not her biographer Kitty Kelley, but *New York Times* super-pundit William Safire.* In his March 2, 1987, column, when Nancy was still in charge of the White House and riding high in the punditocracy, Safire pounced on the First Lady for making her husband "appear wimpish and helpless." Complaining of her "political interference," Safire accused Mrs. Reagan of "extraordinary vindictiveness" and called her "power-hungry" and "an incipient Edith Wilson, unelected and unaccountable, presuming to control the actions and appointments of the executive branch."

Safire's attack on Nancy Reagan was the stuff of Washington legend. Not only did a perceived presidential ally go after the one sacred personage in Reagan's White House, but he challenged conventional wisdom in doing so. It was Nancy, after all, who had just engineered the replacement of evil, incompetent chief of staff Don Regan with likable, effective Howard Baker, thereby allowing the president to cut his Iran-Contra losses and save Washington from much hand-wringing about whether to consider impeachment. A close personal friend to not only George Will but also Katharine Graham and the late Meg Greenfield,

---

*Ever chivalrous, Ronald Reagan, said Nancy, felt Safire's column "was a terrible thing for a man to do to another man's wife." See Reagan, *My Turn*, pp. 333–34.

Nancy Reagan had overcome her early public relations difficulties and blossomed into insider Washington's local hero, maneuvering to try to win her husband the Nobel Peace Prize and perhaps prevent nuclear war as an unintended bonus. Moreover, immediately after that morning's blitzkrieg, Safire refused all television invitations in which he had been asked to discuss his column. The latter move was, if anything, even more shocking than the column itself.

Word for word, William Safire is probably the most influential print reporter in Washington. Any number of writers could have given voice to nasty accusations about Nancy Reagan's behavior, and quite a few had the power and influence to wound the First Lady mortally if they got the inkling. William Safire, however, was the only pundit in Washington who not only could do it, but would. Amazingly, he did nearly the same thing to another president's wife, Hillary Clinton, by calling her a "congenital liar." President Clinton's spokesperson averred that the president wanted to punch the pundit in the mouth. But he didn't. Safire had far more friends in Washington than Clinton did. Well-connected, principled, extremely hawkish, and politically fearless, William Safire was, like Lippmann, an institution unto himself.

The name *Safire* (originally spelled Safir, but too often mispronounced "Say-fur" and since changed) derives from the Yiddish *soifer,* meaning "scribe." The power to make the Nancy Reagans of the world livid derives less from Safire's reputation as a *soifer* than as a *macher.* The journalese translation of *macher* is "bigfoot": the kind of writer who political Washington regards as able to leave footprints on the issues he covers. Some journalists confess to liking this power. None exercises it with greater frequency than William Safire.

Appearing twice weekly on the op-ed page of the *New York Times,* Safire was the only cleanup hitter in the Reagan-era punditocracy whose homerun swing rested solely on the power of his reporting and the force of his argument. Alone among the punditocracy's high-rollers, he did no regular television. Although he attended his share of dinner parties, he was never accused of trading on his friendships. In fact, some of Safire's toughest attacks were reserved for those with whom he had the longest histories. Not only Nancy Reagan, but United States Information Agency (USIA) Director Charles Z. Wick, Attorney General William French Smith, Reagan adviser turned influence peddler Michael Deaver, and former friend and business partner CIA Director William Casey all came under the Safire scalpel during the Reagan years and emerged considerably worse for the operation. When Casey experienced a fatal cerebral hemorrhage on the day that Safire had accused him of being "corrupted by power and secrecy" (despite the fact that Casey had called him three times on a Sunday to try to ask him not to do it), a mutual acquaintance called the pundit and told him not to worry: Casey's seizure came "at least an hour" after reading the column.*

The *New York Times* is credited with having invented the modern op-ed page, but this is only partially true. In September 1970, after much institutional soul-searching, then–editorial page editor John Oakes and publisher Punch Sulzberger decided to clear out the old obituary page and make room for an expanded opinion section to "afford greater opportunity for exploration of issues, and presentation of new insights and new ideas by writers and thinkers with no institutional connection with the *Times*." The innovation was a subtle one. Although the first op-ed page began with Frank Cobb and Herbert Swope at the *World* in the early 1920s, its opinions rarely conflicted with those of the publisher. Non-staff editorials had also been running on the editorial page of the *New York Herald Tribune* for years before it folded in April 1966, but these, too, rarely disagreed with the newspaper's editorial policy and were published on a largely ad hoc basis. What Oakes and Sulzberger invented was the notion of a separate page pairing guest editorials, some contrary to the paper's own editorials, with its regular rotating columnists on a daily basis. Edited initially by Harrison Salisbury, the page inspired many imitators and soon developed into the most prestigious print forum available anywhere.

Although the *Times* remained the world's most influential newspaper by virtue of its readership and the thoroughness of its coverage, in the decade that Reaganism ruled Washington, Safire's column constituted pretty much the sum total of all of the *New York Times'* op-ed page insider influence. The paper's unsigned editorials across the fold carried virtually no weight among insiders until Howell Raines took over the page in the mid-1990s and used it as a forum from which to assault Bill Clinton and defend Kenneth Starr. The guest spots on the op-ed page remained the zenith of the now crowded op-ed page field, but such contributions rarely had much lasting effect. For reasons geographical, stylistic, political, and journalistic, no other regular *Times* columnist enjoyed a fraction of Safire's regularly deployable power, and none was an important player on the insider battleground, where the wars of the Reagan years were fought.

*Safire confessed to "pulling his punches" a little as a result of the calls. See Eleanor Randolph, "William Safire, Right to the Core: The Columnist and His Novel Look at Abraham Lincoln," *Washington Post*, 24 August 1987, Style section, p. 1.

The exile of Safire's op-ed page colleagues at the *Times* from the din-ner tables and policy planning sessions of Ronald Reagan's Washington was apparent almost immediately after Reagan's election. James Reston, approaching his fourth decade as a columnist, was initially put off by the oversimplifications and chauvinism of the Reagan campaign. He worried on the day after the victory that "it had not clarified the nation's prob-lems, but deepened them, not unified the people but divided them." By the following Monday, however, the forces within Reston that sent him like a homing pigeon to the center of debate—regardless of how far over to the Right that center had moved—were already working their way through his typing fingers. Reston latched onto Reagan's superficial rhe-torical nod in the direction of a "bipartisan foreign policy," celebrating the fact that "in the foreign policy field, he has indicated quite clearly that he wants a national partnership." The basis on which such a partner-ship might be forged did not concern Reston as much as the partnership itself. "It has long been recognized here that there is a difference between campaign rhetoric and the more realistic policies that follow an election," he wrote. In other words, like much of what remained of the old establishment, Reston was willing to embrace Reagan as long as he vowed not to act on any of the foolish promises he had made during the campaign. When it became clear that Reagan truly meant what he had been saying—that he really did intend to try to translate his anti-Soviet rhetoric into policy, to fight a few proxy wars regardless of their constitu-tionality, and to gamble the nation's economic future on his untested the-ories, Reston lost his intellectual footing. He remained with Safire at the *Times*' Washington bureau and filed his column for much of the next decade, but he lost most of his clout.

Of the other three political columnists who surrounded Safire on the *Times* op-ed page in this era, none wrote regularly from Washington, and none made much of an impact on the formation of insider opinion. Flora Lewis, the first woman to be given her own column on the page, filed from Paris what was quite possibly the most boring regular column in the history of journalism. It certainly contained no hint that it had been written by a woman. Lewis wrote like Reston, but without his charm, his history, or the implicit indulgence on the part of the reader he inspired. Her gray, leaden prose had a deadening effect on the reader to a point at which it was often a challenge to wade deep enough into her column to determine what her point might be. When the *New Repub-lic* held a "world's most boring headline" contest, its inspiration was a Lewis column entitled "Worthwhile Canadian Initiative," and the editors did not even catch her on a particularly boring day. Shot through with cautious, carefully weighted *Times*-style centrism, Lewis' soul was at one with the Council on Foreign Relations, which she somehow considered to be a beleaguered organization, under threat from "isolationism, know-nothingism and freaky suspicion."* Without being unnecessarily unkind about a person with sound instincts and sensible political judgments, one might say that Lewis was to columnists what Michael Dukakis was to presidential candidates.

The two liberals on the page, Tom Wicker and Anthony Lewis, who had appeared so important during the brief late–Vietnam era interregnum, also entered the decade on a collision course with insider irrelevance. Wicker, whom Reston had groomed to replace him as Washington bureau chief, ran out of steam during the late 1970s. Like his mentor, he kept pitching too long after his curveball started to hang. Wicker greeted Reagan's election by pointing out the intellectual and ideological inconsistencies in the candidate's record and waited patiently for the common sense of the American people to prevail. On the major issues that dominated the Washington debate during the 1980s until his retirement at the end of 1991, Wicker was predictably pacific, tolerant, and racially sensitive. While these qualities make for a fine human being, they were not enough to power interesting columns. "I think after Vietnam people just got tired," he explained in an interview, speaking of his colleagues, and inadvertently of himself. By the early 1990s, when he finally retired, Wicker's presence had already become invisible.

In the case of Anthony Lewis, insider irrelevance was a clearly defined political and intellectual choice. Lewis had never had any intention of being a Washington pundit. He spoke throughout the 1980s as the voice of disinterested morality, of the Constitution, and of the victims of American foreign policy. While he did not have occasion to use the prophetic rage he employed during the Christmas bombings of 1972, Lewis still has enough fire in his belly to light up a corner of the *Times* op-ed page with the kind of political passion that, for most of the Reagan era, was roped off in Washington at marches and rallies.

Michael Kinsley, a liberal who did become quite influential, said he admired Lewis for choosing not to be. "He is not a Washington journalist on purpose," notes Kinsley. "He wasn't marginalized by anybody else. Tony speaks for liberals who want to be told about how they feel about things. And his views percolate back." By refusing to countenance the assumptions of Reagan and Bush rhetoric, Lewis willfully forfeited what-

---

*For some reason, in December 1989 Lewis felt compelled to defend the council from an attack by the nearly moribund John Birch Society. Her final sentence could, in truth, be attached to any one of her columns, regardless of subject: "There has scarcely been a time when American interests more urgently needed the sober, informed thought about foreign affairs the Council promotes." Flora Lewis, 13 December 1989.

ever direct influence over policy his influential perch in the *Times* might have accorded him. Instead, he played the role ostensibly mapped out in the 1920s by Walter Lippmann: to educate the public in the hope that they would make more intelligent choices about their leaders.

An intense conversationalist with an easygoing manner and an unwieldy curly pate, Lewis laughs at the notion that he is the most radical of left-wing political commentators in the American mainstream. "It's absolutely hilarious to me," he admits. "I mean, I'm a pro-capitalist, middle-of-the-road, tepid centrist. I mean, is it Left to insist that presidents and CIA directors adhere to the law? I don't think so. I think it's American." Indeed, for all his commitment to human rights and conflict avoidance, Lewis never called into question the fundamental precepts of the American establishment during the Cold War, except to denounce what he viewed as the self-destructive manner in which the conflict was conducted. He thinks it unfair to expect an organization like the *Times* or the *Post* to reflect anything but the view of the establishment. "All of the people we're talking about," he notes, "are upper-middle-class and establishment figures who tend to share in the selfishness that afflicts the political system. . . . It is hard to escape the economic structure that you live in, and we're not radical in nature. We're not like some outsider journalists in some Third World country. We are part of the system."

Safire, meanwhile, was less a part of the system than his own mini-system mucking up the larger one. He began the Reagan era triumphant. "The silent majority, like a great soaking-wet shaggy dog [or a once-ostracized political columnist], banished from the house during the Watergate storms," he announced two days after the 1980 election, "romped back into the nation's parlor and shook itself vigorously." Safire graded Reagan's inaugural address "a respectable seven," one point below the address he had helped write for Richard Nixon in 1969 but one point above the address he had pounded out in 1973. That Safire could, by 1980, recover from Nixon and the innumerable strikes against him and develop into not only a powerful pundit, but also a respected journalist was one of the most remarkable ironies of the making of the Reagan punditocracy.

After growing up fatherless and near poverty in New York and California, Safire won a scholarship to Syracuse University. After two years, however, during the summer of 1949, he landed a job with Tex McCrary and Jinx Falkenberg, whose many ventures included a personalities column for the *Herald Tribune*. Safire found that he enjoyed interviewing famous writers and politicians more than he did reading about them in school. The nineteen-year-old college dropout did not return to Syracuse until he gave the commencement address there almost forty years later.

Working for McCrary, Safire drifted into public relations work, for which he demonstrated a singular professional genius. At the 1959 American National Exhibition in Moscow, he achieved one of the biggest coups in advertising history when he maneuvered Vice-President Richard Nixon and Soviet Premier Nikita Khrushchev into his client's mock-kitchen for their historic "kitchen debate." Safire then blocked the exits so that the two blowhards would have to blow at each other and finally took the picture himself that ran on the Associated Press wires.

Safire quickly became a name in the public relations world, hiring eager young assistants like Barbara Walters and working for clients that ranged from Nelson Rockefeller to Ex-Lax. When the "new Nixon" ran for president in 1968, the increasingly conservative Safire went to work on selling the president. Hired as a speechwriter in the Nixon White House, Safire likes to joke that his real job was to walk into the empty Oval Office and call out, "Do the popular thing, Mr. President. Take the easy way out." Then he would walk back into his own cubbyhole and write into Nixon's speech, "My advisers counsel me to do the popular thing, to take the easy way out."

As a political wordsmith, Safire was a whiz, but he is best remembered as an accessory to the Nixon administration's crimes against the English language. By far the worst of these occurred when Spiro Agnew asked him for a colorful epithet for media gloomsters. Safire offered the incipient language felon a choice between "hopeless, hysterical hypochondriacs of history" and "nattering nabobs of negativism." Agnew chose both.

Safire's career hit bottom when, after retiring from the White House in 1973 to write a memoir of the Nixon years, he saw his president self-destruct and his massive memoir rejected by his publisher with a demand for the return of its advance. The book was eventually published, and when both the *Times* and the *Post* began beating on his doors with the request that he please say whatever he wished for their op-ed pages twice a week, his life began to take on a sunnier cast.[*]

"There was lots of outrage," recalled former *Times* editorial page editor Jack Rosenthal of Safire's hiring. "Not so much because he was a conservative voice in this temple of the eastern liberal establishment, but that he had been a hired gun for the Nixon administration. They thought he was just a shill." All of the *Times* editors polled advised the publisher against the move. As Safire recalls it, "When I walked through the city room of

[*]When Arthur Krock, the *New York Times'* conservative Washington columnist, began to falter in the mid-1960s, Punch Sulzberger attempted, unsuccessfully, to recruit William F. Buckley, Jr. When this proved unworkable for contractual reasons, the *Times* publishers waited more than seven years until Safire, an acceptable conservative, became available. (Harrison Salisbury, interview by author.)

the Washington bureau, silence fell. My new colleagues were unfailingly civil, a few even friendly, but my written opinions were ill-received; some *Times* reporters took pride in the paper's willingness to publish the unpopular views of 'a Nixon apologist,' but most felt the publisher had been suckered." Feelings were so strong that only one member of the Washington bureau, Safire's boyhood friend Martin Tolchin, would even eat lunch with him.

Life inside the office began to improve after a summer office party at which Safire ruined a good suit fishing a flailing child out of a swimming pool, but the column floundered. Safire had begun inauspiciously, accusing Nixon's critics of being McCarthyites and calling on the president to burn the White House tapes. At the end of his first two-year contract, Sulzberger summoned him to New York and told him it just wasn't working out. Unless the column improved, Safire would be out of work. "Bill had not learned to be a columnist yet," recalls his editor, Harrison Salisbury. "He was still writing like a PR flak for the Republican right wing." When Safire left the publisher's office, he was completely despondent. "He didn't want anything but to be a *New York Times* columnist," says Salisbury, "and he was blowing it." Safire went back to his office, sat down at his desk, put his head in his hands, and wondered how the hell he was going to save his job. Then he looked up and, lo and behold, saw his salvation: the telephone. Safire knew everybody in Washington and he knew how everything worked. So he made a few calls. Soon Washington had its most effective pundit in a generation.

Safire's influence as a pundit during the Reagan years derived from many sources. He combined far-right political principles with the distrust of the Far Right itself. He demonstrated an investigator's bloodlust for the powerful and arrogant, but blunted it with an admirable sense of humor and a felicitous sense of style. Throw in the fact that he happened to be writing in the most influential print organ in the world, and you have a pundit with unique credibility and respect across the political spectrum.

Safire has been feared by the German government, beloved by the Israelis, and viewed with affection but not trust by the conservatives during the past five American administrations. On the wall of his Chevy Chase home is a framed Safire column vigorously annotated by then-president George Bush. Washington political consultants read him the way swamis read tea leaves, grilling their candidates twice a week on Safire's pet issues and daily obsessions to head off the predictable Safire-inspired questions from the traveling press. Unlike most pundits who take a coach-tour attitude toward issues ("If this is Tuesday, it must be nuclear proliferation"), Safire has no qualms about returning day in and day out to the same subject if he thinks doing so will raise the hackles of those he suspects. Bert Lance lost his job this way, winning Safire a Pulitzer in the process. So, in some measure, did Jimmy Carter.

Perhaps most alarming from the perspective of his opponents, Safire was a wonderful writer, and in this respect was almost alone in the punditocracy for many years. While he may be the most feared and respected media presence in Washington, Safire is known to the majority of *Times* readers as the paper's Sunday language columnist, where his pieces draw an incredible eighteen thousand letters a year. An inveterate punster, he is responsible for a healthy percentage of the wit allowed to bypass the *Times*' Wit Police over the past two decades, as well as some of the worst puns in pundit history. Among those unearthed by Victor Navasky for an *Esquire* profile were porn-free, tongue in chic, radical-sheik, columny, pressycophants, trendustry, journafiction, ukasy char, Spock-marked generation, the President's populism and the First Lady's momulism, Peking-too-soon, Hizayatollah, sycophancy network, and Haigemony. The classic Safirism of all time appeared atop a column on Saudi Arabian oil minister Sheikh Ahmed Zaki Yamani. Safire called it "Yamani or Ya Life."

Not above making himself tremendously rich, Safire also gives speeches for astronomical fees. When questioned about his fee in his Century Club–like office in Washington, Safire pooh-poohs the money. His fee, he says, is based on what it costs him to park at the *Times*' garage on Washington's I Street. "Every time parking goes up a quarter," he explains, "my speaking fee rises a thousand bucks." Whatever the money goes toward, it certainly is not his wardrobe, which could double for that of some of the city's more sartorially careless plumbers.

If all the Washington news media shared Safire's love of combat, his intellectual seriousness, and a fraction of his wit and brilliance, this book would not be necessary. But because there is only one William Safire, his shortcomings are magnified within the punditocracy by the lack of any equally powerful opposition. The straight-jacketed rules of objective journalism exist because reporters are not trusted to leave their own personal and professional agendas out of the story they are covering. Columnists are exempt from these rules, excluding libel and slander laws, and are subject only to the sanctions of their papers and the value of their reputations. When the paper is the *Times*—which does not interfere at all with the content of its columnists' columns—and their reputations are as imposing as Safire's, the sanctions are strictly internal.

One problem with Safire is political. However engaging and talented the man may be, he has developed over the years into a political extremist by virtually every measure save that used within the Washington punditocracy. On occasion, this has tended to cloud his journalistic judgment.

Safire was thrilled with Reagan's first term, reveling in what he called its "years of stable growth" while either ignoring or failing to understand the long-term costs to the economy that precisely such a facade involved. At the heart of Safire's worldview, moreover, was the same impossibly myopic vision that gave the Soviets credit for everything deemed unpleasant by American right-wingers from Managua to Mars. Safire bought into Claire Sterling's misrepresentations of a fabricated "KGB/Bulgarian connection" to the Pope's attempted assassination and then misrepresented even Sterling's own specious claims. On a larger scale, he celebrated Reagan's Star Wars fantasy without ever addressing the question of its obvious technical limitations. He admitted to being "elated" over Reagan's "evil empire" rhetoric because this pointless posturing somehow "brought moral pressure to bear on international mischief-making in Afghanistan, Nicaragua, Angola, and the Middle East," as if Oliver North and his cronies were setting up nursing homes in those places.

The Reagan administration disappointed Safire precisely when it behaved most responsibly. Safire likened Reagan's belated effort to join Mikhail Gorbachev in winding down the Cold War to "the failing Roosevelt with 'Uncle Joe' Stalin at Yalta." He cried "appeasement" at the announcement of every negotiating success. On issues related to Israeli security, Safire was frequently holier than Jerusalem itself, often siding with the revanchist Ariel Sharon against the rest of the civilized world.[*]

Safire's ethics as a journalist also have been the subject of some speculation. Michael Kinsley called Safire a "bully with the soul of a PR man" when Safire beat up on the hapless USIA director Charles Z. Wick ("by all accounts, a jackass," said Kinsley) for tapping his phone calls without telling people. Kinsley then damned Safire for printing the contents of Wick's taped conversations, thereby vastly magnifying the invasion of pri-

---

[*]Safire's devotion to Israel has led to two of his most serious mistakes in the column. In 1981, when the Israelis destroyed Iraq's nuclear reactor, Safire quoted "Baghdad's official newspaper" as insisting that the reactor was "not intended to be used against Iran but against the Zionist enemy." The quotation, however, was an invention of the Israeli Foreign Ministry, and Safire was forced to issue a personalized correction at the bottom of a later column. More recently, in 1990, when a group of Israeli tourists were slain in Egypt, Safire wrote that the Palestinian Liberation Organization (PLO) had "condoned last week's slaughter of Israeli tourists in Egypt." Yet, according to four separate stories in the *Times* and the *Post*, PLO spokespeople had "denounced the attack," "strongly condemned the assault," "denounced the attack" (again), and "formally distanced itself from the assault." This time no corrections ran. See Victor Navasky, "Safire Appraised," *Esquire*, January 1982, p. 50, and William Safire, 12 February 1990. The PLO quotations noted above appeared in Joel Brinkley, "A Grieving Israel Pushes Politics Aside," *New York Times*, 6 February 1990; Allan Cowell, "Attack on Israelis Upsets Palestinians in Egypt," *New York Times*, 7 February 1990; Caryle Murphy, "Egypt Pledges to Pursue Talks," and Jackson Diehl, "Israel Postpones Peace Moves after Attack," both in the *Washington Post*, 6 February 1990, p. 16.

vacy that so upset the bigfoot pundit in the first place. Safire's series of patented insinuating interrogatories, imputing corrupt fund-raising practices to Wick (which were later picked up by Mary McGrory and the *Washington Post* editorial page) also peeved Kinsley, as they rested on what then appeared to be the slenderest shred of evidence. Wick survived the ensuing investigation with the help of a considerable number of $250 hours contributed by Washington superlawyer Leonard Garment—like Safire, a Nixonian who had managed to spin Watergate dross into Reaganite gold—but Kinsley pronounced Safire guilty of "misusing the power of his august office."* (The fact that Kinsley was defending the Reagan administration while Safire was bashing it goes some distance toward explaining why these two remain the most interesting pundits in Washington.)

Another problem with Safire's modus operandi is the liberties he grants himself with regard to the deployment of his own power. According to sources quoted in the *Washington Post,* Safire once had trouble getting then–Under Secretary of State William Clark to call him back. Furious, he allegedly told Caspar Weinberger that he was "going after" Clark, which he did—calling him "miscast," "inexperienced," and "a living example that still waters could run shallow." Safire calls the incident a "Rashomon thing," where many people have differing recollections of the same event. In another variation on the same theme, during the 1984 campaign Safire lobbed a verbal hand grenade at then–Vice-President George Bush for "ducking questions" and campaigning in a "media-free cocoon" when Bush declined to return Safire's call regarding the administration's position on the ill-fated merger of Libya and Morocco. The fact that the vice-president was en route from Paducah to Houston when Safire called did not impress the columnist. He told a staff member to have the vice-president use the Secret Service telephone at the bottom of the ramp and call him immediately after landing. "There is no doubt that not returning calls in my mind is evidence of being either fearful of calling back or contemptuous," argues Safire. "I don't buy that they're too busy."

Those are awfully imposing words for a mere columnist, but they are probably true. Few insiders doubt that William Safire is the most influential and respected pundit alive. When the point is made to Safire himself, he does not dispute it. During the opening days of the Bush administration, then–Chief of Staff John Sununu went through the elaborate charade of pretending to refuse a call from the president so

*Wick later invited Kinsley to lunch. When Kinsley said he was surprised by this, given that he had called Wick a jackass, Wick replied, "I don't mind criticism from the press, as long as it's accurate." See Michael Kinsley, *The New Republic,* 30 January 1984, p. 4, and *Curse of the Giant Muffins* (New York: Summit Books, 1987), p. 10.

as not to interrupt a Safire interview. When Safire felt like going to Riga to interview Latvian independence fighters, the Latvian Thomas Jefferson put down the draft of the Latvian Declaration of Independence he was writing to spend a few hours talking with him. When Safire traveled to Bir Zeit University on the occupied West Bank to meet Palestinian nationalists there, he simply knocked on a door, called out "Safire, from the *Times*," and was treated to a first-class tour of Palestinian misery. This was regardless of the fact that he, as much as any American pundit, has been responsible for supporting Israel in its imposition of that misery on his hosts. From Riga to Nablus, from Pennsylvania Avenue to South Capitol Street, William Safire is known to everyone whose name might one day appear in a newspaper as one tough SOB. When asked if he would one day like to be secretary of state, Safire responds, "Why step down?"

Safire admits that he has gone beyond the bounds of fairness on a few occasions and says he feels particularly badly about a "cheap poke" he once took at Ted Kennedy. He also confesses to pulling his punches occasionally, but "perhaps not often enough." "In this business," he philosophizes, "it's OK to take a hard shot if you show your hand when you do it." The power, however, he recognizes, is real and considerable. "This is the *New York Times*. It's powerful. If you abuse or misuse it, it's like abusing power in the White House, so you've got to be careful. . . . You can't just take a pop at a little guy."

The contrast with Will here is particularly telling. Safire turned down the request from the Reagan debate team in 1980 that caused Will so much heartache. During the period when Safire was relentlessly beating up on Nancy Reagan in his column, she could frequently be spied at the Jockey Club, consoling herself with Will. Safire, also unlike Will, is a brilliant reporter. Liberal *Washington Post* columnist Richard Cohen recently wrote, "Most opinion columnists cannot be relied upon for breaking news. That, by common agreement, we leave to William Safire." Is it any wonder that Ben Bradlee, who said he would have fired Will if given the chance during Debategate, and who once denounced Safire as a "master of the cheap shot" who "automatically impugns the motives of everybody he thinks is against him," named Safire the only pundit whom he would have liked to steal for the *Post*?

Philosophically, Safire came to conservatism from a position almost diametrically opposed to Will's. On foreign policy, both men are uncompromising hawks. But with regard to the proper role of government in society, where Will sees the state as the moral tutor of the masses, Safire calls himself a "libertarian conservative" and says his "political mindset resists the intrusion of government into the individual's moral decisions." This libertarianism has led him to attack the arrogance of "the Christian Republican party," who, led by "Reverend Reagan," committed the "Constitutional sin" of refusing to distinguish between politics and morality. Safire's endorsements of gay rights, abortion rights, pot-smoking rights, and a whole host of other rights during the Reagan administration had the dual effect of driving social conservatives in the Reagan coalition to distraction and earning Safire the respect and admiration of those who rarely agree with him. This, in turn, made him all the more valuable to the same right-wingers when he deployed his hard-earned mantle of thoughtful iconoclasm on behalf of the administration's militant foreign policy.

Safire spent the Clinton administration back in opposition, but neither his luster nor his access was much dimmed during this period. The pundit kept plugging away at what he viewed to be unconscionable corruption of the Clinton campaign finance machine, while being more generous than most regarding l'affair Lewinsky. Initially he argued, "We should presume him innocent, not merely on high-minded judicial principle, but because it's hard to conceive of this deft politician being so reckless as to carry on an 18-month affair with a White House intern a few years older than his daughter, and then to raise it to the level of Federal crime by suborning perjury. But to take the senseless risk of abusing the trust of a young girl down the hall? I just can't believe that."

Nevertheless, during the height of the crisis, all of power Washington gathered to roast Safire to benefit the Spina Bifida Association of America. Secretary of State Madeleine Albright, White House Counselor Rahm Emanuel, House Appropriations Committee Chairman Bob Livingston (soon to be briefly elected Speaker of the House), Senator John McCain, and Jimmy Carter's budget chief Bert Lance all took the opportunity to show their respect (and fear) by throwing rhetorical marshmallows at him. Livingston played the harmonica, or what Safire called the "mouth organ," for an "Oh, Susanna" parody whose lyrics included the line "he's a Foggy Bottom feeder, he sucks blood so liberally."

Everyone laughed, no one harder—or better—than Safire.

Politics aside, the obvious question to be asked about William Safire's column is why the *Times* has only one of him. An important reason may be that while the job of columnist for the *Times* op-ed page is difficult to attain, it is even harder to lose. As former *Times* op-ed page editor and columnist Leslie H. Gelb explains, "The publisher chooses people who they think have something to say and stands by them for their journalistic careers. The column itself goes up and down." The only way to lose one's appointment is to reach retirement age, as Reston and Flora Lewis have, or to use one's column to attack the *Times* itself, as former metro columnist Sydney Schanberg did.* Moreover, the publisher's efforts to improve the page during the 1980s were sidetracked by the decision to give a column to his forcibly retired editor-in-chief, Abe Rosenthal, a man whose newsroom during his later years was casually likened to Stalinist Russia and Castro's Cuba.

On January 6, 1987, Rosenthal's first column ran under the self-written headline "Please Read This Column." If it struck readers as a mite pathetic, it in no way prepared them for the masochistic experiences they would endure were they to accede to Rosenthal's plea on a regular basis. Rarely in the history of any industry has a man once so powerful humiliated himself so publicly as Abe Rosenthal has done with "On My Mind" (nicknamed "Out of My Mind" by *Times* staffers) on the op-ed page.

The *Times* advertising copy promised its readers, "Whatever it is that's on Mr. Rosenthal's mind, it's going to be interesting." That may or may not have been true on any given day. One had difficulty judging because Rosenthal hides his thoughts behind a writing style made up of short staccato outbursts that resemble sentences only at great distances. In praising

---

*The hero of the film *The Killing Fields*, Schanberg refused to cozy up to his publisher's pals and, rather amazingly, did not exempt the *Times* itself from criticism. Shortly before he went on vacation in July 1985, Schanberg wrote three columns in a row on subjects of particular sensitivity to the *Times* management. In the final one, he attacked the paper's news judgment in ignoring a series of scandals involving the construction of the Westway superhighway on Manhattan's West Side at the same time that it devoted fawning coverage to the chef of a popular new Cajun restaurant facing licensing problems. The *Times* editorial page, along with most of the city's power structure, was committed to Westway. That "the city's newspapers, like the big politicians" had "ignored most of the scandal" was part, in Schanberg's view, "of the shame of Westway." When Schanberg returned from his fishing trip in upstate New York, he was summoned to the office of publisher Punch Sulzberger's assistant, Sidney Gruson. There he was given the bad news: there would be no Sydney Schanberg column the next day. Shocked and angered, Schanberg wanted to fight. He told Gruson, "You cannot keep your trust by killing a voice. An op-ed page is dedicated to diversity," he insisted. "You have put a taint on the *Times*." Gruson remembers telling Schanberg that he and the publisher "found the tone of the column to be too shrill." Nor did Gruson or Sulzberger approve of the way Schanberg returned to the question of New York real estate developers "day after day." Finally, to imply, as Schanberg had, "venality on the part of the *Times* with regard to Westway, that was more than we could accept." When Schanberg asked just how the paper planned to announce this, Schanberg says Gruson replied, "I'm not going to tell anyone. Are you going to tell anyone?"

This account is based on the author's interviews with Sydney Schanberg and Sidney Gruson. It is not inconsistent with the version published in Joseph Goulden, *Fit to Print: Abe Rosenthal and His Times* (Secaucus, N.J.: Lyle Stuart, 1988), pp. 243–48, which relies primarily on Gruson. Schanberg nevertheless insists that "I am ashamed of Sidney Gruson for all the lies he told to Joseph Goulden about me and my departure from the *Times*." Gruson says he cannot reply to Schanberg's charge without knowing what he is alleged to have lied about, but he denies telling any lies, either to Schanberg or to Goulden or to the author. See also Sydney Schanberg, 27 July 1985.

his friends in the media and hires at the *New York Times*, Rosenthal once committed the following paragraph: "Even Barbara Walters could not have done better—no higher compliment. And Larry Tisch once more is a hero at CBS." Another four-month period saw three Rosenthal columns entitled, respectively, "How to Be Stupid in New York," "How to Be Crazy in New York," and "How to Love New York." All three were sentimental paeans to the outgoing mayor, Ed Koch. Like Rosenthal, Koch was an insecure Jewish neoconservative, obsessed with critics of Israel and intensely critical of civil rights leaders, other outspoken liberals, and people of color. To Rosenthal, Koch was "the saint of Gracie Mansion," and "the best mayor" New York ever had.

To say that Abe Rosenthal had an exalted sense of the importance of his own judgments is to utter one of the great understatements of our age. Rosenthal columns have sought to hook readers with this opening: "The City of Washington is quite interesting," or this headline, quoted in its entirety: "Something Is Happening." Shortly after the column began, the late *Village Voice* writer Geoffrey Stokes counted thirty-nine uses of the personal pronoun in a single Rosenthal column. In one column written later in his career, Rosenthal used it three times in the first sentence. In yet another historic column, Rosenthal achieved the hitherto unimagined literary feat of quoting himself quoting himself.[*]

Under most circumstances, Rosenthal might inspire a degree of pity among the good-hearted. Not only was he booted from the job he loved so dearly, but it was given to his rival, Max Frankel. At the end of Rosenthal's brilliant but erratic reign as editor of the paper, he was greeted with the publication of a trashy biography, which drew heavily on the intimate recollections of his long-time mistress, whom he jilted after allegedly promising marriage. When Rosenthal did finally divorce his first wife and remarry, his new romance coincided with the appearance of the satirical New York monthly magazine *Spy*. There, Rosenthal's enemies have chronicled the adventures of Abe "I'm writing as bad as I can" Rosenthal and his wife, Shirley "bosomy dirty-book writer" Lord, to a degree that was sometimes painful to read. *Spy*'s spies regularly reported on the columnist's unpopularity with his colleagues, his exacting interior decorating standards, his inexplicably emotional behavior at society dinner parties—even the poor man's renting of adult videos.

Any sympathy Rosenthal might have earned based on *Spy*'s treatment and the awful biography, however, was soon squandered by his uncom-

[*]See Jonathan Alter, "Abe Speaks His Mind," *Newsweek*, 9 March 1987, p. 54; A. M. Rosenthal, "On My Mind," 17 March 1989; and the author's "The Pat and Abe Show," *The Nation*, 5 November 1990. For the three *I*s, see A. M. Rosenthal, 19 March 1991.

promising self-righteousness and inability to countenance differences of political opinion. When Rosenthal began the column, well-wishers had hopes that he would develop along the lines that Safire had; a conservative with contacts who would ask tough questions and dig out the answers. Instead, he metamorphosed into a twice-weekly version of Norman Podhoretz, but without the self-deprecating wit and charm. By far the most exasperating aspect of Rosenthal's bloated sense of self derives from his apparent belief that he has been anointed by American Jewry as the official ambassador of its angst. Rosenthal lectures the goyim incessantly on the importance of Jewish sensitivities, almost always mixing up his own personal paranoia with the fate of millions of Americans and Israelis. In his hysterical haranguing of those he deems to be either anti-Semitic or anti-Israel—he recognizes no distinction—Rosenthal's column frequently puts one in mind of a character in Franz Lidz's memoir about growing up in postwar New York with his four daffy Jewish uncles. Attending his first baseball game, one uncle sees a line drive career off Mickey Mantle's bat in the direction of his seat and starts screaming that Mantle, with the assistance of Yankee manager Casey Stengel, is planning a pogrom.

Thus, because of his confusing writing style, self-important pronouncements, and social embarrassments, Rosenthal's influence within the punditocracy was virtually nil. The main beneficiaries of the introduction of Rosenthal's column have been the op-ed pages of the *Washington Post* and the *Wall Street Journal*, whose relative improvement, through no fault of their own, appears unarguable on the days when Rosenthal appears in the *Times*. The main losers have been Rosenthal, the *Times*, and the business of columnizing itself. Says Lars-Erik Nelson, Washington columnist for the blue-collar *New York Daily News*, "Rosenthal is an embarrassment to the *Times* and an insult to all columnists. The idea that he was given the job as a sort of going out to pasture. . . . It shows a basic contempt for informed commentary."

In the Clinton era, the page remade itself once again. Leslie Gelb left to take the top job at the Council on Foreign Relations. Lewis and Rosenthal were cut back by the publisher to once-a-week columns. Although Safire remained vital—his intellectual and journalistic juices pumped by the fresh injection of Democratic scandal, the paper was given new life by the appointment of a new generation of columnists to its pages: Bob Herbert and Frank Rich in 1993, and Thomas Friedman and Maureen Dowd in 1995.

Herbert, the *Times*' first black columnist, wrote a straightforward liberal column that focused on urban issues, primarily those concerning the plight of the poor, the weak, and the darker-skinned. It preserved the Schanberg tradition, minus the criticism of *Times* editors, and occasionally caused considerable consternation to corporations who mistreated their workers, particularly Nike. But Herbert wrote from New York and played no role in the insider discourse. He rarely took on major national issues from a new or interesting point of view and did not have the power or influence to make or break an issue or politician. His column was strongest when his subject was smallest, usually in the case of a particular injustice against an individual. Beyond such cases, it was difficult to discern a larger impact on any issue of national importance.

Frank Rich, formerly the paper's theater critic, had a major impact on the page on two counts. He brought to it a sense of literary style that had not been churned into mush by a career as a news reporter—to say nothing of a career as a *Times* reporter. Rich also brought a critic's eye to the drama of national politics, which allowed him to step back and observe machinations behind the entire system—the media conglomerates included—involved in the mind-boggling spectacle that had become American politics. He brilliantly dissected the moral posturing that lay behind the right wing's "family values" agenda and bared its hypocrisy on issues from gay rights to abortion to censorship. He also devoted a great deal of space to the nexus between politics and entertainment, pointing out how frequently the news corporations that owned the rights to broadcast over the public airwaves confused the two to their own advantage. Although like Herbert he wrote from New York, Rich, a Washington native, understood the political rhythms of the city well enough to weigh in at critical points in the discussion and help to shape the conversation from without. A critical Clinton supporter, he proved an important counterweight to the page's moral scolds, as well as to most of the heavyweights in the punditocracy.

Tom Friedman, author of a Pulitzer Prize–winning book based on his coverage of the Middle East, also proved a boon to the page's influence and reputation. Friedman wrote about foreign affairs with a razor-sharp intelligence and a powerful command of the emerging post–Cold War agenda. His column soon became the most influential foreign affairs column anywhere in the media. Initially sympathetic to Clinton, he became furious at the recklessness of the president's behavior and his seat-of-the-pants conducting of foreign policy. Freidman hoped that a president of Clinton's talents would pay sustained attention to foreign issues, but Clinton, for many reasons, proved unable to satisfy him. When Friedman turned on Clinton, therefore, the president had an entirely new problem in winning support for the establishment in any of his foreign policy initiatives. Friedman was worth any number of Congressional chairmen on the critical foreign policy questions of the day.

Maureen Dowd is the pundit who probably made the biggest splash, day-in, day-out, during the Clinton administration. Curiously apolitical, Dowd was a flashy stylist who covered politics as if she were writing personal diary entries or perhaps letters to her mother. If Rich viewed politics as theater, Dowd saw it as sitcom. She commented on the style of the actors but never took seriously what any of them had to say. Sometimes a given actor would infuriate her by breaking some moral rule that Dowd did not consider to be among the forgivable sins.

Even though her politics were impossible to discern, Dowd enjoyed outsized influence throughout the punditocracy, in large measure owing to her audacious style and unique perspective. When Dowd wrote a column calling Clinton the devil, McLaughlin began his show by asking, "Is Bill Clinton commander in chief? Or is he . . . the Prince of Darkness?" He read the column on the air and asked, "If Dowd [is] right, and Clinton is, in a manner of speaking, Satan. . . ." This no doubt attracted the attention of the First Couple, who kept her off the list for the White House Christmas party.

Dowd's treatment of the Lewinsky scandal was most curious. When it first exploded, she worried that the White House would seek to "destroy That Woman." A week later, Dowd herself called Lewinsky "a ditzy, predatory intern," a "mall rat," "the girl who was too tubby to be in the high school 'in' crowd," and a "dithering shopaholic who thought she was having a high school romance with the president, like, of the United States." Observations like these won her a Pulitzer Prize.

Dowd was, no doubt, floored when she happened to run into Lewinsky in a restaurant and the young woman asked why she insisted on being so hurtful to her. Dowd could only answer, "I don't know." After pillorying the president throughout the scandal, Dowd did a complete 360-degree turnaround after the release of the Starr report. Presidents she wrote, should not be impeached for offenses so tawdry. And the pro-impeachment forces lost their most biting and eloquent voice. But she never did let up on poor Monica; after the 1998 elections, when impeachment became a matter of merely disposing of the charges with some modicum of due process for all concerned, Dowd returned once again to the subject of the woman she described as "looking like an upscale bag lady" on a "shopping and eating tour," focusing on her "zesty feasts on leg of lamb and polenta with chocolate sauce." Dowd just would not let Monica rest. "Poor girl," she continued, "No wonder she's in a bad humor. Her commercial window of opportunity is slamming shut. . . . Monica must be in a panic to squeeze the last drop of profit from this sordid tale. . . . There are lawyers to be paid, not to mention Bloomingdale's, Ann Taylor, Bergdorf's and personal trainers." Why one of the most envied journalists in America would stoop to this kind of treatment of an obviously confused young woman, already victimized beyond belief by a tabloid-driven mass media, is a question one could only hope Ms. Dowd will some day take up.

CHAPTER SEVEN

Glass Houses and Revolving Doors

When Donald Graham ascended to the job of publisher of the *Washington Post*—a position for which he had trained nearly his entire life—his first major initiative was to replace editorial page editor Philip Geyelin with Geyelin's deputy, Meg Greenfield. That move, made in August 1979, would provide a strong foundation for the ideological shifts within the punditocracy that characterized the Reagan era.

The decision was a painful one for both Graham and Geyelin, and neither one would discuss it. Chalmers Roberts' semi-official history of the *Post* quotes Katharine Graham, Donald's mother and a major power behind the paper, complaining that the page had become "too gelatinous, too much of 'on the one hand, on the other.' " Unlike Geyelin, a Lippmann protégé drafted in large measure to lead the *Post* away from its misconceived support of Lyndon Johnson's war, Greenfield was expected to take a harder line on foreign policy issues than her predecessor. A Seattle native, Greenfield had worked for eleven years at Dow Jones' *Reporter,* a snappy, liberal, anti-Communist magazine, before coming to the *Post.*

Donald Graham says he picked Meg Greenfield for her "wide-ranging, free-thinking, and interesting mind and indeed, she had won the Pulitzer Prize for editorial writing a year earlier." A close confidant of both Grahams, Greenfield ruled the editorial and op-ed pages of the *Washington Post* with a degree of freedom enjoyed by few of her peers. A thoughtful neoconservative on foreign policy issues and a chastened liberal domestically, Greenfield described herself as "at the right-ish edge of each of the arguments" of the Reagan era.

Although Greenfield, who passed away in May 1999 from lung cancer, was no ideologue, the page over which she presided nevertheless came to be dominated by the voices of the Right sometime during the 1980s and has remained that way ever since. The shift occurred because the page's liberals were either confused or uninspired, and its centrists unwilling to challenge the conservatives' assumptions. Greenfield wrote that "true audacity is having the daring to question the tired assumptions in which most politicians nest." But for virtually the entire decade, her columnists' independence of spirit seemed to derive only from the far Right. Many of the ideas that originated from that direction, however, turned out to be awful ones. Supply-side economics, Star Wars, the deregulation of the savings and loan industry: all of these disastrous Reaganite innovations received considerable support from the most influential denizens of the *Post* page. In some cases, merely by publishing its regular right-wing columnists, the *Post* helped legitimate views that, before Ronald Reagan came to town, were considered just this side of lunacy. The mere appearance of Evans and Novak in so prestigious a forum, for instance, invested them with instant and wholly undeserved credibility.[*]

The paper's unsigned editorials, meanwhile, also overseen by Greenfield, enjoyed extraordinary influence among insiders and in Congress. (Fully aware of their power, the writers would occasionally direct their prose at wavering senators and representatives.) The influence derived in part from Greenfield's extraordinary reputation within the punditocracy and in part from knowledge of how close a personal and intellectual relationship she had developed with Katharine Graham. The latter remained chairwoman and chief executive officer of the permanent Washington power elite throughout the 1980s and into the 1990s.

Owing largely to the old-fashioned liberalism of Herb Block's editorial cartoons, which appeared beside the lead editorial, and to the conservative political tactic of labeling moderates as "liberals" to decertify their true opposition, the paper managed to retain its reputation as a bastion of the liberal establishment throughout the Reagan years. Donald Graham makes a persuasive case that the *Post* deserved its reputation, at least on domestic matters. The *Post*, argues the publisher, endorsed both of Ronald Reagan's opponents, consistently called for tax increases, opposed the death penalty, supported increased funding for

---

[*]In their April 25, 1991, column, for instance, the boys argued that the federal trial of junk bond swindler Michael Milken demonstrated that America, "while far from totalitarian, is only semi-free."

social programs, and remained committed to civil rights legislation. But on the crucial foreign policy issues of the decade—Nicaragua and the MX missile, for instance—*Post* editorial policy led to the sawing off of one leg after another out from under the foundation on which establishment liberalism had once rested.

In race and gender, the op-ed page remained a relic of an earlier America. Of the twenty-six regular contributors to the *Post* op-ed page, three were women and two were black. But even this was deceptive. Of the women, Greenfield published bimonthly, while Ellen Goodman and Jeane Kirkpatrick wrote weekly. Of the two blacks, Carl Rowan was also only sporadically published. Thus, over an eleven-week period, approximately 8 percent (8.4%) of *Post* op-ed columns were authored by a woman and fewer than 12 percent (11.8%) authored by a black. Zero percent, in this city of black and female majorities, were written by black women.[*]

But the ethnic makeup of the *Post* op-ed page is of less intrinsic interest than its ideological composition. The ability of the Right to dominate the politics of the *Post* editorial page was not a matter of majority rule. Ever since the *Washington Star* folded in the summer of 1981, the *Post* has carried so many regular columnists that any attempt to map out a coherent theme would come to despair. Among the page's contributors during the 1980s were pacifist vegetarian Colman McCarthy and radical civil libertarian Nat Hentoff (both on Saturdays only); liberals Hobart Rowen, Mark Shields, Michael Kinsley, Richard Cohen, and Mark Alan Stamaty; mainline establishmentarians James Hoagland, Philip Geyelin, Edwin Yoder, Stephan S. Rosenfeld, David Broder, and Robert Samuelson; the moderately conservative African American William Raspberry; neoconservatives Jeane Kirkpatrick, Charles Krauthammer, Henry Kissinger, and Greenfield herself; and Goldwater-style right-wingers George Will, Rowland Evans, Robert Novak, James J. Kilpatrick, William F. Buckley, Jr., and W. Emmett Tyrell. In the fall of 1991, Lally Weymouth, Mrs. Graham's daughter, who specializes in politically charged Evans and Novak–style foreign reporting was also awarded an op-ed page column.

---

[*]In fairness, Donald Graham points out that at least three other black staff writers, Courtland Milloy, Dorthy Gilliam, and Juan Williams, were given the opportunity to vent their opinions in the newspaper, although none of them appears regularly on the op-ed page. "The *Post* has a number of very fine black columnists," Graham notes, "and I'm very proud to put their views in the paper." (Donald Graham, interview by author.) Also, in fairness, these statistics would probably read similarly if either the *Times* or the *Journal* were the subject of analysis. The calculations derive from data in Christopher Simpson, "Content Analysis and Commentary of the Op-Ed Page of the *Washington Post*," unpublished manuscript, December 1988. Simpson's article is based on the op-ed pages of September 1, 1988, through November 15, 1988.

In the 1990s, Greenfield dumped Colman McCarthy's column on the Left and Emmett Tyrell's on the Right. Kilpatrick retired, Rowan retired, and Stamaty was lured away by *Time*. Rowland Evans retired, but Robert Novak continued to file the column from far-right field. Kinsley, the star liberal, left for the greener fields of Redmond, Washington, where he founded the on-line magazine *Slate*. The page's major addition during this period was the vociferous Clinton-hater Michael Kelly, who was fired from his job as editor of the *New Republic* for his inability to control his obsession. The net effect of these changes, not surprisingly, was to push the page's politics further to the Right.

If the Right succeeded in dominating the politics of the *Post* page during the 1980s, it was because only writers who appeared on television (Safire excepted) and who shared the general principles of the Reagan administration were considered relevant by the city's movers and shakers. George Will, the king of the television hill, was obviously important. So were Evans and Novak. So, particularly, was Charles Krauthammer, who began his column in 1984, invented the Reagan doctrine in 1985, won the Pulitzer Prize in 1986, and soon thereafter replaced Will as the cast intellectual on *Inside Washington*.

The quality of the page during the Reagan era was wildly uneven. Its most consistently original contributions, Michael Kinsley's column and Mark Alan Stamaty's brilliant "Washingtoon" saga, were reprinted from other sources, although Greenfield does deserve credit for recognizing their talent and, in Stamaty's case, for inspiring his idea. Will and Krauthammer wrote elegantly and often thoughtfully on the conservative side. Of the page's own liberals, however, only Richard Cohen maintained the capacity to surprise. But Cohen suffered, for much of the decade, from a professional identity crisis. Having been moved by Donald Graham from the metro page onto the op-ed page against the wishes of Greenfield, Cohen sacrificed the engaging nebbishness of his earlier voice in an ill-fated attempt to achieve what he apparently considered to be a more serious tone befitting an important political pundit. By the time he regained the disarmingly self-effacing tone that had made him a star on the metro page, the 1980s had pretty much come and gone. (Mary McGrory, perhaps the most elegant writer and sharpest wit on the entire *Post* staff, filed her liberal opinions and reportage by her own choice on page two.)

A few of the pundits carrying on the *Post*'s centrist traditions would occasionally demonstrate the ability to see an operational defect in a Reagan policy in a fresh light. James Hoagland's columns out of Paris, although no less doggedly moderate than those of Flora Lewis, were nevertheless vastly superior because he accompanied his consensual political instincts with some excellent reporting. Rosenfeld, Geyelin, and Yoder had their good days as well. But by and large, the *Post* op-ed page began the 1980s in a slump and remained in one for most of the decade. This was all the more unfortunate because, along with the *New Republic*, the *Post* op-ed page provided the punditocracy with the lion's share of its most influential members.

The decline in the page's quality could be traced to three factors. The first was economic. As columnists grew increasingly wealthy from television and corporate appearances, they found themselves with less time and energy to devote to producing a well-reported or originally conceived column. Second, too many of the *Post* regulars were so powerfully tied to the mindset of the government that they effectively conceded the ability to critique it effectively. Finally, and most damagingly, Greenfield opened up the paper's pages to professional Reaganite politicians, such as Henry Kissinger and Jeane Kirkpatrick. Unlike Safire, these operatives had no intention of making their careers as journalists or pundits but saw their columns as an additional means to rewrite the historical records of their performance in office and to retain the public eye. The result was a further diminution of the perceived integrity of the pundit profession, with absolutely no consequential improvement in the quality of the page's analysis.

Because the insider community is itself so small and geographically concentrated, its television stars cut far more imposing figures in the city's social hierarchy than their equivalents do in Manhattan or even Hollywood. In a town whose social structure is not unlike that of a suburban high school, they are, James Fallows points out, the varsity.

Owing to the stern *Times* television prohibitions, a regular column in the *Post* has become the most effective blast-off platform for the television/lecture circuit financial stratosphere. Its denizens can often be viewed at various transit points between the punditocracy's four rings. *New Republic* editors Charles Krauthammer and Michael Kinsley saw their columns in the *Post* lead to regular television appearances, thereby transversing all four rings simultaneously. (Both writers were also enormously well-paid monthly contributors to *Time*.) A particular advantage for *Post* writers in this regard is the company's ownership of *Agronsky and Company/Inside Washington*. *Post* contributors Krauthammer, Will, Kilpatrick, Rowan, and former editorial writer Juan Williams were all tapped for that peculiar star-making institution. Other *Post* writers with regular television gigs include Mark Shields (*The NewsHour with Jim Lehrer* and *The Capital Gang*); Will (formerly of *Nightline*, the *ABC Evening News*, and *Agronsky and Company*, and still a regular on *This Week*); and Novak (formerly of *The McLaughlin Group* fame and the short-lived *Money Politics*, now consigned to *The Capital Gang*, *Crossfire*, and the *Evans and Novak Report*, where he

appears with his *Post* partner, Rowland Evans, and Buckley of *Firing Line*).
Writing in August 1983, Tory curmudgeon Henry Fairlie observed:

> The repetitiveness and predictability of most of the op-ed page of the *Washington Post* are directly related to their unimportance in the eyes of their authors. They are hackwork, which, if their authors were not media stars, any self-respecting editor would drop. . . . They have become mere adjuncts to the paper's main interest in them, that they are written by media names.

Television, however, is only the half of it. Evans and Novak, as has been noted, were less a journalistic enterprise than a small multinational conglomerate. As Fairlie observed, the effect of this corporate expansion has been devastating for the quality of the *Post*'s op-ed page. It is television, and television alone, that lays the groundwork for $20,000 speaking engagements. Time wasted writing interesting or unorthodox columns detracts from speaking engagements. Or, worse, such a column might offend some potential conventioneer somewhere and thus stand in the way of an offer. Richard Cohen shed some light on this phenomenon when he grappled with a hypothetical speech offer from a group whose position he was about to bash:

> But wait! Will this column endanger my speech engagement? I think. I ponder. I check my bank account and, with a ruler, measure the pile of bills on my desk. I decide: It's time to write about the glories of spring in Washington.

Cohen argues that this situation corrupts high-powered punditry, and he is right. He also argues that "the public, my readers, will perceive nothing," because columnists always kill a few days a year with rhapsodies about cherry blossoms and so forth. In the short term, he has a point. But over the long run, readers will likely perceive an increase in exactly the kind of toothless, milquetoast punditry that characterized many *Washington Post* pundits during the Reagan era and after.

To the degree that a newspaper can be said to have a soul, that of the *Washington Post* can be found in the columns of its venerable political reporter and pundit, David Broder. The dean of the Washington press corps, Broder carries on the Reston tradition with spunk and verve that belie his four decades in the business.

Consensual, generous, and moderate to an almost Confucian degree, Broder expresses an unflagging enthusiasm for political reporting that is widely recognized as a model for young reporters in journalism schools across the nation. With his unfailing integrity and willingness to admit error, Broder, a 1973 Pulitzer Prize winner, is viewed across the political spectrum as a guardian of journalistic ethics and traditions. According to a *Washington Journalism Review* poll, Broder was the most admired political reporter in the city, with a six-to-one margin over the nearest competition. The fact that he is both a reporter and a pundit does not seem to confuse anyone, because most of his columns are so politically balanced and consciously anti-ideological that they could run just as easily in the news section.

The son of a dentist, Broder grew up in Chicago in a family of Roosevelt Democrats who talked politics constantly at the dinner table. As a teenager, he published a weekly political newspaper and peddled it around the neighborhood. When he attended the University of Chicago, he led the liberals to victory over the Communists and gained control of the campus newspaper. Broder trained at the *Bloomington (Ill.) Pantograph*, coming to work for *Congressional Quarterly* in 1955 and later the *Washington Star*. He was hired at the *New York Times* in 1965 but resigned a year and a half later to go to work at the *Post*. For this act alone he is revered by his colleagues.

Numerous journalistic legends about Broder's political acumen have arisen. During the 1972 campaign for president, Broder bet gonzo journalist and McCarthy partisan Hunter Thompson $100 that Hubert Humphrey would win a crucial Democratic primary. Thompson kept the bet a secret, however, for fear that if Broder's judgment became known within the traveling press corps, it would tilt their reporting of the race in favor of Humphrey. Broder's greatest moment as a journalist came when he walked out on an interview with Henry Kissinger, then secretary of state, because the latter insisted that their discussion be considered off the record.

A famously honest and hard-working reporter, pundit Broder nevertheless operates from an alarmingly romantic notion of how power in Washington is exercised. As what his colleague Richard Cohen calls "the Olympian voice of the mainstream political community," Broder maintains an almost religious devotion to the idea that the salvation of the American political system lies in the rejuvenation of America's two political parties. Like Reston, he sometimes seems to revere the successful manipulation of the process, irrespective of the content of the legislation for which it is being manipulated. A man of the floating center, Broder considers all ideologies (save the unspoken ideology of the pragmatist) to be anathema. He finds accusation of bias, either Left or Right, on the part of the media to be "laughable." "There just isn't enough ideology in the average reporter," he insists, "to fill a thimble."

Despite the political upheavals of the 1960s and 1970s, Broder remains wedded to a narrow vision of political participation, which results in an inability to appreciate the significance of forces that fall outside the purview of traditional party politics. His manner of dealing with maverick politicians and political movements usually involves a mixture of scorn and denial. On the launching of Eugene McCarthy's insurgent effort to dethrone Lyndon Johnson in 1967, Broder harrumphed that "the frenzy of the anti-Johnson Democrats has now reached the point where it degrades the Democratic Party and those involved in the mutiny as much as it hurts the President himself." The fact that the mutineers felt they had an unconstitutional war to end apparently did not impress Broder. "Those Democrats," he lectured, "ought to realize that their own reputations are being affected by their behavior."

Seventeen years and thousands of political interviews later, Broder took much the same tack during the brief 1984 candidacy of George McGovern, who, at the time, was suggesting that Walter Mondale's calls for higher taxes to pay for essentially Republican goals were not indicating the best direction for his party to take. When McGovern distinguished himself, before withdrawing, by forcing the rest of the candidates to direct themselves to a panoply of issues they would have preferred to ignore, Broder demonstrated the personal and professional class for which he is rightly famous by issuing an apology in his syndicated column.[*] But the tendency remains in the DNA structure of Broder's reporting.

An even more troubling problem for Broder's brand of punditry is its frequent inability to distinguish between the surface and reality of a political maneuver. Like most successful insiders, Broder is a sucker for a smooth-talking political operator. This makes him notoriously easy to manipulate, even when he is upholding the highest standards of his profession. It is not that Broder was unaware of the lengths to which the Reagan administration was willing to go to mislead the public, just that he never mentioned it when it was taking place. Consider the *Washington Post*'s Outlook section on March 22, 1987. On page one, the newspaper carried a thoughtful rumination by one David Broder on the dangers of White House manipulation, drawn from his book *Behind the Front Page.*

> The White House propaganda machine has . . . enhanced the power of the communicator-in-chief. And it has raised to even greater importance the unmet challenge for the press to provide an alternative, non-propagandistic view of the presidency. This is a challenge we in the Washington press corps—and our editors and bosses—cannot afford to ignore.

[*]McGovern framed it and hung it on the wall of his dingy campaign office above a Dupont Circle Greek deli.

Yet, on the last page of the same section of the *Post*, Broder found himself helpless before that very phenomenon. Of Reagan's speech earlier that week, during which the president continued to adhere to his preposterous notion that he had not intended to trade arms for hostages or to encourage his administration to contravene any laws on behalf of the contras, Broder commented:

> The White House has repaired the damage from the Iran affair explosion and reopened for business. President Reagan's news conference on Thursday night provided the strongest evidence yet that the proprietor of the shop has regained a good measure of his emotional balance and is ready to reclaim his role at the center of government. The president did not change his story—or add much to it. But he showed the steadfastness and confidence that had been so conspicuously missing in the final months of 1986. Now Reagan can begin refocusing the nation's attention on his policy agenda without being accused of trying to avoid That Painful Subject.

What is Broder actually saying here? He does not claim that Reagan offered any coherent explanation for the Iran-Contra debacle or for his own role in it. Neither does he explain what has changed inside the White House to prevent such occurrences from taking place in the future. Instead, he appears to be endorsing Reagan's attempt to downgrade the importance of the administration's willful subversion of the Constitution and its conduct of an illegal proxy war against Nicaragua. All Reagan truly demonstrated to Broder was the fact that, after five months of hiding, he could collect himself sufficiently to play the role of president for approximately forty minutes without lapsing into gibberish. Broder considered the Iran-Contra revelations to be not just a well-deserved comeuppance for a group of politicians who behaved contemptuously toward the Constitution, but a "disaster . . . and calamity for the nation." Thus, he was particularly eager to grant the president, on the basis of this pathetic scale of performance, a pass for all of his dissimulating during the Iran-Contra affair and to encourage him to "reclaim his role at the center of government."*

Similarly, during the trial of Oliver North, Broder wondered why "we are going through this expensive legal exercise" when "clearly the courts

---

*More worrisome, perhaps, is the fact that Broder's statements were not defensible even in the limited sense he intended them. Reagan's public approval ratings remained, at the time, twenty points lower than they had been before the scandal. For the political elites to which Broder was addressing himself, Reagan's political reputation was thoroughly destroyed. See Robert N. Entman, *Democracy without Citizens* (New York: Oxford University Press, 1989), pp. 70–71. See also Broder's attack on Kinsley and Buchanan for enjoying Iran-Contra too much, quoted in the *New York Times*, 29 December 1986.

do not lack work." Ignoring both the importance of completing the historical record on Iran-Contra and any "debt to society" owed by North for his crimes, Broder wondered "what more could be gained by sending [North] to Allenwood or one of the other federal prisons for white-collar criminals?" Historians might wish to examine that statement when seeking to explain how Ronald Reagan and George Bush consistently managed to evade responsibility for the actions of their own administration.

Broder's inability to examine the forces underlying political behavior virtually paralyzes his analytical abilities, leaving him in thrall to the strictly show-business elements of American politics. Broder was unimpressed by George Bush's 1988 presidential campaign until Bush gave what Broder thought was a good speech at the New Orleans convention. With this single speech (and, lest we forget, his appointment of Dan Quayle to be his running mate), Bush succeeded, in Broder's eyes, in dispelling his image as "the 'wimp' of the Doonesbury cartoons." "Republican Senate Minority Leader [and failed presidential candidate] Bob Dole called him a 'tough, aggressive' candidate"; few, argued Broder, "would disagree."

That Broder thought it noteworthy for Dole to praise his party's presidential nominee is astonishing. Every loser in every presidential campaign has made the same gesture. Given the historical standards for this type of insincere flattery, Dole's limited concession constituted faint praise indeed. That Broder could be so impressed by a single speech—a speech that was, after all, written by Peggy Noonan under the direction of James Baker—is depressing. It indicates just how powerfully surface-level television images have replaced a politician's record as the ultimate arbiter of character and competence, even in the eyes of the most experienced and high-minded critics of the process.*

No one can doubt that David Broder is sincerely devoted to reversing the deteriorating foundations of American democracy. But by offering the politicians themselves such an overpowering degree of sympathy, however pure his motives, Broder contributes to that deterioration by playing the role of a toothless watchdog. Moreover, because Broder is generally considered to be the very archetype of a responsible liberal pundit in Washington, his failings have consequences far beyond the shortcomings of his own reportage. In addition to his prominence at the

---

*When I raised this issue with Broder, he tried to point out how foolish I was being (without hurting my feelings). "There is no way to be polite about this," he told me. "To say that somebody is simply reciting a speech that somebody else writes is to totally misunderstand the process by which a speech gets put together. It suggests that there is only one speech, that it is handed to him, that he is passive about it. . . . I have to say respectfully that that is a simple-minded view of American politics." (David Broder, interview by author.)

Post, his syndication in more than three hundred papers means that Broder is the only non-right-wing pundit to begin to challenge the circulation numbers of the likes of Will, Kilpatrick, and Buchanan. Setting aside the inanity of television, the "responsible" political dialogue on the Great Issues of the Day is, thus, often perceived to fall between Will on the one hand and Broder on the other. Nowhere in this constricted conversation—at least until the attorney general explained it himself—was there room for the possibility that the president was conducting a secret war, selling missiles to our sworn enemies. American politicians, it is assumed by all sides, are simply too honest, too committed, and too sensible to play such childish games. And even if such shenanigans were conceivable, certainly none of the politicians involved would dare lie to David Broder about it.

Broder's saving grace is his complete lack of pretense. If Washington insiders wish to take his ruminations overly seriously, that is their fault, not Broder's. He is just a reporter with a column. "I am not a terribly interesting or fluid writer and I don't have any deep philosophical thoughts . . . so if I didn't do the reporting," Broder claims, "I couldn't do the column."

Given Broder's untouchable reputation for judiciousness, modesty, and moderation, it came as a shock to insider Washington when, in November 1988, the usually soft-spoken, mild-mannered reporter emerged from his phone booth of the soul to launch a decidedly immoderate attack on the ethics of a number of his colleagues. At a black-tie dinner in his honor given by the National Press Club, Broder took to the podium and lashed out at "a new hybrid creature, an androgynous binding of politician and journalist called The Washington Insider. One day, he or she is a public official or political operative; the next, a journalist or television commentator." Broder worried that if "the people . . . see us as part of a power-wielding clique of Insiders, they're going to be resentful as hell that they have no way to call us to account." Broder concluded his speech with the observation that he could not fathom why journalists would want to become insiders when "it's so damn much fun to be outsiders—irreverent, inquisitive, impudent, incorrigibly independent outsiders—thumbing our nose at authority and going our own way."

Broder was no doubt operating from a frightfully exaggerated notion of just how impudent he and his incorrigibly independent colleagues had been during the previous decade. After all, it was at the very same dinner that secretary of state–designate James Baker read a note from the president-elect remarking that Broder had "come a long way" since the Bushes, the Broders, the Bakers, and others spent weeks touring China together in 1977 "as a kind of private, bonding experience." "Read my lips," concluded Bush, using the phrase that during the presidential campaign signaled an approaching falsehood, "David, you're a pro."

However black his own pot may have been, Broder put his finger on one of the hottest kettles in the ongoing degradation of American political commentary: the plethora of professional politicians who have been able to negotiate themselves into the punditocracy without first renouncing any further political ambitions.

In the old days, when high officials would lose their posts, they would retire to the relative obscurity of a Wall Street law firm or a university institute. The Wise Man model, Dean Rusk, withdrew to a foreign policy institute somewhere in Georgia and was not heard from again for a quarter-century. Even Clark Clifford, who remained a lifetime player at a K Street law firm, still had the good taste to devote himself to making money the old-fashioned and, until he was indicted, much quieter way.

But, beginning with the Nixon administration, losers gave up the graceful habit of slinking quietly into the night and began to offer their services as pundits. Some of them—Safire being the obvious case—turned out to be terrific. But most did not. Few were able to write without an eye over their shoulder toward their employers' (and often their own) place in history. Fewer still were trained as journalists or displayed any respect for the honest conventions of the trade. Moreover, one could not be certain that these ex-officials were not temporizing their judgments in the hopes of an even higher-level reappointment some day. Journalist-pundits had never been immune to these dangers, but the politician-pundits represented a completely higher order of corruption.

This trend, manageable under the Nixon, Ford, and Carter administrations, exploded beyond reasonable proportions during the Reagan years. Kenneth Adelman, Richard Perle, Mona Charen, David Gergen, Caspar Weinberger, Edwin Meese, Patrick Buchanan, Jeane Kirkpatrick, and Henry Kissinger (briefly) were all Reagan administration officials who came to enjoy the fruits of syndicated pontification. Kirkpatrick and Kissinger, however, are the only two who enjoy it in the *Post.* Their results ranged from merely bad to fundamentally corrupt.

As an ostensibly honest pundit, Jeane Kirkpatrick was so inept that her work was actually instructive. No pundit cliché was safe in her presence. Concerned about the post–Cold War evolution of the German psyche? Don't worry; "a Berlin taxi driver assured [her], 'we have learned that the civilized way to express power is in the economy.' " Curious about how the entire continent of Europe is "feeling" about German re-unification? Ask Dr. Kirkpatrick: "Europe is feeling ambivalent." Kirkpatrick's column manifested some of the same stylistic problems as Abe Rosenthal's, but she lacked his engaging flair for self-dramatization. Like Rosenthal, Kirkpatrick had a schoolchild's fondness for adjectives and a bad poet's love of alliteration. The result, as when Kirkpatrick described young Chinese demonstrators as "hunted, haunted, and hollow-eyed," recalled no one so much as Eliza Doolittle.

Laziness was also a problem. In attempting to offer Margaret Thatcher some strangely racially exclusive encouragement, Kirkpatrick called her "the only woman to achieve the position of Prime Minister or President of an Anglo-Saxon or European democracy." This led one *Post* reader to wonder if, in Kirkpatrick's judgment, "a) Norway is not in Europe or b) Norway is not a democracy or c) Norwegian Prime Minister Gro. Harlem Brundtland is not a woman." More serious was Kirkpatrick's habit of attempting to rewrite reality to fit the political and ideological contours of her past and future political career. In March 1986, after a dishonest Philippine election stolen by forces loyal to Ferdinand Marcos, a typically attractive "authoritarian" government according to the Kirkpatrick doctrine, the former U.N. representative accused American liberals of orchestrating a "campaign . . . to suggest the existence of an anti-Marcos 'consensus' inside the United States government." The effect of such "meddling" was "interference in Philippine politics." Americans should "cease" their "interference," she insisted, or they could expect to suffer the fate of the explorer Magellan, who was "hacked to death" by "the Philippine tribes." The day before the column appeared, however, Reagan administration officials began edging away from their embrace of Marcos on the Sunday morning talk shows. Kirkpatrick, out on a shaky limb, quickly sent out a revised version of the column in which she observed that "charges of fraud destroyed [the] perception" of "a creditable election." The two columns appeared simultaneously the next day in various newspapers.

In another column, this one on El Salvador, Kirkpatrick promised her readers that "there was no question" that President José Napoleon Duarte would do any of the things with regard to the upcoming Salvadoran elections that he had, unbeknownst to her, announced he would do the previous evening. In this case, however, there was no time even to attempt a rewrite.

Henry Kissinger, as always, presented a unique set of problems. Standards had become so lax within the punditocracy by the 1980s that the fact that Kissinger lied to and placed wiretaps on various journalists while in office did not appear to disqualify him as an ostensibly honest pundit. Nor did Kissinger's service on Ronald Reagan's Foreign Intelligence Advisory board, which offered him full access to the nation's most sensitive secrets and was simultaneous with the launching of his column. When a Kissinger controversy finally did erupt, in the spring of 1989, it was not over these issues, or even because Kissinger had, during the Reagan administration, served as its Central American adviser; rather, it was his reaction to the Tiananmen Square massacre in China.

After the massacre, Kissinger wrote that "no government in the world would have tolerated having the main square of its capital occupied for eight weeks" and that "a crackdown was therefore inevitable." America's ability to ignore the murderous force with which the "inevitable" took place, keeping in mind "the extraordinary sensitivity of any Chinese leader to what appears to be foreign intervention" became, in Kissinger's eyes, "a test of our political maturity." China, according to Kissinger, remained "too important for American national security to risk the relationship on the emotions of the moment."

Three aspects of Kissinger's analysis stood out immediately. First, he hoped to whitewash the mass murder of a people by its government with an appeal to alleged American geopolitical interests. Lives sacrificed on the altar of "national security" were nothing new for Henry Kissinger, but it had become an increasingly tired excuse in the aftermath of Mikhail Gorbachev's dismantling of the Soviet military empire. Second, Kissinger proved to be demonstrably wrong. The governments of Czechoslovakia, East Germany, Bulgaria, Nepal, and even Gorbachev's Soviet Union all witnessed massive demonstrations in their public squares in the aftermath of the Tiananmen crackdown. These resulted in forced concessions and a transition to a more democratic rule. Even the neofascist government of Augusto Pinochet in Chile—whose existence owed so much to Kissingerian diplomacy—saw the wisdom, in 1989, of handing over the reins of power to its opposition in the streets. Only in Romania did the dictators adhere to Kissingerian principles, and that decision set off a brief civil war.

What damaged Kissinger, however, was not the substance of his analysis, but the atmospherics that surrounded it. The *Wall Street Journal* revealed that as he was apologizing for the Chinese regime, Kissinger was sitting on an announcement of a limited partnership called China Ventures to pool $75 million raised from U.S. investors for joint ventures with the China International Trust and Investment Corporation. While Kissinger said he had put the initiative on hold after the bloody events of June 6, the timing smelled bad to everyone. As head of the super-secret consulting firm bearing his name, Kissinger had long given super-secret advice to foreign corporations for hundreds of thousands of dollars in super-secret fees.* But

---

*Kissinger did this, however, not because he liked to, but because he had to. "Making money is actually boring," he complained in his final words to diplomatic adversary Andrei Gromyko, "even if it is necessary." See Andrei Gromyko, *Memoirs* (New York: Doubleday, 1989), p. 394.

this time, his timing was so egregious and his words so offensive to Americans who had seen the young heroes killed live on their television sets that, for the first time in decades, Kissinger felt compelled to defend himself in public. Kissinger blamed the charges on those who sought to "blacken" his reputation. He described as "McCarthyism" any attempt to link his views on China to his business interests. Deputy-Kissinger Winston Lord rose to his friend's defense with a ringing statement of the decidedly unobvious. "No one can question his motives," insisted Lord. As always, the grumbling continued, but Kissinger came out on top.

When asked in the aftermath of the China episode how he felt about the fact that Henry Kissinger was now published regularly in what was then his newspaper, Ben Bradlee sighed, looked up at the ceiling, and slowly replied, "I feel badly about it." He should have, but the appearance of Kissinger and Kirkpatrick in the *Washington Post* was not Bradlee's decision but Greenfield's. Geyelin, Greenfield's predecessor, accuses both Kirkpatrick and Kissinger of "recycling old ideas and tending toward their place in history." In some ways, though, both columns were useful. As with caricature and portraiture, sometimes only through exaggeration are the features of an object made sufficiently clear to reveal its essence. Kirkpatrick and Kissinger provided the clearest example of the most egregious violations of the ethics journalists profess to live by. But the *Washington Post* op-ed page is filled with writers and political operatives who transgress these rules on a less grandiose scale virtually every day.

Broder's noble efforts notwithstanding, the *Washington Post* op-ed page is literally the worst place in the world from which to launch a campaign against insiders. No institution did more during the Reagan era to invest insiderdom with a false authority that derived simply from its proximity to power. None did more to legitimize notions of governance that were not merely untested, but in many instances contrary to common sense. It is significant that Broder worries that people will start to see the media as a "power-wielding clique of Insiders." What would be truly dangerous would be if the Washington media—specifically the punditocracy—really did constitute a "power-wielding clique of Insiders," and the public, still in thrall to the myths of a politically and intellectually independent Fourth Estate, failed to perceive it.

CHAPTER EIGHT

We Are the Wild Men

During the 1990s, the editors of the *Wall Street Journal* were among the harshest critics of President Clinton anywhere in the media. They were relentless about investigating every nook and cranny of the various scandals that perplexed the administration, from "Whitewater" to "Filegate" to Paula Jones, campaign finance, Chinese influence-buying, Hillary Clinton's health care plan, and Bill Clinton's alleged rape of Juanita Broderick twenty-one years ago. The extreme animosity the editorial page demonstrated toward the first Democratic administration to come to power in twelve years was surprising to some. It should not have been. By the 1990s, the *Journal* was operating in an atmosphere in which it was one powerful conservative voice among many. Yet, back in the 1970s, it played an enormous role in creating the political atmosphere that allowed so many conservative flowers to bloom. What follows is the story of how the *Journal*'s editors did it.

Ray Shaw, the onetime president and director of Dow Jones & Company, may or may not have had strong feelings about the complex and convoluted lines that divide punditry from politicking. But when he found himself on a New Jersey commuter train platform one balmy June evening in 1978, confronted by a *Wall Street Journal* editorial writer handing out campaign literature for a Republican senatorial candidate, he knew instinctively that something was amiss. Jude Wanniski, the writer in question, had allowed himself to become so convinced by the righteousness of his cause—that of the nascent economic philosophy labeled "supply-side"—that he had jettisoned all journalistic decorum. Wanniski was, in fact, writing speeches, brokering political deals, and reportedly throwing the paper's weight around quite crudely in Washington.* On the leafleting matter, Wanniski recalls that it took place during what he remembers to be "my most manic phase. The only way I could see to elevate the supply-side idea was in the political realm. Without it, the United States would not find a path back to economic growth and the whole world would implode. You know, war and depression, the whole thing." Of course, supply-side economics did eventually triumph and, as readers will be aware, war and depression were by and large avoided. But this did not save Wanniski's job; he left the paper to form a consulting firm shortly thereafter.

The story of the ability of the *Wall Street Journal*'s editorial page to reverse decades of official U.S. economic doctrine in the late 1970s and early 1980s has few historic precedents. According to economic historian Wayne Parsons, the *Journal* "had an absolutely vital role to play in disseminating and legitimating the ideas which became associated with Ronald Reagan, and without its support it is difficult to see how the supply-side argument could possibly have achieved such a leading position in the economic policy debates." The closest parallel, the victory of John Maynard Keynes over classical economics in the late 1930s and early 1940s, had been decades in the making. Moreover, Keynesianism entered the political lexicon the hard way: by breaking through the walls of orthodoxy at the Harvard economics department. It received important but hardly decisive support in the public arena from young Walter Lippmann in the *New Republic* as well, but it was not until after the Great Depression—and the complete ruination of the old system—that Keynesian assumptions began to supplant the ruling elite's conventional economic wisdom.

Wanniski and the supply-siders at the *Journal*'s editorial page played a completely different ball game. They bypassed academia entirely, propagating their ideas only via regular contributors to their own page and at seminars with tiny groups of like-minded politicians and counter-establishment think-tank analysts, particularly those at the Heritage Foundation and the Hoover Institution. And although the 1970s did see the first prolonged period of stagflation—what one econ-

---

*The *Journal*'s Washington bureau members complained to their boss of Wanniski's preaching to the representatives they were trying to cover. Some representatives reportedly insisted that Wanniski had twisted their arms with threats of favorable or unfavorable publicity. At the 1976 Republican convention, Wanniski wrote Jack Kemp's floor speech and did his utmost to broker a deal between the Kemp and Reagan forces. According to Kemp, however, it was done without his permission.

omist called the "diabolic double helix" of rising unemployment coupled with rising inflation—this can hardly be compared to the political and intellectual wreckage that lay strewn on the road to the New Deal. Few events in recent American history demonstrate more succinctly the new power of the punditocracy than the replacement, in the 1980s, of Harvard, Brookings, and Keynes as the nation's traditional guardians of economic policy by Jude Wanniski, Robert Bartley, and the *Wall Street Journal.*

The *Journal's* role within the punditocracy is a paradoxical one. According to a Brookings Institution study, the *Journal* is read daily by approximately one-half of the Washington press corps and 60 percent of "high federal officials." Nationally, fewer than 30 percent of the paper's readers pay regular attention to the editorials, less than half the number who say they buy it for its business news. Among Washington insiders, however, these numbers are quite probably reversed. Business news is important in Washington largely to the degree that it affects politics. At least until the recession of 1991, the insider Washington economy has been almost fully insulated from that of the rest of the nation.

The prestige of the *Journal's* Washington bureau grew enormously during the 1980s under the direction of its high-profile chief, Al Hunt. But, ironically, it was Hunt's own avocation as a pundit on *Washington Week* and *The Capital Gang*, coupled with his power marriage to anchorwoman Judy Woodruff, that propelled him into the punditocracy stratosphere. As for the *Journal* itself, against all the rules of insiderdom, the unsigned opinions of its editorial page have, under Bartley, carved out a tremendously influential perch in the insider dialogue without so much as a Washington office or even a widely recognized face. Bartley himself quietly tends to business in his spacious, oak-lined office atop the World Financial Center in Battery Park, Manhattan. He does not appear on television and is amazed, he says, at just how "dumb" friends like Mark Shields and Robert Novak sound when they do. Indeed, it is difficult to imagine Bartley, a soft-spoken man with a patrician's gentle demeanor, managing even to complete a sentence on *The McLaughlin Group.*

But Bartley's manner has little in common with his politics or, for that matter, his style of argument. "We are the wild men," said his comrade, Wanniski, of the supply-siders centered around the *Journal,* and he wasn't kidding. Beginning in 1972, when the Midwestern conservative firebrand was given de facto control over the *Journal's* editorials (the title "editor" did not follow until 1979), they have had a harsh and unforgiving tone. Throughout the Bartley era, *Journal* editorials have been among the most dependable allies of the far-right elements of the Republican party on both foreign and economic issues in the entire punditocracy, going so far as to attack other journalists in advance of their published works when they fail to hew to the administration line.*

Quite frequently, ideology drove Bartley's page so relentlessly that it appeared to blind him to the facts published in his own paper. In 1980, a *Journal* reporter broke a story proving that an alleged $100 million tax-administration cost offered up by a group of California oil firms protesting a new state tax was, in fact, a wildly exaggerated estimate of the actual expense. Two days later, the editorial page noted that "according to one estimate, enforcement of the tax would cost taxpayers $100 million. . . ." The pattern repeated itself in 1984 when Washington reporter David Rogers discovered that the CIA had been illegally mining Nicaragua's harbors. The story ran on page six and was picked up by the *Washington Post*. Six days later, the editorial page, standing foursquare behind the contra war, criticized members of Congress for leaking the information to the *Post*.

Ben Bagdikian, former dean of the journalism school at the University of California, Berkeley, explained the dichotomy between the editorial page and the news pages as follows:

> Executives and stockholders really do want to know the unpleasant truth about corporate life when it affects their careers or incomes. At the same time, however, most of them are true believers in the rhetoric of free enterprise, whose imperfections and contradictions are standard content in the *Wall Street Journal*. By reporting critical stories about realities in particular industries in the news columns, but singing the grand old hymns of unfettered laissez-faire on the editorial pages, the *Journal* has it both ways.

Bartley himself attributes the occasional conflicts to the fact that "the front page has its own sources and we have ours. We do our own reporting, and I have never quite figured out how the reader suffers by having access to two sets of sources."

As is typical of most neoconservatives, Bartley stuck to the straight and narrow on most Reaganite matters, with the significant exception of those issues involving the religious Right. The paper strongly supported

---

*Donald Graham says he enjoys reading Bartley's editorials, but he would be "very uncomfortable if the tone of the *Post* editorial page was as harsh and intolerant as the typical *Journal* editorial." Donald Graham, interview by author.

the various Reagan Doctrine counterinsurgencies of the 1980s and plowed considerable ground beneath the construction of Reagan's Strategic Defense Initiative (SDI) program. "Mutual Assured Destruction is immoral," Bartley insisted, "and we tried to keep the issue alive until Reagan proposed SDI." Wanniski attributes what he terms Bartley's "softness on social issues like abortion" to the editor's desire to "take some of the 'throw the orphans into the snow' pressure off of the Right Wing." In Wanniski's view, however, this was eventually accomplished far more effectively by his ex-boss' embrace of supply-side economics.

Determining the influence exercised by financial punditry within insider Washington is an even murkier matter than determining that of the political punditocracy. Most insiders, like people in general, understand little about economics. Editors, moreover, can't seem to make up their minds about whether economic news is of special or general interest to its readership. The *Times* consigns its financial pundits to the paper's business section, where they have little impact on the high politics of the Washington insider debate. The *Post* does publish its business writers on the op-ed page, but they are not considered to be among the page's heavy hitters.

Newsweek probably did more for the institution of economic punditry than any other publication when, in September 1966, it invited Milton Friedman and Paul Samuelson to contribute regular triweekly columns. Samuelson stuck to Keynesian assumptions but tended to explain rather than preach. He was Restonian in his prejudice in favor of good sense. His ideological predilections generally tended toward, "This is not a time for taking chances or laissez-faire. It is a time for prudent action."

Milton Friedman could not have been more different, either in temperament, ambition, or intellectual inclination. Through his *Newsweek* column, along with his bestselling books and a few strategically scheduled television series, Friedman established himself during the 1970s as perhaps the single most influential American economist in history.

Friedman was a Keynesian in the sense that he believed in the power of ideas to move society. He hurled himself into the Keynesian conventional wisdom with popular tracts relentlessly attacking the notion of positive government interference in the economy, beginning with *Capitalism and Freedom* in 1962 and sustaining this consistent line through the bestselling election-year tracts *Free to Choose* (1980) and *The Tyranny of the Status Quo* (1984), both coauthored with his wife, Rose. Friedman's ideas were generally considered beyond the pale of reason when he began his attack on the Keynesian orthodoxy; he was the only member of the profession to advise Barry Goldwater in 1964. But through

Newsweek, the books, his television series, and his association with counter-establishment think tanks, particularly AEI and the Hoover Institution, this bald, diminutive professor managed to reeducate a nation on the principles of economics. As his intellectual adversary, John Kenneth Galbraith, observed, "the age of John Maynard Keynes gave way to the age of Milton Friedman."

Friedman's academic delineation of what he termed "Monetarism," in which the health of the economy rested on the government's ability to provide a stable, tightly controlled money supply, eventually divided the profession between various factions of monetarists and Keynesians (with occasional Marxist outliers in selected institutions) and in 1976 earned Friedman the economists' equivalent of a Nobel prize. But Friedman's most important contributions came in the political arena. Most significant was his sustained attack on the efficacy of government intervention in the economy. "I know hardly any do-gooder legislation . . . which on examination of its full consequences, does not do more harm than good," he told readers. "We have heard much these past few years about using the government to protect the consumer," he explained. "A far more urgent problem is to protect the consumer from the government."

Previous to the Reagan administration's walk on the supply side, Friedmanite experiments had been undertaken by three different national governments. All vastly increased, at least in the short and medium term, the economic misery of the masses.* "It is possible," worried William F. Buckley, Jr. at the time, that Friedmanite theories "suffer from the over-riding disqualification that they simply cannot get a sufficient exercise in democratic situations—because it takes longer for them to produce results than the public is prepared to wait." To the growing number of conservatives in Friedman's corner, Buckley's diagnosis underscored a particularly serious problem for a nation addicted to instant gratification. Before Friedman's monetarist prescription could be considered politically palatable in the United States once again, it would require a kind of sugar-coating, one that would offset its harsh side effects long enough to allow the medicine to take hold.

Supply-side economics, as preached by its evangelists at the *Journal*, was not simply sugar-coated; it was the sweet gooey essence of the stuff. As outlined in the *Journal* editorial pages by Wanniski, Bartley, Arthur Laffer, Paul Craig Roberts, Norman Ture, and George Gilder, supply-side economics seemed a money tree. The less the government taxed, the more

*The three experiments were conducted by Richard Nixon, Augusto Pinochet, and Margaret Thatcher.

money it received.* Counterintuitive, perhaps, to those educated in the shadow of Lord Keynes, yet in truth, the idea was one of the oldest in economics. (Indeed, it was taught as gospel to all students who, like Ronald Reagan, passed through Eureka College between the years 1928 and 1932.) Deriving from the writings of Jean-Baptiste Say, a French follower of Adam Smith, supply-side economics reintroduced the classical notion known as Say's Law: Supply creates its own demand. Keynes had buried Say under an avalanche of counter-examples drawn from the Great Depression in his *General Theory of Employment, Interest, and Money* (1936), but the supply-siders were able to resurrect him amidst the stagflation of the 1970s.

The story of how supply-side economics came to be the official doctrine of the government of the United States of America with virtually no support from the economics profession has already been documented. What is important to understand about the doctrine is its Holy Grail aspect. After half a century of orthodoxy in which it was always assumed that fiscal and monetary policy presented a Hobson's choice on the Phillip's curve between inflation and unemployment, the hard-headed captains of industry at the *Journal* were suddenly promising painless gain. Philosophically, this was as un-Friedmanite as it was anti-Keynesian. But politically, it turned out to be irresistible. Whatever its murky intellectual justification, supply-side economics promised an end run around the primary dilemma that had plagued the American government since the "escalation without taxation" policies of the Johnson administration: how to provide a level of services and military forces far beyond that for which Americans were willing to pay.

The new theory offered the new counter-establishment something for everyone. During the post-Vietnam/pre-Reagan interregnum, the insider mind had often appeared to be drowning in a sea of Jeremiads, from Christopher Lasch's *The Culture of Narcissism* to Lester Thurow's *The Zero-*

---

*Wanniski and other supply-side partisans would insist that this is a caricature of their ideas. It isn't. The argument of the Laffer curve is that high taxes are a disincentive to work. On a curve plotted with taxes on one axis and government revenues on the other, the latter will equal zero at two points: that of no taxes and that of 100 percent taxes. The goal for policymakers is to locate the point on the curve at which sufficiently low taxes provide the greatest level of revenue. If the nation is already above that point, as the supply-siders clearly argued the United States was in 1980, then the entrepreneurial forces unleashed by a tax cut would indeed raise government revenues. In the spring 1981 *Cato Journal*, Laffer wrote of the proposed Reagan tax cuts that "it is reasonable to conclude that each of the proposed reductions in tax rates would, in terms of overall revenues, be self-financing in less than two years. Thereafter, each installment would provide a positive contribution to overall tax receipts." Arthur Laffer, "Government Exactions and Revenue Deficiencies," *Cato Journal* (spring 1981): p. 21.

Sum Society, the Club of Rome's infamous *Limits to Growth*, and Jimmy Carter's all-purpose malaise. Supply-side economics provided the equivalent of a psychological lifeboat.* For Friedmanites, it promised a close watch on the money supply to control inflation and keep interest rates low. For conservative politicians, it provided an irresistible election issue: lower taxes. For wealthy voters and campaign contributors, it promised free money. For Bartley and the *Wall Street Journal* editorial page, supply-side economics provided a stick with which to beat the paper's enemies and a vehicle by which it could distinguish itself as the most influential economic voice in the national political dialogue.

Under the previous editorial regime, headed for decades by two-time Pulitzer winner Vermont Royster, the page had been a dependable repository of conservative conventional wisdom. In economics, that meant unlimited support for free enterprise and opposition to government interference. Monetary policy was broadly Friedmanite. When Robert Bartley took over the editorial page in 1974, he was consciously searching for a way to shake up his readership. Under Irving Kristol's tutelage, Bartley wanted the page to adopt a more combative tone toward what he considered to be the liberal establishment—to "capture some of the intellectual appeal traditionally associated with liberalism." To this end, he recruited a bevy of prestigious regular contributors. They included Kristol; economists Walter Heller, Paul McCracken, Herbert Stein, Martin Feldstein, and Charles L. Schultze; and the liberal historian, Arthur Schlesinger, Jr. Later, whipping boys Hodding Carter, Michael Kinsley and, most astoundingly, the Stalinist Alexander Cockburn were added to this list.[†] These additions had the effect of livening a page that had been drifting like deadwood for decades. Instead of being merely America's best business newspaper, the *Journal* became the counter-establishment's newspaper of ideas.

---

*Supply-side mania, hardly coincidentally, corresponded almost exactly with the reheated Cold War of the neoconservatives and the social offensive of the Christian New Right as a means of redefining the political dialogue on the basis of "traditional American values." In this case, the values were laissez-faire economics and unquenchable Yankee optimism.

†The appointment of the Stalinist ladies' man as a regular columnist aroused feverish opposition on the part of many of the paper's readers and Bartley's ideological allies. For a brief time, Bartley even printed up "Alex Cockburn complaint cards" to give to the complainers. Cockburn's romance with Lally Weymouth, daughter of Katherine and Philip Graham, and his marriage to the novelist Katherine Kilgore, the granddaughter of Barney Kilgore, the famous *Journal* editor of the 1940s and 1950s, inspired what must be the cleverest observation Joseph Sobran ever made: "Alex Cockburn's scorn for the men who created the wealth of America is exceeded only by his admiration for the women who inherited it." Quoted in Charlotte Hays, "Alex Cockburn's Popular Front: *The Nation*'s Wittiest Soviet Apologist Has an Eye for Rich Men's Daughters," *Policy Review*, summer 1984, p. 60. In a 1989 interview, Bartley allowed that, personally, he found the column to be "not as interesting as [it] used to be." He discontinued Cockburn's column in January 1991.

Bartley's very first move, he recalls, was to try to hire as an editorial writer "a young assistant to Senator Gordon Allott by the name of George Will." When Will demurred, wishing to remain closer to the seat of national power, Bartley went after Jude Wanniski. The son of a Pennsylvania coal miner, raised on the streets of Brooklyn, Wanniski came to the *Journal* by way of newspapers in Alaska and Las Vegas and, finally, Dow Jones' own *National Observer.** He had gone off in search of journalistic fortune, hoping to emulate his hero, the mild-mannered centrist pundit James Reston. But he returned from his sojourn with the fiery eyes of a zealot without a cause. Initially, when Bartley made the offer, Wanniski protested that he knew nothing of editorial writing. "All it takes is arrogance," replied Bartley. That, all agree, the good Lord had given Jude Wanniski in generous measure. George Will, no slouch in the confidence department himself, once said of his competition, "I wish I were as confident of something as he is of everything."

An ebullient character of almost limitless enthusiasms—one of his most recent being Louis Farrakhan—Wanniski taught Bartley what the latter calls "the power of the outrageous." Nowhere was this more apparent than in the area of monetary and fiscal policy. Wanniski had no formal economic training himself, but on arriving in Washington he had found a willing tutor by the name of Arthur Laffer. Laffer had served under George Shultz in Richard Nixon's Office of Management and Budget (OMB), where his unorthodox forecasting method had briefly made him a laughingstock.† He returned to the University of Chicago, where his life went from terrible to much worse. Compulsively overeating from nervousness, Laffer ballooned in size. To welcome him home, his department sponsored a lecture by Paul Samuelson entitled, "Why They Are Laughing at Laffer."

Soon afterward, the department leaders decided that Laffer, who had been the youngest member of the Chicago economics faculty to be given tenure, had misled them about the completion of his doctorate. "It was horrible," Laffer wrote; "I knew there was no way on God's earth that I could make it in the profession. So, I went other routes—the press, the political process, consulting." Fortunately for Laffer's national reputation, Jude Wanniski, ostensibly just an editorial writer at the *Journal*, had a talent for all three.

By the time Bartley hired Wanniski at the *Journal*, he had become more than just a supply-side convert: he was a dedicated disciple in the

---

*Dow Jones published the weekly *National Observer* from February 1962 through July 1977.
†The predictions that caused Laffer so much heartache, those for the 1971 gross national product, turned out to be far closer to the mark than the predictions of any of his competitors at the time.

fully religious sense of the word. Laffer, building on the teachings of his Canadian mentor, Robert Mundell, was pushing a policy mix that called for a simultaneous (Friedmanite) contraction on the money supply and an enormous (Keynesian) reduction in the rate of personal income taxes on the wealthy. The former method was intended to control inflation; the latter to spur investment. The combination of lower taxes plus a stable money supply would, insisted the supply-sider, unleash a flood of pent-up entrepreneurship, displacing inefficient government spending with an explosion of growth in the private sector.

It took Bartley nearly two years to convince himself of the wisdom of Wanniski's new vision. But once Bartley was in for his own dime, the page was in for all of the *Journal*'s dollars. The *Journal*'s economics columns soon became a kind of tribal drum for the businessman's new theology. Wanniski would call Laffer every morning and, with Bartley's guidance, write supply-side editorials on the basis of their conversations. "It was our story," recalls Bartley with undue modesty, "and we ran with it."

The first full revelation of the supply-side Word, Wanniski's "The Mundell-Laffer Hypothesis: A New View of the World Economy," appeared, quite appropriately, in Kristol's neoconservative policy journal, the *Public Interest*, in 1975. Before Wanniski's article, neither of the two economists knew they had fashioned a hypothesis and, in any case, the piece was met with a yawn within the academic community, given its lack of a rigorous theoretical basis or mathematical modelling. Conventional wisdom at the time—as embodied by the Brookings Institution—attributed the breakdown of traditional Keynesian relationships to "outside shocks" to the system. The most prominent of these shocks were the impact of the trebling of oil prices in 1973 and 1979 and the delayed inflationary impact of the surreptitious funding of the Vietnam War. But Wanniski and Bartley soon won over a small cadre of Washington politicians, a group that Wanniski would call "the cabal." In time, this cabal would conquer the most important intellectual territory in the land: the "mind" of the 1980 Republican presidential candidate.

Within the upper reaches of the Republican Party, supply-side economics was not a difficult sell. Potential presidential candidates looking for an issue with which to defeat Jimmy Carter were not skittish about embracing the notion of an enormous tax cut as a campaign plank. The success of the 1978 tax revolt initiative in California, Proposition 13, implied almost revolutionary potential for the issue. Quarterback turned conservative Republican congressman Jack Kemp had picked up the tax-cutting ball and begun to run with the issue with Nagurski-like abandon—soon moving it to the top of his party's agenda. What the politicians lacked, however, was a respectable economic theory to justify their political intuitions.

Political prayers were answered in the form of a chance meeting between Wanniski and Kemp. Irving Kristol had suggested that Wanniski stop in and see Kemp, whom the editorial writer had previously considered to be little more than "a Right-Wing football player." Wanniski stopped into Kemp's office while researching another story at ten o'clock one morning, spent the rest of the day with Kemp, and later went home to the congressman's house for macaroni and cheese. "I think I've just fallen in love," Wanniski told a friend that night. Before Jack Kemp, "I was just ammunition in search of a weapon." Kemp assumed the role of an all-but-caped supply-side crusader, with his staff members, economists Paul Craig Roberts (soon to be Wanniski's replacement at the *Journal*) and Norman Ture, sharing the role of Robin. Soon all three began preaching the gospel on the campaign trail and throughout the halls of Congress.

After the conversion of Bartley and Kemp, the road to Reagan proved a relatively straightforward one. The candidate himself was an easy mark. He had never learned Keynesian economics, and he experienced extreme emotional discomfort at the thought of taxing a rich person. The underlying psychology of supply-side economics resonated perfectly with the mythology of a once-potent, self-sufficient capitalist class in America that had been tied by the tenterhooks of intrusive government interference. This was Cowboy Capitalism with a vengeance.

Moreover, to keep Kemp from challenging him, Reagan and his handlers had straightforward political incentives to hitch their wagons to the supply-side star. There was some confusion in the Reagan camp, but, as David Stockman later recalled, once Kemp, Laffer, and Wanniski had "thoroughly hosed [Reagan] down with supply-side doctrines . . . it set off a symphony in his ears. He knew instantly that it was true and would never doubt it a moment thereafter."

From 1974 through much of the 1980 presidential campaign, the *Journal* held a near monopoly on the supply-side discourse. Professional economists refused to take the notion seriously, and the nation's other op-ed pages, with the significant exception of the fire-breathing Evans and Novak, saw no reason to do so, either. One could argue, quite convincingly, that the economics profession's decision to ignore supply-side economics was both arrogant and short-sighted. However unscientific it may have seemed, particularly with regard to the dense econometric modeling that dominated economic discourse in Cambridge and New Haven, supply-side was the only train leaving the station. Keynesian explanations no longer sufficed. It was up to the professionals to either derail it or jump on board; but they could not even bring themselves to look up from their econometric models and wave. As a result, nowhere was the theory subjected to anything like the rigorous testing one would expect before the world's largest economy literally bet its future savings on it. For the better part of the half-decade during which the assault was under way, the *Journal*'s editorial pages provided virtually all of the public discourse regarding the doctrine that would soon govern the organization of the American economy. In fact, the only serious academic discussion of the model during this period appeared in an article by Kemp aide Paul Craig Roberts in the summer 1978 issue of Irving Kristol's journal, the *Public Interest.* It should surprise no one that the author provided an altogether favorable view.

Liberal economists involved in the political process viewed Reagan's supply-side rhetoric with undisguised contempt. Speaking to the *Washington Journalism Review* in the spring of 1980, MIT Business School Dean Lester Thurow called the Reagan economic plan "absolute nonsense" and observed that its policies "don't make any sense from the point of view of conservative economists, much less anybody else." But, like most observers, Thurow probably expected Reagan to cave in to the old Keynesian orthodoxy once tutored by the responsible members of Washington insiderdom. What this view missed, however, was the degree to which the old establishment had exhausted itself fighting the losing battles of the 1970s. Once the Reagan entourage came to town, exuding confidence and cloaking their economic policies in patriotic metaphors, the emasculated political class, tired of feeling helpless in the face of economic equations it could no longer understand, simply threw up its hands and shot craps with the nation's monetary and fiscal policy. Although most insiders did not even pretend to understand it, they were sufficiently riled up by the supply-siders' apocalyptic rhetoric to act on the ever-present American compulsion to do something. As monetarist Herbert Stein wrote in the *Journal*'s op-ed page,

> Economists cannot say that they know with certainty that the Kemp-Roth tax cut would not raise the revenue. They can, or should only say that the available evidence makes the outcome extremely improbable. It may turn out that there is human life on Mars. But I would not invest much in McDonald's franchise on the planet, and I wouldn't bet the nation's economic policy on the assumption that the tax cut will increase the revenue.

Whatever defects Wanniski or Bartley are likely to admit regarding the "riverboat gamble" they helped inspire, they blame on the manner in which it was implemented. Wanniski says he tried to warn Stockman that "interest rates would not come down without recession, unless there was a monetary reform, that it was not a fiscal problem, and deferring the tax cuts would only invite recession and expand the deficits." But Stockman, who, according to Wanniski, "never really understood the supply-side framework," was determined to do it his way, with budget cuts and massive military spending increases and without controlling the money supply. The result was a kind of super-heated military Keynesianism, replete with exploding government debt, declining savings, decreased national investment, and a major redistribution of national income from the poorest Americans to the richest. In short, the plan accomplished none of what its promoters had promised and made our economy's most important problems worse. "The big problem with Dave," Wanniski later insisted, "was his youth."

Stockman's various decoys and dissimulations during the early days of the supply-side adventure at least had the virtue of demonstrating for all to see just how supine the punditocracy can be in the face of a concerted White House propaganda barrage. When then–*Washington Post* editor William Greider published then–OMB director Stockman's confessional (in which Stockman admitted that the entire exercise had been an intentional hoax) in the November 1981 *Atlantic Monthly* nine months into the Reagan administration, insider Washington reacted as if the president had suddenly been found to be selling arms to the Ayatollah. In language that anticipated the upcoming savings and loan scandal—the legislative basis of which the *Journal* editorial page had supported wholeheartedly just six months earlier—Stockman observed that the Reagan administration had "lost control" of its supply-side tax-cut policies, leading powerful and influential "hogs" to "feed" on the new Reagan ideology.* That supply-side economics had been, as Stockman said, nothing more than a "Trojan horse to bring down the top rate" of taxation for America's richest citizens should have come as no surprise to those insiders plugged in to the political process. All that was required was an ability to read the coded dialogue of administration press leaks. Yet, as Greider noted, "it was as though editors and reporters had no memory of what they themselves had been reporting for months."†

---

*With regard to the savings and loan scandal, the *Journal* promised in June 1981 that "complete deregulation would allow [the thrifts] to do all the things that banks can do: make all types of loans and enlarge the scope of their investments." In what may go down as the worst prediction in all economic forecasting history—quite a statement, I know—Bartley and company observed, "the beauty of these solutions is that they're cheap." See "Thrift Sale," *Wall Street Journal,* 29 June 1981.
†"It's kind of hard to sell 'trickle down,' " Stockman explained to William Greider, "so the supply-side formula was the only way to get a tax policy that was really 'trickle down.' . . . Supply-side is 'trickle-down' theory." For the most thoughtful account of Stockman's role in the implementation of supply-side economics, see William Greider, *The Education of David Stockman and Other Americans,* rev. ed. (New York: New American Library, 1986). These quotes appear on pages 47, 48, and 55.

Clearly, the economic pundits failed the American public. They had no inkling whatever that the man most responsible for turning the president's confident economic philosophy into policy viewed the entire episode as a cynical manipulation of the public's gullibility for the purpose of raiding the treasury and feeding the hogs. But they had kept their innocence by fooling themselves as well. The relentless amnesia of the American political process was never more apparent than in the days that followed the Stockman article's appearance. The president's men concocted a story line in which young Davey was taken to a metaphorical "woodshed" by an angry but forgiving president who whipped some sense into his errant young adviser, presumably eliciting a promise never to tell the truth to the American people again. In fact, Reagan never expressed much anger toward Stockman; the "woodshed" meeting was a complete fiction generated to take the political heat off the moment and submerge the truths laid bare in the Stockman story into the mythical image of Reagan as a strong but merciful patriarch.

The substance of Stockman's story could hardly have been more devastating to the Reagan administration. Stockman was saying that, at base, the entire edifice was phony. There was no "there" there. Literally "no one" knew "what was going on with the numbers." The costs of the willful self-deception involved in inferring competence in the Reagan administration would be demonstrated over and over again during the course of the next eight years, but the insider dialogue continued to focus almost exclusively on the alleged personality conflicts. It did not even matter, as in the case of Stockman, that these conflicts existed only in the fevered imaginations of the president's image consultants. No story, it appeared, was too trivial, too clichéd, or too far-fetched to excite the passions of the punditocracy, as long as it had good guys and bad guys and the right ones won out at the end.

Robert Bartley, it should surprise no one, thinks the supply-side experiment turned out just fine. Bartley learned to live with, if not quite love, the deficits approaching $350 billion a year during the 1980s. In the first place, he insists, they were a "secondary issue," irrelevant to what takes place in the "real sector." Second, they were a matter of spending policy, rather than tax policy, and could have been closed by "moderate budget restraint." Third, rather than condemn the deficits and the interest payments they demand from the tax payer, Bartley wants to know what those funds would have gone toward. "It's certainly true that the government can spend money to increase production or on defense which increases production. But, on the other hand, if it's going to spend it on increased transfer payments, I'd rather have them pay it out in interest and let the private economy use it."

What Bartley is in effect saying here, as Wanniski puts it, is that "there are deficits and there are deficits." He would rather see Americans pay a healthy percentage of their taxes to the rich foreigners who hold our debt than have the money available for rebuilding our public infrastructure, cleaning our air and water, providing resources to keep our neighborhoods safe from drugs and crime, improving our national education system, and retraining our workers to compete in the global economy. This is, historically speaking, a respectable philosophical position within the conservative camp. But it is hardly one that the majority of the country can be expected to embrace.

The economist Herbert Stein is credited with being the first to affix the newfangled name of "supply-side fiscalism" to these policies, in 1976, and George Bush, in a brief moment of lucidity four years later, called them "voodoo economics." These characterizations have a nice ring to them, but a more accurate depiction might employ a more old-fashioned term, one that remained taboo within the punditocracy during the entire Reagan era: *class warfare.*

CHAPTER NINE

Even the *New Republic* ...

I don't know if any of you have heard of a magazine called *The New Republic*," said then–treasury secretary Donald Regan to an assembled group of reporters in early 1985, but, as he soon made clear, this hallowed home of historic heartbleeders, this perfidious parlor of pointy-headed pinkos, this effete embankment of Eastern Establishment elitism had just "endorsed" Ronald Reagan's tax reform plan. What a victory for common sense.

Of course, Regan, the no-nonsense former chief executive officer of Merrill Lynch, did not bother with the rhetorical flourishes above. But the thrust of his comments was clear. It was a thrust that the Reagan administration and its allies found extremely useful during the 1980s whenever they needed to demonstrate just how silly and sectarian their adversaries were being. "My god," opponents of the nuclear freeze, proponents of the MX, boosters of the contra war, critics of the civil rights movement, etc., could now say, "even the liberal *New Republic* understands this issue well enough to see we're right. What can possibly be the matter with my distinguished opponent?" Michael Kinsley, editor for much of the period, once suggested that the magazine change its name to "Even the liberal *New Republic* ..."

The degree of cultural hegemony exercised by the *New Republic* over right-thinking Washington insiders during the 1980s was difficult to explain outside the purview of its tiny empire. The ubiquitous presence of Michael Kinsley, Charles Krauthammer, Morton Kondracke, Fred Barnes, and Leon Wieseltier throughout the punditocracy during this period added up to considerable collective influence. The overall effect is even greater than the sum of its parts. Tastemaker *Vanity Fair* instructed its readers on two separate occasions between 1985 and 1988 that no fashion-conscious politico could aspire to hipness without "the smartest, most impudent weekly in the country" and the "most entertaining and intellectually agile magazine in the country." A *New York Times* cultural critic observed that the magazine's influence, as the 1990s began, seemed "to be at, or certainly near, a new height." Right-wingers, in particular, could not get enough of this liberal magazine. Norman Podhoretz called it "indispensable." George Will referred to it as "currently the nation's most interesting and most important political journal." Buckley's *National Review* thought it "one of the most interesting magazines in the United States." The Reagan White House had twenty copies sent over by messenger every Thursday afternoon, minutes after the magazine returned from the printer.

As the above statements testify, the *New Republic* was, during the 1980s, the single most important repository of ideas and political ideology in the entire insider constellation. Excluding the nonpartisan *National Journal*, the *New Republic* was the only regularly read Washington-based magazine in which ideas and policy problems could be fleshed out to a degree that even remotely reflected their contextual complexity, allowing for possible objections and meeting them with fully reasoned responses. Moreover, in a town where the standards of literary eloquence are embodied by General Accounting Office reports with titles like "Administrative Systems: NASA Should Reassess Its Automated Information Management (AIM) Program and Rescind Its IBM-Compatible Policy" (May 1990), the damn thing was actually fun to read. The *New Republic* was well written, perfectly attuned to the rhythms and genuflections of the insider dialogue, and extraordinarily—often diabolically—clever. Even those offended by its know-it-all tone or rightward political leanings could not help but admire its zippy writing style and engaging humor.

The *New Republic*'s victory as the heavyweight champion of pundit-powered publications was partially a reflection of the state of its competition. Other magazines published important articles, but their influence rested largely on the reputations of their authors.[*] The only weekly periodical with cachet comparable to that of the *New Republic* was the *London Economist*. Although American journalists read the *Economist* with a degree of reverence that borders on worship, no magazine written and published across the Atlantic could seriously expect to be a decisive influence in the opinion-shaping game in Washington. The insider dialogue responds to

---

[*]*Foreign Affairs* and *Foreign Policy*, being specialized quarterly publications, speak to a slightly different audience.

stimuli so capricious and arcane that no one who is not fully immersed in it can expect to master it in a meaningful way for other insiders. Former *New Republic* editor Mickey Kaus once lamented the difficulty of attempting to keep track of the insider dialogue from Los Angeles. "By the time you've heard Pat Caddell is touting Bruce Springsteen for president," Kaus bemoaned, "he has already switched to Dwight Gooden."

To the degree that the *New Republic* had any competition in the big idea business, it derived not so much from other publications as from television's two "quality" television interview programs, *Nightline* and *The MacNeil-Lehrer NewsHour*. In terms of pure star-making ability within the punditocracy, *Nightline* host Ted Koppel fell just a few percentage points behind God. Because the program surreptitiously hatched itself amidst the media chicanery surrounding the Iran hostage crisis of 1979, Koppel and company managed to forge a truly unique combination of highbrow respect and network financial support. To be interrupted in a meeting by a call from *Nightline* became the ultimate insider status symbol. To be invited on the show was akin to winning the lottery. Best of all was to be asked to discuss a subject in which one had no particular expertise, which meant that Koppel had anointed you all-purpose wise man. During the 1980s, *New Republic* editors Michael Kinsley, Hendrik Hertzberg, Charles Krauthammer, and Leon Wieseltier all enjoyed this honor repeatedly. But *Nightline* did not set out to shape intellectual fashions as much as to mirror them. For that reason, it suffered from many of the same defects that plague most objective journalism. Most of its invited experts were either public officials or former public officials. In an era dominated by conservative administrations, their minions enjoyed a considerable *Nightline* advantage.* Moreover, because many of the Reagan administration's battles were fought between its incumbent "pragmatists" and "ideologues," the Left/Right split that television producers customarily sought for their guest spots usually featured a "liberal" supporter of the Reagan administration along with someone representing a position so extreme that not even Ronald Reagan could sign off on it.

The *New Republic* occasionally divided along these lines as well. Despite all evidence, Morton Kondracke continued to insist during this period that he was not a conservative, and so, in the magazine's syndicated radio program, he would set himself up as the liberal in order to support Reaganite foreign policies. As late as August 1991, extreme conservatives like James J.

---

*In an examination of *Nightline*'s guest list for the period from January 1, 1985, to April 30, 1988, the most frequently called-on guests were Henry Kissinger, Alexander Haig, Elliott Abrams, and Jerry Falwell. Eighty-nine percent were men, and ninety-two percent were white. See William Hoynes and David Croteau, *All the Usual Suspects: MacNeil/Lehrer and Nightline* (New York: FAIR, May 1990).

Kilpatrick were still touting Kondracke's liberal bona-fides in celebration of his endorsement of their views. Were this the sum total effect of the magazine's efforts to undermine liberalism in the 1980s, it could be considered merely a pale, unimportant version of *The McLaughlin Group*. But the magazine's assault on liberals and liberalism was far more interesting—and confusing—than that seen anywhere else in the punditocracy.

Somehow, during the 1980s the *New Republic* managed to carry on its masthead at least half a dozen of the most interesting and original liberal writers in America, while at the same time providing conservatives with their most potent political and ideological weapons in the punditocracy's war of ideas. The *New Republic* argued the Reagan administration's case with far greater sophistication and nuance than did the administration itself. Moreover, by publishing hard-line Reaganite views alongside those of its traditional liberal writers and insisting that both formed part of a single project designed to rejuvenate liberalism, the magazine succeeded in giving the fundamental precepts of Reaganite foreign policy—the military buildup, the proxy wars, the contemptuous unilateralism—what former editor-in-chief Hendrik Hertzberg called an important dose of "intellectual cachet." Proponents of old-fashioned liberal values—nonintervention, multilateralism, social justice, and redistribution of wealth—were left with nowhere to go but the *Nation*, which, because of Cockburn's prominence, was considered so politically extreme that most insiders were afraid to pick one up without lead-lined gloves.

The act of retaining a liberal readership while publishing a flagship conservative publication was by definition a delicate one. The magazine's answer to its ideological conundrum was to seek refuge in a term that previously had been taken to indicate a severe psychological disorder. Owner and president Martin Peretz bragged that "some people say we are schizophrenic, yet these are times when even the most thoughtful people are ambivalent."

In addition to *schizophrenia*, the magazine's editors had great success in renegotiating the political connotations of the word *unpredictable*. This term, for which *Roget's Thesaurus* offers "capricious, careless, immature, irresponsible, undependable and untrustworthy" as imperfect synonyms, became, during the reign of the *New Republic*, the certifying adjective: the word that admitted formerly boring liberals into the exclusive club of the politically relevant and culturally chic. To be predictable—that is, to remain consistent with some definable set of principles or worldview—became, in the lexicon of the *New Republic*, akin to cowardice, lily-livered nostalgia, soft-headedness, and stunted mental growth. The *Nation* was predictable. Feminists were predictable. Civil rights leaders were predictable. But "the one sure thing," promised Peretz, "about this unpredict-able magazine is that we will go on being unpredictable."

The unpredictable/schizophrenia strategy won the magazine the new, influential audience it sought without driving away too many of the liber-als who formed the backbone of its readership. It was also extremely helpful to the magazine's ability to secure corporate advertising. Freed from what its then-publisher Jeffrey Dearth called the "philosophical albatross" of the "dead-weight of knee-jerk liberalism," the *New Republic* was able to woo new corporate advertisers to its pages. More to the point, however, was its ability to sway the insider dialogue. Just how, through the personality of its writers and editors, the magazine arrived at its "iconoclastic" definition of modern liberalism was a subject of endless speculation on the insider cocktail circuit in Washington. Everyone read the magazine, liberals angrily and conservatives with ill-concealed glee. Feminists, although put off by its Harvard frat-boy atmosphere—Henry Fairlie once compared it to an ancient Greek gymnasium—nevertheless appreciated its pro-feminist politics. Radicals on both sides of the politi-cal divide agreed that the only reason Washington seemed to find the magazine's arguments so fascinating was the fact that its conservatives insisted on calling themselves liberals. As *Nation* columnist Christopher Hitchens complained,

> The preface to this was always to be able to say, "Look, I've been a liberal all my life, it is in my roots, my fingertips and my hair, and it is in that capacity that I say I like the contras, or I like the MX, or what's so wrong with Ivan Boesky?" These are statements which would be perfectly trite on their own—they almost would have some distance to go before reaching trite—but because of the "I'm a liberal" preface, they are invested with a kind of daring and appear brave.

Right-wing writer Dinesh D'Souza concurred:

> Articles triumphantly circulated on the Right would probably be ho-hum items if they appeared in *National Review* or the *American Spectator*. . . . Per-haps *TNR*'s only new idea is that its old ideas aren't very good. . . . But if *TNR* articles give credibility to the Right, perhaps the magazine considers this a small price to pay for getting itself taken seriously by conservatives—who happen to be in power.

However unimpressed critics like these were, the benefits of calling oneself liberal while endorsing Reaganite goals were manifestly apparent at the magazine's November 1984 seventieth anniversary party. There, among the silk cummerbunds and caviar blinis, editors heard themselves praised by such liberal luminaries as Patrick Buchanan, Jeane Kirkpatrick, Irving Kristol, and Henry Kissinger. Dr. K (to whom, in 1977, the magazine had bid farewell with an editorial entitled "Good Riddance") complained with a straight face that the evening had been "traumatic" for him. "I have been photographed with so many liberals, my semiannual visits to the White House will now be even less frequent."

One of the enduring mysteries about the *New Republic*'s role in the political and cultural wars of the 1980s was the fact that, while its liberals were considered more talented and interesting than its conservatives by far, it was the latter whose political views defined the magazine's stature within the punditocracy. This was even stranger given the fact that, for much of the period, its editor-in-chief was the writer widely recognized as the most talented liberal pundit in more than a generation.

To say that former editor-in-chief Michael Kinsley has led a charmed life is to commit oneself to considerable understatement. Compared to Kinsley, Dobie Gillis grew up in downtown Baluchistan. Loving parents, suburban Detroit childhood, private schools, Harvard, Rhodes scholarship, Harvard Law School, five summers working for Ralph Nader, one summer as managing editor of the neoliberal *Washington Monthly* and, finally, at the ripe old age of twenty-five (and still in law school), managing editor of the *New Republic*. With a weird kind of glamorous nebbishness that frequently put him at the top of Washington's most eligible bachelors lists, Kinsley somehow lived up to all the myths that New Republicans tried to create about themselves. He was ideologically anti-ideological. He had an unerring eye for cant, hypocrisy, and sanctimony. He was hysterically funny and, perhaps most important, politically fearless.

Kinsley turned sacred cows into hamburger without regard for political or ideological affinity. During the 1980s, he scorched the earth on targets ranging from Jonathan Schell's high-minded nuclear apocalypticism to his own magazine's infatuation with anti-Communist guerrillas, welfare programs for the wealthy, and the unfairness of the social security tax. His column on the latter issue inspired Daniel Patrick Moynihan to introduce a bill cutting the tax, thereby throwing the Democratic Party into yet another unsolved identity crisis and forcing the entire Congress to calculate the size of the deficit slightly less dishonestly. His satires on the self-important stupidity of such Washington pundits as Hugh Sidey and the cast of *Agronsky and Company* were funnier and more biting than anything in this book.

But however talented a writer or critic he may have been, Kinsley did not inspire. He laughed, he cajoled, he mocked, and he satirized, but even the most astute reader of his work would have had a hard time conjuring up what motivated Kinsley's political zeal. Kinsley credited neoliberal guru and *Washington Monthly* editor Charlie Peters with inspiring his personal philosophy, but after three decades of neoliberal proselytizing, its fundamentals still appear decidedly fuzzy. Kinsley was against overtaxing poor people and subsidizing wealthy ones. He was an ardent free-trader and believed that capitalism would benefit from a collapse in real-estate prices. He admired Ralph Nader, his former employer, whom he viewed as "operating on the mental fringe where self-abnegation blurs into self-obsession." But Kinsley himself was obsessed by nothing. He dedicated himself simply to delineating the foibles of contemporary Washington life. Kinsleyism might fairly be called Dukakisism with a sense of humor. However satisfying it may have been for upper-middle-class yuppies, it was not the foundation of a resurgent liberalism.

Whenever Kinsley got fed up with taking orders from Peretz, he would resign as the magazine's editor and be replaced by Hendrik Hertzberg.[*] Kinsley had no competition as the most talented liberal pundit in Washington, but if he had, it would have been Hertzberg. Emanating from a less ambivalently bleeding heart, Hertzberg's politics derived from exactly the emotionally driven sense of commitment that was lacking in Kinsley. A one-time *New Yorker* editor and Carter speechwriter, Hertzberg was a traditional social democrat who wrote with a keen eye, an engaging sense of humor, and a wonderful feel for unintended irony. Here is Hendrik Hertzberg on the 1988 Iowa primary:

> The big Democratic winner, of course, was Richard Gephardt, a man who puts me in mind, unreasonably to be sure, of an earthling whose body has been taken over by space aliens. I keep expecting him to reach under his chin and peel back that immobile, monochromatic, oddly smooth face to reveal the lizard beneath. Perhaps the aliens are from the planet Bryan. How else to explain the fact that Gephardt, who until a few months ago was sort of a neoconservative, neoliberal, has suddenly begun talking, in his slow robotic voice, like a devotee of Populism?

Rounding out the liberal stable at the magazine during the 1980s were Sidney Blumenthal and Leon Wieseltier. Blumenthal, who spent much of the decade at the *Washington Post*, nevertheless contributed to the *New Republic* a powerful ability to mine the underlying cultural elements of American politics and a deep devotion to the presidential can-

---

[*]The reverse was also true until Hertzberg retired again in September 1991 and Kinsley, ensconced at *Crossfire, Time,* and the *New Republic*'s TRB column, was no longer available.

didacy of Bill Clinton. (He would later work directly for the president.) Wieseltier, a brilliant Jewish medieval scholar whom Peretz plucked from the elevated vines of Harvard's Society of Fellows, was an extremely ambivalent liberal who tended to arrive at conventional liberal political positions via almost Hegelian intellectual complications.[*]

If the four writers discussed above had been given free rein to write and publish the *New Republic*, supplemented by thoughtful liberal contributing editors such as Ronald Steel, Robert Reich, and Robert Kuttner, the magazine most likely would have been exactly the challenging liberal publication that American politics so sorely lacked in the 1980s. Such a magazine would have been decidedly less radical than the *Nation* but better able to integrate moral, political, and social questions into a policy framework. Such a magazine would also have been at the cutting edge of Democratic Party politics, helping the more progressive elements of the debate fashion a coherent response to the breakdown of the social contract that for years ensured the primacy of the New Deal coalition. But then, of course, no one would have had occasion to beat down liberal opponents by insisting that "even the *New Republic*" understood the necessity of whatever Reaganite measure happened to be on the table.

When Martin Peretz took over the *New Republic*, each had reached a political and philosophical dead end. Peretz had attended Brandeis before becoming a left-wing (graduate) student activist at Harvard. A dedicated Zionist with many millions of dollars at his disposal, he had given up trying to overthrow the system and was now ready to work within it. Peretz and the New Left parted company when black revolutionaries began to condemn Israel as a racist and imperialist outpost. He felt a deep devotion to the Jewish state, explaining to Henry Kissinger during the 1967 Arab-Israeli war that his "dovishness stopped at the delicatessen door."

Peretz and his second wife, the Singer sewing machine heiress Anne Labouisse Farnsworth, had funded some of the decade's most ambitious political efforts along with some of its most disastrous ones.[†] Peretz had

---

[*]This was truer later in the decade than it was in the early part. Wieseltier supported aid to the contras and the MX missile, but his cultural revulsion with Reaganism led him further and further toward the liberal side as the decade wore on.
[†]According to Gwenda Blair, Peretz married Linda Heller, a Brandeis classmate and the daughter of a wealthy citrus grower, in 1962. The marriage lasted "a year or two," and then Peretz moved into Kirkland House, a Harvard residential hall. He married Farnsworth in June 1967 after she separated from her first husband in the mid-1960s. It was at this point, according to Blair, that Peretz became "a husband again, a stepfather, and a very rich man." Blair, "Citizen Peretz," pp. 89–90.

invested himself wholeheartedly in both the arguments and the personal style of the movement, and its collapse left him at loose ends. One freshman at Harvard in 1966, James Fallows, who says he was "straight off the boat" from the Goldwaterite conservatism of his Southern California upbringing, applied to join a seminar Peretz was conducting on the Vietnam War. Fallows recalls feeling Peretz's "withering contempt" for someone who, like this California rube, was not "sufficiently or stylishly anti-American in his view of the war."* But by the early 1970s, with Peretz's academic career stymied and his politics moving on a rightward arc, the couple was looking for new political investments.

The *New Republic*, meanwhile, had drifted into a kind of courtly irrelevance. Its post-Lippmann zenith had taken place more than a decade earlier when the handsome young president emerged from Air Force One ready to lead the free world, holding a copy of that week's issue beneath his arm. But ideological ferment of the 1960s, coupled with the failure of liberalism's wars—on the Vietnamese in Indochina and on poverty in America's cities—had left its most venerable institutions exhausted and confused. The *New Republic* was no exception.

The Peretzes purchased the magazine from owner-editor Gilbert Harrison in 1974, with the understanding that Harrison would remain editor for three years. That arrangement lasted ten months. One day Harrison entered the stately Nineteenth Street townhouse to find his Queen Anne desk and John Marin paintings in the hallway and Martin Peretz sitting in what had until the day before been Harrison's office. The *New Republic*'s era of unpredictability had begun.

In the beginning, there were the words. On taking over the magazine, Peretz would frequently subject the holdover staff to profane verbal abuse before firing them, says Philip Terzian, an editor whom Peretz fired and whose recollections may be colored by his unmitigated hatred for the man. Harrison's staff feared that Peretz would turn the *New Republic* into a liberal version of *Commentary*, with all issues decided on the basis of what was "good for the Jews." Peretz went so far in this direction, says Terzian, that he instructed his editors to pick up material from the Israeli embassy that he would later run as *New Republic* editorials.† "It

---

*"The contempt is more or less the same now," Fallows said twenty-five years later. "It's just pointed in the opposite direction." Historian Barton J. Bernstein, who attended graduate school with Peretz in the early 1960s, adds, "It's funny. Most of the people, pro and anti, who've known Marty over the years see him the same way—as somebody on the make. The dispute most often is on the value of whatever his cause is." Author's interviews with James Fallows and Barton J. Bernstein.

†This assertion could not be confirmed by anyone else who worked at the magazine at the time, although at least two employees did consider it to be plausible. Peretz declined to speak to this or any other issue raised in this book.

was a very wild place," recalled Henry Fairlie, who remained close to Peretz until his death in 1990, "run by a sort of Jewish cowboy with an open shirt."

Peretz originally told the *Washington Post* that he planned to "toughen the *New Republic*'s liberalism with more aggressive, sharply argued opinions now being exploited by conservatives." But the most obvious manner in which these positions were sharpened and toughened up was by heaving them overboard. The political retooling of the magazine began immediately but proceeded fitfully during the Ford and Carter eras, and not always according to political principle. This confused readers and writers alike. Speaking of a book review commissioned more than a dozen years earlier, Peretz recalled to the literary critic Alfred Kazin in 1989 that, "the worst thing I ever did to you was when I suppressed your [negative] review of Lillian Hellman. She scared me shitless."

While Peretz allowed Kinsley and his cohorts a generally free hand with much of the magazine's domestic agenda, he gradually reshaped its foreign policy to reflect the contours of the emerging counter-establishment realignment. Michael Ledeen, a shadowy, failed academic who was accused of perjury by his colleagues and maintained still-murky ties to the Italian Secret Service, began to appear prominently in the magazine.[*] Kenneth Adelman, Reagan's future anti–arms control adviser, also saw his right-wing polemics featured frequently. Other invited neoconservatives included Jeane Kirkpatrick, Edward Luttwak, and the ubiquitous Irving Kristol. The only point of contact between the old liberals and the New Rightists was a consistently pro-Israel hard line.

Unlike Norman Podhoretz's monochromatic *Commentary*, Peretz's neoconservative leanings stretched him in many directions simultaneously. First came the most conventional: Peretz hired Morton Kondracke from the *Chicago Sun-Times*, and the reporter quickly converted from liberal to neoconservative in tune with the tenor of the late Carter era. When Kondracke left on his brief *Newsweek* sojourn, he was replaced by the even more conservative Fred Barnes. When Kondracke returned, Barnes remained. Both men made their livings by professing faith in the conventional wisdom of the moment. Neither one proved

---

[*]This is the same Michael Ledeen who helped broker Oliver North's arms sales to the Ayatollah. It is also the same Michael Ledeen who once offered to put the author's head "through the living room window" if the author asked him another question about why Ledeen had ended his academic career under a cloud of plagiarism charges at the University of Washington at St. Louis. See the author's "Michael Ledeen: His Shadowy World Is None of Your Business," *Regardie's*, April 1987, p. 38.

an intellectual match for the magazine's liberals, but each had qualities that endeared him to insiderdom.

The charitable explanation for Morton Kondracke was simply that he was a likable fellow who had fallen in with the wrong crowd. Kondracke worked hard but suffered from a built-in homing device for conventional insider thinking, regardless of the issue. Without trying or perhaps even being aware of it, Kondracke speaks, as Kinsley has noted, with the voice of "official" Washington.* As one *New Republic* editor put it, "Central America is wherever Mort is."

Fred Barnes, a born-again Christian, was less a member of the close-knit Peretz mishpacha than Kondracke, but he excelled as the kind of inside pooper-scooper who kept the *New Republic* on the punditocracy's cutting edge. White House sources knew his to be a sympathetic ear and thus went to great efforts to fill it early and often. They would leak to him on Tuesday to make his *New Republic* deadline and then again on Friday morning for *The McLaughlin Group.*

Barnes and Kondracke kept the magazine current, but it was Charles Krauthammer who undertook a five-year mission to shape its liberal philosophy and boldly take it where no liberal had gone before. Almost alone among the *New Republic*'s neoconservative stable, Krauthammer brought both arguments and an intelligence that were taken seriously by its liberal half. As Kinsley put it, "Before I know my argument is sound, I like to run it hypothetically through Charles."

Krauthammer had been chief resident of Psychiatric Consultation Services at Massachusetts General Hospital before coming to Washington with one of his professors in 1978. After a stint as Walter Mondale's speechwriter, he joined the *New Republic* as a senior editor, later expanding his portfolio to op-ed pages, newsweeklies, and pundit sitcoms. As with most neoconservatives, Krauthammer was never willing to give up his insistence that he was the real liberal. Hendrik Hertzberg, whose job it was to argue with him, calls Krauthammer a "Left-Wing Neocon on domestic matters and a hard-Right Neocon on foreign policy." This is in contrast to Peretz, who, according to Hertzberg, had been a "Left-Wing Neocon," both foreign and domestically, during the 1980s. These distinctions are important. As Kondracke reveals, although both he and Krauthammer began as "disciples of Peretz at the outset, increasingly Peretz and I became inspired by Krauthammer."

*The quote from which I derive this view reads, "I think we can hear the official view making itself heard through my friend Mort Kondracke in last week's *New Republic.*" Michael Kinsley, "Yes, We Have No Bananas," *The New Republic,* 24 November 1979.

During the Krauthammer ascendancy, *New Republic* editorials took a progressively harder line and developed a frequent habit of questioning the motives of its opponents. The sentiments underlying these editorials often recalled a McCarthy different from the one whom Peretz had helped bankroll in 1968. Those who did not see things the magazine's way became "second-rate thinkers"; "self-indulgent, solipsistic"; "Sandinista sympathizers"; and "fellow-travellers and their ilk." One editorial accused "Democrats, including some in Congress," of "positively identifying with the Sandinistas, their social designs, their political ends and even their hostility to the United States." This tactic infuriated Wieseltier, who explains,

> Charles' great contribution to the debate was to question the motives of his opponents. One of the great Neoconservative habits—[Norman] Podhoretz has perfected it—was that since your own view is obviously correct, anyone who disagrees with you must suffer from a human frailty. The explanation cannot be intellectual, it must be psychological. Because if the intellectual differences were granted, that would imply there was something to argue about. But there is nothing to argue about. So it is obvious that there must be something the matter with that person, and so you look to his ambitions, his motives, his wife. Something.

The questioning of liberal motives during the Reagan years was part of a frontal assault by the magazine on the chastened, post-Vietnam internationalism that characterized the Democratic Party's mainstream. At the beginning of the Reagan administration, when its opponents coalesced behind a proposal for a mutual, verifiable freeze on the production and development of nuclear weapons, the magazine attacked both the proposal and its partisans. When the conference of Catholic bishops proclaimed nuclear deterrence to be immoral, the *New Republic* wrote that "there are few greater sins against sanity than the weakening of deterrence. Like the president, the bishops have sinned." "Utopian thinking has always offered lofty rationalization for risk, for tampering with the foundations," explained the *New Republic*'s editors in yet another editorial that equated the willingness to negotiate a reduction in arms with the Soviets with "utopianism" and "risk," but "this time the risk is too great, the foundations too shaky."[*]

Opposing the peace movement and arms control caucuses within the Democratic Party, the magazine threw its considerable persuasive

---

[*]"Nuclear Fantasies," *The New Republic*, 18 April 1983, p. 10. Needless to say, had Mikhail Gorbachev thought this way, we'd still be fighting the Evil Empire.

powers behind the construction of two new intercontinental ballistic missiles, the ten-warhead MX missile, and the single-warhead midgetman. In 1983, when the Reagan administration engineered the "Scowcroft Report"—a propaganda document conceived by one of the decade's many bipartisan commissions of conservative Democrats and Republicans to build support for otherwise insupportable Reagan administration policies—the *New Republic* wrote, "The Commission has accomplished nothing less than a revolution in doctrine." What this revolution constituted in political terms, however, was merely the agreement of the administration to build midgetman missiles in addition to its beloved MX. The *New Republic* professed to detest the MX, observing at one point that "only if we wish to start a nuclear war—do we need the MX." But it was willing to endorse its development as a means to persuade the Reagan administration to build a fleet of midgetman missiles as well. The "revolution," however, never arrived. The Reagan administration got its MXs, to be sure, with crucial New Republican Democrats supporting it. But none of the administration's promises with regard to the Scowcroft Commission's report was ever fulfilled.

Although it was passionate in support of the continuance of the nuclear arms race, the magazine reserved much of its most vociferous rhetorical support for the administration's proxy wars in Central America. With regard to El Salvador, the magazine's editors managed to convince themselves that by 1986, "the military and police, which rightist thugs once dominated, are slowly but meaningfully becoming more professional and apolitical." El Salvador, wrote the editors, "is a democracy in the process of becoming, and it is therefore a big credit on Ronald Reagan's ledger—and also on the ledger of moderate Democrats who weren't afraid to cross the partisan line." In fact, in 1986 El Salvador was still a hellish country, run by exactly those thuggish elements the *New Republic* sought to whitewash. According to figures assembled by the human rights office of the Catholic Archdiocese in San Salvador, in the period from 1980 to 1989, government-sponsored or -assisted death squads killed 41,048 citizens. The equivalent figure for the left-wing guerrillas, including kidnappings, was 776. When in November 1989 these same U.S.-equipped and -trained "professional and apolitical" soldiers chose among their victims six Jesuit priests, the priests' cook, and the cook's daughter and then, after their grisly murders, conspired to cover up their responsibility and protect the guilty parties, the magazine (with the exception of Kondracke) began to backpedal. With between fifty thousand and seventy thousand lives and nearly $6 billion wasted in the endless Salvadoran civil war, the country made a mockery of the magazine's 1986 insistence that "what has happened there should cheer all who welcome the strengthening of the democratic center in Central America."*

While the *New Republic* fought hard to win support for the Reagan administration's policies in El Salvador, its heart belonged to the contras. For the *New Republic*'s neoconservatives, the Nicaragua of the 1980s was not a country but an existential opportunity. In the overblown rhetoric used by contra supporters during the various battles, one could hear echoes of Seville, Saigon, and Munich. Nicaragua was where good and evil were facing off for what promised to be a final showdown: the "Communist totalitarians" versus the "Democratic resistance."

It was through the invention of the Reagan Doctrine, with its ire focused on tiny Nicaragua, that Krauthammer and the *New Republic* decisively demonstrated how central punditry had become in the formation of the insider consensus that ruled American policy in the 1980s. The idea steamrolled through all three rings of the punditocracy, aided considerably by Krauthammer's unmediated access to each of them. The advantage of having a "doctrine" to defend their lies and dissimulations was considerable to William Casey, Oliver North, Elliott Abrams, and their allies in the bureaucracy. They could sell it to private contributors, manipulate it in confidential white papers, and seize on it as a justification for trading arms for hostages, diverting the money to their friends, and lying about it before Congress and the American people. Details about this or that massacre or drug-smuggling operation could be swept under the rug on behalf of the exalted moral calling that the "doctrine" invoked. Most people like to think that they are toiling on behalf of some idea larger than themselves—larger, even, than the country for whose interests they labor. Krauthammer's creation not only flattered these peo-

*"Democrats and Commandantes," pp. 7–10. The figures come from Charles Lane, "The War That Will Not End," *The New Republic*, 16 October 1989, p. 23. Immediately after the massacre, Kondracke tried to blame the Jesuits' murder on the rebels. Speaking on *The McLaughlin Group*, he noted, "You can either say it was the right-wing death squads, and that's what the Communists will say and that's what the left wing in the United States will say, but it could have been the [rebel] FMLN." He made this statement despite the fact that just five days later, he authored a *New Republic* editorial that admitted that the army had "almost certainly" been responsible. When asked about this apparent contradiction, Kondracke replied, "I sort of hope, frankly, that the left did it." A November 1991 investigative report authored by House Democrats found what it termed to be "strong circumstantial evidence" that the crime was plotted at the highest levels of the Salvadoran military, including, perhaps, its defense minister at the time, General Rene Emillio Ponce. Kondracke's explanations come from an interview by the author. See also the author's "Shooting from the Lip," *The Washington Post Magazine*, 18 March 1990, p. 30, and Clifford Krauss, "Panel Links Chief of Salvador Army to Jesuit Killings," *New York Times*, 17 November 1981, p. 1.

ple, it inspired them; some so much that they were later indicted by a Washington grand jury.

But more than a higher calling was involved. Washington public relations firms—the people who are paid good money to understand these things, however subliminally—knew a cash cow when they saw one. They flew the Reagan Doctrine flag and lobbied administration officials to include their high-paying anti-Communist clients on the list of U.S.-funded Reagan Doctrine "freedom fighters." Rival public relations firms adopted Marxist regimes as their clients in order to compete. Thus, Reagan's closest friend, Robert Gray, head of the powerhouse Gray and Company, adopted the cause of the Marxist government of Angola, only to give it up when young Reaganites picketed his stately Georgetown offices. Soon, the South African creation in Mozambique, Renamo, and the non-Communist guerrillas in Cambodia attached themselves to the Reagan Doctrine teat, basking in all the pro-freedom and pro-democracy rhetoric that passionate supporters of the Afghans and contras were generating. Right-wing adventurer Jack Wheeler revealed something of the value of Krauthammer's service to the cause when he told Sidney Blumenthal, then of the *Post*, that "we had him [Krauthammer] in for an off-the-record lunch with the president. He popularized the term, a rallying point for conservatives. . . . I love that guy Krauthammer for inventing the 'Reagan Doctrine.' "[*]

Although the Reagan Doctrine knew no borders, the object of its most passionate affections was always Managua. When push came to shove on a crucial congressional vote, virtually the entire edifice of the nation's foreign policy seemed to rest on these agrarian democrats. According to one Krauthammer-authored editorial, "the liberation of Angola, Afghanistan, and Cambodia would not have one-tenth the geopolitical importance—and psychological importance for other oppressed democrats—that the replacement of the Sandinista regime with a democratic government in Managua would." The upcoming vote somehow became "one of the most important foreign policy votes of the decade."

Charles Krauthammer's Nicaragua editorials are among the most significant documents of the entire era. They embraced all of the clichés of

[*]Quoted in the *Washington Post*, 29 June 1986. Krauthammer's specific response to these criticisms—he has responses to all the other criticisms as well—is that all of the cases he chose were "tentative, leaky colonies that did not quite have legitimacy and who engendered authentic, indigenous resistance." He specifically left out Renamo in Mozambique and felt considerable discomfort with regard to Cambodia. As to Nicaragua, "Yes, much of the leadership was Somocista and America-guided. But by the mid-eighties, Arturo Cruz, who is someone I respect, said it had become an authentic peasant army." Author's interview. Note: Cruz was on Oliver North's payroll at the time, although he explicitly denied this at a press conference attended by the author.

the Reaganite mindset with regard to both the "moral equivalent of our founding fathers" in Nicaragua and the functional equivalents of Neville Chamberlain at home. Krauthammer rested the contras' Jeffersonian bona fides on the allegedly "impeccably democratic" shoulders of their civilian directorate, Arturo Cruz and former Coca-Cola magnate Adolfo Calero. He did so despite the fact that Robert Owen, the right-wing congressional aide appointed by both Abrams and Oliver North to act as a go-between for the contras and the American government, was describing the civilians in a secret memo as "a creation of the USG [United States government] to garner support from Congress." Those Americans who observed that the Soviets and Cubans were more than ready to match our own military commitment in Nicaragua were smeared as "the council of pure defeatism." To those who noted that Nicaragua's neighbors preferred a peaceful solution, Krauthammer and company insisted that these countries were merely reading the tea leaves of liberal cowardice. Seeing "an isolationist Congress and a rising military power in Managua," they fell into the grip of public appeasement and private duplicity. Secretly, the *New Republic* assured its readers (and apparently on the basis of mass mental telepathy), Nicaraguans were "desperate to see the United States get rid of the Sandinistas for them."

The editorial was, contra supporter Wieseltier noted, "the worst piece of agitprop writing I have read since I got here. It talked about the other side's motives, and it made the case in the administration's words, rather than in our own." Twelve *New Republic* contributing editors apparently agreed, and they banded together to sign a letter of protest that was summarily buried in the magazine's back pages. Kinsley ripped the editorial to pieces in his own column, calling the logic it used "preposterous," "fatuous," and a "logical contortion." Hendrik Hertzberg did not critique the piece in public but believes that sentiments such as these finally led him to resign as editor of the magazine. "The magazine was playing a role," he explained, "where I just couldn't be the front man for it anymore."

What Hertzberg had in mind here was not merely the Krauthammer-Peretz powers of persuasion evinced in the magazine's editorials, but also the efforts of a group of formerly liberal political operatives to use these powers. Saluted in the pages of the magazine as "a handful of young Democratic intellectuals and activists, Robert Leiken, Bernard Aronson, Bruce Cameron and Penn Kemble [who] will have been found . . . when the history of the American debates over Nicaragua is written . . . to have transformed both public discussions and public policy," these apostate liberals worked closely with Abrams and Oliver North to try to sway the swing votes in Congress. Their vehicle of choice was the *New Republic*. As Sidney Blumenthal observes, these "pro-contra operatives were able to use the pages of the *New Republic* to develop a public strategy to complement a political strategy that they were working on inside Congress. This gave legitimacy to the whole effort." It also helped Aronson earn Elliott Abrams' old job in the Bush administration. Not a bad day's work for a magazine whose editors lectured poor Salman Rushdie that "it is the place of the writer and the intellectual to be outside, not inside; not to be a part of, but to be not a part of."

Because the endless contra debate in Congress focused on the votes of fewer than two dozen swing Democrats in the House of Representatives, these interventions would prove absolutely crucial in convincing Congress to approve military aid. Pat Buchanan was calling the Democrats "the party of Communism" at the time, and Norman Podhoretz insisted that "in a conflict where the only choice is between Communists and anti-Communists, anyone who refuses to help the anti-Communists is helping the Communists." The Democrats could not allow themselves to be perceived to be responding to threats quite this vulgar, but they were looking for cover from them nevertheless. The most influential of these swing votes, House Armed Services Committee Chair Les Aspin and Coalition for a Democratic Majority Member Dave McCurdy, were particularly susceptible to the compliments heaped on them by the editors of the *New Republic*, who noted that these "moderate Democrats . . . weren't afraid to cross party lines" and were willing to "lead and to take risks." Aspin even hired Leiken, briefly, as an informal adviser and paid his way to Nicaragua to survey the situation. Together, they prevailed upon the key swing Democrats to back contra aid and allow the war to continue at crucial moments in the debate. This pattern repeated itself for two years, until Oliver North and Robert McFarlane put an end to it with a Bible and a birthday cake in Tehran.

When the contra cause crumbled, Krauthammer and company only heated up their rhetoric even further, using language that turned out to be wholly inaccurate but that should have sent shudders down the spines of those dedicated to free public debate. Borrowing a page from Podhoretz, Krauthammer compared contra-Sandinista cease-fire accords to "the similar speedy peace" that "Congress brought Indochina in 1975." Going back even further in the history of stab-in-the-back politics, he also promised that "who lost Central America will become an issue some day and on that question it is worth keeping the record straight and the memory fresh." Democratic Speaker Jim Wright had, in Krauthammer's evocative words, "made Central America safe for Communism."

Aside from the violence it inflicted on the English language, the most significant damage done by the neoconservative view of Latin America was the inexplicable importance it placed on pathetic little Nicaragua, to the exclusion of the rest of the region. The magazine's friend and confidant, assistant secretary of state for inter-American affairs and admitted liar Elliott Abrams, said he spent almost half his time on this one tortured nation. In the meantime, staggering economic debt in Latin America, coupled with extremely fragile democratic development and environmentally unsustainable investment patterns across the continent, were undermining the long-term viability of the truly strategic nations of the region. In Argentina, by the end of the decade, inflation had reached 3,700 percent and the government had accumulated an unpayable debt of $65 billion. Brazil, another nation of enormous strategic importance, saw its inflation rate rise to 1,765 percent in 1989, with an accompanying debt of $100 billion. Closer to home, Mexico, a nation of millions of potential economic refugees, saw its debt shoot up to $107 billion in 1987, with a relatively modest inflation rate of 160 percent. The Andean nation of Peru, a supplier of much of the U.S. cocaine market, experienced an inflation rate of 2,275 percent and a 10 percent drop in growth in 1989 alone. Bolivia, another cocaine-producing nation, may have set the all-time world's record with an annual inflation rate of 8,170 percent in 1985. Environmental destruction in these places also approached crisis proportions. In Peru, farmers were razing sections of the Amazon rain forest to sow coca crops for export to America's cities. All of these countries are unarguably more important to the future economic and political security of the United States than either Nicaragua or El Salvador. Yet, owing in part to the punditocracy's Reagan Doctrine–inspired obsession with these two countries—including, particularly, arguments calling this or that contra vote "one of the most important foreign policy votes of the decade"—not one of them attracted a fraction of the attention necessary to fashion a coherent American response.

It is impossible to write about the *New Republic* without coming to grips with Peretz and Israel. It is not enough to say that the *New Republic*'s owner is merely obsessed with Israel; he says so himself.* But, more important, Peretz is obsessed with Israel's critics, Israel's would-be critics, and people who never heard of Israel but might one day know someone who might someday become a critic. "Israel, lion of nations, loyal ally and democratic outpost, Israel, gateway of Meccas, is, of course, a land of religious resonance and geopolitical significance," wrote James Wolcott, trying to describe Peretz's mindset on the subject. He understated the case considerably.

---

*"My own passions coincided with those of the founders, the cause of a free Israel among them. My critics say it is an obsession. I confess. It is my obsession. And why shouldn't it be?" Taken from subscription appeal from Peretz to American Jews, July 1991.

One could, if one were sufficiently conspiracy-minded, draw a political *New Republic* map of the world based wholly on the Israel connection. The Sandinistas were bad because they accepted PLO advisers. The United Nations was useless because it invited Yassir Arafat to speak. Jesse Jackson was dangerous because he sang "We Shall Overcome" with West Bank Palestinians and spoke up for their right to statehood. The Salvadoran government was deserving of U.S. military support because it accepted Israeli military trainers and voted with the Israelis in the United Nations. Bill Moyers was a fraud because he once spoke up for the right of Arab-Americans to criticize Israel in the media.*

Of course, the *New Republic*'s flight into the arms of the Right was based on political and psychological factors far more complex than just Israel, but the notion retains a kind of subliminal credibility. Since he gave up on revolution, Peretz has devoted himself to fighting for Israel on all fronts, a crusade not uncommon among neoconservatives. Influential intellectuals of both the Right and Left in Western Europe hold the rather oversimplified and unsophisticated view that the entire rightward drift of American liberalism during the 1960s and 1970s can be viewed as a result of the change in Israel's geopolitical status from the spirited socialist David of its early years to the pro–American empire, post-1967 military Goliath. (The Six Day War was important to the birth of neoconservatism, but so were the New York City teachers' strike and the blatantly anti-Semitic rhetoric of much of black America's most vocal leadership.) Still, there are uncountable ironies involved in the *New Republic*'s treatment of Israel's critics, not least of which is the fact that, although few people are so frequently reviled in the *New Republic*'s editorials as those who openly call for the establishment of a Palestinian state living in peace alongside Israel, no fewer than four of the magazine's editors during the 1980s—Kinsley, Hertzberg, Blumenthal, and Wieseltier—said they would have supported the establishment of such a [demilitarized] state.

---

*The Moyers case is of particular interest because it is the one example where the *New Republic* attacked somebody wealthy enough to buy more than equal response time in the magazine. In defending his unsuccessful attempt to destroy Moyers' reputation as a thorough reporter and an honest man, the writer the *New Republic* commissioned to the job, Andrew Ferguson, admitted that he "could not afford the three or four hours it would have taken [him] to get to Mr. Moyers," who had offered him a face-to-face interview, and thus rejected the opportunity to interview the subject of his hatchet job in person. This did not appear to bother the magazine's editors, who ran the article beneath the self-revelatory tag-line, "Bill Moyers, Liberal Fraud." See Andrew Ferguson, "The Power of Myth," *The New Republic*, August 19 and 26, 1991; the correspondence pages; and Moyers' paid response in the October 7, 1991, issue.

The *New Republic*'s role in the Arab-Israeli debate is both simple and complicated. Norman Podhoretz has argued that "the role of Jews who write in both the Jewish and general press is to defend Israel." Critical reporting of Israel, Podhoretz insists, "helps Israel's enemies—and they are legion in the U.S.—to say more and more openly that Israel is not a democratic country." Peretz has never advocated anything quite this explicit, but one could argue, not wholly inaccurately, that his primary task as editor and owner of the *New Republic* has been to praise Israel and subvert those he deems to be its opponents.

Marty Peretz does not like Arabs. They have, he argues, "a national characterological inability to compromise" and tend toward the "violent," "fratricidal," "unreliable," "primitive," and "crazed." Even worse, however, are Palestinian Arabs. The *New Republic* editorials often treat the word "Palestinian" as a synonym for "terrorist." In an interview with the Israeli newspaper *Ha'aretz* during the 1982 Israeli invasion of Lebanon, Peretz explained that the Israelis should administer to the PLO

> a lasting military defeat that will clarify to the Palestinians living in the West Bank that their struggle for an independent state has suffered a setback of many years. [Then the] Palestinians will be turned into just another crushed nation, like the Kurds or the Afghans . . . [The problem] is beginning to be boring.[*]

When asked what he objected to most about the magazine he edited, Michael Kinsley responded, "I have a problem with some of the needlessly vicious things about Arabs that we publish."

Another significant responsibility Peretz has undertaken on behalf of Israel's interests has been the ideological policing of the American media. Peretz calls U.S. media coverage of the Middle East, "an obsessive wound in my heart." If so, he has managed to offer this pain considerable balm in the editorial pages of his magazine. This wound accounts for what one *New Republic* editor calls "Marty's ridiculous obsession with [*New York Times* columnist] Tony Lewis."[†] It also seems to account for the magazine's shameful vilification of I. F. Stone over a period of decades. During

---

[*]See Peretz's interview with Benny Landau, published in *Ha'aretz*, 9 December 1982. Note Peretz's implied analogy between the moral behavior of the Israeli occupying forces and those of Saddam Hussein and the pre-Gorbachev Soviets. Note also that after the Persian Gulf War, Peretz authored an article vociferously objecting to any comparison between the Kurds, whom he insisted were entitled to their own state, and the Palestinians, who were not. See Martin Peretz, "Unpromised Lands," *The New Republic*, 3 June 1991, pp. 20–23.
[†]Author's interview. Lewis says, "I don't understand what it is about me that so enrages Marty. I don't think it is a difference in policy or theology. I think he is kind of obsessed with me." Anthony Lewis, interview by author.

the 1982 Israeli siege of Beirut, during which Israel turned off all water and electrical services to the Moslem sections of the city, Peretz spotted Stone's name on an appeal for "the victims, including hundreds of thousands trapped in West Beirut without water, essential services and medical supplies." Peretz singled out Stone, a devoted friend of Israel's peace camp, from the list of signatories and accused him of caring "only" for those "trapped in West Beirut," whom he insisted were trapped not by the surrounding Israeli army but by the PLO. "So this is what I. F. Stone has come to," wrote Peretz, "asking his admirers to put up money so that the PLO can continue to fight, not simply against Israel but against the possibility of a peaceful Lebanon." "I do think sometimes we attack people unfairly," admits Wieseltier.[*]

Peretz's most ambitious media enforcement operation of the 1980s came during the Israeli invasion when he authored a cover story entitled "Lebanon Eyewitness." After being treated to a brief tour of the war zone by Israeli military intelligence, Peretz assured his readers that the news reports they had read and television coverage they had seen were simply false. He would single out for particular opprobrium the *Washington Post* and ABC News. One cannot hope to judge how many journalists fudged their stories or did not report them at all to avoid being singled out for treatment like this. "We're the cops" on Israel, explains one *New Republic* editor. "Marty really put the fear of the devil into the media after Lebanon."[†] With more than $4 billion in aid monies riding on perceptions of Israel in Congress each year, the importance of this kind of police work can hardly be overestimated.

But Peretz is only half the story. Leon Wieseltier is correct when he says, "There is no question that on Israel we have had it a million ways. Yes, our rhetorical heat has been out front, but we have published some of the most anti-Israeli policy stuff anywhere." The *New Republic* has published a cover

---

[*]Author's interview with Leon Wieseltier. During the Persian Gulf War, Peretz complained in a column entitled "Blacklisted" that, despite repeated efforts to volunteer his services, he was perhaps "the only writer on the Middle East who had not been invited by PBS or NPR to speak about the Gulf," while other writers with less "definite views," such as Anthony Lewis and Harvard professor Roger Fisher, had been extended invitations. Peretz apparently neglected to ponder the possibility that, with the exception of fellow millionaire magazine owner (and Israel partisan) Mortimer Zuckerman, he was also the "only writer on the Middle East" who owned, published, and edited the forum that so prominently featured his views. See Martin Peretz, "Blacklisted," *The New Republic*, 15 April 1991, p. 42.
[†]Author's interview. Peretz also trumpets his magazine's reception of an accuracy award from an organization called CAMERA—The Committee for Accuracy in Middle East Reporting. As most journalists covering the area can attest, the word "accuracy" in CAMERA's title is about as relevant as the word *Pravda* ("truth") was in the Communist Party's official publication. CAMERA is an enforcement organ of the Israeli right wing, but it uses tactics far more vulgar and transparent than anything that has appeared in the *New Republic*.

with a map of the Middle East featuring a Palestinian state on it. Wieseltier, Irving Howe, and Michael Walzer have all written articles extremely critical of the policies of the Israeli government. During the 1980s, the magazine called on Begin to resign and made an enemy of Yitzhak Shamir. It has published Robert Kuttner's attack on the "unholy alliance" between Jewish political action committees and far-right politicians on the cover as well. In a seminal issue published during the height of the intifada in March 1988, Wieseltier endorsed many of the PLO's demands for a mini-state alongside that of Israel. Even Peretz declared "the policy of occupation and settlement" to be "in ruins." It fell to Krauthammer to defend the hawkish ground that the *New Republic* had historically occupied, arguing that to cede any territory to the current generation of Palestinian leadership would constitute "surrender" to "rioting."

The *New Republic*'s dovish pieces on the Middle East, particularly those by Wieseltier, have been tremendously important within the American Jewish community in legitimizing the kind of dissent from the Israeli party line that Peretz and Krauthammer have made a career of attacking. On the one hand, this is a confusing phenomenon. Why would Peretz— whose attacks on the likes of Stone, Lewis, Edward Said, and others associated with criticism of Israel or support for Palestinian rights are almost unparalleled in their bile and venom—allow his magazine to be used to publicize similar positions in the mouths of others? Part of the answer lies in the magazine's celebration of political diversity, which, in the matter of Israel, extends beyond the parameters of its American agenda. Perhaps more significant, however, is the fact that support for a Palestinian state or criticism of Israel's occupation is not the point. The point is who is doing the criticizing. Those whom Peretz determines to be criticizing Israel out of genuine concern for its best interests are generally left alone. Those whose primary concern appears to be the conditions of Palestinian life are savaged within an inch of their professional reputations.[*]

One question liberals asked constantly during the 1980s was why, if a primary function of the *New Republic*'s liberal editors-in-chief was to make the magazine's neoconservatism more palatable, did they stick around for the party? The answers, like everything at the *New Republic*, are complicated. Kinsley says that his decision to edit a magazine whose political thrust he did not support was, in essence, "a Faustian bargain." The bargain amounted to the fact that he could publish whatever he wanted:

---

[*]For the record, the author puts himself in the former category.

The price was I had to publish things I didn't want. I thought that was a pretty good arrangement. It comes out every week. There is a lot of crap in it, but if I have anything I want said or want to say, I can say it in a national magazine without having to pay the bills. Yes, the war in Nicaragua bothered me as did our endorsement of it, but I was considerably soothed by being able to publish the opposite view, and it seems to me that anybody reading both would think that I was right.

Hertzberg's refusal to adopt Kinsley's stratagem (i.e., to publish a liberal magazine within a conservative one), led to frequent "Fuck you, Ricks" and "Fuck you, Martys" shouted in the hallways of the magazine during the early 1980s, with Hertzberg telling one reporter that Peretz was "oafish and bullying." "The initial way I dealt with the tension," recalls Hertzberg, "was to resign. . . . I became sufficiently disturbed with the role of TNR and the general thrust of the role that I was playing in the Reagan years that I left. I didn't feel alienated to the point that I wasn't perfectly happy to write for the magazine, but I didn't want to be a front man for it any longer."

In addition to the contras, Hertzberg was angered by the public role played by the *New Republic* in undermining the nuclear freeze movement and supporting the MX missile. "I wanted our position to be one of critical support rather than critical opposition. Instead, the magazine showed contempt for its arms-control thinking and questioned the backgrounds of many of the movement's leaders." It does not bother Hertzberg that the magazine subjects civil rights or social-policy organizers to fine-toothed scrutiny. "What the magazine should be criticized for," he allows, "is for not subjecting power to the same kind of criticism."

Beginning in late 1986, the magazine began to draw itself away from Reagan and Reaganism and concentrate a bit more of its fire on "power." The magazine's October 13, 1986, editorial on "The Reagan Hangover" was among the first frontal attacks on the legacy of Ronald Reagan in the mainstream media and among the only ones that preceded the revelations of the Iran-Contra scandal. But during the 1988 election, the *New Republic's* editors, like much of the punditocracy, focused on the wholly irrelevant question of which Democratic candidate would likely be toughest on the Russians. They attacked Dukakis for his willingness to "parrot the left isolationist line," his "standard issue McGovernite left worldview," and his refusal to endorse the *New Republic* theology on the nuclear freeze, the MX missile and, most particularly, the Reagan Doctrine. The magazine chose as its favored candidate former Peretz student and midgetman booster Albert Gore of Tennessee. Gore ran a perfectly conceived neoconservative campaign, talking tough to the surrendering Gorbachev and prostrating himself before the Shamir government to curry favor with New York's Jews. Advised extensively by Peretz and Wieseltier, his campaign fizzled in New York, where even the Jews found his hawkishness a bit too kosher for comfort. With its anemic 10 percent of the total Democratic vote, the Gore campaign in the end proved to be a kind of metaphor for just how far the *New Republic* had drifted from the concerns of the sophisticated Democratic voters for whom the magazine's editors had, for the previous decade, pretended to speak.

Beginning in 1995, the right-wing Australian media magnate, Rupert Murdoch, invested a few of his millions in a new conservative weekly for the capital, to be edited by William Kristol. The *Weekly Standard* soon became for conservatives what the *New Republic* had once been (but no longer was) for liberals, setting their agenda and helping to develop young stars.

The *Standard* took Fred Barnes and Charles Krauthammer away from the *New Republic*, just as Michael Kinsley, Hendrick Hertzberg, Jacob Weisberg, Sidney Blumenthal, and others also severed their relationship with the magazine. The result was a much weaker publication that spent the 1990s enduring one professional humiliation after another. First, one of its star young writers, Ruth Shalit, was accused of a string of plagiaries. Next, its high-profile "gay-Catholic-Tory"-editor, Andrew Sullivan, was fired for professional incompetence. Sullivan was deemed by staff members to care more about posing for Gap ads than editing the actual magazine. The changes he did bring to the magazine were almost uniformly awful. He put a young man named Stephen Glass, who turned out to be a serial plagiarist, in charge of fact-checking. He featured Charles Murray's racist pseudo-science on the cover and encouraged essays by Camille Paglia in which she wrote of "Hillary the man-woman and bitch goddess." Michael Lewis wrote a piece in 1994 about the "weird degradation" of being married to a beautiful part-time model, Kate Bohner. One conservative writer compared the magazine under Sullivan to "watching a middle-aged accountant try on a pair of nipple rings."

Not much improved under Michael Kelly, whom Peretz chose to replace the fired Sullivan. In the press release announcing his hiring, Peretz compared Kelly to Thucydides. Alas, it would be difficult to find a less apt role model in all human history. Under Kelly, twenty-five-year-old Stephen Glass continued to publish fiction as reporting, while his editor attacked the integrity of those who raised questions about his work. To one critic, Kelly wrote, "You lied because lying supported your thesis, and you attempted to cover up your lie. You have shown that you are willing to smear someone's professional reputation without any concern for truth. . . . I await your apology to Stephen Glass and to this magazine." It turned out that twenty-seven of Glass' forty-one stories contained considerable fabrications.

But Glass was the least of the *New Republic*'s problems under Kelly. It turned out that in Michael Kelly Martin Peretz had managed to hire an editor for America's most venerable liberal magazine who happened to hate liberals. In his inaugural "TRB" column, written shortly after the 1996 election, he wrote that liberalism had become an "ideology of self-styled saints; a philosophy of determined perversity. Its animating impulse is to marginalize itself and then to enjoy its own company. And to make it as unattractive to as many as possible; if it were a person, it would pierce its tongue." Kelly shared Peretz's animus toward affirmative action and consistently attacked the nation's civil rights establishment, in much the same way that Peretz would beat up the Palestinians. Black people seemed to be causing trouble nearly everywhere you turned, according to the *New Republic*'s coverage under Kelly. And the beating that Kelly gave Clinton was so relentless and so obsessive that Peretz could no longer stand it—particularly when he was so heavily invested in Al Gore's 2000 candidacy. What's more, the old delicate balance of having a smart liberal edit a neoconservative magazine was destroyed. The *New Republic* was a liberal magazine at the end of Kelly's reign only in memory.

When Peretz finally pushed Kelly over the side, he was replaced by longtime contributor Charles Lane, who quieted the clamor, firing Glass and allowing Shalit to take her leave. But in letting go of liberalism and destroying its reputation for high-quality journalism, the magazine succeeded only in making itself invisible. True, Leon Wieseltier's literary pages remained the best anywhere in America, but politically speaking the magazine ceased to matter. The magazine's best conservative writers had gone off to form the nucleus of Rupert Murdoch's *Weekly Standard*. The liberals had gone either to the *New Yorker* with Hertzberg or to *Slate* with Kinsley. The latter's brilliant TRB columns and razor-sharp editing and the former's passionate prose were now part of a distant past. The flagship of American liberalism, at the end of the century, had lost its reason for being.

CONSEQUENCES:
THE BUSH AND CLINTON YEARS

"I miss it, the Cold War. It gave you a reason to get up in the morning."

—Harry "Rabbit" Angstrom, in John Updike's
Rabbit at Rest (1990)

CHAPTER TEN

The Man with No New Ideas

Drawing on fragments by the Greek poet Archilochus, Isaiah Berlin divided Russian thinkers into foxes, who know "many things," and hedgehogs, who "know One Big Thing." Each point of view has its advantages, but the world is probably a safer place with fewer hedgehogs. Being a fox can be uninspiring, but being a hedgehog is often worse. What happens when your One Big Thing turns out to be wrong?

In March 1985, Eduard Shevardnadze, Mikhail Gorbachev's closest friend and adviser, turned to his new boss, the general secretary of the Communist Party, and blurted out the fact that had eluded virtually the entire Soviet leadership since Stalin's time. "Everything's rotten," observed Shevardnadze, "it has to be changed." Through their willingness to accept this awful truth into their collective political psyche, the two men converted themselves from hedgehogs into foxes. Gorbachev was not exaggerating in the slightest when he explained that things were so bad that "everything pertaining to the economy, culture, democracy, foreign policy—all spheres—had to be reappraised."

The pre-Gorbachev Communist Party had known One Big Thing: Soviet-style Communism was the highest order of ideological and economic development known to man. This knowledge blinded the party's members to facts that were obvious to any tourist who spent more than a week traveling the country: the Soviet experiment, initiated in 1917, was over. It had ended in almost unmitigated failure. Although the

Gorbachev "revolution from above" was also a failure in many important respects, it at least created a political space for the even more revolutionary efforts of Boris Yeltsin and the final, incredible implosion of 1991. For all its fits and starts, it was an effort of almost unprecedented existential audacity.

The Reagan-era punditocracy, meanwhile, comprised no fewer hedgehogs than the Brezhnev-era politburo. Its consensus also insisted on One Big Thing: that America's "long twilight struggle" in the Cold War took precedence over all competing national priorities and goals. By the mid-1970s, however, this view was only slightly less useful in determining the true interests of the United States in a multipolar and economically driven world competition than Stalin's constitution was to the Soviets. Although certainly not "everything" in American economic and political life had become rotten, many things had, and more were in the process of becoming so. The rot permeated the nation's manufacturing industries, its environment, and much of its political and social structure. But because of the dramatic difference in degree between our own problems and those faced by the Soviets, the United States failed to produce any leadership with the vision or clarity of purpose necessary to pierce its intellectual delusions. Incredibly, not even the public surrender of the enemy proved sufficient to disturb our self-satisfied complacency.

During the final years of Ronald Reagan's presidency, the punditocracy withdrew even more deeply into its insider cocoon. The central problem of American political life, it insisted, remained the need to educate and fortify the attentive public to resist the implacable expansion of international Communism. The United States, as the only Western power with both the will and the means to resist this expansion, would continue to be required to expend vast amounts of blood and treasure in this never-ending conflict.

The doctrines that ruled the mindset of the punditocracy were in most cases internally consistent. This enabled its members to fit virtually any development anywhere in the world into its basic model without upsetting any core assumptions. That core formed the minimum intellectual requirements for admittance into the club of the politically relevant. Yet despite the rigidity with which they were enforced, many pundit beliefs were unique to insider Washington. The combination of the intensity with which these notions were held and their frequently tangential relationship to reality often left European and other observers shaking their heads in astonishment.

The worldview through which punditocracy perceptions were filtered was a mixture of the pre-Vietnam centrism coupled with the hard-line revisionism of the Reaganite counter-establishment. Where the former gave way to the latter was not in its recognition that the United States was engaged in a timeless duel to the death with the Soviet Union—this was already a given—but in the Whittaker Chambers–like pessimism with which it regarded the likely outcome.[*]

Zbigniew Brzezinski, who, as Jimmy Carter's national security adviser, approached the dovish edges of respectability, published a guide to U.S.-Soviet relations in 1986, positing as its "central proposition" that "the American-Soviet contest is not some temporary aberration but a historical rivalry that will long endure." The contest was being fought, in Brzezinski's view, for "nothing less than global predominance," and would long ago have been settled by war were it not for the deterrent power of nuclear weapons. "Never has there been a contest," including that between the United States and Nazi Germany, Brzezinski argued, "between two powers so fundamentally different" as these two.[†]

The reasons to doubt the eventual triumph of good over evil in this contest lay in what one neoconservative writer called our country's "excess of virtue." Democracies were fickle fighters and unwilling to sacrifice themselves for total victory. Jeane Kirkpatrick argued in her seminal essay, "Dictatorships and Double Standards," that "the history of this century provides no ground for expecting that radical totalitarian regimes will transform themselves." Kirkpatrick's was a perfectly rational reading of history, but it came to be understood during the Reagan years to mean simply that, whereas democracies were fragile flowers, Communist dictatorships, like diamonds, were forever. Jean-François Revel, a right-wing French intellectual who became to the punditocracy of the 1980s what Regis Debray was to the student movement of the 1960s, saw democracy as "a historical accident, a brief parenthesis that is closing before our eyes." In his influential text, *How Democracies Perish*, Revel complained that while democracies face an "internal enemy whose right to exist is written into the law itself," Communism was both "durable and immutable." "Totalitarianism liquidates its internal enemies," wrote Revel, "or smashes opposition as soon as it arises; it uses

[*]Chambers worried that Communism (which, more than three decades before Ronald Reagan, he called "the focus of the concentrated evil of our time") was certain to triumph over freedom because "the world outside Communism, the world in crisis, lacks a vision, and a faith." See Whittaker Chambers, *Witness* (New York: Random House, 1952) pp. 3–22.
[†]Zbigniew Brzezinski, *Game Plan: How to Conduct the US-Soviet Contest* (New York: Atlantic Monthly Books, 1986), pp. 8, 12–15. In the book, Brzezinski argued on behalf of a military strategy designed to maintain what he modestly supposed necessary to achieve an "integrated capability" for "surface, sea, and space combat as the central point of departure for the waging of an enduring and consuming political contest for earth control" (p. 259).

methods that are simple and infallible because they are undemocratic. But democracy can defend itself from within only very feebly; its internal enemy has an easy time of it because he exploits the right to disagree that is inherent in democracy."

Revel's ideas were much popularized by George Will. Arguing that time was not "on the side of the bourgeois societies of the West," Will insisted that totalitarian regimes, "for all their stupidities have one strength, staying power." After a mere six decades in power in the Soviet Union, the Communists had "achieved the closest approximation to permanency in politics." When, in the early 1980s, Senator Joseph Biden argued on behalf of keeping U.S. sanctions on the Soviet Union as long as their troops remained in Afghanistan, Will guffawed. "Biden, 37," he predicted, "will not live to see the troops withdrawn."

The irreconcilability of Soviet and American systems coupled with the enemy's immutability added up to only one of two possibilities: we had either to fight or switch. Under Jimmy Carter, went the argument, the country had come dangerously close to switching. Under Ronald Reagan, we would be fighting again.

Because nuclear weapons had raised the cost of typical world wars to prohibitive levels, the third world war was conducted by means of military spending and proxy warfare. Throughout the 1980s, the leading voices of the punditocracy argued on behalf of vast increases in America's weapons budgets, the rapid expansion—into outer space if possible—of its nuclear weapons capabilities, and a series of U.S.-funded and -supplied proxy wars against Soviet military clients. The justification for these efforts rested on the allegedly urgent need to demonstrate to friend and foe alike that we had every intention of resisting Communist expansion. The punditocracy's Cold War became a war of symbols, to be won not merely with blitzkriegs or flanking maneuvers, but with line items, flow charts, and disinformation.

Aside from the disastrous intervention in Lebanon, a couple of bombing missions in Libya, and a holiday takeover of the nutmeg-producing island of Grenada, the only fighting and dying done on behalf of this strategic vision was done by foreigners. Throughout the period, however, a number of the punditocracy's most distinguished members were itching to go further. The Soviets, said Irving Kristol, were driven by "a self-conscious and fully articulated secular-messianic religion." Kristol recommended a U.S. invasion of Nicaragua to teach the mini-messiahs there a lesson. Edward Luttwak, the punditocracy's favorite military strategist, lamented that military pacifists had been successful in making even tactical nuclear weapons unfashionable in U.S. military doctrine. "Unless we refute the counsel of impotence," he insisted, "the only possible choices left to us will be appeasement or outright retreat."

The problems in even the most moderate versions of this worldview were threefold. First, because it was not shared by the very allies we were hoping to impress, our demonstrations of will and resolve proved counterproductive: not unlike that of a man who tries to win a vegetarian woman's affection by showering her with steaks and pork chops. Second, it proved extremely expensive, in real terms as well as in its opportunity cost. Third, it had precious little relationship to the alleged object of its attention—the phenomenon of post-Stalinist Soviet Communism. It therefore demanded sacrifices of the American people and the victims of its proxy wars that were wholly unnecessary and doubly self-defeating for being so.

As amazing as it sounds, the most important country in the world to the Reagan/Bush punditocracy, excluding the Soviet Union itself, was brave little Finland. Throughout the decade, the example of Finland was held up as the ultimate threat to the safety and security of the American people—the geopolitical dagger we saw before us. Finland, argued Charles Krauthammer, "had earned its independence at the cost of its dignity." It lived behind not an Iron Curtain, explained William Safire, but "a kind of beaded curtain . . . subservient to Soviet security and foreign policy domination." The theory of "Finlandization" was an existential version of the domino theory: Communist conquests came in the form not of small subjugated Asian countries, but of psychologically dispirited Europeans. Unless the United States showed itself willing to do all the things the neoconservatives were demanding of it, they warned, Western Europeans would lose heart and decide that they, too, had no choice but to purchase their independence at the cost of their dignity. It is this logic that explains George Will's otherwise wholly nonsensical statement that "if Cuba cannot be 'Finlandized' by the United States, then Western Europe eventually will be by the Soviet Union."[*]

---

[*]George F. Will, 7 November 1983. The official manifestation of the Finlandization argument can be seen in Ronald Reagan's April 27, 1983, insistence, in a speech to a joint session of Congress, that "if we cannot defend ourselves [in Central America], we cannot expect to prevail elsewhere. Our credibility would collapse, our alliances would crumble, and the safety of our homeland would be put in jeopardy." This argument was an even greater exaggeration of those put forth by his predecessors in seeking to justify the American war in Indochina. When defending his 1970 invasion of Cambodia, Richard Nixon argued that "if, when the chips are down, the world's most powerful nation, the United States of America, acts like a pitiful, helpless giant, the forces of totalitarianism and anarchy will threaten free institutions throughout the world." Similarly, Lyndon Johnson defended his escalation of the Vietnam conflict by insisting that if the United States did not prevail there, "We'll lose all of Asia and then Europe, and then we'll be a rich little island all by ourselves. That means World War III." For a useful discussion of the legacy of these doctrines in American life, see the afterword in Jonathan Schell, *Observing the Nixon Years* (New York: Pantheon, 1989). The Nixon and Johnson quotes appear on pp. 254–55.

The Finlandization argument was originally trotted out during the Carter presidency by members of the Committee on the Present Danger on behalf of the MX missile, and it reappeared as late as June 1989, in a Jeane Kirkpatrick column. As with its larger strategic umbrella, it suffered from no end of difficulties when confronted with the realities it alleged to address. For starters, it painted a wholly false picture of Finland. That frozen nation, as William Pfaff and George Kennan have noted, actually served to deter Soviet expansion, so that by the 1980s Soviet influence over Finnish affairs had declined precipitously.[*]

The audience at this costly spectacle, the Europeans themselves, found the entire intellectual exercise to be so vain and misguided that it often seemed to call into question both the judgment and the values on which the Atlantic partnership was alleged to be based. To observant European elites, the concept of Finlandization lacked both simple cogency and elementary dignity. Its primary purpose, in their eyes, was to provide an all-but-transparent gloss for the Reagan administration's own deadly crusades in Central America.[†]

But the most serious problem with the argument was its catastrophic misreading of the basis of Soviet power. The image of the insatiable Russian bear, whose power was increasing with every unchallenged conquest, bore little relationship to the exhausted, emaciated economy on which the Soviet military rested. The punditocracy was by no means solely responsible for this situation. Soviet secrecy had created a kind of black box in the American imagination into which all our fears and neuroses were poured. Certainly some of these were justified, as the writings of Aleksandr Solzhenitsyn among others attest; so do the easily observable miseries of Afghan and Eastern European life. But these fears, coupled with the difficulty in acquiring dependable data from the Soviets themselves, led the government's national security apparatus to invent a capa-

---

[*]Finnish security was guaranteed by the Finns themselves, who, through a variety of political, economic, and military measures, successfully raised the cost of Soviet domination to prohibitive levels. See Pfaff, *Barbarian Sentiments*, p. 88, and George F. Kennan, *The Nuclear Delusion: Soviet-American Relations in the Atomic Age* (New York: Pantheon, 1982), pp. 70–72. Moreover, for all the very real danger to Finland from Soviet power, it nevertheless managed to achieve an average per capita income higher than that of the United States and, according to a 1991 U.N. survey, scored higher on an international "freedom" index. According to the statistical supplement to the *OECD Observer,* June/July 1990, Finnish per capita income stood at $21,266, while that of the United States was pegged at $19,558. According to the U.N. Human Development Report for 1991, the United States ranked thirteenth based on the forty criteria chosen to measure international freedom. Finland ranked fourth, behind only Sweden, Denmark, and the Netherlands.

[†]In the summer of 1986, a top official of Margaret Thatcher's Foreign Office—a representative of the only government that even pretended to support U.S. global counter-revolution—complained to a visitor, "If you Americans want to behave like brutes in Central America, go ahead. But for goodness sakes, leave us out of it!" Author's interview.

bility for the Soviet Union that vastly exceeded its pathetic economic output. As a result, the Pentagon regularly flooded the American media with a steady stream of falsehoods regarding the Soviet military machine, and the CIA provided enormously inflated estimates of Soviet power throughout the bureaucracy. The 1989 edition of the *Statistical Abstract of the United States*, citing the CIA, reported the per capita gross national product of East Germany to be larger than that of West Germany. The CIA's annual *Handbook of Economic Statistics* reported that the growth of the Soviet economy during the years 1981–1985 exceeded that of the European community by more than 25 percent. Using such figures, the White House, State Department, and private defense contractors and consultants operated what former neoconservative Senator Daniel Patrick Moynihan called a "national security state" based on a "vast secrecy system which basically hid from us our own miscalculations."

Building on the false figures and the infectious atmosphere of government secrecy, the punditocracy's vision of an implacable enemy on an immutable march toward our shores caused American politicians to inflict enormous damage on American long-term interests. While the investment-oriented societies of East Asia and northern Europe were laying the groundwork for their massive industrial expansions in the 1980s and 1990s, the United States engaged in the most expensive military buildup in peacetime history. Coupled with massive increases in luxury consumption inspired by the supply-side tax cuts, this had the effect of accelerating the deindustrialization of the nation at a time when massive public and private debt made ever larger demands on our dwindling productive capacities. The net result was a steady decline not only in the economy's annual productivity gains but, more concretely, in the living standards of most Americans—a decline that becomes more difficult to reverse with every passing moment.*

Strobe Talbott, then a *Time* magazine pundit and well-respected guru on Soviet affairs, published a brave mea culpa in early 1990, in which he deplored the fact that

> for more than four decades, Western policy has been based on a grotesque exaggeration of what the Soviet Union could do if it wanted, therefore what

---

*Real weekly earnings in 1987 per average American family were no higher than they were in 1973, despite a major increase in the number of two-income families. See Bennett Harrison and Barry Bluestone, *The Great U-Turn: Corporate Restructuring and the Polarizing of America* (New York: Basic Books, 1988), pp. 6–7. Excluding the wealthiest 20 percent of Americans, family incomes began losing ground in 1987 and declined steadily throughout the end of the decade. See Louis Uchtelle, "Not Getting Ahead? Better Get Used to It," *The New York Times Week in Review*, 16 December 1990, p. 1. (Data based on U.S. Bureau of Labor Standards.)

it might do, therefore what the West must be prepared to do in response . . . where the West thought the Soviet Union was strong, it was in fact weak.

Conversions such as Talbott's and Moynihan's, however admirable, were not sufficient to overcome the punditocracy's ideological preoccupation. For, according to the ideology of the 1980s punditocracy, the very idea of Mikhail Gorbachev was impossible. Almost until the very moment the Berlin Wall came crumbling down in November 1989, there was simply no room in the insider mindset for a weakening base of Soviet power, an end to the Cold War, and the possibility of a cooperative superpower relationship. Regardless of what the Soviets may have said or done, the punditocracy knew better.

On the balmy Moscow morning of March 11, 1985, members of the Central Committee of the Communist Party of the Soviet Union gathered inside the Kremlin to choose a new leader. The contest proved a seesaw battle between the top two contenders and, according to Yegor Ligachev, "a completely different decision could have been made" had all the eligible voters shown up. When it was over, the victor was fifty-four-year-old Mikhail Sergeyvich Gorbachev. Two days later, as Chopin's *Funeral March* drifted through Red Square, mourners marched to the burial of the morally and intellectually barren Brezhnevite, Konstantin Chernenko. With him was buried Moscow's collaboration in the construction of the Cold War ideology that had sustained the American leadership class since the end of World War II. As François Mitterrand, Helmut Kohl, Margaret Thatcher, and George Bush stood quietly by, Mikhail Gorbachev threw in the first shovelful of earth.

On the opposite side of the world, in northwest Washington, D.C., the punditocracy scrambled to reconstitute itself into its "something's up in Russia" mode. For approximately two weeks thereafter, a window to the inner rings of the punditocracy opened into which climbed those Sovietologists and former officials who had made the final cut on the Rolodexes of the senior producers and op-ed page editors the last time a general secretary had died. Fax machines hummed and satellite hook-ups buzzed with the juice of instant strategic analysis.

In a rare moment of both humility and candor, on the day of Gorbachev's appointment, Henry Kissinger admitted to a *Washington Post* reporter that "nobody really knows what the younger generation thinks in the Soviet Union. We don't have any contact with them." America would have been well served by its Sovietology industry if Kissinger and company had just stopped there. Alas, that was not an option. "It will be two to four years before he can consolidate his power," Kissinger continued. Minor-league Kissingers took a similar line. "There will probably be a long period of transition to adjust to the new generation," explained former Secretary of State Alexander Haig. "It will be more like three years or so for the new leader to establish himself in a position of pre-eminence," noted former Secretary of Defense Harold Brown.

Complete ignorance of Gorbachev's views was not considered a serious handicap in the punditocracy. Its ideological assumptions told the chosen pundits all they needed to know. Soviet leaders came in only two categories: just as bad and even worse. Thus, virtually all the expert reactions solicited in the media during this period fell into one of two persuasions: boredom and alarm.

The bored pundits complained that Gorbachev was simply old hat. How could he be anything else? The man was a product of assembly-line totalitarian immutability. Carnegie Endowment Sovietologist Dimitri Simes forthrightly stated to reporters that Gorbachev had "no new ideas." "You don't survive the winnowing-out process in the Politburo unless you are cut from the same cloth as your fellow members," explained former CIA man George Carver; "[George] McGoverns and Jimmy Carters do not rise to the top in the Soviet Union." "You don't get into the Politburo by being a liberal," seconded Russian historian Peter Reddaway. "The real question," added *Time*'s Talbott, "was not whether he will pursue a course different from that taken by his predecessors, but whether he will pursue it more effectively."

A more alarmist tone was taken by a second faction of Soviet experts. As former Kissinger aide Helmut Sonnenfeldt explained, the Soviets had "an advantage now that they have a living, breathing leader who can deal with European leaders." Sonnenfeldt was alluding to the fact that the first five years of Reagan's presidency had been conducted opposite three sick, aged Soviet leaders who could barely muster the strength to stand up. Gorbachev's ability to walk up and down the Kremlin steps without assistance, coupled with what these experts perceived to be the American public's desire to love their adversary, could, if not thwarted in time, lead to catastrophe.[*]

The problem, according to Arnold Horelick of the RAND Corporation, was that "everyone is waiting for someone to appear on the Soviet side in whom you can invest some illusions." Punditocracy Sovietologists put the kibosh on that one almost before you could say Henry Wallace. Georgetown's Angela Stent warned that it was "very dangerous to think

[*]Midge Decter explains "Americans always love Soviet leaders—not Chernenko, but we didn't really get the chance. But beginning with Khruschev . . . Khruschev was a terrific guy. We really loved that guy." See The Committee for the Free World, *Does the West Still Exist?* (New York: Orwell Press, 1990), p. 19.

that Gorbachev will be any more 'liberal or flexible' on foreign relations" than his predecessors. Zbigniew Brzezinski promised that the United States could expect "a much more skillful, energetic—but in many respects, more dangerous—sort of leader." Adam Ulam, head of Harvard's Russian Research Center, predicted that "Gorbachev may be even more rigorous with intellectuals, writers and dissidents than in the past." His colleague, Marshall Goldman, added his view that in his acceptance speech Gorbachev had called for "an intensification of social production . . . and the economy," which, according to Goldman, was "usually a catch phrase meaning 'more discipline.'"[*]

These statements all have a number of characteristics in common. Most obviously, they were incorrect. But they were incorrect in important ways. Almost all seem to preclude the possibility of alternative interpretations. Moreover, all share the assumption that any optimism with regard to the de-escalation of Cold War tensions is both foolish and dangerous and deserves no place in the discussions of serious men and women. Aside from the special case of the émigré Dimitri Simes, those Sovietologists who had spent extended periods of time in the United Soviet Socialist Republics (USSR) during the previous decade, or who had significant contacts at numerous levels of Soviet society and understood the broad middle-class stirrings for change, were generally excluded from adding their strokes to the burgeoning Gorbachev portrait. The more dovish inhabitants of ex-officialdom not only were not consulted but were held up as objects of ridicule. George Carver had only to mention the names "McGovern" and "Carter" to discredit any views that diverged from the punditocracy hard line.

To the degree that American attitudes were capable of influencing the behavior of the Soviet leadership, these views may have been self-fulfilling. As was true of the Soviet belligerence quoted and magnified in the American media, hawkish words from one side feed and empower hawks on the other. This symbiosis was demonstrated time and again by comments like those of the retired dovish Soviet army colonel who explained to a British journalist in 1984 that "we need an economic reform. We need to expand human rights in our country and to further develop Soviet democracy. And we can only make headway in tackling our problems under conditions of prolonged détente. We need détente, lots and lots of détente."

---

[*]Goldman added, "If he masters the system—rather than its mastering him—this may augur bold moves in domestic and foreign policy. Don't bet on it." Marshall I. Goldman, "Will Gorbachev Be Brezhnev II?" *New York Times*, 12 March 1985, op-ed page.

The Soviets didn't get much détente from Ronald Reagan or the Reagan-era punditocracy. But in Mikhail Gorbachev, they had happened on something truly new in the history of great power politics. Throughout the next four years, the most influential members of the punditocracy virtually tied themselves to the mast of Stalin-era Manicheism, dismissing what were once colossally unthinkable Soviet concessions as mere propaganda moves designed to confuse Western audiences or to thwart our sense of purpose. When the charade could no longer be maintained, the world had changed forever: Geopolitics had entered an entirely new era, and the United States, the primary architect of the previous one, had been dragged along kicking and screaming.

The period between Gorbachev's initial rise to power and the final American agreement to accept the Soviet forfeit of the Cold War was one of endless confusion within the punditocracy. It was as if a slow-motion earthquake were shattering its ideological foundation brick by brick. With each falling fragment of the edifice, pundit after pundit scrambled to deny either the reality or the significance of the bricks, insisting all the while that the lumps they appeared to be taking were part of some larger pattern—a pattern that, despite all evidence, they had predicted all along.

Addicted to a wholly superficial level of analysis, the pundits sealed themselves off from the wide-ranging ideological debate that had commenced in Moscow. This dialogue, which encompassed not only military strategy, but also the entire economic and social structure of the Soviet Union, contained within it the seeds of an astonishingly broad social and intellectual revolution within much of the Soviet leadership class.* Had U.S. experts been willing to tap into this discussion, it might have been possible in certain limited instances to try to influence Moscow to move in more pacific and cooperative directions. The inability of the punditocracy to even consider the possibility of internal change within the Soviet civil and military mind helped lead to a series of belligerent statements and actions that impeded the progress of those Soviet leaders and intel-

*This analysis relies heavily on that put forth by Michael McGwire in *Perestroika and Soviet National Security* (Washington, DC: Brookings Institution, 1991), pp. 115–258. It is not inconsistent with those in Stephen M. Meyer, "The Sources and Prospects of Gorbachev's New Political Thinking on Security," *International Security*, fall 1988, pp. 124–63; Robert Legvold, "War, Weapons and Foreign Policy," in *Gorbachev's Russia and American Foreign Policy*, ed. Seweryn Bialer and Michael Mandelbaum (Boulder, CO: Westview Press, 1987), pp. 97–133; Jack Snyder "The Gorbachev Revolution: A Waning of Soviet Expansionism," *International Security*, winter, 1987/88, pp. 93–127; Matthew Evangelista, "The New Soviet Approach to Security," *World Policy Journal* (fall 1986): pp. 561–89; and Raymond Garthoff, "New Thinking in Soviet Military Doctrine," *The Washington Quarterly*, fall 1988, pp. 131–58.

lectuals who were arguing for a whole new focus for Soviet strategy. Once the strategic shift was finally accomplished, the punditocracy's inability to perceive it crippled Washington's ability to help shape it and pursue U.S. interests accordingly.

Skeptical observers can be forgiven for failing to embrace the changes represented by Mikhail Gorbachev purely on the basis of a new rhetorical style. Soviet leaders had long demonstrated an embarrassing affinity for a kind of surreal flower-power rhetoric that could not have been more inconsistent with the country's behavior. But if Gorbachev rewrote the Soviet stylebook in his speeches, it was his actions that provided more serious evidence that something profound was under way in the Soviet Union. And it was the significance of these actions, rather than the new rhetorical style, to which the punditocracy willfully blinded itself.

The punditocracy's reaction to Gorbachev during his first four years in power can be roughly divided into three segments. First came the "it's all a trick" period. When this was no longer sustainable, the "he's just resting," or peredyshka, interregnum took over. When this justification collapsed, the pontificators returned with a new theory: Gorbachev was a fine fellow, yes, but unfortunately he was about to be overthrown. Proving that he was always a man slightly ahead of his time, Charles Krauthammer came close to rolling all of these genuflections into three consecutive sentences in November 1987, when he observed that "We don't know if Gorbachev is sincere. If he is, we don't know whether he will succeed in winning over his bureaucracy. If he does, we don't know if he will last." Under any and all of these conditions, however, the proscribed American response remained the same: stand tall, remain firm, keep your powder dry, avoid "euphoria" and, most important, do nothing.

The new era of U.S.-Soviet relations can be dated approximately to April 17, 1985, when Gorbachev proposed his first moratorium on nuclear testing. Three months later, in July, he announced a unilateral testing moratorium, promising to extend it indefinitely should the United States follow suit. Two months later, he proposed a chemical weapons "free zone" in Central Europe, offering to destroy Soviet stocks in exchange for a reciprocal gesture by the North Atlantic Treaty Organization (NATO) powers.

All of these measures were viewed in Washington as simple propaganda, no different than the cynical and insincere crowing that Gorbachev's predecessors regularly undertook on behalf of the "peace-loving peoples of the world." That Gorbachev might have something new in mind did not really occur to anyone within the punditocracy until April 1986. Then, in response to Chernobyl, Gorbachev requested assistance from the West German and Swedish governments. On May 14, he proposed a four-point program to strengthen Soviet cooperation with the International Atomic Energy Agency, thereby reversing a decades-old policy of total secrecy in all nuclear-related matters. Soviet experts found this behavior intriguing and were even more surprised when, three months later, Gorbachev released a remarkably candid and self-critical report on the accident.

In mid-December, Gorbachev pulled a final Christmas rabbit out of his fur cap when he phoned Andrei Sakharov in Gorki and told the Soviet Union's leading dissident to return to Moscow and "go back to your patriotic work." Many hundreds of thousands of Americans had campaigned for Sakharov's freedom and were initially overjoyed by the news. This was a foolishly naive reaction, according to punditocracy prognosticators. George Will, little more than a year earlier, had attacked Gorbachev for heading a regime that "tortures its most distinguished citizen, Andrei Sakharov," titling his column on the subject, "Sakharov's Release: It's Just Business as Usual." Dimitri Simes, writing in *Foreign Affairs*, insisted that Gorbachev's decision "changed little" and was probably undertaken only to avoid being "blamed for Sakharov's de facto murder."

The coming winter proved a brutal one for punditocracy ideology. It began in late January 1987 when, in a plenum of the Party Central Committee, Gorbachev introduced perestroika, charging the party with stagnation and systemic failures and calling for the introduction of secret balloting, a choice of candidates in party elections, and experiments in giving Soviet citizens a choice in general elections. Three weeks later, he announced the pardoning of 140 political prisoners, the largest number pardoned at one time since 1956, with promises of more to follow. On February 28, Gorbachev ended the stalemate in the U.S.-USSR intermediate nuclear force (INF) negotiations by simply caving in to all American demands. Lest anyone get the idea that serious change was taking place, Henry Kissinger, invited by *Newsweek* to explain these bewildering developments, harkened back to the much-over-interpreted Kirkpatrick doctrine. "The Soviet Union is a totalitarian state today and it will be a totalitarian state even after the reforms are completed," Kissinger reassured his readers. "They seek efficiency, productivity—not democracy. They need a respite in the international field to accomplish these objectives: they have not been converted to Western pacifist notions."

Still, Gorbachev's response to the Soviet crisis continued unabated. In May, he announced that the Soviet Union would no longer jam Voice of America broadcasts. In June, at another Central Committee plenum, he called for the partial dismantling of centralized economic control and irrational pricing methods. Five days later, on June 30, Gorbachev announced an appeals process for Soviet citizens unjustly treated by party officials. That summer he began withdrawing Soviet troops from Afghanistan. On returning from his summer vacation in September, he invited three American representatives and two journalists to inspect the disputed radar station at Krasnoyarsk, which American officials had long maintained was a violation of the 1972 ABM treaty. Next, in November, after proposing a mutual U.S.-USSR 50 percent cut in nuclear weapons, Gorbachev took the opportunity of the seventieth anniversary of the Bolshevik Revolution to denounce Stalin's terror and to rehabilitate his more liberal adversary, Nikolai Bukharin.

Within the scholarly Sovietological community, excitement regarding Gorbachev's ultimate direction, piqued initially by Chernobyl, was reaching a fevered pitch. "History is on the move again in Soviet Russia," announced the distinguished emeritus professor of politics at Princeton, Robert C. Tucker:

> The signs are abundant, among them the proclaimed need for public openness or "glasnost," steps toward structural economic reform, the legalizing of limited forms of small scale individual and cooperative enterprise, a lively ferment in the arts, a drive against the mass scourge of alcohol abuse, the freeing of some prominent dissidents, the release of Andrei Sakharov to return to Moscow from Gorki exile, and moves on the international chessboard. . . . The fundamental fact about the Soviet Union today is that a struggle is taking place over reform of the established political culture—the customary ways of thinking and acting handed down from the past.

Tucker had the reputation of being a conservative Sovietologist. His article, which appeared in the spring of 1987 in the *World Policy Journal*, was preceded by any number of pieces written by less cautious Soviet experts proclaiming the onset of a new era in Soviet political culture.[*] By September, Robert Legvold, director of the most prestigious center of Soviet study in the country, Columbia's W. Averill Harriman Institute for the Advanced Study of the Soviet Union, explained that he did not "think there is anyone in academic circles who doubts that Gorbachev is committed to far-reaching changes within the Soviet Union, including a re-examination of foreign policy ideas."

---

[*]A special citation is due here to the series of prophetic articles on the emerging changes in the Soviet Union and their implications for U.S. strategy published by Soviet experts Archie Brown, Jerry Hough, Matthew Evangelista, and Michael McGwire that appeared in *World Policy Journal* during the period from late 1986 through 1987 under the guidance of its editor, Sherle R. Schwenninger.

In the American public, too, Gorbachev struck a remarkably responsive chord. Popularity polls indicated that Americans admired him even more than their own leaders. Japanese economic domination replaced Soviet military power as the most feared threat to the country's well being. When Gorbachev came to Washington at the end of the year and stepped outside his limousine on Connecticut Avenue, the nearby pedestrians started screaming, jumping up and down, and reaching over to try and touch the great man's garment.

Yet academic and popular enthusiasm for Gorbachev only seemed to inspire the punditocracy to new heights in its attempts to deny the reality of substantive change. William Safire promised his readers in November that no matter what Gorbachev said about Stalin himself, the general secretary would "break few Stalinist icons." Safire saw glasnost and perestroika as a means not to achieve "peaceful competition but to get a second wind—to carry out their now unspoken mission to dominate the world." Should real trouble break out in Eastern Europe, Safire promised, Gorbachev could be counted upon to "crack down as Mr. Stalin would have, fraternally, rolling in the tanks and shooting the dissenters."[*]

The Springsteen-like reception accorded Gorbachev during the December 1987 summit seemed to drive the punditocracy to desperation. Charles Krauthammer chalked it up to the fact that the city had somehow "lost its head." Americans were "getting dizzy on Gorbachev." George Will relied on a similar explanation: Americans were simply "drunk on détente."

Because Gorbachev seemed to be caving in to American demands on all bilateral issues related to human rights and arms control, post–Cold War Cold Warriors had to reach out to find other important areas of conflict to make their case that the conflict still remained essentially unchanged. The obvious target here was Nicaragua. Because the punditocracy mindset insisted that Third World revolution was, by definition, a function of Soviet meddling, the fact that the Sandinistas did not roll over and play dead as a favor to Gorbachev was seized on as a telling example of the general secretary's true deviousness. Instead of being cast as a mere symbol of the larger ideological conflict between the United States and the USSR, proxy warfare in Nicaragua and, to a lesser extent, Angola, El Salvador, and Afghanistan became the essence of the conflict itself.

The Nicaragua fetish during this period produced a wonderfully emblematic moment in the history of punditocracy strategic analysis. In early November 1987, Edward Luttwak spied a photograph on page one

---

[*]Quoted in Walter Shapiro, "Prolific Purveyor of Punditry," Time, 12 February 1990, p. 62. Safire also noted on March 27, 1989, that "when the Poles or the Hungarians rebel, Russian tanks will likely roll, corking genies and pushing back tooth paste with a vengeance."

of the *New York Times* in which Nicaragua's Ortega was posed beside East Germany's Erich Honecker and Poland's Wojciech Jarulzelski at the opening of the Nineteenth Party Congress in Moscow. The photo, wrote Luttwak in the *Washington Post*, proved that the Sandinistas had been admitted to the "very exclusive club of governments the Soviet Union regards as permanent, organic allies" and thus "settled conclusively" the argument over "the nature of the Sandinista regime and its intent in regard to the peace plan." The problem with Luttwak's analysis of the problem was that the photograph did not exist; neither, as far as anyone else knew, did the club. The *Times* had simply published the two photographs adjacently with only a tiny border between them.[*]

If the punditocracy's stubbornness with regard to Mikhail Gorbachev's 1987 initiatives appeared to have an element of tragedy, its continuation in the face of Mr. Gorbachev's 1988 performance demonstrated a distinct touch of farce. In early February 1988, Gorbachev announced that the Soviets would withdraw unilaterally from Afghanistan. Ten days later, in Yugoslavia, he signed a joint statement in which he blamed the USSR for the two nations' historic conflict, renounced the "pretension of imposing concepts of social development on anyone," and rejected the use of force or "interference in the affairs of other states." In May, Ronald Reagan was invited to lecture Soviet students on human rights at Moscow State University. In June, the Russian Orthodox Church celebrated its one thousandth anniversary with the full support and cooperation of the Soviet Government. At the end of the month, at the first All-Union Communist Party Conference since 1941, Gorbachev outlined his plan for a transition to democracy, which included a plan for local elections and a democratically elected bicameral legislature. Three weeks later, he offered to dismantle the disputed radar station at Krasnoyarsk.

This pattern continued throughout early December, when Gorbachev, demonstrating a true showman's flair for the single dramatic gesture, piled up all of his proscribed doctrinal changes in Soviet behavior and dumped them on an unsuspecting world at the United Nations in New York. For good measure, he threw in a unilateral 20 percent cut in Soviet military forces. His speech out-McGoverned George McGovern with its internationalist rhetoric and electrified both the media and the American people.

But even now, Gorbachev had still not managed to impress the influential Cold Warriors within the punditocracy. Following the U.N. speech, the *Washington Post* op-ed page seemed to mirror the various stages of Gorbachev denial. George Will fell back on the now-dated "he's trying to get

---

[*]Philip Geyelin was the first person to point this out. *Washington Post*, 29 November 1987.

us to drop our guard" standby, arguing that "Gorbachev may, without reversing Soviet economic decline, achieve a relative enhancement of Soviet military power."[*] (Will would hold fast to this line right up through Gorbachev's agreement to dissolve the Soviet Union four years later.[†]) Charles Krauthammer went with the current fashion, the waiting-period argument. He observed that Soviet leaders "always talk this way when they are looking for a period of peredyshka [breathing space]." Sovietologist Dimitri Simes saw a need to get out in front of his nonspecialist colleagues and used the page to argue that Gorbachev was "a beleaguered imperial leader in desperate need of foreign successes to compensate for domestic setbacks." He was, therefore, making "a virtue out of necessity" in order to "use Soviet limitations to enhance Moscow's global influence." No matter what the prognosis, the administered cure never seemed to change. At all costs, insisted Dr. Kissinger eight days later, the thing to do was to avoid "wishful thinking" and, of course, "euphoria." In the end, counseled Kissinger, "peaceful coexistence must be based not on public relations spectacles but on a reciprocal respect for the other side's vital interests."

European leaders found the American response puzzling. A *Manchester Guardian* reporter in Bonn observed, "The German Question is suddenly quite simple: what on earth is the matter with the Americans?"[‡] Unencumbered by the simple moral certainties of the early Reagan era, the Europeans were sufficiently agile, intellectually and diplomatically, to negotiate an entirely new foundation for their relations with the East. The Germans, in particular, achieved once-unthinkable strategic gains from perestroika and new thinking because they were quick to recognize the opportunity and seize it with both fists. They not only united their homeland, but maneuvered themselves into a relationship that left them poised to exploit the Eastern transformations for long-term growth and environmental security.

---

[*]George F. Will, 9 December 1988. This was similar to Safire's line of the day; he noted that the speech was a combination of "audacity and mendacity," while arguing that if Gorbachev were really sincere, he would show it by "tearing down the Berlin Wall." William Safire, 9 December 1988.

[†]"Gorbachev placed only an instrumental value on freedom," Will wrote of the man then being held in captivity in the Crimea. In a column entitled, "So Much for a Master Tinkerer," Will complained that the man he would call a "retrograde force" favored "only small, conditioned doses of freedom, only because and to the extent that they would serve economic efficiency and hence Soviet power." George F. Will, 22 August 1991, and 24 August 1991.

[‡]See W. L. Webb, "West Germans Baffled by American Attitudes," *The Manchester Guardian Weekly*, 28 May 1989, p. 10. Webb quotes one Social Democratic party politician observing, "the Russian enemy image has been the basis of their ideological identity, the one sure thing in an insecure world of daunting debt and declining economic power. Where the Germans offend is in not letting them preserve this image of an enemy."

It is instructive to examine the case of German foreign minister Hans-Dietrich Genscher as an example of just how insistent were the punditocracy nay-sayers in denigrating the possibility of peaceful cooperation between East and West. Genscher saw in Gorbachev the opportunity to make peace and end the division of Europe as early as August 1986. He announced a few months later that if such a chance existed, "It would be a mistake of historical dimension for the West to let this chance slip just because it cannot escape from a way of thinking." "Let us not sit back idly and wait for Mr. Gorbachev to deliver," he advised. "Let us rather try to influence, expedite, and shape developments from our end."

Such talk was heresy at the time in Washington, and Genscher soon became a despised figure in the punditocracy, his name converted into an epithet of unadulterated perfidy. *Newsweek* devoted a cover story to the threat of "Genscherization" of European foreign policy. Evans and Novak quite predictably beat this drum on the *Post* op-ed page, and the usually staid James Hoagland also joined in, calling Genscher "a master contortionist" willing "to mix domestic politics and East-West policies when it helps his favorite cause—himself." William Safire, however, took his place as leader of this particular pack. He warned of "the Genscherite appeasement bloc" led by "Germany's devious foreign minister," a man who saw "a Fourth Reich rising from NATO's ashes to dominate Europe's economy." Using a textbook "When did you stop beating your wife?" construction, Safire inquired whether "the export-loving foreign minister, Mr. Genscher, approve[s] of the way West German missile experts are providing Third World nations with the technical means to build delivery systems for gas bombs." It is a demonstration of just how thoroughly Cold War myopia dominated the punditocracy mindset that its most influential member, Safire, could accuse an allied foreign minister of being "export-loving" and make it sound evil.

Protected by the distance of the Atlantic Ocean and his status as the most popular politician in Germany, Genscher survived the punditocracy's attack. In a front-page story dated July 20, 1990, the *New York Times* reported that while "the man of the hour of German Unity may be Chancellor Helmut Kohl . . . the man who first saw it coming was certainly Foreign Minister Hans Dietrich Genscher." Genscher went on, with Kohl, to achieve not only German unity but, as the *Times* reported, "a comprehensive package of arms reductions, an all-European security structure building on the mechanisms set up in 1975 by the Helsinki Conference on Security and Cooperation in Europe, large-scale Western financial help for the Soviet Union to modernize its economy and a gradual end to the divisions of the continent." Needless to say, none of this would have been possible if Genscher had had a punditocracy to worry about.

As a direct consequence of its inability to adjust to the prerogatives of the new world era, meanwhile, the United States was rapidly losing influence in Europe while excusing itself from the new political and economic arrangements negotiated under the shadow of Gorbachev's new initiatives. The European Bank for Reconstruction and Development was set up under the leadership of the Bundesbank and chaired by Jacques Attali, an adviser to François Mitterrand who considered America to be "Japan's grainery." *Washington Post* foreign editor David Ignatius noted shortly after the Berlin Wall fell that, while America's economic competitors had representatives in Warsaw, Budapest, Prague, and Moscow, "making contacts, making loans, making business," the United States had generally restricted itself to reactions amounting to "Whoopee! We won the Cold War."*

If Mikhail Gorbachev had taught the nation's leading political pundits anything at all, it should have been the value of a little humility. In the years after his 1985 ascension to power, all that would have been needed to embarrass most pundits was to read aloud their previous predictions. Unfortunately, Gorbachev had no more success in reforming the deeply ingrained practices of the punditocracy than he had with Soviet agriculture.

A few pundits were sufficiently honest to own up to the fact that their ideological compasses had veered off-kilter. Shortly before the Berlin Wall came down, Meg Greenfield admitted that "What we are confronting is the destruction of many of our premises and expectations. . . . Our pat arguments don't work anymore. We can no longer put our minds on automatic." Most pundits, however, simply continued to dig themselves further and further into their early-Reagan-era ditches. In February 1989, Zbigniew Brzezinski told the editors of the *Washington Times* that further upheaval in Poland could discredit Gorbachev's efforts at political liberalization to the point at which it would spark a Soviet military takeover in Moscow. A George Will column dated November 9, 1989, the very day of the fall of the Berlin Wall, contained these immortal words: "Liberalization is a ploy . . . the Wall will remain."

When a lost driver asks a pedestrian for directions, only to find out later that his destination is hundreds of miles from the place to which he

---

*Of 940 joint ventures in the Soviet Union reported as of October 1, 1989, U.S. companies had participated in only 97, compared with 595 for Japan and Western Europe. PlanEcon, a Washington-based consulting firm for Eastern Europe–related business, noted that 75 percent of its clients were European or Japanese. See David Ignatius, "While Washington Slept," *Washington Post*, 19 November 1989, Outlook section, p. 2.

has been directed, the driver usually knows better than to go back for more advice. Fortunately for the employment status of the punditocracy, a similar standard does not appear to operate with regard to the American news media and matters of war and peace. The pundits who had blithely predicted that Gorbachev would never do anything he had just done continued to pontificate as if their dismal records had no implications for their newest pronouncements. Yet, so long as their analyses erred on the side of "caution," of "prudence," of doing nothing and, above all, of avoiding "euphoria," the pundits risked little.

To those who argue that what pundits say matters little because the politicians ultimately must make the decisions, the 1988 American presidential election provides a useful demonstration of the strictures that the punditocracy can impose on political debate irrespective of public opinion and political reality. Although he had not yet made his U.N. address or allowed the collapse of his Eastern European empire, Gorbachev had, by the fall of 1988, gone some distance in addressing the major concerns of the United States regarding Soviet intentions. The American people, moreover, were consistently telling pollsters that they no longer worried about the Soviet military. Yet the presidential election was conducted as if none of this were happening.

The campaign was characterized by the bizarre spectacle of each serious contender's seeking to prove his political manhood by demonstrating just how "tough" and "strong" he could be in the face of the surrendering Soviet leader. The less cooperation a particular candidate received in this regard from his punditocracy audience, the more he felt it necessary to take the responsibility upon himself. In a speech before the New Hampshire Knights of Columbus, the Democratic victor, Michael Dukakis, used variants of the word "strength" thirty-eight times in twenty-five minutes. The result was a pathetic spectacle that disintegrated into an argument over whether any of his opponents was sufficiently "tough" and "strong" enough, in Dukakis' words, "to use force to defend our territory," as if a potential military attack on the United States were somehow the most pressing danger facing the next American president.

Early in the race a few candidates had attempted to move their dialogue away from the shopworn penny of Korea-era machismo, but they were quickly slapped back into line. Albert Gore, for instance, began his campaign by speaking of the dangers posed by greenhouse gases and the need for a high-tech infrastructure to support American technological research and development. Gore was laughed off the podium by George Will for addressing issues that "were not even peripheral." Sufficiently chastened, Gore quickly embraced the hairy-chested neoconservative rhetoric crafted for him by his advisers, two of whom doubled as editors of the *New Republic.* This succeeded in convincing Will to endorse Gore as the only Democratic candidate who was "not a foreign-policy naïf." Meanwhile, the public dialogue on America's problems inspired by the race began absurdly and degenerated from there.[*]

An interesting dichotomy developed during this period between reporters and op-ed writers that served to demonstrate just how powerfully the punditocracy's Reagan-era obsessions impeded its members' ability to judge the candidates. While news pages were filled with incredible report after incredible report about the Soviet Union, the pundits kept insisting that such things were simply not possible. This tension was clearly illustrated during the election by the reporting and editorial staffs at the *Wall Street Journal.* Extrapolating from the changes inspired by Gorbachev and the emergence of the economic power of Japan, among other developments, two journalists reported quite undramatically in August 1988 that the postwar era was over. Writing on the newspaper's front page, they noted,

> the containment of Communism and its chief proponent, the Soviet Union . . . tailored to the two-power world of 40 years ago, doesn't fit an era in which the Soviet Union is struggling to restructure its ossified economy, Communism is in decline as an ideology and the American people worry more about economic competition with Japan or terrorist attacks against the U.S. than superpower confrontation.

Yet, a month after the story appeared, the *Journal*'s editorial page savaged Michael Dukakis for allowing even a hint of such a common-sense approach to cloud his vision. "A bipartisan postwar consensus has sustained a policy of 'containment' against Soviet and Communist expansion," argued Mr. Bartley and company. "Mr. Dukakis supports containment in Europe, but he won't support Freedom Fighters in the Third World." These sixteen words constitute a masterpiece of punditocracy subterfuge; they contain three simultaneous intellectual sleights of hand and an attack on their subject for failing to address the phony issues posited in the first place. By insisting on the continued relevance of the "bipartisan consensus" on containment, the editors

---

[*]When Dukakis observed that if a Central American nation wished to have friendly relations with the Soviet Union, this did not constitute an a priori justification of a U.S. military invasion, Gore insisted that this meant "it would be perfectly all right with [Dukakis] for the Soviets to create a client state in the Western Hemisphere." This, in turn, inspired Dukakis to return fire as if preparing for a fifth-grade playground fight: "I don't think he is the toughest," declared Dukakis. "I don't think he's the toughest at all . . . I don't yield to Gore in toughness in any way, shape or manner." See Toner, "Dukakis Talking Tough," p. A19.

ignore the consequences of the Soviets' military's commitment to the doctrines of New Thinking and Reasonable Sufficiency.* (The editors' hero, Margaret Thatcher, declared the Cold War over in November.) The *Journal*'s editors, moreover, equated support for Third World guerrillas with this same outdated policy of containment in Europe, which, when it was still relevant, had been significantly weakened by exactly these adventures. Finally, they insisted on calling those revolutionaries "Freedom Fighters," although their ranks were largely populated by persons whose ideas and motivations can be said to have little or nothing to do with the idea. Jonas Savimbi's "freedom fighters" in Angola were Maoists. The Mujihadeen in Afghanistan were largely Islamic fundamentalists with a heavy concentration of heroin smugglers. The brigades of the Nicaraguan contras were filled with similarly unsavory types, as evidenced by what one reputable human rights organization called their "routine attacks on civilian populations," including "the kidnapping, torture and murder [of] health workers, teachers and other government employees."

Because he had neither the courage nor the vision to defend his own conception of the changes under way in the Soviet Union and the proper role of the United States in a changed world, Michael Dukakis constantly found himself the helpless victim of the punditocracy's 1946 worldview. If he spoke of his intention to move away from Reagan-era confrontation, these sentiments were attributed to his softness—they were "standard-issue McGovernite Left," in the words of the *New Republic*; "pure McGovernism," as William F. Buckley called them; or even vintage Henry Wallace, as *Journal* editors intimated.

But if, in contrast, Dukakis folded completely and endorsed the punditocracy viewpoint that Ronald Reagan's toughness had won whatever meager concessions Mr. Gorbachev had offered, he was attacked for having opposed most of these policies in the first place. After noting that Gorbachev would never reject terrorism or permit freedom of religion or free emigration as Dukakis would "challenge" him to do, Charles Krauthammer noted that "Reagan's successes, which Dukakis is quick to applaud, happened not because he challenged the Russians to be nice but because he forced them to give in." In what must qualify as one of

---

*"Reasonable sufficiency" consisted, according to Robert Legvold, of "paired-down nuclear arsenals capable only of launching a secure second strike; conventional forces capable of defending, not conducting major offensive operations, and interventionary forces capable of deterring an aggressor in regional crises but insufficient to prop up a regime incapable of defending itself." These ideas were footnoted to articles published in the Soviet press between June and September 1987. See Robert Legvold, "War, Weapons and Foreign Policy," in *Gorbachev's Russia and American Foreign Policy*, ed. Seweryn Bialer and Michael Mandelbaum (Boulder, CO: Westview Press, 1987), p. 113.

the least flattering presidential endorsements in American history, Krauthammer and his *New Republic* colleagues noted that their candidate, as
president

> would have endorsed the nuclear freeze, thereby denying us the INF treaty
> that saw the removal of Soviet missiles in Europe. He would have cut off the
> contras early on, leaving us today with a consolidated and expansionist Marx-
> ist regime in Nicaragua. Whether a Dukakis foreign policy would have pro-
> duced the Soviet pullout from Afghanistan, the impending settlement in
> Angola, and other successes of the Reaganite hard-line is dubious at the least.

The obvious loser in this process was not Dukakis but the American
political process. William Safire says he thinks his political influence is at
a peak during election season. This is because the candidates must campaign for many months before they face an electorate. Voters are not
invited into the process until the shape of the debate has already been
determined. The pre-campaign campaign is about two things: money and
recognition. The former often follows the latter. While handlers, pollsters, money men, and volunteer workers all have a role to play, the pundits are the only constant determinant of how much and what kind of
attention each candidate can be expected to receive.

Thus, it was wholly irrelevant to the 1988 campaign that vast majorities
of the American people had ceased to view the Soviet military as an
important threat to their well-being. Nor did it turn out to matter much
that economic power and influence had come to play a far more important role on the world stage in determining a nation's well-being than the
size of its military and that more than two-thirds of Americans surveyed at
the time felt that way.[*] To William Safire, George Will, Charles Krauthammer, Henry Kissinger, most of the panelists on *The McLaughlin Group*, and

---

[*]Both of these statements are evident in *Defining American Strength: Results of a Survey of American Voters Conducted by the World Policy Institute, October 15 through October 20, 1987* (Washington, DC: Mellman and Lazarus Research, 1987). See also Stanley Greenberg, "Looking
Toward '88: The Politics of American Identity," *World Policy Journal* (fall 1987). These numbers, moreover, remained firm throughout the year. According to a later poll, taken in May
1989 and therefore more than six months before the fall of the Berlin Wall, a full 4 percent
of Americans surveyed considered "Soviet aggression in the world" to "pose the greatest
danger to America today," whereas just 2 percent selected it as "the most important problem
facing America today." The response to the latter question was one-tenth that for "education" and one-seventh that for "rising costs for young families." Recognizing this, a full 73
percent of those surveyed wanted the government to "recognize that the greatest threat to
American security is the economic challenge posed by Japan, and we should shift military
spending to favor domestic investment." See "Defining American Priorities," in *Results of a
Survey of American Voters Conducted for the World Policy Institute by Greenberg-Lake* (The Analysis
Group, 18–23 May 1989).

the neoconservative editors of the *New Republic*, the rise of Mikhail Gorbachev did not fundamentally affect the power calculation that lay at the root of all great power politics. The American purpose, as it were, remained resistance of Soviet Communist domination. Candidates who refused to place this contest at the very center of their political agendas—and who refused, therefore, to subordinate all other national problems to its achievement—were to be dismissed as foolish, naive, and "McGovernite." Their funding and, hence, recognition levels diminished accordingly.* A candidate who sought to engage Gorbachev in ending the Cold War or merely to subordinate what remained of the East-West competition to what appeared to be more pressing domestic and international needs was not to be taken seriously. The environment, our education system, our economic infrastructure, the health of our cities, our ability to compete on a par with Germans and Japanese—these were issues that, when push came to shove, were "not even peripheral" when compared with the long twilight struggle of the never-ending Cold War.

Thus, when Michael Dukakis debated George Bush for the presidency of the United States, both spoke as if Mikhail Gorbachev did not exist. American Sovietologists regarded Gorbachev as the most remarkable development in the past two centuries of Russian history. The American people considered him among the most impressive men on the planet. But because neither group had the means to puncture the closed circle of self-reinforcing punditocracy ideology, neither group's views proved relevant to the electoral discussion. The Cold War therefore lived on in the American political imagination long after it had ended in the geographical space it was said to occupy, crippling our political dialogue and warping our national priorities.

In 1988, the American people elected a man who attributed the rise of Mikhail Gorbachev solely to "our strength . . . steadiness . . . our resolve" but nevertheless compared negotiating arms control treaties with the man to ignoring the lessons of Auschwitz. His running mate told reporters that he considered perestroika to be "nothing more than refined Stalinism" and Gorbachev to be "no different than Brezhnev or anybody else." The brazen foolishness of these statements was made possible by three years of punditocracy denial, distortion, and distrust. As a result, the United States entered the 1990s with an intellectually crippled political leadership, incapable of even acknowledging, much less addressing, the fundamental challenges we faced as a nation.

*Jesse Jackson is obviously a special case.

CHAPTER ELEVEN

Operation Pundit Shield

Few events in recent American history demonstrate the destructive power of the punditocracy with greater clarity than America's decision to go to war with Iraq in January of 1991. Casting about for a replacement of its One Big Thing in the aftermath of the Cold War, the punditocracy found itself at sea in a world without clear enemies to condemn or a credible international crusade to plan. Dogged by increasing evidence of protracted decline and diminished international influence, the insider political dialogue manifested a kind of inchoate desperation—not altogether unlike that communicated by George Bush's syntax. "If only we knew who the bad guys were," the pundits seemed to be saying, "we'd know who we were again."

How the extrication of the Iraqi army from the kingdom of Kuwait came to be the most important priority of the American people in the winter of 1991 can only be understood in this context. George Bush's success in leading the American public into war might never have been possible without the energetic cooperation of the punditocracy, who, for a brief shining moment, found a new Big Thing to demonstrate its self-worth. The punditocracy's role explains not only the delusion of omnipotence that seized the nation in the aftermath of the hundred hours' fighting, but also the presumably serious insistence on the part of almost everyone who appeared in the media at the time that the defeat of a nation with a gross domestic product the size of Kentucky's somehow represented America's "defining moment."

During the six months which George Bush, Dick Cheney, Colin Powell, and Norman Schwartzkopf laid the groundwork for their successful assault on Saddam Hussein's army, a tiny cadre of neoconservative pundits performed a similarly delicate operation on elite Washington opinion. Although it was undoubtedly President Bush's actions that spoke loudest in this period, the punditocracy's battle plan proved, in many respects, no less effective. The pundits concentrated their fire on a few superficially simple issues in this Arabian drama and treated them in highly inflammatory fashion, thereby simultaneously constricting and distorting the war's public discourse. In the debate that led to Congress' decision to declare war, as well as during the fighting itself, the punditocracy shaped the political dialogue in a manner that substituted the Iraqi bogeyman for their fallen Stalinist icon and celebrated American military prowess with a degree of reverence that bordered on worship. Then, in the war's aftermath, they proceeded to ignore many of its considerable costs, as well as almost all of the fundamental questions it should have raised about America's future.

In the languid months that preceded the Iraqi invasion of Kuwait, Washington was having a difficult time convincing itself that it still mattered. David Broder helped get the year off to a depressing start by telling the city's power-mongers—in a front-page article no less—that they didn't matter anymore. "Nation's Capital in Eclipse," explained Broder's headline, "as Pride and Power Slip Away."

In the White House, tempers were flaring over the re-emergence of the dreaded "wimp issue," just in time for midterm elections. The exploding budget deficit forced the president to publicly repudiate his "no new taxes" pledge, infuriating conservatives, who began once again to search for a potential challenger. One of their favorites, Patrick Buchanan, could be seen every day on television accusing the president of "refusing to stand up and lead our side in the great fight" and looking "like a wimp on the tax issue." Meanwhile, as Bush watched his approval ratings sink to new depths, his son Neil became embroiled in the ever-burgeoning savings and loan debacle. Neil Bush took to defending himself by making abusive phone calls to reporters in the middle of the night and treating live television cameras to the kind of language unheard from presidential family members since the heyday of Billy Carter.[*]

Life was no prettier in the punditocracy. Robbed of its Big Thing, its ideological flailings had the character of Churchill's pudding: they

---

[*]Neil Bush charged that the accusations leveled against him were "absolute bullshit." His taped performance was shown on *The McLaughlin Group*, 14 July 1990.

lacked theme. Of course the pundits hated environmentalists, tax-and-spenders, terrorists and, particularly, drug-smuggling dictators, but passions were waning. One well-known Cold Warrior speculated about trying a second career as a novelist or a jazz critic. The beat went on, but the thrill was gone.

Tax hikes, oil spills, flag burners, Jesse Helms, and the controversial NEA-funded *Piss Christ*: every issue seemed more depressing than the last. Just days before the Iraqi invasion, the McLaughlin group spent a good portion of the show discussing what should be done about Roseanne Barr's mangling of "The Star-Spangled Banner" at a baseball game. Morton Kondracke insisted that Americans boycott her sponsors because Ms. Barr was "unpatriotic" and "down on the country."

As if sent directly from Central Casting, Saddam Hussein rode in on his black horse and rescued Washington from all this. The gratitude was almost palpable. Ben Wattenberg headlined his column, "Thanks Saddam, We Needed That." "In a way," observed the editors of the *New Republic*, "Saddam Hussein did the world a favor. . . ." Suddenly Washington was in the grip of what *New York Times* bigfoot R. W. Apple called "the heavy speculation, the avid gossip, the gung-ho, here's where it's happening spirit that marks the city when it grapples with great events." "Hey, whaddya know," quipped Michael Kinsley, "we're not declining after all." America was "back," yet again.

Hussein, among others, had a right to be surprised by all this. Right up until the day he invaded Kuwait, the very same Mr. Hussein had been considered a valued commercial customer and regional balancing force by at least three American presidents. Both before and during his invasion of Iran, Hussein had enjoyed private screenings of U.S. satellite intelligence data. When the war with Iran ended and he turned his poison-gas pellets on his own Kurdish population, Hussein continued to receive sophisticated American technology and taxpayer-subsidized grain.

Although it could not compete with Hussein's regime in cruelty and aggression, Kuwait, meanwhile, was not exactly the ideal place to mount a principled American defense of freedom and democracy. The ruling al-Sabah family ran a theocratic dictatorship in which Jews and Christians enjoyed virtually no rights. Its leader, the emir, made a regular practice of "marrying" young virgins on Thursday nights, the eve of the Islamic Sabbath, and "divorcing" them the next day. In the United Nations, the Kuwaiti regime attacked the United States with greater frequency and often stronger rhetorical violence than did the Soviet Union. And when one of our ships, the U.S.S. *Stark*, was torpedoed by Iraq while protecting Kuwaiti shipping in 1987, the Kuwaitis refused to allow America's dying sailors the right to use their hospital facilities.

President Bush's motivations in deciding to opt for war are not fully knowable. A late-afternoon meeting with Margaret Thatcher on August 2 was apparently quite influential, as were the parallels drawn in the president's own mind between Hussein and Hitler.[*] Foreign policy crises, moreover, were not exactly unwelcome in the Bush White House, for the president's approval ratings took a nose dive whenever he was forced to deal with domestic matters. His chief of staff at the time, John Sununu, called the prospect of a short, successful conflict "pure gold" for the president.[†] The evidence is sketchy, but one can also postulate an important contribution by the punditocracy. James Fallows, for instance, discerns a powerful combination of Bush's own political and psychological weaknesses with hairy-chested pundit rhetoric to transform the president from wimp to war hero. "Following Bush's conversion," observes Fallows,

> Instantly, all the pundits who had been grumbling about Bush wimping out on "no new taxes" and insisting that he had no backbone were now talking about how he had been transformed into the man of greatness standing up to Iraq. Bush's turn-around seemed to me to be a virtually—almost structurally—pundit-driven activity, and it confirmed his two worst tendencies: not wanting to get involved in domestic politics and thinking that this was the transcendent issue of all time.

Whether Bush himself was swayed by the punditocracy's intimations regarding his political manhood, the issue's transcendence is explicable only in terms of the particular ideological framework constructed for the invasion by Bush and his neoconservative allies in the punditocracy. The ability of both of these parties to manipulate the public dialogue—the pundits by word and Bush by deed—ensured that the truly essential questions about the war and U.S. national interest would never be asked. Instead, the debate was driven by the president's willingness to unilaterally ratchet up the size and scope of the American commitment and by the pundits' ability to reinforce the pro-war agenda at crucial moments in the debate. The latter contribution turned out to be crucial during the belated congressional debate in early January 1991, when a deeply divided Congress accepted the punditocracy's definition of the stakes of the conflict and acceded—reluctantly—to the president's war plans.

*   *   *

[*]"Remember, George," was President Bush's recollection of the soon-to-be deposed prime minister's warning, "this is no time to go wobbly." George Bush, quoted in Martin Walker, "Victory and Delusion," *Foreign Policy* 83 (summer 1991): p. 167.

[†]As, indeed, it was. John Sununu, quoted in Elizabeth Drew, "Letter from Washington," *The New Yorker*, 4 February 1991, p. 83.

In the immediate aftermath of the Iraqi invasion of Kuwait, America's media discovered two facts about the U.S. political debate that it apparently found surprising. First, the Reaganite coalition of Old Right conservatives and New Right neoconservatives was in the process of imploding and, second, the debate's center of gravity could now be found in the punditocracy.

In the latter case, editors and news reporters who had historically prided themselves on ignoring their own editorial pages suddenly found themselves interviewing columnists and talk-show regulars with the respect and attention they would normally reserve for representatives and cabinet secretaries. When they asked one another why they were doing this, the answers came back, "Congress is out of town," or "the Democrats are afraid to undercut the president." Both were true, but neither fully explained why the reporters had no choice but to rely on the punditocracy. The real reason was that there was no other debate to report; the punditocracy was it. Not only was the only coherent opposition to George Bush's initial decision to deploy two hundred thousand troops to the desert pundit-centered, but, with the exception of Stephen Solarz's and a few others', so, too, were the only coherent explanations of why war was necessary. Not coincidentally, Solarz's most complete and cogent presentation of the "war is necessary" argument appeared in the *New Republic*.

The displacement in the public debate of Congress and the old-line political establishment by the punditocracy had been evident for more than a decade. Widespread recognition became necessary in August 1990 only because the stakes were suddenly so high. On an issue as large and symbolically potent as taking the country to war—a war that had been unimaginable until just days before its planning began—most of the nation's hypercautious, poll-driven politicians were helpless to form independent judgments without first hearing the parameters of the debate communicated to them by the pundits. As Patrick Buchanan explained beneath a *New York Times* headline reading, "The Battle of the Columnists: Telling Leaders How to Think,"

> The war between the interventionists and the neo-isolationists has moved to the weekend talk shows and the op-ed pages. It is not only among journalists, like Buchanan and Safire, but between Brzezinski and Kissinger, and it moves onto shows like *The Capital Gang, Crossfire, The MacNeil-Lehrer News-Hour*, David Brinkley's Sunday show and *Nightline*. This is where the debate is played out. It is an unrecognized sea change in American politics.

Jude Wanniski, now a consultant and media critic, concurred: "In order to narrow down the options for where the country should be moving, it is important that the intellectual cadre be engaged in discussion to do that. Politicians no longer have time, so it is the business of the professional opinion leaders—the pundits."

Similarly, the Old Right-neoconservative coalition had been crumbling for quite a while as the glue of anti-Communism grew increasingly less cohesive. With the Soviets down for the count, neoconservatives were eager to press for the establishment of a global Pax Americana—the "universal dominion" of the United States, in Charles Krauthammer's phrase, whereby America and its Western allies would undertake the liberalization of foreign nations across the globe by political, military, and economic means. Much of the Old Right, however, had reverted to its pre–World War II "America first" roots. Led by Buchanan, they were not interested in spreading democracy, but only in defending their vision of it at home. Buchanan accused the neoconservatives of practicing what he called "democratism," a form of "idolatry" that substituted "a false god for the real, a love of process for a love of country."

Between the neoconservatives and the isolationists lay a host of post-Reaganite positions that embraced neither one. The fervently anti-Soviet Zbigniew Brzezinski reconsidered his support for U.S. policy based on "earth control" and retreated into a more modest vision of global security via an American/European/Japanese trilateral compact. Edward Luttwak, the strategic genius behind so many punditocracy war plans of the 1980s, had, by August 1990, come around to the view, originally enunciated by Sherle R. Schwenninger four years earlier, that traditional geopolitical conflicts such as that between Iraq and Iran no longer had much relevance to the overall security and prosperity of the nation. In the "main struggle of the main arena of international life," Luttwak explained, a nation's power and influence were determined not by its geopolitical assets but by its geo-economic ones. "Disposable capital is increasingly displacing firepower, civilian product development is displacing military innovation, and market penetration is displacing the possession of foreign garrisons and bases" as the coins of the strategic realm.

Clearly, ideological fault lines had shifted. While Ronald Reagan could count on a popular punditocracy front to support him in every foreign endeavor involving the U.S. military, the contingent working the field for George Bush was considerably smaller. Fortunately for the president's war plans, Washington's post–Cold War intellectual transformation remained for practical purposes largely rhetorical. Although the Soviet threat was gone, the minds shaped by the Cold War remained programmed for permanent crisis. Even as some of the most influential members of the punditocracy were evolving into neo-isolationists and geo-economists, the Cold War consensus they helped to create came back to haunt them. The idea of conservatives opposing a war thus produced a kind of cognitive dissonance in insider Washington that, however interesting, enjoyed little influence in the system itself. As "the unchallenged superpower . . . the center of world power" and "the apex of the Industrial West," in Charles Krauthammer's evocative phrasing, we simply had to do something. And given a mindset shaped by the Cold War, that something had to be military. Professor Moynihan dissected this phenomenon on the Senate floor:

> What we find is a kind of time warp in which we are acting in an old mode in response to a new situation. . . . It is in that mode of which we are in a bipolar, permanent crisis with the enemy. It used to be totalitarian, Leninist Communism. Without a moment's pause almost, we shifted the enemy to this person at the head of this insignificant, flawed country whose boundaries were drawn in 1925 in a tent by an English colonial official, an artifact of the Treaty of Sevres.

What is easy to forget in light of the obliteration of the Iraqi army is just how shocking the idea of war was in the first place. Indeed, when Washington first received word of the Iraqi campaign, few insiders seemed to be aware that any "defining moments" might be in the offing. On *The McLaughlin Group*, Fred Barnes predicted that "it would be crazy to think that we're going to send troops over there and defend Kuwait." He was joined by fellow inside-dopester Robert Novak, who promised, "We're not going to send troops in there. C'mon, there's no chance of that." These observations were consistent with the early readings of the president as well. After an early morning meeting of the National Security Council, President Bush told the press that intervention was "not being considered," and "we're not contemplating such action."

Outside of the Gulf itself, world reaction was hardly thunderous. In Germany and Japan, both of which lack the internal oil resources enjoyed by the United States, the invasion was a ho-hum affair. As Japanese consul general Msamichi Hanabusa explained, "Who will control oil . . . is not a very serious issue for Japan. It is of course better that oil is in friendly hands. But experience tells us that whoever controls oil will be disposed to sell it . . . oil is a fungible commodity." If awoken at all by news of the invasion, our economic competitors simply turned over and went back to sleep.

Virtually alone in Washington, William Safire and the neoconservative pundits called for immediate war. The groundwork for Operation Pundit Storm actually began three months earlier, shortly after Hussein threatened to "incinerate half of Israel" with a gas attack should he be attacked first. This alerted the powerfully pro-Israel neoconservatives to the fact that they had an enemy in the Middle East to whom they had been paying insufficient attention. William Safire, much to the amusement of less principled commentators, had been raising hell about Hussein's gassing of the Kurds in 1988 and the United States' generally shameful history with respect to the Kurds' unhappy struggle for autonomy.[*] Safire, with Jim Hoagland, also conducted a lonely campaign during the first two years of the Bush administration to expose Hussein's manipulation of U.S. banking and agricultural credits to feed his military appetite and intimidate his neighbors. Once the threat to Israel was made explicit, however, they were joined in this campaign by A. M. Rosenthal, Mortimer Zuckerman, Charles Krauthammer, and others. The latter holds the honor of first affixing the adjective "truly Hitlerian" to Hussein, almost a week before the invasion.[†]

Once news of the invasion came through, so, too, did the neoconservative calls for Saddam's head. The editors of the *New Republic* recommended an immediate "massive bombing campaign" launched "at the slightest provocation" to destroy Hussein's military machine. "The United States must act," they insisted, "the sooner the better." Krauthammer predicted that if Saddam were not stopped by force, the United States would face "a nightmare not just of indiscriminate aggression, but of indiscriminate aggression with missiles, poison gas, and soon nuclear weapons." He chastised the president for being unwilling to stop this "thug on the loose" because Bush was "not eager to get bogged down in a land war in a God-forsaken patch of desert" and anyway had been "shamelessly propiti-

---

[*]Of all the egregious actions for which Safire has forgiven his friends Richard Nixon and Henry Kissinger during the past two decades, none should have been more difficult than the moral callousness with which they manipulated the doomed rebellion of Iraq's Kurds almost twenty years before George Bush did so. At a May 30, 1972, meeting in Tehran with the Shah of Iran, Nixon and Kissinger agreed to institute a $16 million CIA covert aid program to aid the rebellion in order, in the Shah's words, to "help the Kurds make life difficult for our Iraqi neighbor and enemy." In fact, neither the Shah nor Kissinger, who acceded to the request, had any interest in seeing the Kurds succeed. According to a bipartisan congressional investigation commission, "the President, Dr. Kissinger and the foreign head of state [the Shah] hoped that our clients [the Kurds] would not prevail. They preferred instead that the insurgents simply continue a level of hostilities sufficient to sap the resources of our ally's neighboring country [Iraq]. The policy was not imparted to our clients, who were encouraged to continue fighting." U.S. aid to the Kurdish rebellion was, in Kissinger's words, "merely an instrument to dissuade Iraq from international adventurism." When, in 1975, both the Shah and the CIA cut them off, the rebels were summarily slaughtered. Kissinger's explanation: "Secret Service operations are not missionary work." See Karl E. Meyer, "Kurds Are Not Pawns," *New York Times*, 6 March 1991, p. A17; Christopher Hitchens, "Why We Are Stuck in the Sand," *Harper's*, January 1991, p. 71; and Seymour M. Hersh, *The Price of Power: Kissinger in the Nixon White House* (New York: Summit Books, 1983), p. 542n.
[†]"What makes him truly Hitlerian is his way of dealing with neighboring states." Charles Krauthammer, 27 July 1990.

ating [Hussein] since it helped him win the Iran-Iraq war in 1988." Safire took aim at the president's "past appeasement of Saddam Hussein" as well. He titled his first column "Now or Later?" Fewer than three weeks into the crisis he insisted, "The question is no longer 'Will there be a war' between the world and Iraq but 'What is the best strategy to win the war already begun?'"*

A. M. Rosenthal, positively aflame with war fever, generously granted that "not every Iraqi is an evil dreamer of death," but nevertheless saw U.S. hostages in Iraq—soon to be released unharmed—as "tethered . . . sacrificial goats," at the mercy of "the one, true Muslim conqueror, crying destruction to the Jews, and death to all Arabs who question his vision, course and glory." Like Safire, he insisted that we were already "at war with Iraq." Perhaps the most ambitious of the hawks were Robert Bartley's crew at the *Wall Street Journal*; they recommended that American forces simply "take Baghdad and install a MacArthur regency."

The pro-war punditocracy's first team was rounded out by columnist Ben Wattenberg, Richard Perle, David Gergen, and Mortimer Zuckerman of *US News*; Fred Barnes and Morton Kondracke in the *New Republic* and on *The McLaughlin Group*; the eloquent Johns Hopkins professor Fouad Ajami in both the *New Republic* and *US News*; and James Hoagland in the *Washington Post*.

Two warriors who were a little slow off the mark were Jeane Kirkpatrick and Henry Kissinger. Initially, Kirkpatrick said she saw "no distinctive U.S. interest" in the Gulf, and she cautioned against precipitous action there. Over time, however, she joined Stephen Solarz's pro-war organization and proclaimed in early November that "obviously it is time to begin the defense of Kuwait." Kissinger, as always, proved the most slippery. Three days into the conflict, he predicted that "Iraq [would] have to withdraw" if an "effective" economic blockade were instituted for "several months," recommending that "before we station troops in Saudi Arabia," the United States should "try these other measures." Yet just two weeks later, after what he called Bush's "courageous," "skillful," and "flawless" performance in wholly rejecting his advice, Kissinger reversed himself and became one of the most forceful pro-war pundits in the country. "The United States cannot afford to be diddled," he insisted, "and it simply cannot afford to lose."

---

*William Safire, 7 August 1990, 27 December 1990, and 20 August 1990. The columnist recommended that we "(1) suppress Iraqi air defense; (2) take out war production at the 26 key targets; (3) launch a three-front land-war at the Turkish, Syrian, and Kuwaiti borders, coincident with an internal uprising to establish an independent Kurdistan; and (4) increase the blockade and air attacks to simulate riots and a coup. If we cannot win we should disband our armed forces and rely on Star Wars." William Safire, 22 August 1990.

At times, the punditocracy drumbeat seemed to echo that of the Hearst newspapers' "Remember the Maine" campaign that preceded the Spanish-American War, albeit in far more sophisticated form. Its most potent weapon in this crusade was the same impatience with complexity and nuance that had helped make the growth of the punditocracy's power and influence possible in the first place. Those who questioned the wisdom of threatening war over Kuwait were consistently written off as "pro-isolationism," "pro-appeasement" or, in the case of Patrick Buchanan, pro–anti-Semitism.[*] Those who did so with the added disadvantage of professional expertise were contemptuously branded "Arabists" and "fellow travellers" by *McLaughlin Group* panelist Morton Kondracke.[†]

Guided by the twin influences of these pundits and the president's unilateral measures, the public debate proceeded on an uneven and often uneasy course to war. Bush's own role was paradoxical. On the one hand, by declaring that the invasion "would not stand," deploying two hundred thousand troops in Saudi Arabia, doubling that number four months later, and positioning these forces for an offensive war, Bush restricted the terms of the debate in such a fashion that a decision for peace would have necessitated a humiliating public retreat.[‡] He secured countless votes in Congress and percentage points in approval for the war option in U.S. opinion polls by successfully equating a diplomatically brokered solution with an ignominious defeat for the United States. But however valuable the president's willingness to stretch his constitutional prerogatives may have been, he never proved able to articulate a consistent ratio-

---

[*]Abe Rosenthal's accusation that alleged Jew-hater Patrick Buchanan was guilty of "blood libel" and worse for his contention that those, like Rosenthal, who wanted war were more concerned with Israel than with the United States has already received far more analysis and argument than it deserves—including that provided by the author. Even if Buchanan does have a problem with Jews—a question on which I remain divided—the salient point here is the ugly shadow Rosenthal's hysterical imputations cast over the entire debate. This shadow further constricted discussion and confused the relevant issues at hand. For more discussion, see the author's "Semites and Anti-Semites: The Pat and Abe Show," *The Nation*, 5 November 1991.

[†]This took place on *The McLaughlin Group*, 19 January 1991. It should be noted that in the same discussion, Kondracke praised Martin Indyk as the "smartest person on this." Indyk heads up the Institute for Near East Policy, an outgrowth of the American-Israel Public Affairs Committee (AIPAC). Kondracke did not mention that Indyk's institute sponsored his trip to the Middle East and offered former AIPAC staffer, Seth Carus, to coauthor an article with him in the *New Republic*. The article largely endorsed the agenda of the institute and the AIPAC lobby.

[‡]Despite the approval ratings, Bush did not enjoy a public mandate for a course toward war. A *New York Times*/CBS poll published August 10, 1990, indicated that 68 percent of Americans questioned felt that the United States should not go on the offensive to liberate Kuwait. An August 12 poll found that 40 percent thought that Bush was "too quick to send troops." This figure held a week later. Cited in James Bennet, "How They Missed That Story," *The Washington Monthly*, December 1990, p. 13.

nale as to why this war was necessary. He could not seem to make up his mind about his reasoning and therefore frequently confused people by switching from economic to moral to political rationales from moment to moment. Bush attempted to demonize Hussein as "worse than Hitler," but he sounded small and petty doing so.[*] As Charles Krauthammer complained in late November, "Bush has been so clumsy in advancing his case as to have nearly discredited it." Fortunately for the president, the pundits were more than willing to take over.

Throughout the fall, much of the subsequent public discussion inspired by the president took place on a rhetorical level so silly that many pro-war pundits could not bring themselves to support it. Bush's alleged devotion to the idea of a "new world order" was explicitly disavowed by pro-war pundits from Krauthammer to Kristol to Kissinger. Such talk was directed strictly at what Washington calls "the hustings"—the "flyover" parts of the country that didn't matter—and was taken seriously by almost no one, save perhaps A. M. Rosenthal and the soon-to-pay-for-it Kurds.[†] Going to war "for good against evil," to "combat aggression," or to defend "national sovereignty" also did not enter into the punditocracy's reasoning in any serious fashion.[‡]

A cousin of the "new world order" argument that was taken seriously, however, was the insistence by many liberal pundits that the president was dedicated to the 1940s ideal of entrusting the United Nations to be the primary enforcer of peace in an otherwise anarchic world. This belief was encouraged, no doubt, by the Bush administration's newly minted enthusiasm for the approval of the Security Council for its actions, coupled with its success in convincing thirty-three nations to provide either token fighting forces, materiel, or medical teams to the war effort. These were no small achievements. But when Richard Cohen wrote that "maybe the most important consequence of the Gulf crisis has been the revival of the

---

[*] Sir Michael Howard, considered by many to be the English-speaking world's most distinguished living military historian and a supporter of Bush's war policy nevertheless, called the comparison "demeaning to the president and misleading to the American people." Michael Howard, "The Burdens of Victory," *U.S. News and World Report*, 13 May 1991, p. 48.
[†] At one point during the crisis, Rosenthal published a column entitled "New World Order" that consisted entirely of previously published news reports side-by-side with streams of Rosenthal's ungrammatical consciousness. One such entry read: "Jew kills Arab, Arab kills Jew, big news, Arab kills Arab, who gives a damn? Hypocrisy column? Everybody inured to hypocrisy. Try just clippings, documents." A. M. Rosenthal, 24 October 1990.
[‡] No one in the punditocracy has suggested the United States go to war to end Turkey's military occupation of Cyprus, China's brutal domination of Tibet, or Indonesia's eradication of East Timor. The United States, moreover, is not exactly strategically well-placed among great powers to launch a credible campaign on behalf of wars in defense of another nation's national sovereignty, given recent unilateral U.S. military actions in Libya, Grenada, Nicaragua, and Panama.

United Nations," he demonstrated nothing so much as how easy it had become to snow desperate liberals. It had been a point of pride within the Reagan administration for the entire decade of the 1980s to mock the self-righteous moralizing of that pathetically ineffective debating society on Manhattan's East River.[*] If, after more than a decade of contempt, George Bush had truly gotten religion regarding the United Nations' potential, he could have secured a resolution under article 43 of the body's charter, creating a true U.N. force with a U.N. military staff. Such a path would have helped spread international costs and contributions evenly among the world community and could have saved James Baker the humiliating spectacle of traveling the globe, tin cup in one hand, billy club in the other. But it would also have restricted the president's freedom of action in exactly the fashion envisioned by the U.N. founders. As such, it was never seriously considered.

The "war for oil" argument, although stronger than its new world order counterpart, was never sufficiently powerful to stand on its own. It is hardly prudent to fight a war to ensure one's oil supply, as the Japanese consul general pointed out, when one can simply pay for it. The key weapon in the warriors' political arsenal, therefore, was the fear inspired by the idea of a nuclear-armed Saddam Hussein. William Safire introduced this argument—by coincidence, the only justification for an offensive war, according to a CBS/*New York Times* poll, acceptable to a majority of Americans—just five days into the crisis. Initially, Safire predicted that the Iraqis would have a nuclear bomb ready to deliver to the United States by 1994. ("The first city he will take out is New York.") A few months into the crisis, in the midst of four consecutive columns on the

---

[*]The devotion shown to the United Nations by both the Bush administration and the punditocracy was particularly difficult to square with extremely recent American history. The United States was condemned by the World Court in June 1986 for its "unlawful use of force" in mining Nicaragua's harbors, supporting the contras, and conducting illegal economic warfare there. The United States vetoed the November 1986 Security Council resolution, passed 11 to 1 with 3 abstentions, calling on the United States to observe international law in the case of Nicaragua, and then lost a 94 to 3 vote in the General Assembly calling on it to comply with the World Court's decision. In 1987, during the INF summit, the General Assembly voted 154 to 1 to oppose the buildup of weapons in outer space. It voted 135 to 1 against the development of new weapons of mass destruction. The United States provided the lone dissent in both votes. In the same session, the General Assembly passed a resolution condemning "Terrorism Wherever and by Whomever Committed." The vote was 153 to 2 this time, with Israel and the United States in opposition. The two nations objected because the resolution's text stated that nothing in it "would prejudice the right of peoples, particularly those under colonial or racist regimes, or under foreign occupation or other forms of domination, to struggle for self-determination, freedom and independence, or to seek and receive support for that end." In January 1990, during the first year of the Bush administration, the Security Council voted 13 to 1 (with Britain abstaining) to condemn the sacking by U.S. troops of the residence of the Nicaraguan ambassador in Panama.

subject, the *Times*man moved the deadline up a year, to 1993. Along with his compatriots in the pro-war punditocracy, Safire argued that we were no longer talking simply about oil, peace, order, or democracy: we were "dealing with our own survival."

Unfortunately, neither Safire nor anyone else in the West had any dependable information about the Iraqi nuclear program. The data managed to evade Western experts throughout the war, coming to light only when an Iraqi defector provided blueprints in the aftermath of the war. At the time of the Safire columns, even Colin Powell saw the threat as years away.* Yet, even if Safire's predictions had been based on fact rather than conjecture, his insistence on immediate war begged all kinds of questions about the self-enforcing aspects of nuclear deterrence and the less drastic means at America's disposal for reducing or eliminating Hussein's nuclear threat. In any event, in the course of the war, the United States still failed to eliminate most of Iraq's nuclear infrastructure. Had Hussein really been interested in nuclear blackmail—and his decision to invade Kuwait before his plants achieved operational capability belies this hypothesis—the war would likely have given him his excuse to use it.†

Iraq's invasion of Kuwait did present a complicated problem for the United States. We are dependent on cheap oil from a region that has always been an unfriendly neighborhood, characterized by violent autocracies and unstable political relationships. As Zbigniew Brzezinski noted, "There [was] no easy solution to the crisis." But the Reagan administration and its punditocracy cheerleaders had inoculated the insider dialogue against the idea that there was any problem facing the United States that did not have an easy solution—particularly if the latter included an opportunity to flex American military power. In the case of Iraq's invasion of Kuwait, the punditocracy treated the inherent difficulty of the problem as something that would go away just as soon as the United States proved it meant business.

*　　*　　*

*In December 1990, General Colin Powell said that Iraq was still some distance from joining the ranks of the nuclear powers. A comprehensive survey published in the March 1991 issue of the *Bulletin of Atomic Scientists* also concluded that "Iraq was many years away from developing usable nuclear weapons." Gary Milhollin, head of the Wisconsin Project on Nuclear Arms Control, guessed that "even the earliest estimates are that Iraq probably cannot produce a critical mass of fissionable material in less than four or five years." See Charles William Maynes, "Dateline Washington: A Necessary War?" *Foreign Policy*, spring 1991, and Gary Milhollin, "A Mideast Dilemma: What Is Saddam's Nuclear Timetable?" *Washington Post*, 25 November 1990, Outlook section, p. 5.

†Moreover, the pro-war position implies that an Iraqi invasion of Kuwait was worth a risk of a nuclear attack on the United States, which is a controversial view to say the least.

Throughout the autumn of 1990, the president and the punditocracy worked in tandem to create a heightened sense of crisis regarding the Iraqi occupation of Kuwait and thus an increased sense of inevitability about the war should Hussein refuse to capitulate. Liberals, in particular (along with those pundits unfairly perceived as liberals), were tremendously eager to be seen as supportive of the president during this period. David Broder found it "almost impossible to imagine a more serious, calm, cautious, rational and prudent set of people than those this president has assembled" in his tiny coterie of advisers. Richard Cohen expressed awe over the president's "masterful assembling" of the crisis. Haynes Johnson congratulated Bush for his "skill and sureness of purpose," and Anthony Lewis applauded the president's "wisdom . . . professionalism and care for long-term interests" of the nation. This strategy of rallying 'round the commander in chief backfired, however, when it became clear that Bush had no intention of using his newly discovered mastery, skill, and wisdom, etc., for anything but an offensive war.

As Charlie Peters complained on the *Times* op-ed page, there was nothing inevitable about any of this: "The conditions that created the pressure to go to war were the result of choices made by George Bush." Yet Bush succeeded in constructing his own cage so skillfully that he now seemed to be "its victim rather than its architect." Peters argued bravely and frantically on the morning of January 16, 1991, that the nation did not "have to accept the trap he has created. We can tell him not to go to war." But of course we could not have. Bush may not have had much support for his commitment to war when he first made it.* But once the president committed himself, he committed not just the reputation of one politically savvy individual who happened to occupy the Oval Office at the time; he committed—with the help of the punditocracy—the power and prestige of the United States of America.

Had it been up to George Bush and a healthy proportion of the punditocracy, the decision to go to war would have been left entirely to them. Richard Cheney noted in early December 1990 that, in the opinion of the administration, George Bush had all the authority he needed to go to war, with or without congressional approval. Charles Krauthammer gratefully observed around the same time that Congress had been completely "irrel-

---

*According to an ABC/*Washington Post* poll taken on January 9, 1991, only 39 percent of Americans who were questioned thought that the U.S. should go to war "immediately" after the January 15 U.N. deadline passed. Thirty-five percent thought the crisis could be solved by additional negotiations, and a full 66 percent believed that the United States "should agree to an Arab-Israeli conference if Iraq agreed to withdraw from Kuwait." The poll results were reprinted in the *Congressional Record* of January 12, 1991, as part of a statement by Senator Robert Byrd of West Virginia.

evant" to the decision-making process regarding the war. Fred Barnes argued that "Congress has no business getting involved. They would stew and whine and yap and they couldn't even pass a budget." Morton Kondracke seconded Barnes' analysis, adding "Congress is chicken."

By the time Congress finally did get around to exercising its constitutional prerogative to determine whether to commit the nation to war, it had almost ceased to matter. The punditocracy had succeeded in defining the debate so narrowly and perversely that the antiwar position would be considered the functional equivalent of national humiliation, retreat, denial, and general cowardice in the face of evil.

Twenty-four of the nation's twenty-five largest newspapers endorsed George Bush's strategy to risk war on behalf of Kuwait.* David Broder considered this near unanimity of opinion a mark of maturity, noting approvingly that "almost none" of the president's domestic critics "disputes his decision to intervene. Nor does any Democrat challenge Bush's view that America's vital interests are at stake." Leslie H. Gelb, who inaugurated his foreign affairs column in the *New York Times* at exactly this propitious historical moment, caught the appropriate wave perfectly. As a "liberal," he conceded all the major points of contention to the president. Bush was "right on the fundamental issue. If war is not justifiable here, then where?" The only "realistic alternative" was sanctions. But the advocates of continued sanctions could not "convincingly show that Iraq will crack before the alliance crumbles." Just why Bush was "right" on the fundamental issue, Gelb did not bother to explain. Nor was it necessary for him to demonstrate why it was so important to Iraq to "crack" before the alliance crumbled. Colin Powell reportedly believed that U.S. objectives could be accomplished over time without a war, and Norman Schwartzkopf argued that "if the alternative to dying is sitting out in the sun for another summer, that's not a bad alternative." This view was seconded by the vast majority of living ex–secretaries of defense and ex–chairmen of the joint chiefs of staff. But given the president's rhetorical commitments and the pundits' consistent ideological bombardment, by early January sitting and waiting had become no alternative at all. "Politically," George Bush allegedly explained to his top military officer, "I don't think there is time." Pro-war pundits have a right to a certain pride of accomplishment in the president's statement. When the crisis began, few people save the pundits wanted war. "Politically" the president had had all the time in the world.

---

*The exception was Denver's *Rocky Mountain News*. See Vincent Carroll, "The Scarcity of Anti-War Editorial Voices," *Washington Journalism Review,* January/February 1991, p. 14.

Here was the field on which the congressional debate was finally conducted during the second weekend of 1991. Instead of addressing the difficult considerations about the American national interest the crisis posed, Congress simply asked itself the question Safire had raised more than six months earlier: War "Now or Later?" Senate Armed Services Committee Chairman Sam Nunn had single-handedly slowed the pro-war juggernaut with his late-November committee hearings, but his argument for continued sanctions was not nearly strong enough to stand up to the patriotic crescendo orchestrated by Bush and the pundits. With the honorable exception of Pat Moynihan, most senators were largely mute about just what it was about the tiny, anti-democratic, anti-Semitic, and anti-American kingdom of Kuwait that justified an American-led war on its behalf.* Senator Nunn, the axis around which all Democratic defense debates revolve, disposed of that problem when he explained, "the question is not whether military action is justified. It is." Senate Majority Leader George Mitchell concurred. As he introduced the Democratic position at the beginning of the debate, he reassured the nation that "this is not a debate about whether force should ever be used. No one proposes to rule out the use of force."

David Broder saw fit to laud Congress for dealing with the question of war "in a manner befitting the gravity of the subject" with a debate that "was civil and somber, always serious and often eloquent." Again, this was less a reflection of the subject of Broder's commentary than of the deterioration of his own standards. In fact, no debate worthy of the name even took place. Members read their remarks to largely empty chambers, with little substantive intercourse, exchange of ideas, or engagement of their colleagues' positions. The Republican war supporter, Arlen Specter, complained that "there have not been very many senators on the floor and there has not been the kind of exchange which I think a matter of this gravity deserves." Another senator commented that he did not see "a single senator trying to persuade another senator" during the entire three-day period.†

The body's "debate," moreover, revealed a distinctly Orwellian cast. The war's margin of victory was provided by lawmakers who claimed to prefer continued sanctions. Specter, for instance, said he would have "preferred to give sanctions more time to work and would not have set

---

*As a reward for his courage, Moynihan was greeted immediately after the war with a full-page advertisement in the *New York Times*, paid for by the New York Conservative Party, accusing him of "opposing" the "values of proud Americans" and being a "spokesman for appeasement." 6 March 1991.

†For a useful discussion of the Senate debate, see James Bennet, "The Senate's Lame Doves," *The Washington Monthly*, March 1991.

the January 15 deadline" but voted for war because it offered "a unique opportunity to promote world peace." Republican minority leader Robert Dole insisted that his vote should be considered a vote "to strengthen [the president's] hand for peace, not war but for peace." Frank Murkowski of Alaska argued "that for those who believed in allowing the sanctions to take effect, the only responsible action to take now is to grant the president his request for a realistic threat of force." Senators Bennett Johnston, Albert Gore, and James Jeffords also indicated that they would have preferred continued sanctions but voted for war because the president had already committed the nation so far toward war. Senator John Kerry estimated during the course of the debate that "75 percent or more of those who will vote for the use of force do not want it to be used, and a significant number will vote for it only because they want to prevent the president from being reversed." Kerry may have been right; he may have been exaggerating to strengthen his own argument. But such distinctions were quickly left to the historians once the final vote was tallied up and the bombs began to fall.

CHAPTER TWELVE

Operation Pundit Storm

s the U.S. Air Force lit up the late-night Arabian sky with its eerily beautiful arsenal on the morning of January 17, 1991, George Bush went before the American people to explain why "the world could wait no longer," and the confusion within the American political dialogue achieved a kind of perverse epiphany. False information, incomplete field reports, and raw Pentagon propaganda were transmitted across the American airwaves unfiltered by editors, producers, or any of the traditional gatekeepers of independent journalism. Retired colonels, admirals, and Pentagon consultants paraded through the punditocracy's third ring as the networks' impartial experts and pronounced every aspect of the effort to be an unqualified success—and a morally exemplary one at that. On the op-ed pages and weekend talk shows, the punditocracy discovered in victory not merely the vindication of Bush's war strategy, but a reaffirmation of every dogma its members had ever wanted to believe: America's decline was a myth; military power remained the only important determination of national strength and international influence; and we lived in what would always be, as Ben Wattenberg put it, "the most powerful nation in the world."

The victory in Iraq inspired what seemed to be a metaphysical trend in punditocracy analysis. Even before Hussein's tattered troops made it home from Kuwait, commentary was beginning to exhibit an almost supernatural hue. Fred Barnes called George Bush's performance "flawless, daring, bold, and fantastic," indicative of what he termed to be "the greatest presidential leadership ever." On the same show, Morton Kondracke praised the president's "vision, guts, and grace," naming the U.S. ground war "an act of mercy." Evans and Novak professed to detect a "fearsome, transcendent America emerging from Bush's flawless conquest of Saddam Hussein," coupled with "something . . . intangible and mystical in the new relationship that now appears to bind the president and his country." Pat Buchanan, too, saw George Bush as "the most effective war president of our lifetime"; a man who "doth bestride our narrow world like a colossus." Even allowing for the fully understandable sense of relief inspired by the war's surprising end, one could not help but be amazed, once again, by the precarious intellectual foundation on which America's new political theology was being forged.

Punditocracy discussions of the Gulf War never came to terms with the single most important determinant of their content: the Pentagon censors. Having been shamed and embarrassed by critical reporting of Vietnam, Pentagon public-affairs officers had spent the better part of twenty years thinking up ways to control the flow of news from any prospective battlefield.* After trial runs in Grenada and Panama, they were ready with a smorgasbord of strategies that combined to present an almost perfect version of a Steven Spielberg–like movie called *War in the Gulf*. They were so good at their jobs, in fact, that the media paid their transmission costs.

The Pentagon's information control system had a haphazard quality to it, but this did not adversely affect its effectiveness. Sometimes news

---

*The problem was not, as so many pundits insisted, that the military blamed the media for "losing the war." That opinion may be held by individual officers and servicemen, but, in truth, the war's legacy to the U.S. military is considerably more complex than punditocracy commentary would admit. For instance, the official U.S. Army history concluded that "most of the public affairs problems that confronted the United States in South Vietnam stemmed from the contradictions implicit in Lyndon Johnson's strategy for the war. . . .

"Believing that the press had in most cases supported official policies in earlier American wars, especially in World War II, many members of the military expected similar support in Vietnam. When the contradictions engendered by President Johnson's strategy of limited war led instead to a more critical attitude, the military tended increasingly to blame the press for the credibility problems they experienced, accusing television news in particular of turning the American public against the war. . . .

"It is undeniable, however, that the press reports were still often more accurate than the public statements of the administration in portraying the situation in Vietnam." William M. Hammond, *The United States Army in Vietnam: The Military and the Media* (Washington, D.C.: U.S. Army Center of Military History, 1988), pp. 387–88.

reports were censored.* Sometimes reporters were lied to.† Sometimes they were even arrested.‡ But such extremes were rarely necessary. By creating a pool system whereby a tiny number of favored reporters were allowed to observe and interview pre-selected soldiers in the presence of an all-powerful public-affairs officer, there was little chance that anything terribly unpleasant about the war would turn up in a correspondent's report.** If by some miraculous chance a critical observation did make its way into a pool report, then the officer in charge could send it home via military press headquarters in Dhahran for "security review." There, the military would enjoy yet another opportunity to alter, delay, and otherwise emasculate whatever did not please it. If all that was not enough, the Dhahran office might send it to an air base in Omaha or Nevada for more "review." Given the "degree of surveillance and control the military exercised over the correspondents' reports," *Times* Gulf reporter Malcolm Browne compared his role and that of his colleagues to "the PK," referring to the Propaganda Kompanic, the Nazi propaganda corps, and admitted that for the duration of his experience as a pool reporter, he was little more than an "unpaid employee of the Department of Defense."

Aside from its troubling First Amendment implications, the upshot of this system, from the point of view of public debate, was that the entire game was fixed. Punditocracy discussion of the war was largely a product of tainted information provided by a supremely interested party. The only major outlier in the system of Pentagon information control was Peter Arnett's reports from Iraq. But owing to extensive Iraqi censorship, these

*Malcolm Browne describes an almost comical example of the kind of censorship that was ongoing during the conflict. In a pool report he coauthored, public-affairs officers changed an adjective describing pilots from "giddy" to "proud." The word "fighter-bomber" in the story was also simplified to "fighter," in Browne's estimation so as not to jeopardize funding for the B-2 Stealth bomber by making it seem redundant. After these changes, the story was sent to officials at the Tonopah Test Range in Nevada, where the entire piece was deemed a breach of security. It was cleared twenty-four hours later, however, long since dated and already irrelevant. Malcolm W. Browne, "The Military vs. the Press," *The New York Times Magazine*, 3 March 1991, p. 45.

†When asked about the military's deliberate deception of the media, Pentagon spokesman Pete Williams did not deny the allegation but responded, "We were not trying to deceive the press. We were trying to fool Saddam Hussein." See Jim McNeil, "The Big Ten Gulf Myths," *In These Times*, 3–9 April 1991, p. 12.

‡The *Washington Post* reported on February 11 that *New York Times* correspondent Chris Hedges was detained a day earlier by U.S. military authorities after interviewing shopkeepers in Saudi Arabia. Hedges was held for two hours and then sent back to his hotel without his press credentials.

**The pool from which the pool was chosen was itself pre-selected by the Saudis, who, advised by their Washington public relations staff, frequently denied visas to reporters likely to be too tough on the kingdom.

could hardly be considered much more reliable. Thus, our high-tech weaponry performed flawlessly, because the people paid to requisition it said it did. Loss of Iraqi life on the ground was minuscule for similar reasons. What's more, explained such credible and disinterested television pundits as the recently cashiered Air Force chief of staff and NBC News consultant General Michael Dugan, the United States would never deliberately harm civilians in wartime. The happy circle was completed by civilian analysts such as right-wing Republican congressional aide and former Pentagon employee Anthony Cordesman, who appeared fifty-six times to reassure the skeptics in ABC's viewing audience not to worry, "The Pentagon is giving it to you absolutely straight."[*]

Whatever their individual motivations, were many of these experts giving testimony in a court of law, they would be looking at multiple perjury charges. Even the most celebrated American weapons—particularly the "smart bombs" and Patriot missiles—did not work remotely as advertised.[†] Iraqi battle deaths were enormous, although we will never know just how high.[‡] And a large part of the reason Dugan was available for day work at all was his untimely revelation as chief of staff that in the event of war, the Air Force planned to target such noncombatants as Saddam Hussein's family and mistress. What's more, the massive rout of the Iraqi forces that Americans found so wonderfully surprising may not have been such a shock to those with accurate inside information. Before the war's commencement, the Pentagon leaked vastly inflated estimates of its likely cost, including exaggerated assessments of the number of Iraqi troops dug into Kuwait, the

[*]In most cases, Cordesman was identified not by his employment history, but simply as a professor at Georgetown University, where in fact he is only adjunct. He is quoted in Verne Gay, "Instant Stardom for War Experts," Newsday, 23 January 1991, p. 59.
[†]The Patriot anti-missile system was, in the words of one MIT analyst and former Pentagon adviser, an "almost total failure," causing "greater ground damage" than would have been experienced had the missiles never been fired. According to Professor Theodore A. Postol of MIT, who reviewed technological data provided by the Israeli military, "during the period of Patriot defense there were 15 percent fewer Scud attacks relative to the period when there was no defense, yet the number of apartments reported damaged almost tripled and the number of injuries from attacks increased by almost 50 percent." A second, equally egregious example was the wide reporting of "80%" accuracy of U.S. bombing missions in virtually every news outlet in the early days of the war. In fact, according to a postwar briefing by Air Force General Merrill A. McPeak, of the 88,500 tons of bombs dropped on Iraq and Kuwait, approximately 70 percent missed their targets. See Patrick E. Tyler, "Did Patriot Missiles Work? Not So Well, Scientists Say," New York Times, 17 April 1991, p. 1; William J. Broad, "Critic of Patriot Missile Says It Was 'Almost Total Failure' in War," New York Times, 9 January 1991, p. A8; and Barton Gellman, "US Bombs Missed 70% of Time," The Manchester Guardian Weekly, 24 March 1991, p. 18.
[‡]Even today, no one knows how many Iraqis were killed in the war. Ted Koppel reported on Nightline on January 9, 1992, that despite an official initial estimate by the Pentagon's Defense Intelligence Agency of "approximately 100,000" Iraqi deaths in Kuwait, it is possible that the number may have been as low as ten thousand.

kinds of weapons available to them, and the number of American combat deaths the two together were likely to cause.* The Iraqis' crumbling under the weight of American air power and running for cover during the ground assault were wholly attributed to the brilliance of our strategic doctrine and the awesome powers of America's (Japanese) technology. A better explanation, although one rarely heard at the time, would have been that the Iraqis were never as strong as everyone had been led to believe.

Almost as alarming from the point of view of a sensible, measured debate was the incredible rush to judgment by the pundits, as if the long-term consequences of the conflict could be determined on the morning the fighting began. Within twenty-four hours of the beginning of the initial bombing campaign, the punditocracy concluded that the war had been a brilliant, unmitigated success. Literally hours into the fighting, A. M. Rosenthal started tallying up its political winners and losers. All of the winners, by coincidence, had been on Rosenthal's side of the argument in the first place. George Will, who had opposed the war as ill-considered, was nevertheless swept by away the "technological prowess and moral purpose" of a nation that had become "the symbol of Western political values and of cultural modernity." It was Will's hope that the explosions would provide "the thin edge of a large wedge sufficient to pry parts of Arabia into participation in the modernity" capable of producing such wonders.

Punditocracy commentary throughout the conflict jumped from one false report to another, occasionally pausing long enough to inflate misleading data into a full-fledged doctrine. The wholly misleading progress reports for the Patriot missile kills, for instance, became absolute proof of the efficacy of the Strategic Defense Initiative (SDI)—an argument that would not have made sense even if the Patriots had worked as trumpeted. George Will nevertheless insisted that "there's more to SDI than the Patriot, as you will learn to your pleasure sooner or later." Fred Barnes asserted the same day that the Patriot battles had proved that "we need SDI." "When President Bush goes before Congress for his State of the Union address," added Patrick Buchanan, "he ought to insist on the restoration of full funding for SDI. And entertain no counter-argument. The debate is over." The *Wall Street Journal*'s editors concurred, arguing that

---

*The Pentagon ordered sixteen thousand body bags and told reporters to expect between twenty thousand and thirty thousand casualties. Moreover, it estimated Iraqi strength in Kuwait at 540,000 front-line troops. This turned out to be more than twice the roughly 250,000 ill-equipped, second-rank soldiers who were really there. The vast majority of Hussein's elite Republican Guard remained in Iraq, where they were needed for Kurdish and Shi'ite population control following the war. See "Hunger and the Butcher's Bill," *The Economist*, 8 September 1990, p. 45. Note: Whether these estimates were purposefully inflated is not known at present, but, in any case, intentionality is peripheral to the issue at hand.

"the epic debates over ABM and SDI, after all, were over whether to give American civilians the kind of protection Israeli civilians have just received." Now, even according to the information provided by Israeli military and U.S. defense department officials, the Patriots hit fewer than 20 percent of the incoming Scud missiles launched at the Jewish state. If the United States were to counter a full-fledged nuclear attack equally effectively, Will, Barnes, Buchanan, and the editors of the *Wall Street Journal* would all be incinerated.

Mikhail Gorbachev's desperate attempts, just before the ground war began, to broker a diplomatic solution that achieved virtually all the goals eventually earned by the ground war at immeasurably less cost met a similarly unhappy fate within the punditocracy. Conventional wisdom—with only Anthony Lewis dissenting—assumed that Gorbachev had no real interest in peace, but was only looking to resume his arms pipeline to Hussein while simultaneously spoiling America's triumph and heating up what Charles Krauthammer called "Cold War II" as an added bonus. A dispute arose, however, as to whether Gorbachev had intended to do this all along and had therefore submitted to the entire war effort as a grand set-up, or had merely reverted to Evil Empire form. Evans and Novak straddled their respective horses, detecting a "reversion to old-style diplomacy" and insisting that Gorbachev was "playing a double game all along." A. M. Rosenthal went whole hog with the latter view as well, arguing that Gorbachev was trying to "retain his old pal, Saddam Hussein," because "the Moscow-Baghdad alliance was never dissolved." William Safire did not take a position on the theological dispute, although he did accuse Gorbachev of "perfidy" at a "cost of thousands of American and allied lives." Morton Kondracke, the alleged reporter among the group, went so far as to insist that Gorbachev already was "re-arming Hussein," although of course he neglected to supply any evidence. It was, to say the least, hardly the punditocracy's finest hour.

The U.S.-led ground assault lasted only one hundred hours, but the brevity of the conflict only seemed to intensify the transcendence that the punditocracy's postwar analysis discovered in the victory. We not only "kicked" the Vietnam syndrome, we were the envy of the world. A new era of Pax Americana was in the offing, based on "a single pole of world power" with "the United States at the apex," argued Charles Krauthammer. Pat Buchanan, hardly a stern critic of the excesses of American jingoism, nevertheless recoiled from the "hubris, the sense of omnipotence," he detected in post-Gulf Washington; the "feeling that as Mr. Bush exults in the world today, what we say goes."

Needless to say, this state of affairs owed more to the distortion of fact engendered by the punditocracy's willful self-delusion than to any development that had taken place in the Gulf region. What the punditocracy was trumpeting as a wondrous victory in the Gulf rapidly turned into a quagmire of unending frustration. The war was not without significant accomplishments. The *Economist* numbered these as the need "to stand up to the Iraqi dictator, both to prevent him from extending his tyranny to countries beyond Iraq and Kuwait and to deny him the wealth of oil that would have fueled that extension and to deter other aggressors who might have taken inspiration had they seen him get away with such a rich grab." The magazine's editors had insisted all along that these gains could not have been achieved without war, but that hypothetical statement can never truly be answered. Let us grant it for the sake of argument. A real accounting would weigh these accomplishments against the enormous physical destruction and human dislocation the war produced. But because of the punditocracy's intoxicated embrace of the conflict as the ultimate demonstration of American power and beneficence, such an accounting became impossible.

Had the pundits been willing to examine the results of the war from the perspective of a strict, non-ideological cost-benefit analysis, the claims of any kind of meaningful "victory" would have become less overwhelming with each passing day. True, fewer than three hundred Americans died overall in the war, a much smaller number than anyone publicly anticipated. But one does not judge the wisdom of a given war on the basis of how many casualties each side experienced. Millions died in World War II in a thoroughly worthy military conflict. Conversely, the U.S. Army suffered far fewer battle deaths than its enemy in Vietnam, but it lost the war nevertheless. The proper question regarding battle deaths is not how few died relative to one's enemy, but whether the war turned out to be a strategically prudent and morally sound use of military force.

Take, for instance, the case of oil. Although not the primary justification for the war, the need to assure a secure supply of petroleum nevertheless transformed Kuwait from a nasty little autocracy into a "vital interest" of the United States. Unless we were willing to go to war, the *New Republic* editors argued at the outset of the crisis, a "large scale American military presence in the Persian Gulf" would be necessary "to protect the oil."

In fact, the war significantly decreased the amount of oil available for U.S. import for at least the next five years by destroying or inspiring the destruction of much of Kuwait's production potential and even more of Iraq's. Saudi Arabia and the rest of OPEC moved quickly to take advantage of this state of affairs on March 12, 1991, by announcing that member production would be further curtailed. By the spring of 1991, the price of a barrel of oil reached nearly $21—almost exactly the level Saddam Hussein had been demanding of OPEC just before the invasion. A few months later, the Saudis cut production by another one hundred thousand barrels a day.

The allies did succeed in briefly weakening Saddam Hussein, but they did not by any stretch of the imagination cripple him. CIA Director Robert Gates told a Senate committee in early 1992 that Hussein's military forces remained "a great challenge" to the United States, armed with "a cadre of scientists and engineers . . . able to reconstitute any dormant program rapidly." After the ground war, Hussein retained at least 700 tanks, 1,400 armored personnel carriers, 340 artillery pieces, and 20 divisions, including Republican Guard divisions, who remained wholly untouched by the fighting and who could hardly be said to be at "peace" with the Kurds and Shi'ites. Most of the Iraqi Air Force sat out the war as well. Within a year of the triumph, hawkish columnists James Hoagland, A. M. Rosenthal, and William Safire were calling for yet another war against Hussein, this one to accomplish all the things the last one had failed to do. Hussein would continue to menace the region throughout the decade.

In the region, the war's benefits were no less murky. Turkey, a nation whose strategic importance dwarfs that of Kuwait, panicked under the threat of a massive Kurdish exodus from Iraq—a threat that became even more dangerous when Hussein decided to start arming Turkey's Kurds in revenge. Iran, meanwhile, emerged as the dominant power in the region, as Iraq's role as a buffer against the export of Islamic extremism passed into history. Its revolutionary regime began purchasing massive amounts of discarded Soviet weaponry and pursuing its own nuclear research program after the war. The war also complicated the Middle East peace process, high-profile conferences notwithstanding. Although it did weaken the forces of Arab rejectionism—in part the result of the Palestinians' foolish and self-defeating support for Hussein's murderous invasion—it nevertheless hardened them in Israel. The Shamir government used the war to invite an avowedly racist party into its coalition, to jail a moderate Palestinian philosophy professor for three months without charge, and to break ground on a massive series of new Jewish settlements in the occupied West Bank, confiscating many thousands of acres of Palestinian farmland in the process.

However costly the victory may have been, argued Charles Krauthammer in mid-April, "the primary gains of the war—the liberation of Kuwait and the destruction of Iraq's potential for aggression—remain." But Krauthammer's latter claim is simply untrue. The war did not destroy Hussein's potential for aggression; it merely caused him to confine it, quite briefly, to those unlucky enough to live within his borders.* As for the much-publicized "liberation" of Kuwait, this is a curious choice of words to describe a nation that does not enjoy freedom of speech, freedom of assembly, freedom to vote, or freedom of much of anything else; where outspoken advocates of democracy are shot in the streets; where the penalty for wearing a politically incorrect T-shirt is fifteen years in jail; and where Charles Krauthammer would be denied entry because he is a Jew.

More than half of Kuwait's citizens did not bother to show up for their liberation. By early May, nearly a third of those who had stayed in the country during the occupation also departed, leaving perhaps one hundred thousand to five hundred thousand actual Kuwaiti nationals in their own homeland. To the degree that these few remaining patriots did consider themselves free of their Iraqi oppressors, they were liberated to live under what are perhaps the most oppressive environmental conditions in human history. The war created an ecological catastrophe that poisoned the air, land, and sea of the entire Gulf region and could threaten the health of millions of people. Kuwait may have been freed from Iraqi plundering, but, from a public health standpoint, saving the country all but destroyed it.

To the degree that the remaining Kuwaitis felt any sense of well-being, their good fortune was purchased at an extraordinarily expensive price in innocent human misery. The most immediate victims of Kuwaiti freedom were the tens of thousands of soldiers and civilians who died during the war and its buildup. The number of Iraqi casualties remains murky, but perhaps as many as two thousand Iraqi conscripts, according to Pentagon calculations, were simply buried alive. A second set of victims were those Palestinian, Iraqi, and Jordanian nationals who had the misfortune to find themselves alive and unprotected in liberated Kuwait. According to human rights organizations present at the time, these innocents were the victims of widespread kidnapping, rape, torture, and occasionally murder—treatment that sounds quite similar to the horror stories told by Kuwaitis of the Iraqi occupation. Additional victims would have to include the roughly 18 million Iraqi civilians who saw their country bombed into conditions a U.N. commission termed "near-apocalyptic." To liberate tiny, anti-democratic, anti-Semitic, and anti-American Kuwait, allied bombing turned the city of Baghdad into a hellish cauldron. Sanitation systems failed, infectious disease thrived, food became scarce, and child mortality figures almost tripled. The only crime these children committed, let us recall, was to be born inside a country governed by Saddam Hussein.

*In addition to the unhappy fate that befell the Kurds and the Shi'ites, Hussein also began arming Kurdish fighters on Turkey's Southern border, turning them from a "rag-tag terrorist band," according to one Western diplomat, to a "viable guerrilla army." See Chris Hedges, "Iraqis Are Arming the Rebel Kurds in Turkey's South," *New York Times*, 20 October 1991, p. 1.

Then there were the betrayals. George Bush repeatedly called upon the Iraqi people to "take matters into their own hands" and force Hussein to "step aside." The "Voice of Free Iraq" radio station, broadcasting from Saudi Arabia under what is universally assumed to be CIA sponsorship, encouraged the rebels to form a unified military command and "to swoop in on the regime of the Saddam Hussein gang and destroy it." But when the Shi'ia Moslems of southern Iraq heeded this call, the U.S. Army was ordered to stand by silently just a mile away from the killing grounds as Hussein's murderous minions slaughtered them by the tens of thousands. In the north, the Kurdish rebellion against the man Bush called "worse than Hitler" was met with official U.S. indifference; the president took a fishing vacation simultaneously with one of the worst man-made humanitarian disasters in modern history. Nearly 2 million Kurdish refugees were created almost overnight after the president's decision to allow Hussein's forces to use rotary attack planes in their merciless slaughter of the men, women, and children who had paid heed to Bush's call for an uprising after the president had publicly promised that the choppers would not fly. The predictable result here was yet another massacre, with deaths numbering in the tens of thousands and the heart-wrenching sight of pregnant women, babies, and small children freezing and starving to death in the mountains. The president explained himself by professing an unwillingness to "intervene militarily" in what he called "Iraq's internal affairs." As he uttered these words, the U.S. military occupied between 15 and 20 percent of Iraqi territory. By the time Bush reversed himself and joined Britain and France in helping to construct refugee camps for the wretched survivors, the president succeeded in earning the United States the worst of both possible outcomes: our military stood by in the face of genocide, and it still risked involvement in a long-term, long-distance quagmire. A year after the war ended, more than eight hundred thousand Kurds remained homeless in northern Iraq. Meanwhile, to accomplish what the Kurds had intended to do in the first place with their uprising—the overthrow of Hussein—Bush reverted to crippling economic sanctions, thereby further punishing the innocent victims of Hussein's megalomania. The sanctions, which Bush and the punditocracy had insisted would never dislodge Hussein from Kuwait, were now alleged to be the mechanism through which we would dislodge him from Iraq.

The punditocracy did not spare George Bush any of its capacity for moral outrage over his willingness to sit back and allow the Kurdish massacre to take place. William Safire compared it to the Bay of Pigs. Haynes Johnson chose the Hungarian uprising of 1956. Charles Krauthammer preferred the metaphor of Tiananmen Square. A. M. Rosenthal borrowed the parallel of the Red Army at the Vistula, going so far in another column as to promote the Kurds to the status of honorary Jews. But for all of the anguish voiced by the punditocracy during this period, questioning the wisdom of having started the war that helped set all of these simultaneous catastrophes in motion in the first place remained beyond the parameters of the dialogue. Apart from the extremes of the "Buchanan/McGovern axis" (Pat Buchanan, Anthony Lewis, Tom Wicker, and Mary McGrory), almost no one in the punditocracy asked whether, after all was said and done, the war had been a mistake.*

It was certainly too bad about the Kurds, though. Jim Hoagland complained that the Kurds and Shi'ites had "embarrassed" George Bush and "tarnished the glory of the victory of Operation Desert Storm," with George Bush "accomplishing less than he did in Panama."† Charles Krauthammer admitted only to "enormous disappointment," after "seven months of brilliant, indeed heroic presidential leadership." The punditocracy's argument seemed to rest on a distinction in which Bush had conducted the war beautifully, only to choke somewhere near the finish line. "Brilliant, heroic, flawless, fantastic, daring, bold, masterful" George Bush had launched the war. But the wimp had retaken possession of the president's body before the final mopping up could be completed. The post-Iraq political spectrum lay somewhere between Morton Kondracke, who argued in the *New Republic* that "although the Democrats were wrong to oppose America's war against Saddam Hussein, they have every right to second-guess the administration's handling of the postwar endgame," and Charles Krauthammer, who denied pre-war critics the right to postwar criticism. "Erstwhile antiwar critics" he argued, were "quite prepared to consign Kuwait to the fate they now bemoan in Kurdistan" and would thus do better to hold their tongues.

---

*The punditocracy view of the war throughout the conflict, it is worth noting, was largely at odds with that voiced in the public opinion polls. The majority of the American people were initially opposed to the president's decision to launch the war immediately after the U.N. deadline came up; they supported the organization of a pre-war peace conference to deal explicitly with the Palestinian issue; ten days before the ground war was launched, they expressed themselves against the idea by a nine-to-one margin; and, within a few weeks of the war's end, they had already decided that it could not in good conscience be called a "victory." For the early war and Palestinian peace conference poll figures, see the January 9, 1991, *Washington Post*/ABC poll reprinted in the *Congressional Record* of January 12, 1991, by Senator Robert Byrd of West Virginia. For the poll figure regarding the ground war, see the CBS/*New York Times* poll cited in Charles Krauthammer, 1 March 1991. For the figure on Americans believing the war was not a "victory," see Morton Kondracke, "Gun Shy," *The New Republic*, 20 May 1991, p. 19.
†Jim Hoagland, 22 April 1991. Regarding Bush's magistral accomplishment in Panama, we learn that, according to U.S. and Panamanian police and military officials, "just 16 months after American troops invaded Panama to free it from the domination of cocaine lords, it has again been turned into a narcotics center by Colombian drug cartels and associates of ousted dictator, Manuel Antonio Noriega." Kenneth Freed, "Panama Is Seen As a Hub of Drug Traffic," *Los Angeles Times*, 28 April 1991, p. 1.

None of the war's promoters in the punditocracy appeared willing to recognize that the unhappy fate of the Kurds, the Shi'ites, and even the innocent, tortured nationals of pro-Saddam nations inside Kuwait was visited upon them directly as a result of the American decision to launch a war for Kuwait. The chaos and suffering caused by the war were thus treated in the American political dialogue as if they had come about wholly independently of the war that had sown them.

Even more dangerous than the war itself to long-term American interests, however, may be its political legacy. The war's end saw the pro-war pundits' influence reach its pinnacle inside Washington, just as the assumptions underlying their analyses grew ever more remote from the realities they were alleging to interpret.

Initially, the war seemed to imperil the future of the two-party system. Richard Cohen gloated over the party's "isolationist chickens coming home to roost." David Broder insisted that the war "showed the nation once again that Democrats cannot define the destiny of America." The *Wall Street Journal*'s editors wondered how "so many elected members of a political party could end up on the opposite side from the American people? Especially after so many of them endured a failed tryout of this act with the invasion of Grenada." A. M. Rosenthal's barely coherent fulminations contained this warning: "A party that is not strong enough to fight evil abroad cannot be trusted to fight evil at home." There was simply no way "that Americans would put their affairs into the hands of a candidate who not only opposed military action against Saddam Hussein but is too murky-minded or arrogant to drop the heavy baggage of that mistake and goes staggering on under it, crying, 'What mistake? What baggage?'"

Leaving aside the fact that the more serious consequences of the war were not and could not possibly be apparent just one week after the initial cease-fire had been announced, these analyses were also flatly contradicted by public opinion polls at the time.[*] But because they accurately reflected punditocracy conventional wisdom, the Democrats by and large accepted their punishment quietly and tried to keep their heads down. At the Democratic Leadership Council meeting in early May, the "centrist" delegates dropped plans to make pre-war support for Bush an explicit litmus test for

---

[*]A poll taken by the *Los Angeles Times* at the height of the war euphoria in early March found that only a tiny plurality (19 to 21 percent) of those questioned thought that a vote against war had been an exercise of "good judgment." Asked how the war had affected their impression of the Democrats, 11 percent said they were less favorably inclined toward the Democrats, 3 percent said they were more favorably inclined toward the Democrats, and 85 percent said their view of the Democrats had not changed. E. J. Dionne, "Democrats Remain Split over Policy," *Washington Post*, 17 March 1991, p. A6.

a presidential race but passed a resolution saluting their political adversary for his "well conceived and superbly executed strategy" in the war anyway. As the organization's favorite son, Arkansas Governor Bill Clinton, put the finishing touches on his pro-war presidential candidacy, such previously vocal opponents as Senators John Kerry and Barbara Mikulski offered up mea culpa mass mailings celebrating the war and intimating that they, too, had been on board, sort of, right from the start.

In the longer term, the punditocracy used the war to shape the overall direction of American strategic policy. Enough of doomsayers, conservationists, butter-before-guns types, and liberals who whined about bad schools and unmanageable debts. Everything was just fine. The war had proven us to be, in Ben Wattenberg's words, "the most influential nation in history." In the sands of Kuwait, the punditocracy decided, it had finally found incontrovertible proof that those nagging declinists had everything wrong. Charles Krauthammer argued that the defeat of Iraq demonstrated that the very idea of American decline was "nonsense." He deployed as his sole piece of supporting evidence the relative difficulty the United States had faced defeating North Korea in 1950 in comparison to defeating Iraq forty years later. The war had proven, added Michael Novak, "the end of the decline . . . the decline of the declinists . . . the daughter of disaster for the declinists."

These arguments were so transparently specious that the fact that such respected and influential political intellectuals felt no compunction in offering them is itself evidence of the alarming decline of the standards of Washington debate. As a basis for a sensible, prudent comparison of America's relative power in 1950 and 1990, Krauthammer's analogy is intellectually indefensible.* As for Novak's claim, widely endorsed throughout the punditocracy, it asks much merely to be

---

*The Korean War, he noted, "lasted three years, cost 54,000 American lives and ended in a draw." The Iraqi War lasted six weeks, cost 196 American lives, and ended in a rout." "If the Roman empire had declined at this rate," he quipped, "you'd be reading this column in Latin."

Cute, but for starters, Krauthammer might have acknowledged that the Korean War was fought not only against Koreans but against the massive army of Mao's China as well. Second, he might also have noted that a significant proportion of the fifty-four thousand Americans who died in Korea died not from battle wounds but from sickness and disease— something only Iraqis died from in the Gulf. Third, Krauthammer would have done well to deal with the fact that the United States could not and did not initiate a worldwide embargo against Korea before going to war, thereby depriving its military of key spare parts and maintenance equipment. Fourth, Korea had not just exhausted itself in an endless war against its neighbor, as had Iraq against Iran. Fifth, the North Koreans had the Soviets in their corner, offering a degree of support and materiel that is still unclear, while the Soviets were allied with us against Iraq. Sixth, the United States ended military action in the Gulf after it liberated Kuwait. Had the army stopped after liberating South Korea, the war would have ended within four months. General MacArthur captured Pyongyang, the North Korean capital, on October 19, 1950, a little over three months after U.S. and allied troops initially landed. For something approaching the whole story, see Bruce Cumings, *The Origins of the Korean War,* 2 vols. (Princeton, NJ: Princeton University Press, 1981–91).

taken seriously. None of the supposedly humiliated declinists on whose graves he is so eager to dance remotely implied that as a result of its inability to fashion a decent education system, a healthy economy, or a stable urban society, the United States would be incapable of winning a war against so pathetically mismatched an opponent as Iraq. The argument, rather, insisted that America's obsession with military force at the expense of its economic, social, and environmental health had undermined its productive capabilities and ensured the long-term degradation of its living standards. And that argument stands.

History is replete with examples of empires mounting impressive military campaigns on the cusp of their impending economic collapse. Spain sent a massive army to Germany in 1634 to fight in the Thirty Years War, Paul Kennedy reminds us, but the kingdom was bankrupt within a decade. Britain demonstrated a daunting "force projection" capability when it transported three hundred thousand troops from all over the world into the Transvaal in 1899–1900. Yet it, too, had already begun its decline and started to come apart fourteen years later.

Punditocracy celebrations of the "unity of purpose" Americans allegedly achieved during the Gulf War were similarly woolly-minded. In a *National Review* column ominously titled "Rebirth of a Nation," Reagan/ Bush appointee and newly minted neoconservative pundit William Bennett posited that the war's success would henceforth become "one of the defining events in the American psyche." The foundations for this much-expressed hope were sketchy, but it appeared to rest primarily on the fact that Americans watched greater than usual amounts of television during the war and told pollsters of their near-unanimous approval of Bush's conduct of the conflict. Yet even were this more than wishful thinking on the part of the punditocracy, it is doubtful that it would have any significant implications for addressing the sources of America's predicament. Michael Howard observes that Britain achieved its greatest moment of "national unity" under Winston Churchill in 1944–45, after its victory in World War II, yet this period coincided with Britain's most pronounced national economic decline.

From the standpoint of the problems that truly threaten the nation's future prosperity and security, the Persian Gulf War was little more than a wasteful diversion from the difficult tasks at hand. While the nation remained focused on Scud attacks and Patriot kills, the remaining productive forces within the economy continued on their steadily deteriorating path. According to Commerce Department figures, real gross national product in the United States dropped at an annual rate of 2.1% during the buildup, making for the largest single downturn since the 1981–82 recession. This slide worsened during the months of the war and its aftermath. The number of Americans applying for unemployment insurance also reached an eight-year high. Banks went bust at record post-Depression rates, and business failures jumped more than 20 percent. The big-three auto companies lost a total of $2.4 billion between them in the same quarter that George Bush went to war, and $4.5 billion during the entire crisis. The United States, for the first time in twenty-seven years, dropped out of the world's top five machine tool manufacturers. Overall, roughly 1 million jobs disappeared from the American economy in the six months it took George Bush to amass his fighting force on the Kuwaiti border alone.

Inside our cities, the number of people gunned down during the one hundred hours of Desert Storm equaled our battle casualties in the Persian Gulf. More than one in eight American children were found by one study to be going hungry. The number of families requiring aid for dependent children hit an all-time public record. As the war wound down, the state of Maryland announced that 9,300 women and children would be cut off from receiving free milk, cheese, eggs, juice, and peanut butter each month because of decreased funding in the federal government's nutrition program. Similar cuts had been announced in Virginia a week earlier.

The balance of American foreign policy in the non-Gulf world suffered from malign neglect during this period as well. The punditocracy barely paid attention as the most important political development of the postwar era—the political experiment under way in Mikhail Gorbachev's Soviet Union—became unglued, and the Soviet Union slipped into what appeared to be unending chaos. U.S. public debate treated these dramatic developments almost exclusively in terms of their implications for Bush's Gulf War script. As the fate of perestroika hung in the balance throughout the fall and winter of the war months, and conservative coup-plotters in Moscow gathered strength, attacking Gorbachev and Eduard Shevardnadze for behaving as American handmaidens in the Gulf, the punditocracy could hardly be roused to notice, except for a few ritual denunciations of Gorbachev's peace-making perfidy. As British journalist Martin Walker noted during the height of the ground war, the failure of Gorbachev's reformist agenda was at least in some measure the cost of Washington's "obsession with the essentially regional problem of Saddam Hussein." Had the August coup turned out differently, the reformist impulse in the Soviet Union might have been the final victim of the punditocracy's fatal preoccupation in the Gulf.

In most of these cases, the punditocracy's sins were those of omission rather than commission. Only A. M. Rosenthal went so far as to criticize the few journalists who did continue to discuss America's more serious problems. The unfortunate "sob-sisters of journalism, politics and academia," cried Rosenthal, were still offering "sophomoric lectures" about "how the war would still leave us with all the domestic problems bedeviling the country: drugs, crime, race, AIDS, savings and loan bank failures, homelessness, recession, teen-age pregnancy, graffiti, garbage, loud radios, and paper cracklers at the movies," when they should, like him, have been devoting their columns to dewy-eyed tributes to the manliness and grace of their president.

Perhaps the most dangerous idea to emerge from the detritus of Baghdad's destruction was the notion that the Gulf War provided a worthwhile model for a future international security system. Despite the obvious costs involved, the idea of the United States serving as the gendarme of the Western World, putting our massive military might at the service of Western interests, swelled punditocracy breasts with pride. Anthony Cordesman, who won William Safire's award for the most impressive television pundit of the war, greeted *New York Times* readers on the morning after the cease-fire with a paean to "America's new combat culture," based, at least in Cordesman's hope, on what would be a further redistribution of money and resources to military means. Charles Krauthammer sketched out the contours of this culture's foreign policy in his plea for a new "Pax Americana" based on unilateral U.S. military intervention on a worldwide basis. "Our best hope," argued Krauthammer, "is in American strength and will, unashamedly laying down the rules of world order and being prepared to enforce them," with the ultimate goal being the use of American "dominance to achieve American ends throughout the world." As always, Krauthammer's candor and eloquence were instructive. His use of the word "dominance" does not refer to economic dominance, political dominance, or even the kind of intellectual or cultural dominance to which Americans once aspired. It refers explicitly and exclusively to military power. By the time of the Gulf War, it was military power, and military power alone, in which the United States remained the world's premier nation.

"Every other nation on earth would like to be in our position," insisted Charles Krauthammer, who, in the wake of the war, had come closest to fulfilling Lippmann's mantle as the most influential intellectual voice in elite political culture. "Why not enjoy it?" Both the statement and the question are an invitation to complacency. If we are the envy of the world, then why worry about the quality of our schools, our environment, our underclass? Although the enemy had self-destructed and his stand-in had proven to be a fraud, the system was predicated on eternal enemies, and the system worked. There would be no new thinking in Washington as long as the punditocracy reigned.

CHAPTER THIRTEEN

All Monica, All the Time

*Is it not exceedingly strange that Paula Jones and Monica
Lewinsky are the nails in the shoe of the horse in the skirmish in
the battle in the war for which, wanting them, Western civilization may be, to some degree, lost?*

—Mark Helprin in the *Wall Street Journal*

During the House Judiciary Committee's initial debate
about the wisdom of an impeachment inquiry in October
1998, Representative Robert Wexler, defender of Presi-
dent Clinton, was caught in an argument with Representative Bob Barr, an
almost hysterical proponent of impeachment. Instead of replying to one of
Barr's arguments, however, Wexler instructed his colleagues that he would
be saving his arguments for a really important occasion: that evening's episode of *Crossfire*. "In an effort not to ruin the show tonight, I'm going to
wait to respond to Barr's comments earlier until we get on the show," Wexler said. He was not kidding. A month later, when their dismal showing in
the November elections led the House Republicans to dump their leader,
Newt Gingrich, and elect a new Speaker, that election was also conducted
over the air, in the debating chambers of the punditocracy, rather than in
the congressional caucus rooms. Christopher Cox announced his candidacy for the job on *Larry King Live*. Bob Livingston, the eventual, but brief,

winner (and a participant in a roast of pundit William Safire arranged by pundit Al Hunt) appeared on the Sunday shows to reply. If anyone had any idea that these shows were aimed at nationwide—rather than strictly insider—audiences, they were quickly disabused. So were those naive souls who believed that it was in Congress—rather than among the new, expanded punditocracy—that such debate took place.

In many ways, the late 1980s and early 1990s can be seen as the prelude to the great punditocracy explosion of the Clinton/Lewinsky era. When I first sat down to survey the pundit universe for a 1988 article in *World Policy Journal,* the phenomenon, although significant in influence, was nevertheless tiny when measured in numbers. Located exclusively in the most elite publications and network news programs, virtually the entire punditocracy could be assembled in a White House briefing room for its Friday morning spin-control operations. Today, that meeting would need to be held in RFK stadium. Back in 1988, the group did not even have a name—no one had thought to separate it out from the rest of the pack of allegedly objective journalists. Although each respected punditocracy outlet did make a conscious effort to include a woman or an African American on its panel—occasionally both at once—in most cases, the punditocracy was very much an old, white, and largely conservative boys' club.

The key sparks setting off the explosion were economic, technological, and cultural. In the first realm, communication conglomerates that controlled the world of broadcast and cable television discovered that they could produce pundit programs more cheaply than almost any other kind of television. Virtually all the costs were those initially put into building and production facilities. Once these were amortized across a sea of talking heads, the costs of each show fell to nearly nothing. The hosts commanded serious salaries, true, but, more often than not, the guests appeared for free. NBC News converted this insight into twenty-seven hours of news and punditocracy programming per day across one broadcast and two cable stations by 1996. (CNBC and MSNBC did not exist a decade earlier.) Fox did much the same with its programming when it created Fox News Channel in 1996. CNN, the granddaddy of the fly-by-night pontification program, was, by 1998, broadcasting not only its signature station, but also CNN Headline News, CNN International, CNN fn, CNN/SI, CNN en Español, two radio networks, seven Web sites, CNN Airport Network, the Better Health Network, the College Television Network, and a syndicated news service called CNN Newsource. People were needed to fill up all that airtime with opinions, speculations, accusations, and insinuations, and those people, ipso facto, became pundits. These networks cut into the major networks' audience share and threatened their traditional dominance of the news business. Only 38 percent of those polled in 1998 claimed to watch the national nightly news on one of the three major networks, compared to 60 percent just five years earlier. Despite the relatively tiny audiences the cable news shows commanded in terms of actual viewers, their influence over the rest of the news business was immense. Through a process of electronic cross-fertilization—the networks were closely watched within the punditocracy and by all Washington news operations—the cable news shows transformed the culture of the network news operations and gave a face to their unspoken fear of extinction.

The second great spark to this explosion was the creation of the Internet as a mass phenomenon. A decidedly double-edged sword in terms of the communication of reliable news and informed opinion, the Internet proved a remarkable tool for the democratization of political commentary and gossip. The Internet hit a kind of milestone on September 11, 1998, the day the Starr report was released to the world through the new medium. Everyone with a computer and a modem soon had the information as quickly as Tom Brokaw and Dan Rather did, eliminating the middleman. And so, theoretically, the value of pundits to the outside world was considerably diminished. But the true power of pundits is inside the punditocracy, rather than in the so-called real world. The Internet, by providing a worldwide megaphone for any number of irresponsible voices and assorted crazies, degraded the quality of the conversation without decreasing its power. Together with the increased popularity of right-wing talk-radio shows in the early part of the 1990s, these Internet commentaries combined to coarsen political discourse in America, through both osmosis and invitation: witness the decision of Tim Russert, host of NBC's *Meet the Press*, to invite both Rush Limbaugh and Matt Drudge to the much desired and respected position of commentator on the show's post-interview discussion portion.

The third great transformation occurred in 1994, when former football star O. J. Simpson either did or did not murder his ex-wife Nicole Brown. Before O. J., the only way a cable network like CNN knew to ensure ratings was to cover U.S. involvement in a real war in real time. Operation Desert Storm had caused the network's ratings to skyrocket. The United States did not get into many wars, and so this was not a viable strategy for general use. But with the dramatic footage of the police chasing Simpson's white Bronco up and down the Los Angeles freeways, pundit programming rediscovered its audience. The ensuing trials, both criminal and civil, combined true-life elements of crime, celebrity, sex, race, and suspense. They captivated the nation and created an insatiable demand among viewers for legal commentary and explanation. When they finally ended, the networks, particularly the cable news networks (including CNN, Court TV, CNBC,

MSNBC, and Fox News Channel), embarked on an endless search for other trials to cover that might generate some of the same kind of excitement—and ratings—among viewers. As a result, the prepubescent beauty queen, JonBenet Ramsey, mysteriously murdered in her home in Boulder, Colorado, soon became a household name in the United States. So too did Louise Woodward, the British nanny from hell, who either did or did not accidentally murder the suburban Massachusetts child entrusted to her care. Even the question of whether sportscaster Marv Albert's biting of a prostitute on the back constituted a form of rape was deemed to be of sufficient national import to justify endless hours of pontification by twenty-four-hour talking heads.[*] At the same time, Americans appeared—according to the judgments of the same news executives—to have lost all interest in any event that took place beyond the nation's borders. Foreign news reporting, the typical prestige beat, fell by more than 50 percent after the end of the Cold War. The ensuing headlong descent into tabloid fare had the effect of demoralizing much of the old guard, who thought of themselves as carrying on the traditions of Walters, Cronkite, and Lippmann; it increased the value of those pundits able to combine "news" with qualities previously associated with carnival-barking and professional wrestling. Ted Koppel's pain was Geraldo Rivera's gain.

Consistent with the spirit of the new era, the Lewinsky story broke first not in any traditional media outlet, but in *The Drudge Report*, the Internet's leading cybergossip publication, at 1:11 A.M. on January 18, 1998. But because Matt Drudge had already developed a well-deserved reputation for recklessness—he has admitted to not bothering to check out many of the tips he receives from anonymous sources—it did not have much of an impact until a major news organization was able to verify it. Still at the stage of unverified gossip, voice was first given to the story in a respectable punditocracy outlet when *Weekly Standard* and ABC News panelist William Kristol mentioned it the following Sunday on *This Week*. Kristol was immediately interrupted by former Clinton adviser George Stephanopoulos, who noted that Drudge had long ago discredited himself. (Drudge was, at the time, defending himself against a $30 million lawsuit by White House adviser and former *New Yorker* pundit Sidney Blumenthal, who Drudge had falsely reported to have a history of spousal abuse. Drudge had not bothered to check out the story—even with Blu-

[*]As a paid MSNBC talking head from July 1996 through April 1998, I, too, found myself spouting off on each and every one of these subjects. I cannot say that the quality of my analysis, however superior or inferior to the rest of the available punditocracy fare, made any difference whatever in the world at large.

menthal—before posting it on his Web site.) Noting that *Newsweek* had decided not to run the story over the weekend, Sam Donaldson changed the subject, and the story died—for forty-eight hours.

Finally, the following Tuesday night, ABC News broadcast the outlines of the affair during a 12:45 A.M. radio report, with the *Washington Post* and the *Los Angeles Times* following suit in far more detail the next morning. The same day, *Newsweek*'s editors reconsidered their previous decision to hold off on printing what was by far the most detailed version of the story—one in which Linda Tripp and Lucianne Goldberg had cooperated in planning the taping of Lewinski's phone calls—and instead sent it off into the world via the magazine's Web site on America Online. This last move, which gave more information than all the rest of the news reports combined, would have been impossible for a weekly news magazine just a few years earlier.

That January morning, the news hit the punditocracy like a tidal wave. CNN, MSNBC, and Fox News Channel provided live coverage—with commentary—of White House spokesman Mike McCurry's daily briefing, only to see Sam Donaldson inquire as to whether the president was planning to cooperate with an impeachment inquiry. Drudge kept the rumors flying, and Rush Limbaugh read them aloud to his audience, hot off the computer screen. Most of the network anchors and their star producers had been in Cuba to cover the Pope's dramatic visit there. But at approximately 3:30 P.M., ABC's Peter Jennings broke into the network's daily schedule to broadcast President Clinton's interview with PBS's Jim Lehrer. Two minutes later, NBC's Tom Brokaw did the same. CBS, much to the shame of its executives, waited a full twenty minutes before bringing Dan Rather on the air. Rather later explained in an interview on CNN that he felt he had two choices: he "could get back to Washington and cover this big breaking story, or ask for asylum in Cuba."

Soon, Ms. Lewinsky was everywhere, hugging the president from beneath a blue beret, in what quickly became perhaps the most frequently replayed ten seconds of television footage in the medium's history. *Newsweek*'s Michael Isikoff (author of the article that was briefly delayed before being relayed on the Internet) appeared on *NBC Nightly News, The News with Brian Williams, Today, Imus in the Morning,* and MSNBC's daily broadcast (replayed repeatedly during the day), in the space of just fourteen hours. He also gave regular commentaries on the daily broadcasts on MSNBC. Although only NBC had Isikoff, the story consumed the complete energies of almost every news outlet, pushing not only the Pope's Cuba visit but virtually the entire world off the media agenda. Yassir Arafat was shown looking on, confused and helpless, during a long-scheduled Oval Office meeting, as reporters threw questions at Clinton about his relations with Lewinsky, rather than the Middle East peace process that Arafat had come to discuss. Thousands of reporters, producers, and editors, meanwhile, worked frantically to try to squeeze a droplet of new information out of the story.

This effort took place twenty-four hours a day, seven days a week, with the news-gathering apparatuses of each of the communications conglomerates thrown at the problem of finding something, anything, new to say about the Clinton-Lewinsky affair. With no new news breaks, opinions quickly became news, as pundits found they could get their comments repeated if they predicted the president's imminent demise in a shorter time than their competitors. MSNBC producers scrambled to create a new nightly show, *White House in Crisis*. This was in addition to the two hours of *News Chat* usually devoted to the crisis, the two hours of *Internight* devoted to same, and the entire day's programming and one-hour evening newscast that were soon dominated by the scandal as well. MSNBC's daily broadcast of *Imus in the Morning* was similarly scandal obsessed. CNBC put up programming by the pro-Clinton Geraldo Rivera ("There is, ladies and gentlemen, absolutely no possibility that a so-called semen-stained dress exists") and the anti-Clinton Christopher Matthews. CNN offered up daily updates on the scandal on *Politics Today* with Wolf Blitzer and arguments over it every night on *Crossfire*, along with an all-scandal focus on most of its regular news broadcasts. Fox News Channel and Court TV did much the same with their programming. Every one of these shows was desperately searching for something new—something sensational—to say about the scandal.

The vast majority of these attempts turned out to be futile or worse. The competitive pressures of the new environment, coupled with the tabloid nature of many of the programs in the first place, combined to inspire a number of news organizations to forego traditional journalistic rules and mores and broadcast all manner of salacious hearsay, most of it unconfirmed and much of it untrue.

Among the highlights were these:

- The *Washington Post*, ABC News, and *Time* magazine all reported that Monica Lewinsky had implicated Vernon Jordan in an attempted conspiracy to get her to lie to the Paula Jones grand jury in return for his help in finding a job. No evidence of this charge was ever produced.
- NBC News, Fox News, and the *Washington Times* all reported that the White House, or someone close to the White House, had provided Monica Lewinsky with a set of "talking points" to help her mislead the Paula Jones grand jury. Once again, this charge was later proved false.
- ABC News and NBC News both broke into their daily broadcasts on Super Bowl Sunday with reports that a third party had interrupted Pres-

ident Clinton and Monica Lewinsky in the act. NBC based its report on the ABC report. On the basis of these reports, the same banner headline appeared in the *New York Post* and the *New York Daily News*. It read, "CAUGHT IN THE ACT." The *Post* insisted that "the witnesses [plural] are Secret Service agents." To date, no witness has materialized.

With allegedly objective news reporters throwing away the rulebook for sourcing and verification, it is no wonder that the punditocracy took the new license a step further. Most of the pundits had grown extremely hostile to Bill Clinton during the six years of his presidency. They had been romantically courted during the 1992 election and had fallen deeply in love with the candidate they thought he was: the one who would call in the middle of the night for their advice, who seemed to like staying up all night and shooting the breeze with pundits and journalists; the one who read what they wrote, complemented them on their insight, and picked up some of their favorite themes. This candidate disappeared on election day, however, and was replaced by a man who hated journalists when he bothered to think about them at all. He felt contempt for what he viewed as their inability to grasp the larger public interest in slighting programs such as universal health care and expanded day care, and for their desire to focus on the scandals of which he believed himself to be unfairly accused. A whole host of issues dominated the Clinton presidency that ended in the word *gate*: "Troopergate," "Filegate," "Travelgate," "Vince Fostergate." And this does not even begin to include the scandals that got him into real political trouble: Whitewater, Paula Jones's sexual harassment suit, and the many violations of campaign spending laws that the president and his party may have committed during the 1996 election.

Inspired by personal anger at the president, as well as the thrill of appearing "relevant" again after years being told that politics had lost the imagination of the vast majority of Americans, a kind of unconstrained glee seeped out from beneath the oh-so-serious demeanor of the punditocracy pontificators. Almost from the moment they woke up on Wednesday morning, the pundits took to the airwaves and op-ed pages to demand that President Clinton resign or be impeached. The case of just one program, ABC's *This Week*, is instructive. Panelist George Stephanopoulos was the first person anywhere to raise the possibility of impeachment if the charges of not only sex but also subornation of perjury turned out to be true. (They did not.) The same week, on January 25, Sam Donaldson declared, "I'm amazed at the speed with which this story is going." But four days earlier, at the hysterical January 21 press conference, Donaldson himself had asked Mike McCurry whether the president planned to cooperate with an impeachment inquiry. On January 25,

Donaldson intoned, "If he's not telling the truth, I think his presidency is numbered in days. This isn't going to drag out. We're not going to be here three months from now talking about this."

The days stretched into weeks, which stretched into months, and the pundits, led by Donaldson and his co-panelists, continued to read President Clinton's political obituary as if they had not misjudged the nature of the crisis from the start. William Kristol followed Donaldson's prediction with one of his own: "We are now in the final days. . . . If the President lied to the American people about having a sexual relationship with an intern, and if it's very clear he's lied, I think he's finished." When this did not pan out, Kristol stalled for time. On CNN's *Larry King* a week later, he admitted, "I'm a little surprised. I'm not sure that people have really thought that through. I think it will be different in a month." A month later came this announcement: "The whole dynamic will change once the truth is known." Five months later, when the truth became known and nothing changed, Kristol was forced to admit that someone had made a mistake. Fortunately, it had not been him. "They're wrong," he explained. "The majority of the American people, at this stage, is wrong." Cokie Roberts had greater faith in her fellow citizens. In January, she insisted that she could not "see how the president slices that [the question of his having had sex with Monica Lewinsky] in a way that people are able to accept it." On August 9, she reminded audiences that President Gerald Ford was doomed by his decision to pardon Nixon, predicting that today's voters would not "put something like this behind them." Meanwhile, George Will insisted that Clinton did not deserve to be allowed to resign from office. Only forcibly removing him would suffice.

By creating a political firestorm and then retreating into sullen silence, Clinton was able to demonstrate what a punditocracy spin explosion looked like when the pundits had only themselves to spin. What drove the story until Starr's final report was finally delivered in September was invariably triple hearsay: what leakers say Monica Lewinsky told Linda Tripp about what Clinton or Vernon Jordan said or did to Lewinsky. Starr's office did its share of leaking, most likely in violation of the law. The Clinton forces countered with their leaks, many of which were deliberately misleading. Linda Tripp and Lucianne Goldberg did their spinning as well, all under the protective cover of anonymity. But because the punditocracy made no distinctions between its own responsibilities and those of the permanent Washington establishment—to say nothing of those of the temporary denizens of the White House—its members felt free to answer their own questions without any bothersome reference to evidence or reporting.

As David Broder would later explain to Sally Quinn, "He came in here and he trashed the place, and it's not his place." Other pundits made similar points. "We have our own set of village rules," says David Gergen, editor at large at *US News & World Report*, who worked for both the Reagan and Clinton White House. "Sex did not violate those rules. The deep and searing violation took place when he not only lied to the country, but also co-opted his friends and lied to them. That is one on which people choke." "We all live together, we have a sense of community, there's a small-town quality here. We all understand we do certain things, we make certain compromises. But when you have gone over the line, you won't bring others into it. That is a cardinal rule of the village. You don't foul the nest." "This is a contractual city," added Chris Matthews. "There are no factories here. What we make are deals. It's a city based on bonds made and kept." The president, he went on, "has broken and shattered contracts publicly and shamefully. He violates the trust at the highest level of politics. Clinton lies knowing that you know he's lying. It's brutal and it subjugates the person who's being lied to. I resent deeply being constantly lied to." "This is a community in all kinds of ways," insisted Cokie Roberts, whose husband is a pundit, whose parents both served in Congress, and whose brother is a high-powered lobbyist. "When something happens everybody gathers around. . . . It's a community of good people involved in a worthwhile pursuit. We think being a worthwhile public servant or journalist matters."

Reporting in a situation where everyone knows everyone else in the "community," and all are thinking pretty much the same thoughts, is somewhat beside the point. Thus, Americans were treated to CNN analyst Jeff Greenfield reporting on what White House staffers are "thinking" but not saying. The network's Wolf Blitzer told viewers that "several" of Clinton's "closest friends and advisers" have concluded that "he almost certainly did have a sexual relationship" with Lewinsky "and are talking among themselves about the possibility of a resignation." The *Wall Street Journal*'s Al Hunt explained that he was "convinced that the allegations against [Vernon Jordan] are false," because "Mr. Jordan, a director of Dow Jones, which publishes this newspaper, is a longtime friend." Toe-sucking political consultant Dick Morris intimated to one reporter that none of this would have happened if Hillary weren't a lesbian. ("Of course, none of what I am about to say is a fact.") On CNBC's *Equal Time*, conservative columnist Arianna Huffington spun her theory about the widow of Larry Lawrence, the former ambassador who was exhumed from Arlington National Cemetery for fabricating a military record. "I've come to the conclusion—we're not there yet in terms of proving it—that Sheila Lawrence has had an affair with the president and that her husband was aware of it and used that to pressure the president and get his nomination," she said. (Sheila Lawrence denied any sexual involvement with Clinton, calling the claim in one statement an "outrageous, scurrilous accusation that is completely untrue." She did so on one of Fox News Channel's pundit chat shows.)

The divide between the public and the punditocracy was never more evident than in the Lewinsky saga. Over and over, the pundits explained to their television audiences just what this story was about. "The story," Cokie Roberts explained, was about reinforcing the lesson "that people who act immorally and lie get punished." The story, said Kristol, was one of the President's "defiance," his "contempt," his "refusal to acknowledge some standards of public morality." On *The McLaughlin Group*, the panel spent some time actually discussing whether Bill Clinton was, in fact, Satan. (I am not making this up.) As early as January, McLaughlin prophesied a scenario in which President Gore would appoint Dianne Feinstein vice-president.

During this entire period, vast majorities of the American people consistently told pollsters that they wished to see Ken Starr's office and the entire impeachment apparatus shut down. Although no one condoned what Clinton has done, neither did fair-minded majorities in any reputable poll profess to believe his behavior had come close to justifying his removal from office. More than four hundred American historians and another four hundred legal scholars signed petitions to Congress making the same argument.

For two decades, conservatives crowed about the gulf that separates the values of the "liberal" media elite and the American people. Put aside the fact that many did so for purely tactical and ideological reasons. (As William Kristol has admitted, "The liberal media were never that powerful, and the whole thing was often used as an excuse by conservatives for conservative failures.") The gulf they identified turned out to be quite real. It derived not from abortion, school prayer, or welfare, but from the following proposition: although the punditocracy is certainly no more moral than the rest of the country, they are a great deal more moralistic. Hence, the virtual unanimity within the punditocracy throughout the Lewinsky period that Clinton needed to be removed from office, owing to what Michael Kelly calls his "great and careless cruelty."

Kelly was speaking for an airtight consensus within the world of twenty-four-hour talking heads. After the defection of Garry Wills and Lars-Erik Nelson, Clinton had no significant defenders anywhere in the mainstream media. "There is rage," Charles Krauthammer rightly observed, "across the political class." The demand for Clinton's head on a plate came from five separate camps of would-be executioners. Most enthusiastic was an increasingly influential Catholic mafia, self-identified by one of its members, William Powers of the *National Journal*. This group's moral absolutism, it believes, compels its members to pass out moral judgments the way Michael Corleone issued death sentences. Kelly, the former editor of the *New Republic*, was this mafia's Capo di Tutti Capi, but Chris Matthews and Maureen Dowd, among many others, were also sending horses' heads wrapped in newsprint to the White House every week. Peggy Noonan's were served inside glossy magazines.

Next came the Paleocons and Neocons, now merged, in the oft-expressed outrage of William Kristol, George Will, Charles Krauthammer, Fred Barnes, and the rest of the Rupert Murdoch/*American Spectator*/*Wall Street Journal* clique. These Beltway boys have hated Clinton so long, and so deeply, that his refusal to act sufficiently contrite has driven many of them to the edge of madness. Listen to George Will bemoaning the "deeply depressing and, worse, dangerous fact that seven months of lies from, and on behalf of, the commander in chief have corroded the usefulness of normal political language in the conduct of the country's business." This from the man who spent a decade defending Ronald Reagan, a president whose lies were apparently excusable by the media, owing to the allegedly adorable innocence with which the "Great Communicator" offered them up.

Much of the punditocracy's anger was less religious or political than personal. Many centrist pundits hated Clinton because of the way he toyed with them during the 1992 election, only to morph into a "big creep" afterward. The *New Yorker*'s Joe Klein was the poster boy for the de-(Gennifer) flowered virgins of the press corps, who imagined dining at Camelot only to find, on the first day of work, that they would be confined to tiny White House cubbyholes. ("Vengeance is mine," sayeth Sam and Cokie.)

Resignations were also demanded from a category of pundits who can only be called willfully blind. Their champion, Lars-Erik Nelson, only just figured out that there was something "inappropriate" in the relationship between a president of the United States and the twenty-one-year-old intern whom he happened to call thirty-seven times at home, often after midnight. Every great melodrama needs its Colonel Renault.

Yet another group of pundits felt compelled to argue that Clinton's impeachment was the only sensible way to keep children from taking away the wrong lesson about American politics. "I'd like to be able to tell my children, 'You should tell the truth,'" Stuart Taylor of the *National Journal* said on *Meet the Press*. "I'd like to be able to tell them, 'You should respect the President.' And I'd like to be able to tell them both things at the same time." His colleague on the program, the punditocracy's professional virtuecrat William J. Bennett, spoke of the "moral and intellectual disarmament" that befalls a nation when its president is not "being a decent example" and "teaching kids the difference between right and wrong." "We have a right to say to this president, 'What you have done is an example to our children that's a disgrace,'" he added. This view was seconded by Cokie Roberts, who explained on *This Week* that she "approach[ed] this as a mother." "This ought to be something that outrages us, makes us ashamed of him," Mona Charen complained to Wolf Blitzer on the CNN show, *Late Edition*. "This casts shame on the entire country, because he behaved that way; and all of the nation seems to be complicit now because they aren't rising up in righteous indignation."

In the wake of Clinton's August 17, 1998, testimony, his insufficiently contrite (as deemed by the punditocracy) apology that same night, and the prospect of the nationwide broadcast of that testimony, the punditocracy's demand for his resignation grew into a steady drumbeat. Although it did not explicitly endorse resignation or the president's forced removal from office, the *New York Times* nevertheless did occupy the most interesting—and perhaps most influential—ideological ground in the punditocracy. Under the leadership of Howell Raines, the agenda-setting newspaper reached new heights of rhetorical velocity in seeking to give a name to the moral and political crimes of which it judged President Clinton guilty. "Until it was measured by Kenneth Starr," thundered the voice of the Paper of Record,

> no citizen—indeed, perhaps no member of his own family—could have grasped the completeness of President Clinton's mendacity or the magnitude of his recklessness. Whatever the outcome of the resignation and impeachment debates, the independent counsel report by Mr. Starr is devastating in one respect, and its historic mark will be permanent. A President who had hoped to be remembered for the grandeur of his social legislation will instead be remembered for the tawdriness of his tastes and conduct and for the disrespect with which he treated a dwelling that is a revered symbol of presidential dignity.

Interestingly, while many commentators saw fit to condemn President Clinton's behavior, both with Ms. Lewinsky and before the grand jury, and that of the independent counsel, Raines and the *Times* abjured this bit of obvious political cover. The only problem with Starr's investigation, opined the *Times*, was "legal clumsiness . . . in the main, Mr. Starr did his legal duty . . . whatever Mr. Starr's failings, they will never achieve the grand malignancy of Mr. Clinton's folly and miscalculations."

Like the *Times*, most of the punditocracy was considerably less interested in the problematic questions raised by Ken Starr's investigation than in the sex and lies he purported to investigate. Starr, Sally Quinn noted, "is a Washington insider, too. He has lived and worked here for years. He had a reputation as a fair and honest judge. He has many friends in both parties. Their wives are friendly with one another and their children go to the same schools." He was a great source for journalists and, as a judge, had handed down a decision in a libel case that saved the *Washington Post* many millions of dollars. At the outset of the crisis, *Newsweek* may even have lost the biggest scoop of the decade in a fit of misplaced deference to the sensitivities of the special prosecutor. The decision to hold an explosive but unproved story, particularly for a newsweekly, is a brave one. But *Newsweek* failed to nail down the story in time to go to press with it because the magazine held off on reporting it earlier in the week, when Starr was still planning to sting Vernon Jordan. According to managing editor Ann McDaniel, "The independent counsel's office pleaded with us not to make calls that would interfere with the investigation. In an effort to find out more about the story, we complied."

At the same time that the punditocracy was demonstrating its oneness with Washington's governing establishment, it effected a merger with what used to be called the *gossip industry*. The result was that viewers were treated to seeing Ted Koppel introduce an evening's *Nightline* by wondering whether "oral sex does or does not constitute adultery," for instance. It was only six years earlier that the *Nightline* host was forced to sneak the Gennifer Flowers story onto the program under the guise of a program about whether it was appropriate for news shows like *Nightline* to be doing shows about things like Gennifer Flowers.*

But the downside of the punditocracy-gossip merger was the seal of approval it offered to information that was frequently false, malicious, and proffered by sleazeballs. The "eyewitness" accounts of apparently imaginary Secret Service Peeping Toms become "facts" by virtue of repetition. Tim Russert allowed the generally excellent *Meet the Press* to fall victim to these dangers when he invited Internet gossipmonger Matt Drudge to join an august panel made up of William Safire, Michael Isikoff, and Stuart Taylor. Drudge, a fan of murder fantasist Christopher Ruddy, defends himself from the charge of libeling Sidney Blumenthal by arguing that he has no professional standards whatever. He proudly admits to publishing the purloined work of other journalists who are still in the process of verifying their stories. Respectfully questioned by Rus-

---

*Talk about changing mores. In 1960, Updike's Rabbit, America's ur–dirty old man, was, in his creator's words, "too fastidious to mouth the words" when begging for his first blowjob. And with all the harrumphing about this story pushing the Pope in Cuba off the front page, why didn't any enterprising reporter consider the obvious and combine the two? "Excuse me, Pontiff, both President Clinton and Newt Gingrich have allegedly testified that blowjobs do not constitute adultery in the eyes of the Big Guy. Any inside dope on that one, Your Holiness?"

sert, he used his NBC-supplied microphone to berate *real* reporters for failing to used his own sleazy insinuating tactics. He then offered up even more unverified information about other women who had claimed to have had sex with Clinton and were about to come forward, and he held up a copy of Rupert Murdoch's *New York Post* that claimed "hundreds" of women might eventually be witnesses. Neither Russert, nor Isikoff, nor Safire, nor Taylor saw fit to challenge Drudge. The executives at Rupert Murdoch's Fox News Channel observed this bizarre performance and decided to give Drudge his own weekend show. Stuart Taylor, moreover, was also tainted, although differently from Drudge. During the course of the crisis, he would reveal that he had long considered an offer from Kenneth Starr's office to write the special prosecutor's final report. He did not, however, feel a need to inform his viewers (or readers) of the offer—or his serious consideration of it—while he was still mulling it over.

In the early autumn, just before the midterm elections, Russert treated viewers to an even more bizarre spectacle by inviting anti-Semitic demagogue Louis Farrakhan to comment on the scandal. Farrakhan told Russert on national television that God would soon punish the country with floods, tornadoes, hailstones, "and the soon to come earthquakes that will destroy whole cities in America." This was due to the fact that the United States was "terrorizing the nations of the world with its inordinate power." God was, therefore, "pouring calamity after calamity on this country, and unless the president atones and calls this nation to atone, then America will go the way of ancient Egypt, Sodom and Gomorrah, Babylon, and ancient Rome. America is in deep trouble." "You're going to have to atone for your wickedness and sins and come clean before God," he warned, "or He will wipe this nation from the face of the earth!"

In truth, Farrakhan was only marginally less connected to the reality of the average American citizen than were many of the other people invited by the media to offer their opinions on the scandal. From the moment the scandal began and the punditocracy pooh-bahs began crowing for Clinton's head, the public remained remarkably serene in the face of the mounting hysteria of their televised interlocutors. Beginning in January, polls demonstrated a surprising consistency in the public's insistence on drawing a clear distinction between private and public character, between the personal and the presidential. For example, 80 percent of a national sample reported in February (Harris poll, February 25) that "in judging Clinton, we should focus on how the country is doing and his policies, and not on his private life." Sixty-five percent "summed up the situation" in an NBC/ *Wall Street Journal* poll (March 5) by saying that the "public has become more realistic and accepts that political leaders should be judged on job performance not personal life." Sixty-seven percent told the same pollsters that the president "should be able to withhold certain private matters." And a majority (59 percent; *New York Times*/CBS poll, February 23) found it "understandable [that] he would not tell the truth about his sex life." When asked what should be done if "it turns out that the president obstructed justice," 38 percent reported that he should either resign or be impeached, 34 percent said he should admit it and apologize, and 21 percent said the matter should be dropped (CBS, March 3). In the absence of such a recasting, even if one supposed that Clinton did have an affair, 66 percent believed that it is "his business and has nothing to do with his job" (ABC/*Washington Post*, February 19). Even when pollsters explicitly asked about ethics, the public/private distinction continued to hold. Fifty-nine percent of those questioned said it is "possible for Clinton to be unethical in his personal life while maintaining integrity as president" (*Los Angeles Times*, February 1). Eighty-eight percent reported that "other presidents have had equally bad private lives" (Harris, February 25). Based, in part, on the conclusion that some of the nation's great presidents have led less than exemplary private lives, 84 percent have told surveyors that "someone can be a good president even if you disapprove of his personal life" (CBS/*New York Times*, February 23). When the Starr Report was released, quickly followed by the president's videotaped testimony, the public grew even more adamant in its rejection of the punditocracy's harsh proposals. A CNN/Gallup poll pegged Clinton's approval rating at 62 percent, whereas an ABC News poll put it at 56 percent in the wake of the report's release. Meanwhile, public support for Congress and Republican congressional candidates dipped considerably as the House of Representatives began a formal impeachment investigation of President Clinton, according to a *Washington Post* survey.

After the impeachment vote, surveys found the president to be even more popular than before. In a Post/ABC News poll at this point, two of three Americans—67 percent—told pollsters they approved of the job that Clinton was doing as president, up from 63 percent in a survey conducted by the same organization in the last week of September. Nearly half of those interviewed in the more recent poll—48 percent—said they "strongly" approved of the president's performance, the highest level of strong support for Clinton ever found by a *Washington Post* survey. The president even made modest gains among Republicans: 39 percent approved of the job Clinton is doing as president, up from 32 percent in September.

In light of the consistency of these polls for the entire duration of the crisis, it should have come as no surprise to the punditocracy—and to the Republican Party—that the Democrats were poised to make strong gains in the 1998 midterm elections. But it did. Virtually every pundit prediction on the election was off by at least ten seats, with each pundit predicting a much better showing for the Republicans than the net six-seat loss in the House of Representatives they endured.* "We were all wrong, all the time," George Stephanopoulos, of ABC News, later admitted to a reporter. "It's true and we probably ought to admit it." He said the commentators consistently misread "the public feeling on the entire issue of Monica and impeachment." "We're better at explaining Washington to the country than the country to Washington," added former Gingrich aide and CNN regular Tony Blankley. "We don't have any greater standing than any other reasonably sentient human being on what 270 million people are going to do about something."

When Newt Gingrich attempted to blame the punditocracy's relentless obsession with Monica Lewinsky for his party's dismal showing in the election, many pundits had a good laugh. After all, this was the man who had declared in April that he would "never again, as long as I am Speaker, make a speech without commenting on this topic" of the White House sex scandal. His House Republicans released the president's videotaped testimony and then voted to launch open-ended impeachment hearings. He approved a final-week blitz of scandal advertisements that aired in thirty key districts. (The ads, he insisted "were in a context created in large part by the news media.") But however flawed the messenger, Gingrich had a point. "Look at all the hours that Tim Russert spent on *Meet the Press* this year on that topic versus the number of hours on Social Security. . . . I don't think hour after hour of details about Lewinsky are very newsworthy."

Although Gingrich was interested only in the narrow point of whether the Republican Party was given sufficient media space to get its message across, his argument held across the board. Not only were the Pope's visit to Cuba and Yassir Arafat's visit to the White House submerged by the tsunami of punditocracy argument over Monica Lewinsky's dress and beret, the entire world beyond the Oval Office and Ken Starr's courtroom seemed to disappear as well. The global economic crisis, which engulfed Russia, Malaysia, Indonesia, and perhaps Brazil and Japan, threatening U.S. prosperity as well, received nothing like the attention granted to questions of impeachment. Nothing did. And given the makeup of the brave new world of twenty-four-hour talking heads, such issues are not ever likely to emerge—their complexity might detract from the excitement of a tabloid-driven discourse that responds only to insider arguments and tiny tics in the cable ratings universe.

*For the record: On *The McLaughlin Group,* John McLaughlin said the GOP would gain thirteen House seats; Pat Buchanan, twelve; Michael Barone, eight; former Gingrich spokesman Tony Blankley, seven; and Eleanor Clift, six. On ABC's *This Week,* George Will said six to twenty seats, and Kristol said fifteen. On CNN's *Capital Gang,* Al Hunt and Robert Novak both saw the Republicans picking up five Senate seats.

After the election, one pundit, driven by conscience, left a million-dollar contract with MSNBC because he just could not take it anymore. Keith Olbermann, host of both *White House in Crisis* and *The Big Show,* said he could no longer bear the "strain. . . . There's no way to rationalize this or get around it. The media in its entirety, we amplified this. We served as a megaphone for the whole process." The result was an attitude that " 'We're going to do this story tomorrow: what's the news going to be?' That corrupts or perverts the idea of news." Olbermann returned to sports anchoring, leaving the Lewinsky field open to those with heartier stomachs.

The very same week, *New York* magazine released a poll in which 50 percent of those surveyed said the media's Lewinsky coverage was "somewhat" or "very" irresponsible. Forty-seven percent said that President Clinton's continued popularity reflects the public's "sending a message to the media that they are tired of this story." Forty-eight percent told the pollsters they were not paying attention to the story anymore; 43 percent said they did not want to hear any more; and a mere 7 percent remained enthusiastic about the story.

"People aren't as sophisticated as they think," explained Bill Kristol, when he was still trying to convince his colleagues on *This Week* that the public would join them in condemning Clinton and demanding his removal from office. After the midterm election, however, the same William Kristol, editor and publisher of the *Weekly Standard,* could be found admitting, "I think I'm not as smart as I thought I was, or at least as I pretended to think I was."

Kristol did not, however, give any indication that he planned to rethink his role as an anointed seer in the punditocracy. And why should he? Being correct in one's analysis has never been part of the job description. Neither has sharing the views or values of the vast majority of the American people. Impeachment continued unimpeded. Aided by the punditocracy, the entire political process spun off its democratic moorings, until finally the Republicans could not muster even a majority of the votes in the Senate, much less the two-thirds demanded by the Constitution.

It was business as usual in post-punditocracy America.

Conclusion

C learly, the problems arising from punditocracy's dominance of our national political dialogue were not just a
fleeting phenomenon of the Reagan years. They are
embedded in our political culture and will remain so, absent a concerted
effort to address them. Moreover, these difficulties are likely to be exacer-
bated in the future. These quixotic pursuits will only further divert attention from the urgent tasks of national economic reconstruction and
ecological protection, thereby inspiring more of the same in an apparently
endless vicious cycle. At the end of this road lies an America unable to cope
with the challenges of securing its own prosperity and security in the
twenty-first century, its intellectual leadership remaining mired in what
George Will terms the "tawdry ferocity" of American public discourse.

There is considerable irony in all of this. The American body politic is
sick and getting sicker as our democratic muscles atrophy from disuse.
The very pundits who bemoan the degraded state of American political
debate are themselves in part responsible for its dilapidated condition.
Except in the most extreme cases, it is the punditocracy, not the general
public, to whom our politicians have become answerable.

As we have seen, excluding questions of major wars or minor taxes, the
public has precious little interest or influence in Washington's insider
debate. Impeachment aside, few Americans bother anymore to inform
themselves about political matters, and those who do are generally stymied in trying to make their influence felt. Congress does face the electorate every few years, but incumbent re-elections have become a
foregone conclusion for all but a statistically insignificant minority. In
between these generally bewildering and frequently demeaning contests,
Congress and the president are graded every day not by the public, but by
the punditocracy. For all the attention paid to polling, it is pundits, not
the public, who administer the daily rewards and sanctions of the political
system and who determine the width and breadth of public debate. That
they do so on the basis of values and ambitions that have precious little
relevance either to the country's primary failings or to the expressed

desires of the American people is perhaps the central sclerotic artery in our political and intellectual paralysis.

The problem does not lie with the American people. Clearly, the public demonstrated a more mature attitude to President Clinton's sexual foibles than did the punditocracy. Decades of public-opinion polling suggests a general public that is in profound ways more sophisticated than its ideological interlocutors. The public recognized opportunities to move beyond the strictures of Cold War thinking long before such ideas were taken seriously within the punditocracy. It was also much quicker to recognize the urgency of economic, social, and environmental threats to its well-being.

Given the punditocracy's intellectual shallowness and political precariousness, one is tempted to argue that simply by bypassing the pundit worldview and appealing directly to the American people, a progressive presidential candidate could conceivably transform American politics as thoroughly as Franklin Roosevelt did in the election of 1932. Attacking the power and arrogance of the punditocracy itself could even serve a useful symbolic function in such a campaign, particularly in conjunction with the time-honored tactics of picking on Wall Street fat cats and corrupt Washington influence peddlers.

Such a campaign would undoubtedly increase the meager excitement quotient of our presidential campaigns. It might even win, but the chances of that are slim. They are even worse for the wholesale transformation of the political dialogue necessary to give such a program a chance to work. For the punditocracy is only one aspect—both a symptom and a cause—of a much larger and more daunting problem, a problem that keeps us from even recognizing the extent of our contemporary crisis, much less beginning the national political dialogue necessary to address it.

Although the pundits are perhaps the most important determinants of the size and scope of the American political dialogue, they cannot in good conscience be credited with full responsibility for the decrepit state of our democratic institutions. Were the punditocracy problem to be solved, by, say, a meticulously placed earthquake or a one-way shuttle launch, this would ameliorate but not end the problem of the mutually reinforcing nonsense that rules the American political dialogue. Large corporations would continue to exercise a preponderance of political power by virtue of the system's dependence on their financial largesse. Television production values would retain their dictatorship over the kinds of information Americans receive through the de facto censorship of the nine-second sound bite. Americans would continue to insist on being ceaselessly entertained and comforted by our politicians, rather than instructed or inspired by them. Tax phobias and racial animosities would also stymie sensible discussion.

Alienated, perhaps irretrievably, from the political realm, half the nation's citizenry still might not bother to show up on election day. And by and large, the American political process would continue to operate on the basis of its own bizarre internal logic, rather than any recognizable representations of the reality beyond most of our narrowly conceived day-to-day lives.

The problem, at bottom, is that even if a political candidate seriously wished to address the country's future, he would have difficulty not only being heard, but also in making himself understood. We have lost the language we need to discuss the reconstruction of our political culture.

The young Walter Lippmann grappled with the forerunners of this problem more than seven decades ago and all but threw up his hands in despair. To Lippmann, the "crisis of Western Democracy" was really "a crisis in journalism." The difficulty derived from the imperfections of journalistic communication coupled with the inability of most people to pay sufficient attention to politics. Together, these forces created a false political consciousness that Lippmann termed a "pseudo-environment." In its pre-television, pre-punditocracy incarnation, this pseudo-environment consisted not of imperfect representations of truth but of "reports, rumors and guesses" about it. Thus, the entire reference for political thought and action had become, in Lippmann's view, "what somebody asserts, not what actually is." People under the influence of this pseudo-environment, Lippmann warned, "lost their grip upon the relevant facts of their environment" and thus became the "inevitable victims of agitation and propaganda." Lippmann had no viable solutions for this problem after he gave up his ill-conceived House of Lords idea, and he ended up merely offering up his own analytical abilities as a kind of thrice-weekly defense.

Today, Lippmann's pseudo-environment is further complicated by the onset of what the historian Daniel Boorstin termed "the pseudo-event." The pseudo-event, whose existence Boorstin proclaimed in 1961, represented an entirely new development in the increasing corruption of political culture. A pseudo-event is not spontaneous, he noted,

> but comes about because someone has planned, planted or incited it. . . . It is planted primarily (not always exclusively) for the immediate purpose of being reported or reproduced. . . . Its relation to the underlying reality of the situation is ambiguous. Its interest arises largely from this very ambiguity. Concerning a pseudo-event the question, "What does it mean?" has a new dimension.

Boorstin's dissection of pseudo-event-driven political culture built on Lippmann's already troubling analysis. Not only was the media confusing and distorting the "pictures in our heads," but its spillage was corrupting "the world outside" as well. The media culture had created its own parallel artificial reality alongside that which had previously constituted "the news." This pseudo-reality was far more comforting for its audience and offered a more clearly discernible story line. Because it was thoroughly artificial, it could be scheduled in advance for the convenience of a television audience or a particular politician's personal ambition. That gave pseudo-events a distinct advantage over "real life," which tended to take place beyond the purview of television cameras and often at inopportune viewing times.

As with cheap money in an inflated economy, pseudo-events drove out much of what was once "true life" from our politics. Interviews and ceremonies came to replace—or at the very least determine—the actual issues they were alleged to address. Budget accords, arms control treaties, and trade agreements were negotiated for no other reason but to present the (televised) appearance of politicians doing something. More often than not, the problems that precipitated these events were ignored. It was probably unavoidable, given these developments, that our political language would succumb to a similarly destructive virus. The "pseudo-language" of American politics today is the by-product of the particular pseudo-environment of the Cold War, filtered through pseudo-events manufactured by a nexus of insider politicians, pundits, and news/entertainment producers. It is political doublespeak overlaid with frivolous Hollywood hoopla, as if the fears implied by George Orwell and Aldous Huxley had materialized in tandem. And the manipulation of this false language has become so crucial to the successful exploitation of the American political system that few of us recognize that it has replaced what once was real politics.[*]

Our political pseudo-language represents an unhappy marriage between what Boorstin had considered contradictory phenomena: pseudo-events and propaganda. According to Boorstin, "a pseudo-event is an ambiguous truth" that thrives "on our honest desire to be informed." "Propaganda," however, "is an appealing falsehood" that "feeds on our willingness to be inflamed." Whereas propaganda substitutes opinion for facts, pseudo-events are synthetic facts that move peo-

---

[*]The historian Gordon Wood identifies a moment during the constitutional debates of 1787 in which the Federalist side decided to "appropriate and exploit the language that more rightfully belonged to their opponents" as the "beginning of a hiatus in American politics and ideology and motives that was never again closed." In doing so, Wood argues, the Federalists created a "distinctly American political theory but only at the cost of eventually impoverishing later American political thought." The argument is brilliantly conceived, but the evocation of a lost Eden of honest and appropriate political rhetoric fails to convince. See Gordon S. Wood, *The Creation of the American Republic, 1776–1787* (New York: W. W. Norton, 1969), pp. 562–64.

ple indirectly by providing the "factual" basis on which they are supposed to make up their minds. Propaganda moves them directly by explicitly making judgments for them.

American political pseudo-language accomplishes all of these tasks simultaneously. It substitutes pseudo-event for reality and judgment for fact to a point at which the honest desire of the citizen to become informed is transformed into a process whereby his or her passions are inflamed and reason impaired. The language itself has become so soaked with the assumptions of the American political pseudo-environment that it becomes almost useless for the purpose of addressing contemporary reality.[*] The consequences of this are far more serious than we have so far been able to admit. Instead of furthering political communication, public discussion within the punditocracy and larger political arena actually thwarts it—surrounding our political conversations with a kind of impenetrable pseudo-linguistic force-field. This explains the otherwise bizarre finding by three University of Massachusetts academics who, while polling 250 people selected at random from the Denver phone book during the Gulf War, discovered that the more television news and commentary respondents claimed to have watched about the conflict, the less they were likely to understand about its causes and consequences.

Our political pseudo-language is not only strained and sentimental, it is deceptive and manipulative. The problem is not merely that we destroy villages in order to save them. At least that level of linguistic contortion still retains the capacity to offend. But much of our political terminology has slipped into Orwellian contradiction without causing any commotion at all. Consider the terms *Freedom, Leadership, Democracy, Strength, Credibility, Security.* All can be said to represent fundamental virtues to which Americans profess allegiance and which American politicians promise to uphold. Yet in the context of contemporary American politics, all have become buzzwords for nothing more than the willingness to go to war, to threaten war, and to fund, subsidize, and prepare for war. We defend tyranny in the name of freedom. We behave obsequiously in the name of leadership. We subvert elections in the name of democracy. We allow ourselves to be crudely manipulated in the name of strength. We lie in the name of credibility. And we poison our beautiful country in the name of our national security.

---

[*]"We are in an odd situation," observes William Pfaff. "At one level of intelligence or consciousness, Americans . . . know their political language is false and their ideas are sentimental." But "it is the only language we have—drained of content though it may be." Pfaff, *Barbarian Sentiments,* pp. 10–11.

Political language, Orwell reminds us, has always been the purview of scoundrels.[*] But in the context of the Washington punditocracy, we have a situation akin to a convent run by sex criminals. The same people charged with upholding the value of our political language, of defending its honor and protecting its content, are the ones who manipulate it most shamelessly. In doing so, they have helped to render our language meaningless and our politics hopeless. And because the terms of our national debate are by necessity formulated according to these perverse linguistic standards, and their definitions are in large measure the purview of the punditocracy, our political process has become in many ways immune to the influence of elections or public opinion. The game is already won or lost by the time the punditocracy has named the players and determined the playing field. How could any American presidential candidate ever rise above these linguistic perversions and "talk sense" to the American people when the words needed to express the values to which he or she would appeal imply their antonyms? How could Americans hear him?

The reconstruction of a coherent political language is, therefore, a necessary condition for the revival of a vibrant American political culture. In the absence of either, our political process will continue to be driven by elements that are essentially theatrical. These may consist of foreign wars, or they may consist of proposed education reforms, but the drill will remain essentially unchanged. Politicians and their handlers will go to great expense to stage-manage their presentations of various issues. The pundits, playing a role not dissimilar to that played by a Broadway theater critic, will inform both the players and the audience the next morning whether the performance can be judged a success. By then, whatever it was that seemed so important will be forgotten, and the players will reconstitute themselves to repeat the same exercise on behalf of yet another impending catastrophe. In the meantime, the original problem will fester, the conditions that forced it briefly into the limelight will deteriorate, and the American people will become further convinced that their government has no useful role to play in improving the conditions of their daily lives. On reaching this conclusion they will be congratulated by the punditocracy for their newfound "maturity," and the nation will sink deeper into decline and despair.

I can offer no solution to this complex web of political contradictions, but I do have one modest proposal. The punditocracy may be irredeemable, but it can be made obsolete.

[*]It is, he wrote, "designed to make lies sound truthful and murder respectable, and to give an appearance of solidity to pure wind." See George Orwell, "Politics and the English Language," in *The Orwell Reader* (New York: Harcourt, Brace, Jovanovich, 1956), p. 366.

The punditocracy's power and influence derive primarily from the prestige accorded its members within insider Washington. This prestige originates, as George Will explained to Henry Fairlie more than a decade ago, from the op-ed pages. Because of the riches, fame, and insider indulgence accorded to these pundits, their frequently ignorant opinions have come to exercise far greater authority over Washington's intellectual universe than the knowledge or expertise that, under normal circumstances, would be expected to inform them. To begin to reconstitute a sensible debate about the challenges we face, it is necessary to destroy the prestige of the instant opinion in Washington and to replace it with a renewed respect for legitimate investigation and scholarship. The best way to do this, I think, is to reformulate some of our ideas about contemporary journalism.

The roots of the modern punditocracy, as we have seen, are split between "objective" and "opinion" journalism in the early twentieth century. Objective journalism was Adolph Ochs' answer to the financial opportunities he gleaned in the commercial and demographic explosions of early-twentieth-century New York. The profession of political punditry came about as a means to fill the vacuum left by the demise of opinionated journalism. For Walter Lippmann, it was the only workable solution he could find to the tangled web of illusion generated by the creation of the American political pseudo-environment. Both developments have helped to make American journalism more reliable and professional and have done a great deal to improve the status of journalists. But their relationship to the quality and vitality of American political culture is more ambiguous.

The belief in "objectivity," explains the sociologist Michael Schudson, implies that "a person's statements about the world can be trusted if they are submitted to established rules deemed legitimate by a professional community. Facts here are not aspects of the world, but consensually validated statements about it." But, as Schudson points out, this is an extremely anachronistic notion for a profession that, unlike medicine or law, requires no special training, licensing, esoteric techniques, or language. What is defined as "objective" in journalism is determined in large measure by market forces. It is hardly the same thing as such humanly achievable goals as "fairness" or "balance," but it has come to be interpreted as such. Instead, objective journalism promotes a thoroughly depersonalized version of events based on what Schudson calls "the ideology of the distrust of the self." Because the "self" in this case is the composite of the journalist's experiences, knowledge, prejudices, and understanding of the contextual environment of a given event, it is difficult to argue that by attempting to rid himself of either relevant context or commonsense judgments, a journalist has somehow served the informational interests of his reader. Unconscious biases remain, of course, but they become shrouded in the guise of objectivity and invested with a kind of farcical authority.

Objectivity, moreover, is an ideology that, in its most pristine form, has no clear preference for fact over fiction. It is notoriously easy to manipulate by unscrupulous sources who place a higher value on their own personal advancement than on the value of the public knowledge. Because politicians tend to fall into this category, the rules of journalistic objectivity are regularly drafted into service on behalf of the most shameless kinds of demagoguery, lies, and outright thievery. Against the concerted efforts of a high public official to mislead the public, the rules of objectivity render the journalist virtually helpless. Joe McCarthy understood this better than anyone. As Russell Baker complained in his memoirs,

> Objective journalism forbade a reporter to go beyond what the great man said. No matter how dull, stupid, unfair, vicious, or mendacious they might be, the utterances of the great were reported deadpan, with nary a hint that the speaker might be a bore, a dunce, a brute, or a habitual liar.

The cult of objectivity is therefore something of a hoax. It is an unachievable intellectual state for our subjective species, even when it is not thoroughly compromised by network pressures, advertising revenues, political influence, and individual ambition. Its pretense nevertheless narrows the spectrum of allowable interpretations and restricts the possibilities of thoughtful contextual analyses in journalistic reportage. The net result is the intellectual impoverishment of our political dialogue.

Lippmann's profession, too, has had a devastating impact on the quality of our political debate. Despite his own brilliant example, the job of the prestigious political pundit has developed into the ultimate triumph of power without responsibility, of opinion over knowledge. The artificial journalistic separation between "fact" and "opinion" deprives our public dialogue of even the most rudimentary conclusions of those professional journalists who spend the greatest time and effort seeking to understand the problems, and it simultaneously elevates those who lack even basic competency in the areas they pretend to illuminate. Were this phony split to be undone, journalists would be free explain their stories as they truly see them, providing enough contextual information for their readers to make more sensibly informed choices. The debate would immediately extend itself into previously taboo areas, and the need for wholly uninformed opinion of the kind provided by so many pundits would decline accordingly. Were today's pundits to retain anything remotely analogous to their current privileged position in the public dialogue, they would be forced to do so on the basis of either legitimate journalistic legwork or superior academic scholarship. William Safire and Michael Kinsley would have nothing much to worry about. Most pundits, however, would have to revert to becoming "real" journalists again, forced to test their desk-hardened opinions against a messy reality. Some might even consider returning to the academy for additional study. There, they could write the occasional op-ed between classes and perhaps inspire their colleagues to return to a level of discourse comprehensible to their fellow, reasonably well-educated citizen, thereby improving the quality of the public dialogue from both ends at once.

Why, moreover, should only multimedia conglomerates be invested with the power to determine the content of our public dialogue? Back in the 1920s, Lippmann proposed the creation of a daily paper by labor and "militant liberalism." Conflicting special interests, including those that make up the Democratic and Republican parties, should also be encouraged to participate in this endeavor—not only to inspire increased voter interest, but also to try to recreate some of the lost communal bonds within American life. One can imagine any number of short-sighted objections to this scheme, but there is really no inherent reason that this kind of journalism should be impracticable in the United States. Europe is filled with politically interested newspapers, and many practice a higher-quality journalism than do their objective American counterparts. The conservative *London Economist* observes none of the rules of objective journalism, yet, by providing its readership with a thorough context for its reporting and respecting its readers' intelligence sufficiently to indulge its many biases, it manages to provide the sharpest and most engaging reporting in the English-speaking world.[*] In our own political culture, public television journalist Bill Moyers manages the almost superhuman feat of delving into intricate social and intellectual questions while managing to avoid virtually all of the theatricality and reductiveness that characterizes the rest of television's public discourse. In a small but significant fashion—if only for demonstrative purposes—Moyers' success demonstrates that the medium does have the capacity to stimulate debate without paying heed to the twin shibboleths of objectivity and infotainment.

By destroying the prestige of pure opinion unsupported by factual investigation, a more honest journalism could deal a mighty blow to the power of pseudo-language, pseudo-events, and pseudo-environments in American politics. None of these is completely eradicable. The dilemmas diagnosed by Lippmann predated the birth of the pundit business, and

---

[*]I say this as someone who shares few of the *Economist*'s biases.

they would undoubtedly outlast its demise. The inanity of television culture, as well as the cozy and corrupt political relationships that help sustain the punditocracy, may still thwart the emergence of a more sensible national debate. But once we withdraw the prestige associated with the utterance of wholly ignorant pronouncements in the media, the burden of proof in a political argument would come to rest on a writer's ability to marshall his facts into a coherent context. In such a situation, a writer who wished to use the word "liberation" in reference to modern-day Kuwait would be forced to provide some justification for this claim. The assertion that the United States prevented Saddam Hussein's continued "aggression" would be expected to take account of his treatment of the Kurds. And proclamations of the type that claim the United States to be "the most powerful nation in the world" or "the most influential country in history" or even that "every other nation would like to be in our position" would require support from something other than a pundit's patriotic fervor. While television talk shows may continue to program theatrical shenanigans pretending to be reasoned debate, they would come to be appreciated strictly for their entertainment value, rather than their pretense of intellectual illumination.

A second justification for the elimination of the pretense of objectivity is the currently lamentable state of journalistic prose. This is not a trivial issue. Many of the country's most prestigious newspapers are also its most boring, resembling what A. J. Liebling once called "Adolph Ochs' colorless, odorless, and especially tasteless [New York] *Times.*" Newspapers are losing readers in America in large measure because young people do not recognize their relevance to their lives. This is not only unfortunate for the papers' stockholders, but it has an insidious effect on the quality of our political culture and the nature of the country's "culture of communication."

When Lippmann's *Public Opinion* first appeared in 1922, it became the subject of considerable controversy. The most important response to the book was a lengthy review published by John Dewey in the May 3, 1922, issue of the *New Republic,* later expanded into a series of lectures and finally published as *The Public and Its Problems.* Dewey rejected Lippmann's delineation of the basis of public opinion and the role of journalism in society. As James Carey explained in *Communication as Culture,* Dewey took issue with what he called Lippmann's "spectator theory of knowledge." Dewey insisted that public opinion was formed not from allegedly accurate representations of the environment, but from the discussion that takes place in community life. Dewey saw the role of the press not to be the imperfect representation of reality, but the stimulation of a culture of community conversation. As Carey puts it, "The purpose of news is not to represent and inform but to signal, to tell a story and activate inquiry.

Inquiry, in turn, is not something other than conversation and discussion but a more systematic version of it."

Drawing on Carey's work, Christopher Lasch argued that the cult of "responsible" journalism "professing rigorous standards of objectivity," for which he blamed Lippmann's argument, is in large measure responsible for the decline of public debate in American political culture. If Lippmann's notion of journalism as the scientific demonstration of an objective or "picturable" reality had not triumphed over Dewey's vision of journalism as the cultural agent of community conversation, the United States might still enjoy some of the significant attributes of the vibrant political culture it had in the earlier part of the century. Lasch dated the beginning of the decline of U.S. voter participation, from more than 80 percent in 1900, to the adoption by American journalism of Lippmann's standards of objectivity. Having embraced Lippmann's idea, the press no longer serves to cultivate what Dewey termed "certain vital habits" in the community—habits that are central to the pursuit of real democracy: "the ability to follow an argument, grasp the point of view of another, expand the boundaries of understanding, debate the alternative purposes that might be pursued."

By attempting to produce an almost scientific representation of political behavior, the cult of journalistic objectivity has plundered the guts out of American politics. Stripped of a comprehensible intellectual and emotional context for the news, Americans lose their personal engagement with politics. Requiring some sort of connection to a larger community, they grasp instead for the vicarious emotional fulfillment of the worship of celebrity. The resulting abdication from politics, coupled with an increasing identification with the culture of celebrity, represents, as much as any single development, the foundation of the punditocracy's opportunity to hijack our national political dialogue and direct it toward goals and ambitions that have precious little relevance to most Americans' lives. Were contemporary journalists able once again to recapture the hearts and minds of their readership, the reconstruction of our community conversation might follow.

It is possible to imagine, in such a scenario, the rejuvenation of the American political process as national issues once again re-enter the emotional and intellectual psyches of ordinary Americans. The return of a journalism of engagement would not by itself cure American politics of its many ailments. But by undermining the prestige of ignorant opinion, by reducing the element of pure theatrics from our politics, and by expanding the parameters of permissible political thought, a new American journalism could help to break down the barriers that currently frustrate our ability to address the tasks that lie before us. We cannot begin to solve our problems until we first learn how to talk about them.

Notes

Introduction

8 the public's views: For a useful discussion of the influence of newspaper editorials on the political views of average citizens, see Robert M. Entman, *Democracy without Citizens: Media and the Decay of American Politics* (New York: Oxford University Press, 1989), pp. 151–53.

8 "No other American": The quote appears in a December 9, 1991, fundraising appeal that Buchanan sent to the author.

9 When Dan Quayle launched: These events are detailed in Bob Woodward and David S. Broder, "The Man Who Could Be President," *Washington Post*, 13–19 January 1992, national weekly edition, p. 8.

9 "Auschwitz in the Sand": William Safire, 16 January 1989.

9 "worth two divisions": Johnson is quoted in David Halberstam, *The Powers That Be* (New York: Alfred A. Knopf, 1980), p. 529; the *Jerusalem Post* is cited in Robert I. Friedman, "Selling Israel to America," *Mother Jones*, February/March 1987, p. 25.

10 these same columnists: See, for instance, Charles Krauthammer, 5 April 1991.

10 planting articles: Buchanan explained this technique to Fred Barnes. Author's interview with Fred Barnes.

10 "he who captures": Walter Lippmann, *Public Opinion* (New York: Free Press, 1922/1965), p. 151.

10 "If politicians": Randall Rothenberg, "The Battle of the Columnists: Telling Leaders How to Think," *The New York Times Week in Review*, 23 September 1990, p. 4.

10 James Fallows . . . recalls: Author's interview with James Fallows.

11 As "freedom fighters": See Charles Krauthammer, "The Reagan Doctrine," *Time*, 1 April 1985, reprinted in Charles Krauthammer, *Cutting Edges: Making Sense of the Eighties* (New York: Random House, 1985), p. 185.

11 "a mass conversion": See George Ball, "The War for Star Wars," *The New York Review of Books*, 11 April 1985, pp. 39–40. Garry Wills argues persuasively that

Reagan's idea for SDI derives from his role in the 1940 Brass Bancroft movie *Murder in the Air*, in which the fearless secret agent played by Reagan protects America's wonder weapon, an "inertia projector" that would render enemy airplanes impotent and obsolete by destroying their electrical systems (*Reagan's America: Innocents at Home* [New York: Doubleday, 1987], p. 361).

11 The fact that 98 percent: See "The Strategic Defense Initiative: An Opinion Survey of Scientists," Cornell Institute for Social and Economic Research, 30 October 1986. The most telling support for SDI came from far-Right pundit Jeffrey Hart, who noted in the *National Review*, "I support SDI even if it doesn't work—at least it would keep money out of the hands of the poor." Quoted in Bob Mack, "The Boys Who Would Be Buckley," *Spy*, June 1989, p. 28.

14 Independent intellectuals: See Russell Jacoby, *The Last Intellectuals: American Culture in the Age of Academe* (New York: Basic Books, 1987).

15 "When I understood": Author's interview with David Halberstam.

16 "Ignorance is correctable": Neil Postman, *Amusing Ourselves to Death: Public Discourse in the Age of Show Business* (New York: Penguin Books, 1985), p. 108.

Chapter One. The Road to Lippmanndom

21 Its metamorphosis: See William Carey Morey, "Reminiscences of 'The Pundit Club,'" The Rochester Historical Society, Publication Fund Series, vol. 2, ed. Edward R. Foreman (Rochester, NY: Rochester Historical Society, 1923), pp. 107–11.

21 Henry Luce, who founded: See William Safire, "Pundit Bashing," *The New York Times Magazine*, 27 May 1990, p. 10. Luce also used it for Thorton Wilder.

22 an irreconcilable conflict: The essential text on this question remains Bernard Baylin, *The Ideological Origins of the American Revolution* (Cambridge, MA: Harvard University Press, 1967). For corroborative and competing interpretations, see also chapter 1 of Gordon S. Wood, *The Creation of the American Republic, 1776–1787* (New York: W. W. Norton, 1969); Pauline Maier, *From Resistance to Revolution* (New York: Vintage, 1972); Jack N. Rakove, *The Beginnings of National Politics* (Baltimore: Johns Hopkins University Press, 1979); Eric Foner, *Tom Paine and Revolutionary America* (New York: Oxford University Press, 1976); and Alfred F. Young, ed., *The American Revolution: Explorations in the History of American Radicalism* (DeKalb, IL: Northern Illinois University Press, 1976).

23 Building on the success: See Claude G. Bowers, *Jefferson and Hamilton* (Boston: Houghton Mifflin, 1925), p. 31; and Mitchell Stephens, *A History of News* (New York: Penguin Books, 1988), p. 260.

23 Philip Freneau: Henry Adams described Freneau as "sharing some of the delicacy if not the grandeur of genius" (*History of the United States, During the Administrations of Thomas Jefferson* [New York: Library of America, 1986], p. 87). For Jefferson's recruitment tactics, see Thomas Jefferson, *Writings* (New York: Library of America, 1984), pp. 997–1000.

25 "a page treating": See Nevins, *American Political Opinions*, p. 112.

26 "We do not mean": Quoted in Willard G. Bleyer, *Main Currents in American Journalism* (Boston: Houghton Mifflin, 1927), p. 240.

26 "to give the news": The *New-York Times*, 12 August 1896.

27 "the fullness": Quoted in Nevins, *American Political Opinions*, p. 452.

27 the paper that had been losing: See Meyer Berger, *The Story of the New York Times, 1851–1951* (New York: Simon and Schuster, 1952; reprint, New York: Arno Press, 1970), p. 109. See also Elmer Davis, *History of the New York Times* (New York: The

New York Times, 1921), and Gay Talese, *The Kingdom and the Power* (New York: Bantam, 1966).

27 Circulation skyrocketed: The *New York Times*, 18 September 1911, and 18 September 1926, cited in Michael Schudson, *Discovering the News: A Social History of American Newspapers* (New York: Basic Books, 1978), p. 114.

27 "well-heeled readers": See Christopher Lasch, "Journalism, Publicity and the Lost Art of Argument," *The Gannett Center Journal* (spring 1990): p. 9.

28 As Godkin's successor: See Oswald Garrison Villard, *Some Newspapers and Newspaper-Men* (New York: Alfred A. Knopf, 1933), p. 8, and Walter Lippmann and Charles Merz, "A Test of the News," *The New Republic*, 4 August 1920.

29 "News comes": Walter Lippmann, *Liberty and the News* (New York: Harcourt, Brace and Howe, 1920), pp. 38–41.

29 "The mass of": Walter Lippmann, *Public Opinion* (New York: Macmillan Paperbacks, 1922), p. 75.

30 "He does not know": Walter Lippmann, *The Phantom Public* (New York: Macmillan, 1924), pp. 13–14.

30 "We must assume": Walter Lippmann, "From *The Phantom Public*, 1925," *The Essential Lippmann*, ed. Clinton Rossiter and James Lare (Cambridge, MA: Harvard University Press, 1982), p. 114.

30 "inevitable victims": Lippmann, *Liberty and the News*, p. 54.

30 At first, in the 1919: Lippmann, *Liberty and the News*, pp. 79, 101.

30 Even if undertaken: Lippmann, *Public Opinion*, p. 362.

30 In Lippmann's plan: See particularly chapters 25 and 26 (pp. 369–97) of Lippmann, *Public Opinion*.

31 "In this": Walter Lippmann, "The Job of of the Washington Correspondent," address to the National Press Club, 23 September 1959, reprinted in *The Atlantic Monthly*, January 1960. The "manufacture of consent" phrase appears in Lippmann's *Liberty and the News*, p. 4.

31 one of the richest: See Ronald Steel, *Walter Lippmann and the American Century* (Boston: Atlantic, Little, Brown, 1979).

32 "a small group . . . identifiable": Quoted in Talese, *Kingdom and the Power*, pp. 229–30.

32 the *New Republic*'s editors: For the story of the founding of the *New Republic*, see David Seidman's *The New Republic: A Voice of Modern Liberalism* (New York: Praeger, 1985); David W. Levy, *Herbert Croly of* The New Republic (Princeton, NJ: Princeton University Press, 1985); John Patrick Diggins, "*The New Republic* and Its Times," *The New Republic* 191, no. 24 (10 December 1984); and Steel, *Lippmann and the American Century*, p. 76.

33 the journalist George Polk: See Edmund Keeley, *The Salonika Bay Murder* (Princeton, NJ: Princeton University Press, 1989). See also Kati Marton's *The Polk Conspiracy* (New York: Farrar, Straus, Giroux, 1990), and Ronald Steel, "A Polk Conspiracy?" *The New York Review of Books*, 26 September 1991, for a lively discussion of Lippmann's role in the affair.

33 a 1933 speech: The Hitler assertion is quoted by George F. Will in *Newsweek*, 11 September 1989, p. 68. The second appears in the CBS transcripts of his interviews, published as *Conversations with Walter Lippmann* (Boston: Little, Brown, 1965), p. 202.

33 As his friend James Reston: Author's interview with James Reston.

34 Henry Luce's prospectus: Quoted in Halberstam, *Powers That Be*, p. 49.

34 not until the 1930s: See John Kobler, *Luce: His Time, Life, and Fortune* (New York: Doubleday and Co., 1968), and W. A. Swanberg, *Luce and His Empire* (New York: Charles Scribner's Sons, 1972).

35 Who can believe: See Steel, *Lippmann and the American Century* (Boston: Atlantic, Little, Brown, 1979), pp. 276–77.
35 "bleeding for the poor": Author's interview.
36 "if we see": Quoted in Walter LaFeber, *The American Age* (New York: W. W. Norton, 1989), p. 378.
36 "The American people": Quoted in Richard J. Barnet, *The Rocket's Red Glare* (New York: Simon and Schuster, 1990), p. 237.

Chapter Two. Lippmanndom

38 But Lippmann submitted: See *Life*, 17 November 1947, and 29 March 1943, quoted in Steel, *Lippmann and the American Century*, pp. 410, 447.
38 "afraid of Russia." "They've": Quoted in Richard J. Barnet, "Clearer Than Truth," unpublished manuscript, 1989.
39 "considerable political advantage": Quoted in Walter LaFeber, *The American Age* (New York: W. W. Norton, 1989), p. 461.
39 "The atmosphere in": Quoted in Walter Isaacson and Evan Thomas, *The Wise Men* (New York: Simon and Schuster, 1986), p. 440.
41 Lippmann's protégé: See Isaacson and Thomas, *Wise Men*, p. 409.
42 Together they wrote: See Steel, *Lippmann and the American Century*, pp. 418–19.
42 "What changed his mind": Author's interview.
44 Pegler's ironically titled: See Charles Fisher, *The Columnists* (New York: Howell and Soskin, 1944), p. 166.
44 "the Washington which": Stewart Alsop, *The Center* (New York: Harper and Row, 1968), p. ix.
44 In July 1947: See X [George Kennan], "The Sources of Soviet Conduct," in *The Foreign Affairs Reader*, ed. Hamilton Fish Armstrong (New York: Harper and Brothers, 1947), and Walter Lippmann, *The Cold War* (New York: Harper and Row, 1947; reprinted, 1972). Lippmann did not, as is commonly believed, coin the term *Cold War*. His editor at the *World*, Herbert Bayard Swope, used it first, in a speech he drafted for Bernard Baruch in 1946. Baruch thought it too strong and did not utter the phrase for another year, by which time Lippmann had begun publicizing it. In a letter to Lippmann, Swope said he first came up with the phrase in late 1939 or early 1940 to refer to "the opposite of a so-called hot war." See William Safire, *Safire's Political Dictionary* (New York: Ballantine Books, 1978), pp. 127–29.
44 "policy of firm containment": X, "Sources of Soviet Conduct," p. 482.
45 "to the status of": George Kennan, *Memoirs, 1925–1950* (Boston: Atlantic Monthly Press, 1967), p. 356.
45 "My strongest impression": See Walter Lippmann, 4 November 1947, reprinted in Lippmann, *Cold War*.
46 Lippmann insisted that: See Steel, *Lippmann and the American Century*, p. 487.
46 "the most powerful voice": Quoted in Merle Miller, "Washington, the World and Joe Alsop," *Harper's*, June 1968, p. 49.
47 "a clerk": Quoted in Miller, "Washington, the World and Joe Alsop," p. 49.
47 "whenever I go": Quoted in the *New York Times*, 29 August 1989, p. B6.
48 "was tactless enough": Alsop, *Center*, p. 7. Alsop added the intriguing detail that "Kennan was seen dancing at a party a few days later over the U.S. decision to commit troops there."
48 "While we sleep": Quoted in Miller, "Washington, the World and Joe Alsop," p. 50.
48 "There is a difference": Quoted in Miller, "Washington, the World and Joe Alsop," p. 50.
48 "Joe was the kind": Author's interview with Tom Braden.

49   "There, that should": Quoted in Meyer, *Pundits, Poets and Wits*, p. xiii.

49   "had gone collectively": Joseph Alsop, 16 March 1968.

49   "you'll be like": Halberstam, *Powers That Be*, p. 449.

50   "He would stalk": Quoted in Tom Wicker's foreword to Arthur Krock's *In the Nation: 1932–1966* (New York: McGraw-Hill, 1966), p. xiv.

50   "There was an old-fashioned": Russell Baker, *The Good Times* (New York: William Morrow, 1989), p. 258.

52   "This is a country": Quoted in Barney Collier, *Hope and Fear in Washington: The Early Seventies* (New York: The Dial Press, 1975), pp. 124–25.

52   "We cannot win": Reston and reviewer Clifton Fadiman are quoted in Talese, *Kingdom and the Power*, pp. 11–12. Reston thinks this is fair (James Reston, interview by author).

52   "He used my legs": Author's interview.

52   "wonderful quick": Author's interview with David Halberstam.

53   "There is one": Author's interview with Tom Braden.

53   "There has not been": Alexander Cockburn, "Pundit to Pasture: James Reston," *The Nation*, 245 (15 August 1987): p. 114.

53   Yes, "Life, tyranny . . .": See James Reston, 20 June 1960. For "sorcery and subversion," see James Reston, 1 November 1961. For "more faith in ourselves," see James Reston, 24 December 1961. For "patient, well-informed people," see James Reston's Gideon D. Seymour Memorial Lecture, University of Minnesota, Minneapolis, 22 February 1955.

53   His first move: See Joseph Kraft, *Profiles in Power* (New York: New American Library, 1966), p. 81.

54   "If you spend": Quoted in Stephen Chapman, "Reston on His Laurels," *The New Republic*, 19 April 1980, p. 24.

54   "compulsory plagiarism": Reston, *Deadline*, p. 378.

Chapter Three. Post-Lippmanndom: The Rest and the Rightest

57   "Could you tell": Walter Lippmann, *Conversations with Walter Lippmann* (Boston: Little, Brown, 1965), p. 3.

57   "Television . . . prostitute of": Walter Lippmann, 27 September 1959, reprinted in *The Essential Lippmann*, ed. Clinton Rossiter and James Lare (Cambridge, MA: Harvard University Press, 1982), p. 412.

58   "They're political bombings": *Conversations with Lippmann*, p. 203.

58   "He must be able": *Conversations with Lippmann*, pp. 15–17.

59   "A program in which": Quoted in Godfrey Hodgson, *America in Our Times* (New York: Random House, 1976), p. 138.

60   Within four years: Quoted in Halberstam, *Powers That Be* (New York: Alfred A. Knopf, 1980), p. 143.

61   "there is one thing": Irving Kristol, "Civil Liberties, 1952—A Study in Confusion," *Commentary* 13, no. 3 (March 1953): p. 229. Shirer's version of his dismissal can be found in William L. Shirer, *Twentieth Century Journey: A Native's Return 1945–1988* (Boston: Little, Brown, 1990).

62   Howard K. Smith, the conservative: The details of these historic events can be found in Barbara Matusow, *The Evening Stars* (New York: Ballantine Books, 1983), pp. 179–83.

62   "access to information" and "the main business": These thoughts are expressed by ABC News executive Av Westin in *Newswatch* (New York: Simon and Schuster, 1983), pp. 156–57.

63 "sticking little needles": Author's interview with Jack Germond.

64 television humming: The figure can be found in Richard Schickel, *Intimate Strangers: The Culture of Celebrity* (Garden City, NJ: Doubleday, 1985), p. 287.

64 a more than two-to-one: Quoted in Joshua Meyrowitz, *No Sense of Place: The Impact of Electronic Media on Social Behavior* (New York: Oxford University Press, 1985), p. 106.

64 "Television has come": See Schickel, *Intimate Strangers*, p. 263.

65 There were ten thousand: The figures are given in Phillip Knightly, *The First Casualty* (New York: Harcourt, Brace, Jovanovich, 1975), p. 412.

65 "necessary illusion": See Reinhold Niebuhr, *Man and Immoral Society* (New York: Scribners, 1952), pp. 221–23.

67 "was based on": See Meyer, *Pundits, Poets and Wits*, p. xii.

67 "was no longer": Walter Lippmann, *Newsweek*, 9 October 1967.

68 "The country has": James Reston, 6 January 1968.

68 "The nation is": James Reston, 6 April 1968.

69 "most of us": Quoted in Godfrey Hodgson, *America in Our Time: From World War II to Nixon* (Garden City, NJ: Doubleday, 1976), p. 375.

69 "the most terrible": Author's interview with Anthony Lewis. Earlier quote is from Anthony Lewis, 28 December 1972.

69 "I realized": Author's interview.

69 "infectious choler": See Mary McGrory, 3 March 1968, and 9 November 1969.

70 "Senators used to tell": Author's interview with Mary McGrory.

70 "And the tragedy": James Reston, 24 May 1973.

70 "If you consider": Quoted in William Safire, *Before the Fall: An Inside View of the Pre-Watergate White House* (Garden City, NJ: Doubleday, 1975), p. 360. The entire text of the memo, dated June 10, 1972, appears in Bruce Oudes, ed., *From the President: Richard Nixon's Secret Files* (New York: Harper and Row, 1989), pp. 474–76.

71 "giving the American": The Nixon/Agnew attack on punditry drew on a proud Republican history. Dwight Eisenhower never got a bigger ovation in his life than he did for the 1952 Republican convention speech in which he scornfully derided "the sensation-seeking columnists and commentators." Agnew is quoted in Jules Witcover, *White Knight: The Rise of Spiro Agnew* (New York: Random House, 1972), p. 47; Eisenhower is quoted in Stewart Alsop, *The Center: People and Power in Political Washington* (New York: Harper and Row, 1968), p. 206.

71 "was not a Conservative": Quoted in William Safire, *Safire's Washington* (New York: Times Books, 1980), p. 7. Halberstam says he was correct to criticize the appointment of Safire, which looked then (and still does) like *Times* publisher Punch Sulzberger's attempt to make "a separate peace" with the Nixon administration. On the other hand, Halberstam considers Safire today to be a first-rate pundit and a tireless reporter (David Halberstam, interview by author).

71 "reestablish the confidentiality": William Safire, 19 July 1973.

72 as Geyelin recalls: Author's interview with Philip Geyelin.

72 "godfatherly moral attention": Author's interview with William F. Buckley, Jr.

73 As children: See David Remnick, "Buckley: the Lion in Autumn," *Washington Post*, 5 December 1985, Style section, p. 1.

73 "conservatism was considered": Author's interview with William F. Buckley, Jr.

75 "scientists, teachers": Irving Kristol, *Two Cheers for Capitalism* (New York: Basic Books, 1978), p. 27.

75 "to explain to": Quoted in William Pfaff, *Barbarian Sentiments: How the Century Ends* (New York: Hill and Wang, 1989), p. 9.

75 "intellectuals to go out": Quoted in Sidney Blumenthal, *The Counter-Establishment: From Conservative Ideology to Political Power* (New York: Times Books, 1986), p. 154.

76 "something that looks": Robert L. Bartley, "Business and the New Class," in B. Bruce-Briggs, *The New Class?* (New Brunswick: Transaction Books, 1979), p. 288. For an extremely learned and trenchant discussion of the New Class war, see Barbara Ehrenreich, *Fear of Falling* (New York: Pantheon Books, 1988). See also Benjamin DeMott's excellent *The Imperial Middle* (New York: William Morrow, 1990.)

77 "Abby Hoffman": The Evans and Novak column is quoted in the author's "Mr. Nice Guy," *The Washingtonian*, November 1989, p. 278. The Nixon memo from the president to John Mitchell, dated June 6, 1972, appears in Oudes, *Richard Nixon's Secret Files*, p. 462.

78 "put politics in command": Author's interview with Alexander Cockburn.

78 The same tendencies: Author's interviews with Rowland Evans, Robert Novak, and Helmut Sonnenfeldt.

80 "The real lesson": William Safire, 11 January 1979.

80 "Western democracies are": George F. Will, 1 May 1980, and 21 May 1978.

Chapter Four. The Triumph of George Will

86 Amidst the violent chaos: See John Judis, *William F. Buckley: Patron Saint of the Conservatives* (New York: Simon and Schuster, 1988), p. 290.

86 The incident drew: Said missives, including a partial transcript of the broadcast, can be found reprinted in their entirety in *Esquire's* history of the 1960s. See William F. Buckley, Jr., "On Experiencing Gore Vidal," and Gore Vidal, "A Distasteful Encounter with William F. Buckley Jr.," in *Smiling through the Apocalypse*, ed. Harold Hayes (New York: The McCall Publishing Company, 1969), pp. 911–65.

86 Kenner admonished: See Judis, *Patron Saint*, pp. 290–95, for all the details.

87 "a snotty-nosed": Quoted in Eleanor Randolph, "George Will, the Oracle at Strict Remove," *Washington Post*, 26 September 1986, Style section, p. 1.

87 "He came along": Tim Russert is quoted in Jane Meyer, "Tory Columnist: Pundit George Will Is a Media Superstar with Plenty of Clout," *Wall Street Journal*, 7 May 1986, p. 1.

87 "perhaps the most powerful": The quote, which was taken from the generally unfriendly front-page *Wall Street Journal* story cited above (Meyer, "Tory Columnist"), appears on the back cover of the paperback edition of George F. Will, *The Morning After: American Successes and Excesses, 1981–1986* (New York: Collier Books, 1986).

88 "demeaning": Author's interview with Philip Geyelin.

88 "like some head of state": Quoted in Eleanor Randolph, "George Will, the Oracle at Strict Remove," *Washington Post*, 26 September 1986, Style section, p. 1.

88 "the infantilism": See George F. Will, *The New Season* (New York: Simon and Schuster, 1988), p. 20.

93 "the undisputed leader": See Charles Krauthammer's review of *The Pursuit of Virtue and Other Tory Notions* by George F. Will, *The New Republic*, 16 June 1982, p. 26.

93 "widely recognized": George F. Will, 10 November 1985.

94 "He said that": Quoted in James Fallows, "Washington's New Celebrities," *The New York Review of Books*, 12 June 1986.

94 "just back from": Nancy Reagan, *My Turn* (New York: Random House, 1989), p. 292.

95 "main feeling": Author's interview with Michael Kinsley.

95 "It is a half-hour": Quoted in Thomas B. Rosenstiel, "Reporters on TV: Is Stardom Weakening the Press?" *Los Angeles Times*, 26 April 1989, p. 1.

95 "Anyone who goes": Quoted in William Henry III, "George Will among the Polysyllables," *Esquire*, January 1987, p. 92.

96 "When Ronald Reagan": Quoted in Thomas B. Rosenstiel, "Columnist Knows Power of Persona," *Los Angeles Times*, 29 May 1986, p. 1.

96 But the First Lady: See Reagan, *My Turn* (New York: Random House, 1989).

96 "The unsurpassed master": George Will, quoted in Meyer, "Tory Columnist," p. 1.

96 "particularly annoyed": George Will, quoted in Lou Cannon, *President Reagan: The Role of a Lifetime* (New York: Simon and Schuster, 1991), pp. 132–33.

96 Phil Geyelin . . . recalls: Author's interview with Phil Geyelin.

97 "journalists are spurning": George F. Will, *Newsweek*, 11 September 1989. William Safire, at least, knew enough to spurn this choice when it was opened to him.

97 "I would have": Author's interview with Ben Bradlee.

97 "I don't": George F. Will, quoted in Meyer, "Tory Columnist," p. 1.

97 Will's face: Author's interview with Robert Kaiser.

98 praised his comrade: Author's interview with Charles Krauthammer, and "Washington Diarist," *The New Republic*, 22 April 1985.

98 "Capitalism undermines": George F. Will, 24 August 1980.

98 "to treat laissez-faire": George F. Will, *The Pursuit of Virtue and Other Tory Notions* (New York: Touchstone, 1982), p. 15.

98 "a toothless": Quoted in Dinesh D'Souza, "Op-ed Artists," *Policy Review* (winter 1985): p. 50.

98 "The United States": George F. Will, *Statecraft as Soulcraft* (New York: Simon and Schuster, 1983), p. 24.

99 He would quiz: The Jesse Jackson interview took place on *This Week with David Brinkley* during the 1988 campaign and is cited in George F. Will, 28 January 1988. The Sartre column appeared 26 February 1976. The Gorbachev quote appeared in Rosenstiel, "Columnist Knows Power of Persona," p. 1. The first "Richard Coeur de Lion" quote appeared in Will's column on December 20, 1979; the second appeared on December 13, 1987.

99 "the most quoted": George F. Will, 10 July 1983. Eight years later, Will's heirs on *Inside Washington* were still seeking to emulate his magnificent accomplishment. On May 14, 1990, viewers saw a bow-tied, bespectacled pundit complaining of a shortage of "candor and cash" on behalf of the Democrats, in contemptuous tones virtually identical to those of Will's historic pronouncement.

101 "Gadzooks!": George F. Will, 1 September 1980; and *Newsweek*, 2 February 1981, and 10 July 1983.

101 "et tu": George F. Will, 8 February 1981, 20 May 1976, 16 February 1987, and 25 March 1990.

101 "one of the most judicious": George F. Will, 26 April 1990, and 7 June 1982.

101 "the Butch Cassidy": George F. Will, 27 October 1980; and *Newsweek*, 2 February 1981.

101 "has been in convincing": Quoted in a 1988 letter by Robert Borsage published in the *Washington Post*. Exact date unknown.

102 "during our watch": Quoted in Andrew Kopkind, "Whose Kissinger Now?" *Zeta Magazine*, November 1989.

102 "terrorism serves": George F. Will, 10 November 1983.

102 "flows not": *This Week with David Brinkley*, 10 June 1985.

102 "it is easiest": George F. Will, 19 September 1983.

103 "born on the farm": Will's Labor Day 1991 column is quoted in Andrew Logan, "Around City Hall," *The New Yorker*, 23 September 1991, p. 103.

103 "Should society": Quoted in Sidney Blumenthal, *The Long National Daydream* (New York: Harper and Row, 1988), p. 34.

104 The columnist insisted: Henry, "George Will among the Polysyllables," p. 90.

105 "Thanks, but": Quoted in Victor Gold, "Look Who's Not Coming to Lunch," *The Washingtonian*, April 1990, p. 65.

Chapter Five. Attack of the McLaughlinites

106 "Sometimes he would": Author's interview.
107 *Rolling Stone* national affairs editor . . . recalls: Author's interview with William Greider.
107 When the group: *The McLaughlin Group*, 29 April 1990.
108 Crocker . . . was forced: Author's interview with Tom Miller.
109 "Don't miss it": The quotations, appearing under the scowling, frightfully serious-minded faces of the four white male regulars, appeared in the *New Republic* on 21 March 1988, p. 4, and 7 September 1987, p. 4.
112 "flesh has an inclination": Quoted in Rudy Maxa, "The Mouth That Roars," *The Washingtonian*, April 1987, p. 127.
112 McLaughlin volunteered: Author's interview with Larry Speakes.
112 McLaughlin called: See the author's "Pundit Power," *The Washington Post Magazine*, 18 March 1990, p. 16.
113 McLaughlin lived: Author's interview with Father William O'Halloran.
113 His friend: I interviewed one such Jesuit grumbler.
113 "the notorious Father": Rowland Evans and Robert Novak, 30 September 1974.
114 Stockman told stories: See Michael Kinsley, review of *The Triumph of Politics*, by David Stockman, *The New York Times Book Review*, 11 May 1986. Novak later replied, "Memoir time is payback time. But Mr. Stockman surprised me and I underestimated him. His book suggests no trace of bad blood between us and contains little if any overt criticism of me. Rather I emerge as his willing tool, described variously as his 'dartboard' or 'bulletin board.' Each of four references to me show me slavishly typing his every wish into the Evans and Novak column. . . . In truth, I got that story from a memo from Treasury. Mr. Stockman writes that Mr. Lewis blamed him for our column's treatment of him, and that he 'agreed not to have breakfast' with me 'for a while.' My calendar reflects no such discontinuation of breakfasts."
115 Among the most historically: Rowland Evans and Robert Novak, 21 May 1986. For a discussion of the columnists' role in protecting North, see Jeffrey L. Pasley, "Inside Dopes: Washington Journalists and Colonel Oliver L. North," *The New Republic*, 23 February 1987, p. 14.
115 An unsuspecting reader: Michael Massing, "The Snob and the Slob," *The New Republic*.
116 During the Iran-Contra scandal: These quotations appear in a profile of Buchanan by Lionel Barber, in the *London Financial Times*, 2 February 1987, p. 10. The "gay men" quotations appear in Patrick J. Buchanan, *Right from the Beginning* (Boston: Little, Brown, 1988), pp. 339–40.
116 "Let the bloodbath": Buchanan, *Right from the Beginning*, p. 3.
117 "McCarthy was cheered": Buchanan, *Right from the Beginning*, p. 93.
117 Buchanan comes from: Buchanan, *Right from the Beginning*, pp. 72 and 15.
117 "Our political and social": Buchanan, *Right from the Beginning*, p. 337.
117 "from the tradition": Author's interview.
118 "people to the right": Author's interview.
120 Did Kondrake mean: Author's interview with Morton Kondrake.
121 "Mort is conducting": Author's interview with Neal Freeman.

121 Why did Richard Nixon: These quotes are all drawn directly from the Kondracke-Nixon conversation: *Richard Nixon Reflects: An American Interests Special,* PBS, 4 May 1990.
122 When asked: *The McLaughlin Group,* 12 January 1991.
124 "are just going": *The McLaughlin Group,* 18 June 1989.
124 "a grade": *The McLaughlin Group,* 29 June 1989.
124 "the more we know": *The McLaughlin Group,* 29 June 1989.
124 McLaughlin became suddenly: See the author's "Pundit Power," p. 33.
124 His assistant: Author's interview with Kara Swisher.

Chapter Six. All the Views Fit to Print

129 Complaining of: William Safire, 2 March 1987.
131 "afford greater opportunity": The *New York Times* editorial page, 21 September 1970.
132 "it had not clarified": He said this at the National Press Club in Washington in June 1988.
132 "bipartisan foreign policy": James Reston, 5 November 1980.
132 "Worthwhile Canadian": Flora Lewis, 10 April 1986.
133 "I think after": Author's interview with Tom Wicker.
133 "He is not": Author's interview with Michael Kinsley.
134 "It's absolutely hilarious": Author's interview with Anthony Lewis.
134 "All of the people": Author's interview with Anthony Lewis.
134 "The silent majority": William Safire, 6 November 1980.
134 Safire graded: William Safire, 22 January 1981.
135 "There was lots": Quoted in the *Washington Post,* 24 August 1987, Style section, p. 1.
135 "When I walked": William Safire, *Safire's Washington* (New York: Times Books, 1980), pp. 7–8.
136 "Bill had not learned": Author's interviews with Harrison Salisbury and William Safire. See also Diana West, "Star Safire," *Manhattan inc,* November 1990, p. 30.
137 Among those unearthed: See Victor Navasky, "Safire Appraised," *Esquire,* January 1982.
137 "Every time parking": Interview with William Safire.
138 Safire bought into: See Carl Oglesby, "Attempt on the Pope's Life: Unpersuasive Case against Moscow," *New York Times,* 24 June 1984, p. 22.
138 "brought moral pressure": See William Safire, 12 January 1989.
139 In another variation: See Peter Teeley, "How to Get an Answer from the Vice-President," *New York Times,* 9 September 1984, p. 24.
139 "There is no doubt": Quoted in the *Washington Post,* 24 August 1987, Style section, p. 1.
140 When asked: Author's interview.
140 He also confesses: Author's interview.
140 "Most opinion columnists": See Richard Cohen, "The Syndicated Columnist," *Gannett Center Journal* (spring 1989): p. 13.
140 Is it any wonder: Bradlee is quoted in Elizabeth Peer and Nancy Stadtman, "Fastest Gun in Op-Ed Land," *Newsweek,* 23 April, 1979, and the author's interview.
140 a "libertarian conservative": Author's interview.
141 "The publisher chooses": Author's interview with Leslie H. Gelb.
143 "Even Barbara Walters": A. M. Rosenthal, 9 June 1989.
143 "the saint": A. M. Rosenthal, 27 October 1989.

144 a character in: See Franz Lidz, *Unstrung Heroes* (New York: Random House, 1991).

144 "Rosenthal is": Author's interview with Lars-Erik Nelson.

146 When David wrote: Lisa De Paulo, "The Devil in Ms. Dowd," *George*, April 1998, p. 98.

Chapter Seven. Glass Houses and Revolving Doors

148 "too gelatinous": Quoted in Chalmers M. Roberts, *In the Shadow of Power* (Washington, DC: Seven Locks Press, 1989), p. 490.

148 he picked Meg Greenfield: Author's interview with Donald Graham.

149 "at the right-ish": Meg Greenfield, *Newsweek*, 25 October 1988.

149 "true audacity": Meg Greenfield, *Newsweek*, 13 November 1989.

149 Donald Graham makes: Author's interview.

153 "The repetitiveness": Henry Fairlie, "How Journalists Get Rich," *The Washingtonian*, August 1983, p. 88.

153 "But wait!": Richard Cohen, "What, Me Worry about Ethics?" *Washington Post*, 26 August 1989, Outlook section, p. 1.

154 During the 1972 campaign: See Timothy Crouse, *The Boys on the Bus* (New York: Ballantine Books, 1972), p. 96.

154 Broder considers: See David Broder, *Behind the Front Page* (New York: Simon and Schuster, 1987), p. 332. The Cohen quote appears in Richard Cohen, "The Syndicated Columnist," *Gannett Center Journal* (spring 1989): p. 14.

155 "the frenzy of": David Broder, 31 October 1967.

155 "The White House propaganda": David Broder, "How Press Secrecy Backfired on Reagan," *Washington Post*, 22 March 1987, Outlook section, p. 1.

156 "The White House has": David Broder, 22 March 1987.

156 Broder wondered why: David Broder, 5 April 1989. Broder later conceded "that there were things that came out of the North trial that improved the historical record—although nothing happened because of it." (David Broder, interview by author.)

157 Bush succeeded: Quoted in Garry Trudeau, "Still a Wimp," *Washington Post*, 4 November 1988, p. A25.

158 "I am not": Author's interview.

158 "a new hybrid": David S. Broder, "Beware the 'Insider' Syndrome," *Washington Post*, 4 December 1988, Outlook section, p. 2. For his trouble, Broder was called "a sermonizing, sanctimonious prig, the Malvolio of the print-heads" by Pat Buchanan. "To say that [Nixon speechwriters] Ray Price and Bill Safire's combined decade in Nixon's NFL means they must defer to Broder is like saying that Frank Gifford of Southern Cal and the football Giants ought to give up his seat in the press booth to some pimply-faced kid who covered the Rose Bowl for the daily *Trojan*." Patrick Buchanan, 6 January 1989. Broder replied, "Buchanan has changed hats so often he's forgotten, if he ever knew, the difference between political propaganda and journalism. In 1980, while ostensibly a journalist, Buchanan joined George F. Will in rehearsing for his campaign debate—a breach of professional ethics so gross even he might be expected to grasp it." David Broder, 11 January 1989.

158 After all: Phil McCombs, "David Broder, Roasted and Toasted," *Washington Post*, 30 November 1988, Style section, p. 2.

159 Concerned about: Jeane Kirkpatrick, 19 February 1990, and 14 May 1990.

160 In attempting to offer: The column appeared 23 April, 1990. Donald F. Graff's letter appeared 28 April, 1990.

160 In March 1986: Quoted in Blumenthal, *Long National Daydream*, pp. 198–99.

160 In another column: See Jeane Kirkpatrick, 27 February 1989, and "Rightists Reject Duarte's Peace Bid," *New York Times*, 28 February 1989.

161 "no government": Henry Kissinger, 6 June 1989, and 1 August 1989.

161 the *Wall Street Journal* revealed: Quoted from an editor's note distributed by the *Los Angeles Times* to subscribers to Henry Kissinger's column.

162 "No one can": Walter Pincus, "Kissinger Says He Had No Role in China Mission," *Washington Post*, 14 December 1989, p. A52.

162 When asked: Author's interview with Ben Bradlee.

162 Geyelin . . . accuses: Author's interview with Philip Geyelin.

Chapter Eight. We Are the Wild Men

164 Wanniski recalls: Author's interview with Jude Wanniski.

164 "had an absolutely": See Wayne Parsons, *The Power of the Financial Press* (New Brunswick, NJ: Rutgers University Press, 1989), p. 149.

165 Nationally, fewer than: Survey cited in J. M. Rosenberg, *Inside the Wall Street Journal* (New York: Macmillan, 1982), p. 204.

165 is amazed, he says: Author's interview with Robert Bartley.

165 "We are the wild men": Quoted in Alexander Cockburn and James Ridgeway, "The World of Appearance," in *The Hidden Election*, ed. Thomas Ferguson and Joel Rogers (New York: Pantheon, 1981), p. 77.

166 "according to one": Quoted in Rosenberg, *Inside the Journal*, p. 206.

166 "Executives and": Ben Bagdikian, quoted in the *Washington Journalism Review*, cited in Rosenberg, *Inside the Journal*, pp. 207–08.

166 "the front page has": Author's interview with Robert Bartley.

167 "Mutual Assured Destruction": Author's interview with Robert Bartley.

167 "softness on social issues": Author's interview with Jude Wanniski.

167 "This is not": *Newsweek*, 22 June 1970.

168 "the age of": John Kenneth Galbraith, *A History of Economics* (London: Hamish Hamilton, 1987), p. 166.

168 "I know hardly": *Newsweek*, 27 July 1970.

168 "We have heard": *Newsweek*, 17 August 1970.

168 "It is possible": William F. Buckley, Jr., 19 August 1971.

169 The story of how: See particularly Parsons, *Power of the Financial Press*, and Sidney Blumenthal, *The Rise of the Counter-Establishment* (New York: Times Books, 1986), on which I have relied for this chapter. For the most exciting, although least dependable, version of events, see Rowland Evans and Robert Novak, *The Reagan Revolution* (New York: 1981).

170 "capture some": Quoted in Blumenthal, *Rise of the Counter-Establishment*, p. 180.

171 "a young assistant": Author's interview with Robert Bartley.

171 "I wish I were": Quoted in Edward Scharff, *Worldly Power* (New York: Beaufort Books, 1986), p. 246.

171 "It was horrible": *Wall Street Journal*, 8 October 1981.

172 "It was our story": Quoted in Blumenthal, *Rise of the Counter-Establishment*, p. 182.

173 Wanniski stopped into: Author's interview with Jude Wanniski.

173 "thoroughly hosed": David Stockman, *The Triumph of Politics* (New York: Harper and Row, 1986), p. 10.

174 "don't make any sense": Lester Thurow, "Watching the Candidates with the Porcupine and Trying Not to Laugh," *The Washington Journalism Review,* July/August 1980, p. 46.

174 "Economists cannot": *Wall Street Journal,* 4 April 1980.

174 Wanniski says: Author's interview with Jude Wanniski.

175 "The big problem": Author's interview with Jude Wanniski.

176 In the first place: The comments are drawn from the author's interview and Bartley's introduction to the third edition of Wanniski's *The Way the World Works* (Morristown, PA: Polynomics, 1990).

177 "there are deficits": Author's interview.

Chapter Nine. Even the *New Republic* . . .

178 Michael Kinsley . . . once suggested: Michael Kinsley, "No Dogs or Journalists," *The New Republic,* 3 June 1985.

179 Tastemaker *Vanity Fair*: See Stephen Schiff, "Patriarch Chic," *Vanity Fair,* April 1985, p. 43, and James Wolcott, "Partisans Reviewed," *Vanity Fair,* November 1988, p. 32.

179 seemed "to be at": See Richard Bernstein, "The *New Republic* Tries to Stay Young at 75," *New York Times,* 26 October 1990, p. C1.

179 Right-wingers, in particular: The Podhoretz quote can be found in Dinesh D'Souza, "Marty Come Lately: The *New Republic* Discovers Old Truths," *Policy Review,* summer 1985. See also George F. Will, 10 November 1987, and *National Review,* 28 December 1984, p. 16.

180 "By the time": Mickey Kaus, "Los Angeles Diarist," *The New Republic,* August 1986.

180 As late as August 1991: James J. Kilpatrick's column appeared in the summer of 1991. Fred Barnes makes mention of the same point in his, *The New Republic,* 24 October 1991.

181 an important dose: See Hendrik Hertzberg, "Journals of Opinion: A Historical Sketch," *Gannett Center Journal* (spring 1989): p. 75.

181 "some people say": Quoted in D'Souza, "Marty Come Lately."

182 "the one sure thing": Quoted in ibid.

182 the "philosophical albatross": Quoted in Janet Meyers, "New Republic Ad Pitch Leaning to the Right," *Advertising Age,* 10 February 1986, p. 32.

182 Fairlie once compared: Fairlie continued, "Marty doesn't take women seriously for positions of responsibility. He's really most comfortable with a room full of Harvard males." Quoted in Gwenda Blair, "Citizen Peretz," *Esquire,* July 1985, p. 91.

182 "The preface to this": Author's interview.

182 "Articles triumphantly": Quoted in D'Souza, "Marty Come Lately."

183 "I have been": Quoted in Elizabeth Kastor, "Hailing the *New Republic*: Left, Right, and Points between at the Magazine's Seventieth," *Washington Post,* 28 November 1984, Style section, p. 1.

184 "operating on": Michael Kinsley, "Saint Ralph," *The New Republic,* 9 December 1985.

184 "The big Democratic": Hendrik Hertzberg, "First Returns," *The New Republic,* 29 February 1988.

185 his "dovishness": Quoted in Blair, "Citizen Peretz," p. 92. With Michael Walzer, Peretz coauthored an article in the July 1967 *Ramparts* entitled "Israel Is Not Vietnam."

186 Peretz went so far: The Terzian comment comes from an interview with him by the author. The Fairlie comment can be found in Blair, "Citizen Peretz," p. 91.

186–87 "It was a very wild place": Quoted in Blair, "Citizen Peretz," p. 91.
187 "the worst thing": Author's interview with Alfred Kazin.
188 "Central America": Author's interview.
188 "Before I know": Author's interview with Michael Kinsley.
188 Hendrik Hertzberg, whose job: The Hertzberg quotes derive from the author's interview. The Kondracke quote can be found in Morton Kondracke, Charles Krauthammer, and James Fallows, "Washington's New Celebrities: An Exchange," *The New York Review of Books*, 26 September 1986, p. 73.
189 "second-rate thinkers": Quoted in Jonathan Kaufman, *Broken Alliance* (New York: Charles Scribner's Sons, 1988), p. 230. The phrase "Sandinista sympathizer" appeared in Fred Barnes, "The Sandinista Lobby," *The New Republic*, 20 January 1986.
189 One editorial accused: "Democrats and Commandantes," *The New Republic*, 28 July 1986, pp. 7–10.
189 "Charles's great contribution": Author's interview with Leon Wieseltier.
189 "there are few greater": "In Defense of Deterrence," *The New Republic*, 20 December 1982, p. 9.
190 "The Commission has": "The Scowcroft Revolution," *The New Republic*, 9 May 1983, p. 7.
190 "only if we": "In Defense of Deterrence," p. 7.
190 El Salvador, wrote the editors: "Democrats and Commandantes," pp. 7–10.
190 According to figures: Cited in Charles William Maynes, "Dateline Washington: A Necessary War?" *Foreign Policy*, spring 1991, p. 162.
192 "the liberation": "The Case for the Contras," *The New Republic*, 24 March 1986.
193 in a secret memo: The memo in question was reprinted in *Harper's* in October 1987. Note: I do not dispute the fact that Cruz, at least, despite his selective memory, was a democrat. He was, however, as Owen indicates, a stooge for the efforts of North, Abrams, and the likes of Somocista commandante Enrique Bermudez. As for the influence of Calero, I quote Owen, who noted that he was surrounded by "liars and greed and power-motivated" people for whom the war was just "a business."
193 "desperate to see": "Case for the Contras."
193 "the worst piece": Author's interview.
193 "preposterous": Michael Kinsley, "Manila, Managua," *The New Republic*, 24 March 1986.
193 "The magazine was": Author's interview with Hendrik Hertzberg.
193 these "pro-Contra": Author's interview with Sidney Blumenthal.
194 "it is the place": Quoted in "Midnight's Confession," *The New Republic*, 21 January 1991.
194 Pat Buchanan was: Quoted in Michael Kinsley, "Debating Rules," *The New Republic*.
194 "moderate Democrats": "Democrats and Commandantes," pp. 7–10.
194 he also promised: The "Who Lost Central America?" phrase appeared in Krauthammer's *Washington Post* column on the occasion of the first ceasefire/peace accord signed by the Sandinistas and the contras. My copy is undated. See also Charles Krauthammer, 10 February 1989.
195 The magazine's friend: Author's interview with Elliott Abrams.
195 staggering economic debt: "How Latin America's Economies Look after a Decade's Decline," *The New York Times Week in Review*, 11 February 1990, p. 3. See also *International Monetary Fund Annual Report* (Washington, DC: International Money Fund, 1989), app. II.
195 In Peru: See James Brooke, "Peruvian Farmers Razing Rain Forest to Sow Drug Crops," *New York Times*, 13 August 1989, p. 1.

195 "Israel, lion of nations": James Walcott, "Partisans Reviewed," *Vanity Fair,* November 1988, p. 28.

196 no fewer than four: Author's interviews.

197 "helps Israel's enemies": Quoted in Friedman, "Selling Israel to America," p. 21.

197 "a national characterological": Quoted in Blair, "Citizen Peretz," p. 93.

197 "I have a problem": Author's interview with Michael Kinsley.

197 "an obsessive wound": Martin Peretz, "Wounds," *The New Republic.* My copy is undated.

198 "So this is": See Martin Peretz, "Usual Suspects," *The New Republic,* 12 July 1982.

198 "There is no": Author's interview.

199 During the 1980s: See Martin Peretz, "Occupational Hazards," *The New Republic,* 14 March 1988; Leon Wieseltier, "Summoned by Stones," *The New Republic,* 14 March 1988; and Charles Krauthammer, "No Exit," *The New Republic,* 14 March 1988.

200 "The price was": Author's interview.

200 Hertzberg's refusal: Quoted in Blair, "Citizen Peretz," p. 91.

200 "The initial way": Author's interview with Hendrik Hertzberg.

200 "I wanted": Author's interview with Hendrik Hertzberg.

Chapter Ten. The Man with No New Ideas

205 Drawing on: Quoted in Isaiah Berlin, "The Hedgehog and the Fox," in *Russian Thinkers* (New York: Penguin Books, 1977). First published in 1951.

205 "Everything's rotten": Quoted in Serge Schmemann, "Shevardnadze Returns as Soviet Foreign Minister," *New York Times,* 20 November 1991, p. A7. See also Eduard Shevardnadze, *The Future Belongs to Freedom* (New York: Free Press, 1991), pp. 41–83.

205 "everything pertaining": See Mikhail Gorbachev, *Perestroika: New Thinking for Our Country and the World* (New York: Harper and Row, 1987).

207 "the history of": See Jeane Kirkpatrick, "Dictatorships and Double Standards," in *Dictatorships and Double Standards: Rationalism and Realism in Politics* (New York: Simon and Schuster, 1982), p. 51.

207 "a historical accident": See Jean-François Revel, "How Democracies Perish," *Commentary,* June 1984.

208 "on the side of": George F. Will, 17 April 1975.

208 "achieved the closest": Will, *Pursuit of Virtue,* p. 17.

208 "Biden, 37": Quoted in Hendrik Hertzberg, "Casualties of War," *The New Republic,* 6 March 1989, p. 4.

208 "a self-conscious": Irving Kristol, "Foreign Policy in an Age of Ideology," *The National Interest,* fall 1985, p. 9.

208 Kristol recommended: Quoted in the *Washington Times,* 2 October 1987, p. 1.

208 "Unless we refute": Edward N. Luttwak, "On the Meaning of Victory" in *America in the World, 1962–1987,* ed. Walter Laquer and Brad Roberts (New York: St. Martins's Press, 1987), p. 157. Previously published in 1982.

209 Finland . . . "had earned": Author's interview with Charles Krauthammer.

209 "a kind of beaded": William Safire, 6 March 1989.

210 and reappeared: Jeane Kirkpatrick, 7 June 1989.

211 The 1989 edition: Cited in Daniel Patrick Moynihan, "The Peace Dividend," *The New York Review of Books,* 28 June 1990, p. 3. See also Franklyn D. Holzman, "How the CIA Concocts Soviet Defense Numbers," *New York Times,* 25 October 1989, editorial page, and Leonard Silk, "Did CIA Distort Soviet Outlays?" *New York Times,* 18 November 1989, Business section, p. 2. For evidence that the practice

may have continued through the 1990 budget cycle, see R. Jeffrey Smith, "Aspin: US Suppressing Data on Cuts," *Washington Post*, 17 November 1989, p. A10.

211 "national security state": Daniel Patrick Moynihan, "How America Blew It," *Newsweek*, 10 December 1990, p. 14. In 1989, according to the Information Security Oversight Office, located in the General Services Administration, the U.S. government classified 6,796,501 new secrets.

211 "for more than four": Talbott's comments were initially made in an interview by the author, and appeared shortly thereafter in "Rethinking the Red Menace," *Time*, 1 January 1990, p. 66.

212 "nobody really knows": Quoted in Don Oberdorfer, "US Experts Expect Little Immediate Change in Soviet Policies," *Washington Post*, 12 March 1985, p. A21.

213 "no new ideas": Quoted in Charlotte Saikowski, "US Analysts Look at Gorbachev and See Shifts in Style, But Not in Substance," *The Christian Science Monitor*, 12 March 1985, p. 1.

213 "You don't survive": Quoted in Norman Kempster, "Gorbachev May Press Drive to Split U.S., Allies," *Los Angeles Times*, 12 March 1985, p. 1.

213 "You don't get into": Quoted in R. W. Apple, Jr., "In West, No Rapid Changes Are Seen," *New York Times*, 12 March 1985, p. A17.

213 "The real question": See Strobe Talbott, "Both Continuity and Vigor," *Time*, 25 March 1990, p. 23.

213 had "an advantage": Quoted in Kempster, "Gorbachev May Press Drive," p. 1.

213 "everyone is waiting": Quoted in Kempster, "Gorbachev May Press Drive," p. 1.

213 "very dangerous": Quoted in Kempster, "Gorbachev May Press Drive," p. 1.

214 "a much more skillful": Quoted in Don Oberdorfer, "US Experts Expect Little Immediate Change in Soviet Policies," *Washington Post*, 12 March 1985, p. A21. (This quote was considered so insightful either by Brzezinski or the reporters who quoted him that it also appeared in Kempster, "Gorbachev May Press Drive," p. 1.)

214 "Gorbachev may be": Quoted in Matt Clark, "The Politics of Art," *Newsweek*, 25 March 1985, p. 45.

214 "We need an economic": Quoted in Stephen F. Cohen, "The Failure of the Hard Line," in *Sovieticus: American Perceptions and Soviet Realities* (New York: W. W. Norton, 1986), p. 151. First published in *The Nation*, 15 December 1984.

216 "We don't know": Charles Krauthammer, "When to Call Off the Cold War," *The New Republic*, 16 November 1987, p. 18.

217 "go back to": Quoted in David Remnick, "The Struggle for Light," *The New York Review of Books*, 16 August 1990, p. 3.

217 George Will . . . had attacked: The first quote appeared in Will's column on 26 September 1985. The Simes quote and the second Will quote can be found in Michael Massing, "Gorbaphobes in the US Media," *The Nation*, 26 December 1988, p. 713.

217 "The Soviet Union": Henry A. Kissinger, "Kissinger: How to Deal with Gorbachev," *Newsweek*, 2 March 1987, pp. 39–47.

218 "History is on": Robert C. Tucker, "Gorbachev and the Fight for Soviet Reform," *World Policy Journal* (spring 1987): p. 179.

218 "think there is anyone": Quoted in Russell Watson, "A Mellower Moscow," *Newsweek*, 21 September 1987, p. 43.

219 "break few Stalinist": William Safire, 4 November 1987.

219 "peaceful competition": William Safire, 9 December 1987.

219 "lost its head": See Charles Krauthammer, "The Week Washington Lost Its Head," *The New Republic*, 4 and 11 January, 1988, and Charles Krauthammer, 3 December 1987.

219 "drunk on détente": George F. Will, 13 December 1987.

221 "always talk": Charles Krauthammer, 9 December 1988.

221 "a beleaguered": Dimitri Simes, "Yes, but," *Washington Post*, 9 December 1988.

221 "peaceful coexistence": Henry Kissinger, 20 December 1988.

222 It is instructive: See Craig R. Whitney, "Kohl Gets the German Spotlight but Genscher Had the Vision," *New York Times*, 20 July 1990, p. 1.

222 *Newsweek* devoted: The "appeasement bloc" quote appears in William Safire, 22 July 1990. The "devious" and "Fourth Reich" comments are in William Safire, 15 May 1989. The *Newsweek* and "export-loving" quotations and the beating-your-wife simile are borrowed from Diana Johnstone, "Washington's Latest Target: Bonn's Hans-Dietrich Genscher," *In These Times*, 11–17 January 1989, p. 9. See also James Hoagland, 18 August 1988.

222 "a comprehensive package": See Whitney, "Kohl Gets the German Spotlight," p. 1.

223 The European Bank: See Jacques Attali, "Lines on the Horizon: A New World Order in the Making," *New Perspectives Quarterly*, spring 1990, pp. 6–8.

223 The apparent inability: See Glenn Frankel, "Europe Views US Crisis as Sign of Economic Ills: Analysts Cite Shift in World's Fiscal Order," *Washington Post*, 7 October 1990, p. A32, and Hobart Rowan, "Dollar's Fall Causes US to Lose Status as a Safe Investment Haven," *Washington Post*, 13 October 1990, p. A1.

223 "What we are": Meg Greenfield, *Newsweek*, 2 October 1989.

223 In February 1989: See Martin Sieff, "Brzezinski Sees Soviet System Eaten from Within," *Washington Times*, 7 February 1989, and George F. Will, 9 November 1989.

224 In a speech before: Robin Toner, "Dukakis Talking Tough, Marches into Dixie," *New York Times*, 17 February 1988, p. A19.

224 "were not even peripheral": Quoted in Sidney Blumenthal, *Pledging Allegiance: The Last Campaign of the Cold War* (New York: HarperCollins, 1990), p. 218.

225 "not a foreign-policy": George F. Will, 25 February 1988.

225 "the containment of Communism": Walter S. Mossberg and John Walcott, "Strategic Shift: US Redefines Policy on Security to Place Less Stress on Soviets," *Wall Street Journal*, 11 August 1988, p. 1.

225 "A bipartisan postwar": *Wall Street Journal*, editorial page, 13 September 1988.

226 what one reputable: See Cynthia Brown, ed., *With Friends Like These: The Americas Watch Report on Human Rights and U.S. Policy in Latin America* (New York: Pantheon Books, 1985), p. 175. For a detailed account of the sustained pattern of murder and torture of innocent civilians carried out by the contras with the full knowledge and tacit cooperation of the CIA and the National Security Council, see Sam Dillon, *Commandos: The CIA and Nicaragua's Contra Rebels* (New York: Holt, 1991).

226 they were "standard-issue": The *New Republic* comment appeared in "Dukakis for President," *The New Republic*, 7 November 1988, pp. 7–9. Buckley made his comment on a special *Firing Line* debate just previous to the 1988 election. The *Journal* comment appeared on 13 September 1988.

226 "Reagan's successes": Charles Krauthammer, 23 September 1988.

227 "would have endorsed": "Dukakis for President," pp. 7–9.

227 William Safire says: Author's interview.

228 "our strength . . . steadiness": Bush speech to the National Press Club, 5 January, 1988.

228 "nothing more than": See David Broder, "Thoughts from Quayle on the Campaign Trail," *Washington Post*, 6 September 1988.

Chapter Eleven. Operation Pundit Shield

230 "Nation's Capital": *Washington Post*, 18 February 1990, p. 1.

230 "refusing to stand up": *The McLaughlin Group*, 28 July 1991, 13 September 1991.

231 Ms. Barr was: *The McLaughlin Group*, 28 July 1990.

231 "Thanks Saddam": Ben Wattenberg, 7 August 1990.

231 "In a way": "The Guns of August," *The New Republic*, 3 September 1990, p. 9.

231 "the heavy speculation": R. W. Apple, quoted in James Bennet, "How They Missed That Story," *The Washington Monthly*, December 1990, p. 16.

231 "Hey, whaddya know": Michael Kinsley, "Kuwaiti Fried," *The New Republic*, 8 October 1990, p. 6.

231 The ruling al-Sabah: See Ernest Hollings, United States Senate, 12 January 1990, and Daniel P. Moynihan's "Letter to New York," 10 May 1991.

232 "Following Bush's conversion": Author's interview with James Fallows.

233 "The war between": Randall Rothenberg, "The Battle of the Columnists: Telling Leaders How to Think," *The New York Times Week in Review*, 23 September 1990, p. 4.

233 "In order to narrow": Author's interview with Jude Wanniski.

234 "democratism" . . . "idolatry": Patrick J. Buchanan, "America First—and Second, and Third." *The National Interest* (spring 1990): p. 81.

234 The fervently anti-Soviet: See Zbigniew Brzezinski, "Beyond Chaos, What the West Must Do," *The National Interest* (spring 1990).

234 "Disposable capital is": Edward N. Luttwak, Testimony before the Senate Armed Forces Committee, 29 November 1990. See also Sherle R. Schwenninger and Jerry W. Sanders, "The Democrats and the New Grand Strategy," *World Policy Journal* (fall 1986).

235 "the unchallenged superpower": See Charles Krauthammer, "The Unipolar Moment," *Foreign Affairs: America and the World*, 1990/1991, pp. 23–24, and his "New World Order: What's New? Which World? Whose Orders?" *The Economist*, 23 February 1991, p. 25.

235 "What we find": Daniel Patrick Moynihan, U.S. Senate, 10 January 1991.

235 "it would be crazy": *The McLaughlin Group*, 28 July 1990.

235 "We're not going to": *The Capital Gang*, 4 August 1990.

235 President Bush told: George Bush, quoted in Martin Walker, "Victory and Delusion," *Foreign Policy* 83 (summer 1991): p. 167, and Thomas Friedman, "Hanging Tough Won't Be the Only Test of Leadership," *The New York Times Week in Review*, 19 August 1990, p. 1.

235 "Who will control": Quoted in John B. Judis, "Burden Shirking," *The New Republic*, 4 March 1991, p. 22.

236 The editors of the *New Republic*: "The Guns of August," *The New Republic*, 3 September 1990, p. 10, and "Fighting Dirty," *The New Republic*, 10 and 17 September 1990.

236 "a nightmare not just": Charles Krauthammer, 17 August 1991, and 3 August 1991.

237 "at war with Iraq": A. M. Rosenthal, 19 August 1990, 23 August 1990, and 9 August 1990.

237 "take Baghdad": Quoted in Otto Friedrich, "The Case against Going to War," *Time*, 10 September 1990, p. 94.

237 "obviously it is time": Quoted in William Safire, 3 September 1990, and Jeane Kirkpatrick, 12 November 1990.

237 "The United States cannot": Henry Kissinger on *Meet the Press*, 5 August 1990, and in his syndicated column, 29 August 1990.

239 "Bush has been so": Charles Krauthammer, 25 November 1990.

239 "maybe the most important": Richard Cohen, 23 August 1990.

240 If, after more than: See George W. Ball, "The Gulf Crisis," *The New York Review of Books*, 6 December 1990.

241 "dealing with our own": William Safire, 5 November 1990.

241 In any event: See Eric Schmidt, "US Says It Missed 2 A-Plants in Iraq," *New York Times*, 10 October 1991, p. A7.
241 "There [was] no": Zbigniew Brzezinski, *New York Times*, 7 September 1991.
242 "almost impossible to": David Broder, 18 November 1990.
242 Richard Cohen . . . : Haynes Johnson, 10 August 1990; Anthony Lewis, 10 January 1991; and Richard Cohen, 23 August 1990.
242 "The conditions that": Charlie Peters, "Stop That Blank Check," *New York Times*, 16 January 1991.
242 Congress had been: Krauthammer made his comments on *Inside Washington* and Barnes and Kondracke, on *The McLaughlin Group*, 11 November 1990.
243 "almost none": David Broder, 16 December 1990.
243 "right on the fundamental": Leslie H. Gelb, 2 January 1991.
243 "if the alternative": Quoted in Lars-Erik Nelson, 25 March 1991.
243 "Politically," George Bush: The conversations between Bush and Powell are reported in Bob Woodward, *The Commanders* (New York: Simon and Schuster, 1991).
244 Senator Nunn: See the author's "Congress' Failure," *Tikkun*, January/February, p. 46, reprinted in James Ridgeway, *The March to War* (New York: Four Walls, Eight Windows, 1991).
244 "this is not": George Mitchell, U.S. Senate, 10 January 1991.
244 "in a manner befitting": David Broder, 15 January 1991.
244 "there have not been": Arlen Specter, U.S. Senate, 10 January 1991.
244 "preferred to give": Arlen Specter, U.S. Senate, 10 January 1991.
245 Republican Minority Leader: Cited in Bennet, "Senate's Lame Doves," p. 45.
245 "75 percent or more": John Kerry, U.S. Senate, 11 January 1991.

Chapter Twelve. Operation Pundit Storm

246 "the most powerful": *The Today Show*, NBC, 26 February 1991.
246–47 Fred Barnes . . . Morton Kondrake: *The McLaughlin Group*, 2 March 1991.
247 a "fearsome, transcendent": Rowland Evans and Robert Novak, 27 February 1991.
247 "the most effective": Patrick J. Buchanan, 28 February 1991.
248 *Times* Gulf reporter: Malcolm W. Browne, quoted in Timothy M. Phelps, "Many of Gulf Press in Shallow End of 'Pool,'" *Newsday*, 23 January 1991, p. 36. See also Browne, " Military vs. the Press," p. 29.
249 What's more: Dugan made this observation on CBS News on February 13, 1991.
250 A. M. Rosenthal started: A. M. Rosenthal, 18 January 1991.
250 "technological prowess": George F. Will, 18 January 1991.
250 "there's more to": George F. Will on *This Week with David Brinkley*, 20 January 1991.
250 "we need SDI": Fred Barnes on *The McLaughlin Group*, 20 January 1991.
250 "When President Bush": Patrick Buchanan, 23 January 1991.
251 "the epic debates": "Bad for Civilians," *Wall Street Journal*, 21 January 1991.
251 the Patriots hit: See Eric Schmitt, "Israel Plays Down Effectiveness of Patriot Missile," *New York Times*, 31 October 1991, p. A5.
251 "Cold War II": See Charles Krauthammer, 21 February 1991.
251 "reversion to old-style": Rowland Evans and Robert Novak, 22 February 1991.
251 "retain his old pal": A. M. Rosenthal, 19 February 1991.
251 "perfidy": William Safire, 21 February 1991.
251 "re-arming Hussein": Morton Kondracke on *The McLaughlin Group*, 23 February 1991.

251 "a single pole": Krauthammer, "Unipolar Moment," p. 24.

251 "hubris": Patrick Buchanan, 28 February 1991.

252 "to stand up to": See "The Hammer of the Kurds," *The Economist*, 6 April 1991, p. 9.

252 a "large scale": "The Guns of August," *The New Republic*, 3 September 1990, p. 10.

253 price of a barrel: Cited in Martin Walker, "Victory and Delusion," *Foreign Policy* 83 (summer 1991): p. 160.

253 A few months later: See Youssef M. Ibrahim, "Saudis Say They'll Trim Oil Output," *New York Times*, 22 January 1992, p. D1.

253 "the United States": James Hoagland, "Bush's America: Welcome to the Post-Gulf World," *Washington Post*, 3 March 1991, Outlook section, p. 1.

253 "peace and the rule": David Broder, 10 April 1991.

253 CIA Director: Robert Gates, quoted in Elaine Sciolino, "Iraq Could Rebuild Weapons Threat Soon, CIA Chief Says," *New York Times*, 16 January 1992, p. A4.

253 Hussein retained: These are U.S. intelligence estimates as reported by Ann Devroy and Molly Moore, "Winning the War and Struggling with the Peace," *Washington Post*, 14 April 1991, p. 1.

253 hawkish columnists: See particularly William Safire, 20 January 1992.

253 The Shamir government: See Jackson Diehl, "Israel Boosts Land Seizures," *Washington Post*, 14 May 1991, p. 1.

253 "the primary gains": Charles Krauthammer, 19 April 1991.

254 By early May: Cited in "Kuwait: The War Within," *Business Week*, 27 May 1991, p. 53.

254 The war created: See Thomas W. Lippmann, "Gulf War Leaves Environment Severely Wounded," *Washington Post*, 2 March 1991, p. 1, and Eric Schmitt, "Fouled Region Is Casualty of War," *New York Times*, 3 March 1991.

254 The number of Iraqi: See Eric Schmitt, "US Army Buried Iraqi Soldiers Alive in Gulf War," *New York Times*, 15 September 1991, p. 8.

254 According to human rights organizations: See William Branigin and Nora Boustany, "Rights Officials: Kuwaiti Soldiers Commit Abuses," *Washington Post*, 16 March 1991, p. 1, and Nora Boustany, "Kuwaiti Hospital Said to Cover Up Torture," 22 March 1991.

254 child mortality figures: See Patrick E. Tyler, "Western Health Study in Iraq Finds Child Mortality Has Nearly Tripled," *New York Times*, 22 October 1991, p. A7.

255 "Voice of Free Iraq": See "Operation Desertion," *The Economist*, 13 April 1991, p. 25.

255 The punditocracy did not: See William Safire, 4 April 1991; Haynes Johnson, 5 April 1991; Charles Krauthammer, 5 April 1991; and A. M. Rosenthal, 5 April 1991, and 9 April 1991.

256 "enormous disappointment": Charles Krauthammer, 19 April 1991, and 3 May 1991.

256 But the wimp: See, for instance, Fred Barnes, "The Old Bush," *The New Republic*, 22 April 1991, p. 13.

256 "Erstwhile antiwar": Charles Krauthammer, 19 April 1991, and Morton Kondracke, "Kurdled, " *The New Republic*, 13 May 1991, p. 10.

257 "isolationist chickens": Richard Cohen, 5 March 1991.

257 "showed the nation": David Broder, 6 March 1991.

257 "so many elected": "Out of Touch," *Wall Street Journal*, 14 March 1991, p. A18.

257 "A party that": A. M. Rosenthal, 15 March 1991.

258 his "well conceived": Quoted in David Shribman and James M. Perry, "Conference of Moderate Democrats Finds Party Full of Factions, Undecided on Road Ahead." *Wall Street Journal*, 8 May 1991, p. A14.

258 "the most influential": Ben Wattenberg quoted in David Shribman, "Victory in Gulf War Exorcises the Demons of the Vietnam Years," *Wall Street Journal*, 1 March 1991, p. 1.

258 "nonsense": Charles Krauthammer, 22 March 1991.

258 "the end of the decline": Novak is quoted in Peter Applebome, "At Home, War Healed Several Wounds," *New York Times*, 4 March 1991, p. 1.

259 "one of the defining": William J. Bennett, "Rebirth of a Nation," *National Review*, 18 March 1991, p. 41.

259 Britain achieved: See Michael Howard, "Churchill and National Unity," in *The Lessons of History* (New Haven, CT: Yale University Press, 1991), p. 159.

260 Banks went bust . . . : For the details of these developments, see Andrew Baxter, "US Drops Out of World Machine Tool Top Five," *Financial Times*, 12 February 1991, p. 4; Louis Uchitelle, "New Jobless Claims at 8-Year High," *New York Times*, 5 April 1991, p. D1; Suen L. Hwang, "Failures in 90 Jumped 20% Due to Slump," *Wall Street Journal*, 13 March 1991; "On Recession's Battlefield, the Economy Is Losing Ground," *Business Week*, 18 February 1991, p. 27; John M. Barry, "Recession Deeper in First Quarter," *Washington Post*, 28 April 1991, p. 1; and John Greenwald, "Detroit's Big Three Are Seeing Red," *Time*, 13 May 1991, p. 40.

260 Inside our cities . . . : See Spencer Rich, "Hunger Said to Afflict 1 in 8 American Children," *Washington Post*, 27 March 1991, p. A4; Robert J. Samuelson, 14 March 1991; Karen Penner, "The Recession Isn't Ready to Pull Out," *Business Week*, 11 March 1991, p. 33; and Brooke A. Masters, "Food Program Cuts Thousands in Area," *Washington Post*, 12 March 1991, p. 1.

260 "obsession with": Martin Walker, "Desert Storm over Moscow," *Washington Post*, 24 February 1991, Outlook section, p. 1.

260 "sob-sisters of journalism": A. M. Rosenthal, 21 February 1991. The column President Bush himself with impressive clairvoyance. On March 6, 1991, the president, speaking before a joint session of Congress, insisted, "We hear so often about our young people in turmoil, how our children fall short, how American products are second class. Well, don't you believe it. The America we saw in Desert Storm was first-class talent."

261 "America's new": Anthony H. Cordesman, "America's New Combat Culture," *New York Times*, 28 February 1991.

261 "Our best hope": Charles Krauthammer, 22 March 1991.

261 "Every other nation": Charles Krauthammer, 22 March 1991.

Conclusion

279 "tawdry ferocity": George F. Will, *Suddenly: The American Idea at Home and Abroad, 1986–1990* (New York: Free Press, 1990), p. xvi.

280 Decades of public-opinion: These figures are taken from the continual surveys undertaken for the project "Americans Talk Security," published in February 1988. They are cited in Stanley B. Greenberg, "The Struggle for a Democratic Vision," *World Policy Journal* (summer 1998): 548–54, and in Bruce Russett, *Controlling the Sword: The Democratic Governance of National Security* (Cambridge, MA: Harvard University Press, 1991), p. 168. For a full discussion of this rich body of polling data, see John Martilla, "American Public Opinion: Evolving Dimensions of National Security," in Edward K. Hamilton, ed., *America's Global Interests: A New Agenda* (New York: W. W. Norton, 1989), pp. 261–316.

280 Attacking the power: William Safire suggests "petulant, Pecksniffian political pundits, preying in packs on protectors of the public." William Safire, "Pundit Bashing," *The New York Times Magazine*, 27 May 1990, p. 10. Both Jesse Jackson and George Bush have already given this tactic a dry run, albeit without Safire's etymological pyrotechnics. At a 1990 Tyler, Texas, campaign stop, the president

lashed out at "the cynics, these Washington pundits that we get on these tiring shows all the time," who were "always telling us everything that's wrong with the United States." Ann Devroy, "Stumping in Texas, Bush Pounds Pundits," *Washington Post*, 6 November 1990, p. A6. Jackson, meanwhile, could not help observing to *Washington Post* reporter Paul Taylor earlier in the year that "the seven million votes I got didn't come from no pundits. . . . When I was talking to a 27-year-old Perdue worker last week who has bursitis in her wrist from plucking 50 chickens a minute and no health insurance, she didn't ask for no pundit."

281 "crisis of Western Democracy": Lippmann, *Liberty and the News*, p. 5.

281 "what somebody asserts": Lippmann, *Liberty and the News*, p. 54.

281 "but comes about": Daniel J. Boorstin, *The Image: A Guide to Pseudo-Events in America* (New York: Macmillan, 1961), p. 9.

282 "a pseudo-event": Daniel J. Boorstin, *The Image: A Guide to Pseudo-Events in America* (New York: Macmillan, 1961), p. 34.

283 This explains the: See Sut Jhally, Justin Lewis, and Michael Morgan, *The Gulf War: A Study of the Media, Public Opinion and Public Knowledge* (Amherst, MA: The University of Massachusetts, Amherst, Center for Studies in Communication, 1991). The survey was done between February 2 and 4, 1991.

285 What is defined: See Michael Schudson, *Discovering the News: A Social History of American Newspapers* (New York: Basic Books, 1978), pp. 7–9.

285 "the ideology of": See Schudson, *Discovering the News*, p. 71.

286 "Objective journalism": See Russell Baker, *The Good Times* (New York: William Morrow, 1989), p. 238.

288 "Adolph Ochs' " : Liebling is quoted in James L. Baughman, "The Press and the Federal Government" (paper presented at the annual conference of the Organization of American Historians, Washington, D.C., 23 March 1990).

288 "The purpose of news": See James W. Carey, *Communication as Culture: Essays on Media and Society* (Boston: Unwin Hyman, 1989), p. 79. See also Dewey's review of *Public Opinion*, by Walter Lippmann, *The New Republic*, 3 May 1922, pp. 286–88, and John Dewey, *The Public and its Problems* (New York: H. Holt and Co., 1927). For an erudite discussion of the Lippmann-Dewey controversy, see Robert B. Westbrook, *John Dewey and American Democracy* (Ithaca, NY: Cornell University Press, 1991), chap. 9.

289 Lasch dated the beginning: See Christopher Lasch, "Journalism, Publicity, and the Lost Art of Argument," *Gannett Center Journal* (spring 1990): p. 9. It is historically overgenerous to credit Lippmann's high-minded critiques with changing the course of American journalism when editors had the fantastic money-making example of the *New York Times* on which to concentrate their minds. The dates in Lasch's voting-pattern argument are better suited to a *Times*-centric critique as well, to say nothing of the influence on voter rolls of new immigrant, black, and women voters. For a discussion of the larger issue, see Michael E. McGerr, *The Decline of Popular Politics: The American North, 1865–1928* (New York: Oxford University Press, 1986).

Index

ABC News, 87, 91, 198, 265. *See also Nightline*
This Week
breaking of Lewinsky story, 265, 266, 267–68
reporting history, 85–86
Abrams, Elliott, 191, 193, 194, 195
Acheson, Dean, 39, 41, 54, 56
Adams, John Quincy, 23
Adams, Samuel, 22
Adelman, Kenneth, 9, 159, 187
Agnew, Spiro, 71
Agronsky, Martin, 60, 63
Agronsky and Company, 13, 152, 183
Center following for, 10, 64
as pundit sitcom, 62–64
Will on, 87, 88, 94, 152
Ajami, Fouad, 237
Albright, Madeleine, 141
Allott, Gordon, 87, 171
Alsop, Joseph, 12, 39, 41, 46–47, 56, 60, 71, 71n, 97
influence of, 47–49
Alsop, Stewart, 39, 47–48
America magazine, 112
American Interests, 122

American public. *See also* Political process and culture
different views than pundits, 280
lack of interest in foreign news and policy, 36, 265
need for political education, 34
Anti-Semitism, 118n, 126–27
Buchanan accused of, 238n
Buckley accused of, 9, 86
Anderson, Maxwell, 34
Apple, R. W., 231
Arafat, Yassir, 266–67, 277
Arnett, Peter, reports on Gulf War, 248–49
Aronson, Bernard, 193, 194
Aspin, Les, 194
Attali, Jacques, 223
Atwater, Lee, 123

Bagdikian, Ben, 166
Baker, Howard, 102, 129
Baker, James, 9, 157, 158, 240
Baker, Russell, 50, 286
Barnes, Fred, 237, 243, 246–47, 250, 251, 272
at Fox News, 14, 121, 127

on *The McLaughlin Group*, 122, 126, 235
at *New Republic*, 178, 187–88
at *Weekly Standard*, 201
Barr, Bob, 262
Bartley, Robert, 76, 225
and economic policy, 165, 170, 174, 175n, 176–77
ideology and style, 165–67, 170
at *Wall Street Journal*, 170–72
Beard, Charles, on Lippmann, 37, 45
Beltway Boys, The, 14, 121, 127
Bennett, James Gordon, 23–24
Bennett, Philip, 43n
Bennett, William J., 259, 272–73
Berlin, Isaiah, 205
Bernstein, Barton J., 186
Biden, Joseph, 208
Bilbo, Theodore, 43n
Blankley, Tony, 277
Blitzer, Wolf, 267, 270, 273
Block, Herb, 149
Bloom, Allan, 7

Novak, Robert, 56, 112n, 122, 150, 151. *See also* Evans and Novak column
  attacks on, 113–14, 123
  and black politics, 127
  career, influence, power of, 14, 77, 85, 115
  on *The McLaughlin Group*, 106–7, 108, 113, 152, 235
  on TV, 152, 153, 165
Nuclear weapons
  buildup, press support for, 190, 200, 208
  Gorbachev proposals concerning, 216–18
Nunn, Sam, 244

Oakes, John, 131
Ochs, Adolph, 26–29, 285
Olbermann, Keith, 91, 127
  withdrawal as pundit, 278
Oppenheimer, J. Robert, 48, 60
Orwell, George, 282, 283, 284
Owen, Robert, 193

Pace, Robert, 47
Page, Clarence, 122
Paine, Thomas, 22
Paley, William, 61
Palme, Olaf, 120
Pastore, John, 112
Parsons, Wayne, 164
Pax Americana, 39, 234, 251
  idea of new, 261
PBS, 63, 121, 266
Pearson, Drew, 36, 43
  senatorial attacks on, 43n
Pegler, Westbrook, 36, 44, 74
Peretz, Anne, 185, 186
Peretz, Martin, 181, 182, 184
  career and experience of, 185–86
  purchase and takeover of *New Republic*, 186–87
  support of Israel, 9, 185, 195–99
Perle, Richard, 237
Persian Gulf War
  affirmation of punditocracy's dogmas and, 246
  Bush's views and policies toward, 230, 235–39
  consequences, and postwar analysis of, 251–57, 258n
  original opposition to, 235
  political legacy of, 257–61

preparations for, 230, 232, 242
  press support for, 243
  and pro-war pundits, 237
  public debate and views on, 238, 242n, 257n
  role of Congress and debate in, 242–45
Persian Gulf War, reporting and discussions during
  Iraqi censorship of, 248–49
  Pentagon control of, 247–48
  pundits' rush to judgment, 250–51
  tainted and false information, 246, 248, 249–50
Peters, Charlie, 184, 242
Pfaff, William, 90, 210, 283n
Phillips, Kevin, 7
Podhoretz, Norman, 74n, 76n, 144, 179, 194
  as pro-Israel, 197
Poindexter, John, 115
Political dialogue and discourse
  coherent, breakdown of and need for, 4, 5n, 279, 284
  commentators' ability to shape, 14, 82, 225, 289
  loss of proper language in, 281–84
  responsible, as lacking or limited, 158, 228
  and propaganda, 282–83
  pundits' dominance of, 233, 261, 262, 279–80
  role of books in, 92
Political process and culture
  diminished by pundits' influence, 227, 228
  Gulf War's effect on, 257–61
  immune to public opinion, 7–8, 284
  proposed changes to, 284–89
  "pseudo-environment," and pseudo-event, 29, 281–83, 285
  quality of, and journalists' impact, 285–86, 287
  replaced by punditocracy, 233
Politics, national, major problems, 4–5, 7–8, 16–17
Polk, George, 33
Postman, Neil, 16
Postol, Theodore A., 249n
Powell, Colin, 230, 241
Powell, Jody, 81n

Powers, William, 272
Public Interest, 172, 174
Pundit(s). *See also* Journalism, journalists in America, history of
  appearing everywhere, 127, 263
  author as, 265n
  early, and growing role of, 32, 35, 71, 72
  as increasingly political, 78–79, 80, 81, 82, 159
  and new layer in 1990s, 201
  origins of word and use of term, 21–22
  political power of, 9–10, 41–42
  with prevailing power and viewpoints, 3–4, 232
  reasons for existence of, 26, 152
  speaking engagements for, 137, 152, 153
  in Washington, role and influence, 39–42, 232, 285
Punditocracy
  defined, 4–5
  diminishment after Gulf War, 257
  disregarding of public's wishes, 271, 275, 278
  ethical code in, lack of, 13–14, 86–87, 95–96
  four circles of, 89–91, 93, 152
  growth of, history and reasons, 11–16, 32, 263–67, 285
  as intellectually impoverished, 15–17, 213, 258
  membership and hierarchy of, 5–8
  merger with gossip industry, 264, 274–76
  need for changes in, 280, 284
  need for new patriotic cause, 230–31
  as only show in town and prevailing voice, 233, 261, 262, 279
  politicians in, 159
  power and influence of, in many forms, 7–12, 13, 82, 229
  self-evaluation of, 277, 278
  and shaping of strategic policy, 258–60